Andw. M. Wilson

Boston

April 2[illegible]

1863

A COMPENDIOUS INTRODUCTION TO THE STUDY OF THE BIBLE:

Being an Analysis of

"AN INTRODUCTION TO THE CRITICAL STUDY AND KNOWLEDGE OF THE HOLY SCRIPTURES," IN FOUR VOLUMES, BY THE SAME AUTHOR.

By THOMAS HARTWELL HORNE.

ELEVENTH THOUSAND.

New York:
PUBLISHED BY CARLTON & PORTER,
200 MULBERRY-STREET.

ADVERTISEMENT

TO THE

LAST ENGLISH EDITION:

THE present Edition has been carefully revised and corrected throughout. A few passages, which were considered too critical to be interesting to general readers, have been omitted; and by condensing that part which treats on the Interpretation of Scripture, the Author has obtained room, without increasing the price of the volume, for various additions:—particularly, a Table of the principal Predictions relative to the Person and Offices of the Messiah, with their Fulfilment, and also a Geographical Index, abridged from his larger work, of the most remarkable places mentioned in the Holy Scriptures, especially in the New Testament. These additions, the Author trusts, will be found to render this Manual more permanently useful as a Compendious Introduction to the Study of the Bible, and not unworthy a continuance of that patronage with which his labours have hitherto been honoured.

PREFACE.

The little Manual, now offered to the Public, has been undertaken in consequence of requests long since communicated to the Author, and frequently repeated, that he would prepare an ANALYSIS, or Abridgment of the four octavo volumes of his larger "Introduction to the Critical Study and Knowledge of the Holy Scriptures;" as an assistant to the studies of Gentlemen, at the Universities and other Seminaries of Theological Literature, as also of those individuals who may respectively possess that work, and to whom such an auxiliary would be acceptable. At the same time, the present volume has been so arranged, as to form a *Comprehensive Guide to the Study of the Bible*, adapted to the use of GENERAL READERS: it will be found to contain,

I. A Summary of the Evidences of the Genuineness, Inspiration, &c. of the Holy Scriptures, refuting the most modern objections of Infidels;

II. An Outline of the Literary History and Interpretation of the Bible;

III. A Compendium of Biblical Geography and Antiquities; and

IV. Introductory Prefaces to the several Books of Scripture.

In preparing this Manual for the press, the order of the larger Introduction has generally been followed: the Parts and Books, into which it is divided, corresponding with the volumes, and parts of volumes in that work. Those bibliographical, critical, and other details only have been omitted, which either would not admit of abridgment, or which would be uninteresting to the generality of English readers.

The Author has subjoined, in an Appendix, a List of Select Chapters of the Bible, forming an Epitome of the Old and New Testaments, adapted to perusal in the family, or in private, together with chronological and other tables; which he trusts, with the Divine blessing on his labours, will contribute to facilitate the devout and attentive reading of "the Holy Scriptures, which ALONE are able to make us wise unto salvation, THROUGH FAITH which is in Christ Jesus."

TABLE OF CONTENTS.

PART I.

ON THE GENUINENESS, AUTHENTICITY, INSPIRATION, ETC., OF THE HOLY SCRIPTURES.

PART II.

ON THE LITERARY HISTORY, CRITICISM, AND INTERPRETATION OF THE SCRIPTURES.

Book I.—On the Literary History and Criticism of the Scriptures.

BOOK II.—ON THE INTERPRETATION OF SCRIPTURE.

PART III.

A COMPENDIUM OF BIBLICAL GEOGRAPHY AND ANTIQUITIES.

BOOK I.—A SKETCH OF THE GEOGRAPHY OF THE HOLY LAND

BOOK II.—POLITICAL ANTIQUITIES OF THE JEWS.

PART IV.

ON THE ANALYSIS OF SCRIPTURE.

BOOK I.—ANALYSIS OF THE OLD TESTAMENT.

BOOK II.—ANALYSIS OF THE NEW TESTAMENT.

APPENDIX.

INDEXES.

COMPENDIOUS INTRODUCTION

TO

THE STUDY OF THE BIBLE,

ETC., ETC.

PART I

ON THE GENUINENESS, AUTHENTICITY, INSPIRATION, ETC., OF THE HOLY SCRIPTURES.

CHAPTER I.

ON THE NECESSITY, ETC., OF A DIVINE REVELATION

I. Revelation defined.

Revelation is a discovery by God to man of Himself or of his will, over and above what He has made known by the light of nature, or reason.

II. A Divine Revelation possible.

No one, who believes that there is a God of infinite wisdom, power, and knowledge, can reasonably deny the possibility of His making a revelation of Himself, and of his will to men, in an extraordinary way, different from the discoveries made by men themselves, in the mere natural and ordinary use of their own powers. To admit the existence of a God, and to deny him such a power, is a glaring contradiction. Though we cannot explain in what manner ideas originate, or are impressed upon the human mind; yet, since we know that this is effected in various ways, it is reasonable to suppose that God *can* act upon the mind, in order to impart to us the knowledge of his will. And, if so, he can do it in such a manner as to give those, to whom such revelation is made, an assurance that it proceeds from himself.

III. The PROBABILITY of such Revelation appears from the two following arguments:

1. From the general sense of mankind in every age, who believed that divine revelations were probable: and from the credit given to pretended revelations, thus evincing a consciousness of their own ignorance, and the need of a supernatural illumination.

2. From the confession of some of the wisest philosophers, that they stood in need of such a revelation, and the hope they expressed that God would at some future time vouchsafe to make one.

IV. Divine revelation is not only possible and probable, but NECESSARY:

1. From the utter inability of mere human reason to attain any certain knowledge of the will or law of God, of the true happiness of man, or of a future state, as is evident from the endless differences and inconsistencies, which prevailed among the most celebrated ancient philosophers, *some* of whom taught immoral doctrines, while the influence of *all* was very inconsiderable, both in rectifying the notions, and in reforming the lives of mankind. Thus

(1.) Their ideas respecting the Nature and Worship of God were dark, confused, and imperfect.

(2.) They were ignorant of the true account of the Creation of the World. Also,

(3.) Of the origin of Evil, and the cause of the depravity and misery which actually exist among mankind.

(4.) Of any Method by which a Reconciliation could be effected between God and man.

(5.) Of Divine Grace and Assistance towards our attainment of Virtue and perseverance in it.

(6.) They had only dark and confused notions of the *Summum Bonum* or Supreme Felicity of man:

(7.) They had weak and imperfect notions concerning the Immortality of the Soul; and also concerning

(8.) The Certainty of the Eternal Rewards and Punishments of a Future State, and the Resurrection of the Body.

2. From the defective instructions of the best of the philosophers, which, moreover, were unsuited to the common people, and which they wanted authority to enforce in practice.

3. From the gross ignorance and idolatry universally prevalent among unenlightened heathen nations.

V. Refutation of the Objection that Philosophy and Right Reason are sufficient to instruct men in their duty.

Answer 1. It is a fact, that the doctrines of Christ have had a more powerful influence upon men, than all the reasonings of philosophers: and though modern opposers of Revelation ascribe the ignorance and corruption of the heathen, not to the insufficiency of the light of reason, but to their non-improvement of that light; yet, if this were true, it would not prove that there is no need of a revelation, because it *is certain* that the philosophers wanted some higher assistance than that of reason.

2. Notwithstanding the pretences of modern deists to superior wisdom, it is a fact that they have borrowed almost all their wise and true observations from divine revelation. It is *one* thing to perceive that the rules of life, which are laid before us, are agreeable to reason, and *another* thing to discover them by the mere light of reason.

3. Besides, the speculations of modern deists, concerning religion, are so glaringly contradictory, and their ethical precepts are so utterly subversive of every principle of morality, as to demonstrate the necessity of a divine revelation *now*, in order to lead mankind to the knowledge of God, and of their duty to one another.

VI. Possible Means of affording a Revelation.

There appears to be only two ways of doing this, viz. 1. An immediate Revelation to each individual; or, 2. A Commission given by God to certain persons to make known his will, accompanied with indisputable credentials of their being delegated by him. The *former* method would be ineffectual: for either the freedom of the will must be destroyed, or else it would fill the world with continual impostures and pretences to revelation. The *latter* method, therefore, is the most eligible and satisfactory; and writing was the best means of transmitting such a revelation, on account of

1. The uncertainty and insecurity of oral tradition.

2. The greater security and permanence of writing.

3. The fairness and openness, which is the result of writing.

4. The importance of the matter, the variety of the subjects, and the design of the institutions contained in the books, which Jews and Christians receive as containing a divine revelation.

CHAPTER II.

ON THE GENUINENESS AND AUTHENTICITY OF THE BOOKS OF THE OLD AND NEW TESTAMENT.

SECTION I.—Genuineness and Authenticity of the Old Testament.

I. GENUINENESS and AUTHENTICITY defined.

A *Genuine Book* is one, that is written by the person whose name it bears.—An *Authentic Book* is one in which matters of fact are related, as they really happened.

There are two classes of proof; 1. Historical Testimony or *External Evidence;* and 2. *Internal Evidence* arising from an examination of the Books themselves.

II. HISTORICAL TESTIMONY, or External Evidence.

1. The persons, contemporary with any Hebrew writer whose books they transcribed, knew by whom they were written; and, having a certain knowledge of the author and of the age in which he lived, delivered them to their descendants, and these again to their posterity.

2. The small number of books, extant at the time when the books of the Old Testament were written, would render fault impossible.

3. The Hebrews or Jews, by testifying that these books are genuine, become witnesses against themselves, and their testimony consequently is unexceptionable.

4. A particular tribe was consecrated for the express purpose of watching over the preservation of these books.

5. The testimony of the ancient Jews, of which we have an unbroken chain; and the *fact* that the Greek version of the Old Testament, usually called the Septuagint, was executed at Alexandria two hundred and eighty-two years before the Christian era.

III. INTERNAL EVIDENCE, arising from an examination of the Books themselves.

ARG. 1. The difference in language, style, and manner of writing, proves that the Books of the Old Testament must have been written at various times and by different persons. As Hebrew ceased to be spoken as a living language soon after the Babylonish captivity, all those books must be nearly as ancient as that captivity: and as they could not all be written in the *same* age, some must be considerably more ancient.

ARG. 2. The multitude of minutely particular circumstances of time, place, persons, &c., mentioned in the books of the Old Testament, is a further argument both of their genuineness and authenticity; because no forger of false accounts superabounds in such peculiarities, or could furnish them; and because such forgeries or falsehoods could be easily detected and exposed.

IV. Proofs of the genuineness and authenticity of the PENTATEUCH in particular.

This is manifest.

1. From the language in which it is written, the simplicity and archaisms of which prove it to be the earliest of all the Hebrew sacred books.

2. From the Nature of the Mosaic Law, as contained in the four last books of Moses.

These books contain a system of ceremonial and moral laws, which, unless we reject the authority of all history, were observed by the Israelites, from their departure out of Egypt until their dispersion at the taking of Jerusalem. Their civil and religious polity are so inseparably connected, and many of their institutions are so connected with historical facts, as to render forgery impossible.

3. From the United Historical Testimony of Jews and Gentiles

[i.] *Jewish Testimony:*—Jesus Christ, Ezra, Daniel, Solomon, David, Moses, and others; to which is to be added the fact, that the law of Moses was received by both Jews and Samaritans *before* they became divided into two kingdoms.

[ii.] *Gentile Testimony:*—Manetho, Eupolemus, Artapanus, Tacitus, Diodorus, Siculus, Strabo, Justin, the abbreviator of Trogus, Juvenal, and many other writers, testify that Moses was the leader of the Jews, and the founder of their laws. The great critic Longinus, and Numenius, a Pythagorean philosopher of Apamea, in Syria, both speak highly of Moses: and Porphyry admitted the genuineness of the Pentateuch. The Egyptian, Greek, and Roman authors concur in relating the tradition respecting the creation, the fall of man, the deluge, and the dispersion of mankind.

4. From the contents of the Pentateuch.

The frequent genealogies prove that it was composed by a writer of very early date, and from original materials.

The geographical details of places bespeak a writer personally present at the transactions recorded.

The frequent repetitions, which occur in the Pentateuch, and the neglect of order in delivering the precepts, are strong proofs, that it has come down to us precisely as it was written by Moses; to which may be added coincidences, so minute, latent, indirect, and undesigned, that they could only have been produced by reality and truth influencing the mind and the pen of the legislator.

SECTION II.—Genuineness and Authenticity of the New Testament.

I. General TITLE of the New Testament.

Every thing we know concerning the belief, worship, manners, and discipline of the first Christians, corresponds with the contents of the books of the New Testament now extant, and which therefore are most certainly the primitive instructions which they received. The collection of these books is known by the appellation of the New Testament or New Covenant, (because it contains the terms of the new covenant, upon which God is pleased to offer salvation through the mediation of Jesus Christ;) in opposition to the doctrines, precepts, and promises of the Mosaic dispensation, which Saint Paul terms the Old Covenant.

II. CANON of the New Testament.

The records, thus collectively termed the New Testament, consist of twenty-seven books, composed on various occasions, and at different times and places, by eight different authors contemporary with Jesus Christ, whose history they either relate, together with the first propagation of his religion, or unfold the doctrines, principles, and precepts of Christianity.

III. The GENUINENESS and AUTHENTICITY of the New Testament are proved, not only from arguments which demonstrate that it is not spurious, but also from positive evidence arising from the impossibility of forgery, and from direct external or historical evidence.

Of all the grounds, that either have been or may be assigned for denying a work to be genuine, not one can justly be applied to the New Testament: for,

1. No one doubted of its genuineness and authenticity when it first appeared.

2. No ancient accounts are on record, whence we may conclude it to be spurious.

3. No considerable period of time elapsed after the death of the Apostles, in which the New Testament was unknown. On the contrary, it is mentioned not only by their contemporaries, but also by succeeding writers.

4. No arguments can be brought in its disfavour from the nature of its style, which is exactly such as might be expected from the writers of its several books.

5. No facts are recorded, which happened after the death of the apostles.

6. No doctrines or precepts are maintained, which contradict their known tenets.

IV. Positive Evidence:

1. The absolute impossibility of forgery arising from the nature of the thing itself; because it is impossible to establish forged writings as authentic where there are persons strongly inclined and qualified to detect fraud, as was the case both with Jews and Gentiles.

2. External or Historical Evidence.

[i.] The Books of the New Testament are quoted or alluded to, times innumerable, by a series of Christian writers as well as by adversaries of the Christian faith, who may be traced back in regular succession from the present time to the apostolic age.

[ii.] The Ancient Versions of the new testament are another important evidence for its genuineness and authenticity, as well as of its antiquity; some of them (as the Syriac and several Latin versions) being made so early as the close of the first, or at the beginning of the second century.

3. Internal Evidence of the Genuineness and Authenticity of the New Testament.

[i.] The Character of the Writers of the New Testament: They are said to have been Jews by birth, and of the Jewish religion, and immediate witnesses of the events which they have recorded. And every page of their writings corresponds with their actual character.

[ii.] The Language and Style.—The *Language* is Greek, which was a kind of universal language, just as the French now is: but it is Hebrew-Greek, *i. e.* Greek intermixed with many peculiarities from the native dialect of the Jews of Palestine, and consequently such as we might expect from the persons, to whom the several parts of the New Testament are ascribed.

The *Style* or manner of writing, too, is such as shows that its authors were born and educated in the Jewish religion.

[iii.] The CIRCUMSTANTIALITY OF THE NARRATIVE, and the coincidence of the accounts delivered in the New Testament with the history of those times, are also an indisputable internal evidence of its authenticity.

SECTION III.—On the Uncorrupted Preservation of the Books of the Old and New Testament.

I. The Uncorrupted Preservation of the OLD TESTAMENT is proved from the impossibility of its being corrupted: for

1. There is no proof or vestige whatever of any pretended alteration: if the Jews had wilfully corrupted the books of the Old Testament *before* the time of Christ and his apostles, the prophets would not have passed such an heinous offence in silence: and, if they had been corrupted *in* the time of Christ and his apostles, these would not have failed to censure the Jews. If they had been mutilated or corrupted *after* the time of Christ, the Jews would unquestionably have expunged the falsified prophecies concerning Christ, which were cited by him and by his apostles.

2. In fact, neither before nor after the time of Christ *could* the Jews corrupt the Hebrew Scriptures; for, *before* that event, any forgery or material corruption would be rendered impossible by the reverence paid to these books by the Jews themselves, the publicity given to their contents by the reading of the law in public and in private, and by the jealousies subsisting between the Jews and Samaritans, and between the different sects into which the Jews were divided. And *since* the birth of Christ, the Jews and Christians have been a mutual guard and check upon each other.

3. The Agreement of all the Manuscripts.

II. The integrity and uncorruptness of the books of the NEW TESTAMENT is manifest,

1. From their contents; for, so early as the two first centuries the *very same* facts and doctrines were univer

sally received by the Christians, which we at this time believe on the credit of the New Testament.

2. Because an universal corruption of those writings was both impossible and impracticable, in consequence of the early dispersion of copies, which were multiplied and disseminated, either in the original Greek or in translations, as rapidly as the boundaries of the church increased, and also of the effectual check interposed by the various sects that existed in the Christian church.

3. From the agreement of all the manuscripts, the various readings in which are not only of so little moment, as not to affect any article of faith or practice; but they also prove that the books of the New Testament exist at present, in all essential points, precisely the same as they were, when they left the hands of their authors.

4. From the agreement of the ancient versions of these books, and the quotations made from them in the writings of the Christians of the three first centuries, and in those of the succeeding fathers of the church.

III. That no canonical books of Scripture have been lost, may be proved by the following considerations, viz:

1. The ordinary conduct of Divine Providence, and the care which the Divine Being has in all ages taken to preserve these books.

2. The zeal of the faithful to preserve their sacred books.

3. The dispersion of these books into the most distant countries and into the hands of innumerable persons.

IV. With regard to the Old Testament, more particularly, we may conclude, that, if any books seem to be wanting in our present canon, they are either such as are still remaining in the Scriptures, unobserved, under other appellations; or they are such as never were accounted canonical, and contained no points essential to the salvation of man. Consequently they are such of which we may safely remain ignorant here, and for which we shall never be responsible hereafter

V. The same observation applies with equal force to the Books of the New Testament; in which some learned men have imagined that they have discovered allusions to writings no longer extant; but on examination, their conjectures prove to be destitute of foundation. Thus the expression Εγραψα *I have written*, in 1 Cor. v. 9, (which has given rise to a supposition that St. Paul had already written an epistle to the Corinthian Church, that is no longer extant,) may probably be put for Γραφω, *I write;* there being nearly one hundred instances in the New Testament, in which the past tense is put for the present.—So also, the expression ἡ Επιστολη εκ Λαοδικειας—*the Epistle from Laodicea* (Col. iv. 16,) which seems to intimate that the same apostle had previously written an epistle to the church at Laodicea, is in all probability that which is called the Epistle to the Ephesians, Laodicea being within the circuit of the Ephesian Church.

CHAPTER III.

ON THE CREDIBILITY OF THE OLD AND NEW TESTAMENTS.

Section I.—Direct evidences of the Credibility of the Old and New Testaments.

I. The writers of the Books of the Old and New Testaments had a perfect knowledge of the subjects which they relate: and their moral character, though rigidly tried, was never impeached by their keenest opponents.

II. If there had been any falsehood in the accounts of such transactions as were public and generally known, it could (and doubtless would) have been easily detected: for these accounts were published among the people, who witnessed the events related by the historians. But this was not the case with the writings, either of Moses and the Prophets, or of the Evangelists.

1. It is impossible that Moses could have asserted falsehoods in his writings: for

[i.] If he had been an impostor, it is utterly incredible that he could have given to men so perfect and holy a law as he did.

[ii.] As Moses had been educated in all the learning of the Egyptians, and was not of a rash, credulous, or superstitious temper, he could not possibly have been himself deceived.

[iii.] It is absolutely incredible that he should or could have imposed on the Israelites, as true, things that were notoriously false, and of the falsehood of which they could convict him: for he relates facts and events which had taken place in the presence of six hundred thousand men; and urges the reality and truth of those facts upon them, as motives to believe and obey the new religion which he had introduced among them.

[iv.] We cannot conceive for what end or with what view *Moses* could have invented all these things. He sought neither riches nor honours for *himself*, and he left neither offices of honour nor emoluments to his children. He did not write to flatter his nation, nor did he conceal his own failings, or attempt to palliate or excuse the errors or sins of his countrymen.

These observations are equally applicable to the writers who succeeded Moses.

2. The credibility of the WRITERS OF THE BOOKS OF THE NEW TESTAMENT is established on evidence equally conclusive with that adduced for the old Testament. For

(1.) The actions ascribed to Jesus Christ in the New Testament are of such a description, that they could not possibly have been recorded, if they had not been true, Plain and unlettered Jews, as the apostles were, though adequate to the office of recording what they had seen and heard, were incapable of fabricating a series of actions, which constituted the most exalted character that ever lived upon earth. It is, indeed, highly probable, that the apostles and evangelists were not wholly aware of that perfection which they themselves have described: for it is not contained in any formal panegyric, but is known only by comparison and inference. Whence it follows, that the actions which are ascribed to Jesus Christ, either are *truly* ascribed to him, or they have been invented for a purpose, of which the inventors themselves were probably not aware, viz. the delineating of a model of perfection; and applied to that purpose by means which the inventors did not possess. And when we further consider that the plan, developed by those facts, was in direct opposition to the notion and expectation of the Jews respecting a temporal Messiah, it is impossible to believe that the apostles could have invented them.

(2.) The apostles *could* NOT *be deceived* in the facts which they have recorded; because

[i.] They were competent witnesses of the facts which they attested: and their testimony respected facts which they had themselves witnessed with their eyes and with their ears. (See 1 John i. 1—3., and 2 Peter i. 16.) They had lived with Jesus

Christ during his ministry; they had heard his discourses; they had seen his wonderful works, and consequently received them on the testimony of their own senses. They had all the same knowledge and in the same degree, and they all agree in the same essential testimony.

[ii.] They were neither enthusiasts nor fanatics.

They were not *enthusiasts:* for they became Christ's disciples, not upon internal persuasion alone, but upon rational conviction, arising from proofs submitted alike to the judgment of their minds and to the evidence of their senses, which enthusiasm could not have counterfeited, and would never have required: and, at every step of their progress, as their faith was called to signalise itself by new exertions, or to sustain new trials, it was fortified by new proofs. Their slowness and caution in giving credit to miraculous operations, particularly the account of their Master's resurrection from the dead, exempt them from all suspicion of being the dupes of delusion and credulity. Throughout their writings the utmost impartiality, sobriety, and modesty prevail; and, contrary to the practice of enthusiasts, they record their own mistakes, follies, and faults.

Neither were they *fanatics.*—This is evinced by the style of the New Testament, which is the very reverse of fanaticism, which is always obscure, arrogant, and violent. Though they insist on the necessity of receiving and believing the Christian system, yet they equally condemn all spirit of persecution and all religious differences.

(3.) As they could not be deceived themselves, so they NEITHER *would* NOR *did deceive* others.

The whole tenor of their lives proved (what their adversaries confessed) that they were men of piety and integrity. If the evangelists and apostles had confederated to impose upon mankind, it is incredible that none of their associates should not have confessed the fraud. They had nothing to gain by obtruding falsehoods; but, on the contrary, they were exposed to the loss of every thing, even of life itself, for preaching the doctrine of the cross, and bearing witness to the truth of Christianity. It is also utterly incredible, that so many precepts of piety and virtue should have been delivered by men of such abandoned principles as they must have been, had they really been impostors. Still less is it to be credited on that supposition, that they performed miracles, (the reality of which was acknowledged by their enemies,) in confirmation of their doctrine. Lastly, if the apostles and evangelists had designed to impose upon mankind, they would have accommodated themselves to the humours of the people whom they addressed; and would carefully have avoided whatever might shock or offend them: whereas they acted in quite a different manner.

(4.) On the contrary, they were men of the STRICTEST INTEGRITY and SINCERITY.

This is evident from the style and manner of their writings, which are characterized by the most rigid impartiality and fidelity. There is in them no preparation of events; there are no artful transitions or connexions; no set characters or persons to be introduced; no reflections on past transactions or the authors of them; no excuses or apologies for what might probably disturb their readers; no specious artifices, no plausible arguments to set off a doubtful action, and to reconcile it to some other, or to the character of the person who did it. They do not dissemble certain circumstances in the life and sufferings of their Master, which have no tendency to advance his glory in the eyes of the world. They announce the miracles of Jesus Christ, with the same dispassionate coolness, as if they had been common transactions, saying nothing *previously* to raise expectation, nor, *after* the recital, breaking out into exclamations.

The same striking integrity marks the conduct of the evangelists, when speaking of their enemies, and also when they are relating any circumstances respecting themselves. Their enemies are barely mentioned, without censure and without resentment; while they record the meanness of their own stations, the inveteracy of their prejudices, the weakness of their faith, their ambition, and, on certain occasions their secular views.

(5.) They appealed to MIRACLES and other notorious proofs, in such a manner, that if they had conspired to impose falsehoods upon the world, they might have been easily detected and confuted. And

(6.) Lastly, they SUFFERED every thing for the truth of their narration, even death itself, and brought many of their contemporaries, (among whom were persons of eminent rank and acquirements,) to a conviction of its truth.

III. The Credibility of the Old and New Testaments is further attested by the principal facts contained in them being CONFIRMED BY CERTAIN COMMEMORATIVE ORDINANCES, or monuments of great celebrity, that existed among Jews and Christians from the very time when the events took place, which they are said to commemorate, and which subsist to the present day in every country where either Jews or Christians are to be found. For instance,

[i.] Among the Jews there are the ordinance of Circumcision and the feasts of the Passover, of Tabernacles, and of Pentecost.

[ii.] In like manner, among Christians, the sacraments of Baptism and of the Lord's Supper, and the festival observed on the first day of the week, in honour of Christ's resurrection from the dead.

IV. The wonderful Establishment and Propagation of Christianity is a most convincing proof of the entire credibility of the New Testament, and of the religion which it establishes. It prevails without the assistance of any temporal power, and it triumphs over all opposition.

In considering all these direct evidences of the credibility of the writers of the New Testament, it is of importance to observe, that there is no opposite testimony to contradict the positive credible testimony of the apostles, evangelists, and multitudes of other persons, to the history and miracles of Jesus. Those persons, therefore, who reject the Gosple, are compelled to maintain, in opposition to positive credible testimony, that the most extensive and important events have taken place, without any adequate cause.

Section II. Testimonies to the Credibility of the Old and New Testaments, from Natural and Civil History.

§ 1.—Testimonies from Natural and Civil History to the Credibility of the Old Testament.

I. *Testimonies to the Mosaic Account of the* Creation of the World.

1. The Heathens had a tradition concerning the primeval chaos and the production of all things by the Supreme Mind. This applies particularly to the Chaldæan, Egyptian, Phœnician, Hindoo, Chinese, Etruscan, Gothic, Greek, and American Cosmogonies.
2. The division of time into *weeks* has prevailed among the Hebrews, Egyptians, Chinese, Greeks, Romans, and northern barbarians.
3. Even the Mosaic method of reckoning by *nights*, instead of days, has prevailed in more than one nation.

II. *The* Formation *of* Man *in the* Moral image *of* God *and his State in Paradise.*

These were the origin of the fabled golden age, which is described by the poets; and may also be distinctly traced in the legends of our Scythian forefathers, and in the age of perfection of the Hindoos. In the classical story of the garden of the Hesperides, we may equally discover a tradition of the Mosaical Paradise, and of the promised Saviour who should bruise the head of the infernal dragon.

III. *The* FALL OF MAN *and the Introduction of Sin into the World.*

The Mosaic Narrative of these events agrees in the most striking manner, both with the obvious facts of labour, sorrow, pain and death. Whatever some may *assert* to the contrary, and however they may attempt to explain away that narrative, · attempt to prove it false; yet the evidently ruined condition of the human race would still remain as an undeniable fact; and the Mosaic Account of the Fall is confirmed by various historical traditions. Thus,

1. From the Fall of the Angels, in all probability, originated the Tradition of the Titans, and giants invading heaven.

2. The Disobedience of Eve is plainly alluded to in the legend of Pandora.

3. The Corruption and Depravation of Human Nature are frequent subjects of complaint among the ancient heathen moralists, philosophers and poets.

4. The form, assumed by the Tempter, has been handed down in the traditions of the most ancient nations, particularly the Persians, Hindoos, Greeks, Egyptians and Scythians, or Goths.

5. A conviction of the necessity of an Atonement for sin has universally prevailed, together with the practice of devoting piacular victims.

IV. *The* TRANSLATION *of* ENOCH

May be traced in the Grecian fables of the translation of their heroes and demi-gods, particularly of Hesperus and Astræa; and in the translation of Dhruva among the Hindoos; of Buddha among the Ceylonese, and of Xaca, among the Calmucks of Siberia.

V. *The* LONGEVITY *of the Antideluvians*

Is confirmed by various heathen writers, mentioned by Josephus: (Ant. Jud. lib. i. c. 3,) and the Mosaic account of *Men of a Gigantic Stature* is confirmed by the Greek and Roman poets and historians, particularly Pausanias, Philostratus, and Pliny.

VI. *The Fact of the* DELUGE *is most completely attested both by Natural and Civil History.*

1. *Testimonies from* NATURAL HISTORY.

The Mosaic narrative of the Deluge is confirmed by the fossilised remains of animals belonging to a former world, which are found in every quarter of the globe, frequently on the summits of the most lofty mountains: and it is worthy of remark, that the remains of animals, belonging to *one* part of the globe, are often found in *another part very distant.* Further, the deep southern indentations on the different continents of the terraqueous globe, and the bold projecting capes on the north, corroborate the account of the ark drifting northwards.

2. *Testimonies from* Civil History.

[i.] The paucity of mankind, and the vast tracts of uninhabited land, mentioned in the accounts of the first ages.

[ii.] The late invention and progress of arts and sciences.

The fabulous nature of early history shows how little credit is due to the pretences to antiquity, made by the several nations among the heathens:—pretences, which have no support whatever from authentic history, but are grounded only on the uncertain calculations of astronomy, in which science they actually had but little or no skill.

[iii.] The universal tradition of this event, which has obtained among mankind in all ages.

The Chaldæans, Phœnicians, Assyrians, Greeks, Romans, Goths, and Druids, the Persians, Hindoos, Burmese, Chinese, Mexicans, Peruvians, Brazilians, Nicaraguans, the inhabitants of Western Caledonia, the Otaheitans, and Sandwich Islanders, all bear testimony to this fact. The deluge is also mentioned by Berosus, Hieronymus the Egyptian, and Nicolaus of Damascus, according to Josephus; and by Alexander Polyhistor, Plato, Diodorus Siculus, and Lucian. It is most evidently alluded to in Ovid's description of Deucalion's flood, and Plutarch relates the same particulars of a dove sent out by Deucalion, as Moses records of the dove sent out by Noah.

Notwithstanding all these testimonies, the Mosaic narrative of the deluge has been objected to, as an improbable event, contrary to matter of fact.

Objection 1.—*The Ark could not contain all the animals which are said to have entered it.*

Answer.—The contrary has been satisfactorily demonstrated. Reckoning the cubit at eighteen inches, Dr. Hales has proved that the Ark was of the burden of 42,413 tons. (Analysis of Chronology, vol. i. p. 328.) *Larger* calculations have been made, but the preceding is abundantly sufficient for our purpose.

OBJ. 2.—*As the same causes produce the same effects, the Rainbow must have existed before the flood.*

ANSWER.—So it may, but not as a sign of the Covenant. The Hebrew word, which in Gen. ix. 13, is rendered *set*, ought to be rendered *appoint*; in which case the passage would run thus:—"I do APPOINT my bow in the cloud to be a sign or token of the covenant between me and the earth."

OBJ. 3.—*If all mankind sprang from one white pair, (Noah and his wife,) it is impossible to account for the origin of the blacks.*

ANSWER.—This difference of colour does not invalidate the Mosaic Narrative: for it has been ascertained that the influence of climate, and the local circumstances of air, water, food, customs, &c. are abundantly sufficient to account for the dissimilarity in the appearance of different nations.

OBJ. 4.—*The peopling of America and of several islands, in which mischievous terrestrial animals have been found, has also been urged as an objection to the universality of the deluge.*

ANSWER.—The straits that divide North America from Tartary are so narrow, as to admit of a very easy passage from one continent to the other: and the resemblance found between the inhabitants of the opposite sides of that passage, and their uncivilised state and rude ignorance of the arts, prove them to have had one common origin.

VII. *The* BUILDING *of the* TOWER *of* BABEL

Is circumstantially mentioned by Berosus, a Chaldæan historian: according to Josephus, it is mentioned by Hestiæus and one of the ancient Sybils; and, as Eusebius informs us, by Abydenus and Eupolemus. That it was constructed with burnt bricks and bitumen, is attested by Justin, Quintus Curtius, and Vitruvius, and also by the relations of modern travellers.

VIII. *The* HISTORY *of the* DESTRUCTION *of* SODOM *and* GOMORRAH

Is attested by Diodorus Siculus, Strabo, Solinus, Tacitus, Pliny, and Josephus, whose accounts mainly agree with the Mosaic Narrative: and their reports concerning the physical appearance of the Dead Sea are confirmed, in all material points, by the relations of all modern travellers.

IX. Ancient historians, cited by Josephus and Eusebius, make mention of *Abraham, Isaac, and Jacob.*

X. *The* Departure *of the Children of Israel from Egypt, and their miraculous passage of the Red Sea,*

Are attested by Berosus, Artapanus, Strabo, Diodorus Siculus, Numenius, Justin, and Tacitus.

XI. *The* Heathen Writers *borrowed images from the accounts communicated in the Scriptures.*

Such are the representations of their deities being veiled in clouds, &c.; together with several religious institutions, and other particulars.

XII. *Many other occurrences related in the Old Testament appear to have given rise to various stories among the ancients*

Thus, the Story of Iphigenia being sacrificed by her father Agamemnon, was borrowed from the circumstance of Jephthah's devoting his daughter. The story of Scylla having cut off the purple lock of her father, Nisus, and given it to his enemy, Minos, was in all probability taken from the history of Sampson's being shaved. Herodotus relates the departure of the sun from its course four times, which seems to refer to the times of Joshua and Hezekia. Numerous other instances occur, in which scripture characters and events are mentioned by heathen writers.

XIII. Lastly, *the* Fertility *of the Soil of Palestine*

Is confirmed by the unanimous testimony of ancient writers, as well as of most, if not all the travellers who have visited that country: and, if Palestine were as well inhabited and as well cultivated as formerly, its produce unquestionably would exceed all calculation.

Besides the attestations from natural and profane history, we may consider the Jews themselves as bearing testimony, to this day, in all countries of the world, to the truth of their ancient history, that is, to the truth of the Old Testament. *Allow* this, and it will be easy to see, why they still persist in their attachment to that religion, those laws, and those predictions, which so manifestly condemn them, both in past times and in the present. Suppose, however, that any considerable alterations have been made in their ancient history, that is, any such alteration as may answer their purposes of infidelity, and their present state will be *inexplicable*.

§ 2.—Testimonies of Profane Writers to the Credibility of the NEW TESTAMENT.

I. *Testimonies of Jewish and Pagan Authors to the* ACCOUNTS *of* PRINCES *and* GOVERNORS *mentioned in the New Testament.*

Thus, Josephus, the Jewish historian, and various ancient writers, mention Herod, Archelaus, Pontius Pilate, and other persons, whose names occur in the New Testament; and they differ but little from the Evangelical Historians, concerning their offices and characters.

II. The Evangelical Writers agree with Josephus, and with profane Authors respecting the SECTS, MORALS, *and* CUSTOMS *of the Jews.*

III. *The* CHARACTERS *and* PURSUITS *of Heathen Nations,* for instance, the Cretans, Athenians, &c. which are occasionally introduced in the New Testament, are corroborated by the testimonies of profane writers.

IV. *Testimonies of* JEWISH ADVERSARIES *to the Name and Faith of Christ.*

1. JOSEPHUS bears testimony to the character, miracles, and doctrines of Jesus Christ, in the eighteenth book of his Jewish Antiquities, Chap. iii. Sect. 3, which passage, though rejected by some writers as spurious, has been satisfactorily demonstrated to be genuine.

2. The TALMUDS, or Books containing the Jewish Traditions, the rabbinical constitutions, and explications of the law, though blended with falsehood, refer to the nativity of Jesus Christ, they relate his journey into Egypt; and do not deny that he performed numerous eminent miracles.

V. *Testimonies of* HEATHEN ADVERSARIES *to the Christian Name and faith.*

1. Mention is made of the LIFE and CHARACTER of JESUS CHRIST in the Acta Pilati, (which were an account sent by Pilate to Rome of the transactions that occurred in his province, and to which the Christian writers, Justin and Tertullian. appealed in their apologies;) and also in the writings of the heathen historians, Suetonius, Tacitus, Pliny, and Ælius Lampridius. And Celsus, Porphyry, and Julian, who were the earliest learned opposers of the Christian Religion, bear evidence to the genuineness of the books received by Christians, and consequently to the truth of the history of the Life and Character of Jesus Christ.

2. To the INNOCENCY of LIFE, and constancy of the first Christians in the profession of their faith, explicit testimony is borne, during the Neronian persecution (A. D. 95,) by Tacitus Suetonius, Martial, and Juvenal: and the celebrated epistle of the Younger Pliny, which was written to the emperor Trajan,

A. D. 107, together with that emperor's reply or rescript, are valuable documents, corroborating the truth of the New Testament, inasmuch as they attest

(1.) The great progress made by the Christian Religion in a short space of time.

(2.) The fortitude of the Christians in suffering, and their steady perseverance in the faith of Jesus Christ.

(3.) That they disowned all the Gods of the Heathens, paid divine worship to their God and Saviour Jesus Christ, and devoted themselves to the practice of moral virtue.

(4.) The innocent and virtuous lives of the first Christians, whose religion was their only crime.

Further, Celsus ridicules the Christians for their worship of Christ, and attests the gradual increase of their numbers. He also acknowledges that there were modest, temperate, and intelligent persons among them; and bears witness to their faith in Christ. Lucian also, another bitter enemy of the Christian Faith, has borne testimony to its principal facts and doctrines, as well as to the upright character of the Christians: and their fortitude and constancy under persecution are referred to by the philosopher Epictetus (**A.D.** 109,) the emperor Marcus Antoninus (**A.D.** 161,) and by Galen. (**A.D.** 200.) Porphyry also, (**A.D.** 270,) and the emperor Julian (**A.D.** 361,) have both attested the truth of many facts and things related in the New Testament.

VI. Refutation of the Objection to the Credibility of the Scripture History, which has been raised, in consequence of the silence of profane historians to the facts therein recorded.

That silence may be satisfactorily accounted for, by *their* great ignorance of facts which occurred very long before their own time, and by the peculiar contempt which several of them entertained both for Jews and Christians, arising from the diversity of their customs and institutions. To these considerations we may add—

1. That many books of those remote ages are lost, in which it is very possible that some mention might have been made of these facts.

2. Some of the Roman Historians, whose works have come down to our time, are defective.

3. That of the few remaining historians, who wrote about the ages in question, most were engaged upon other subjects. Besides, no profane historians, whether Jews or Gentiles, take notice of *all* occurrences.

4. That several of the facts relating to Christ and his miracles, coming from Jews, would be slighted as fabulous by the Gentile writers, especially considering, on the one hand, how common prodigies and magical stories were; and, on the other, how superstitious and credulous the Jews were reputed to be; and

5. That the first appearance of the Christian scheme would

shock them, as seeming so improbable, and so contrary to their received maxims, that it cannot excite surprise, that many of them cared but little to inquire into the evidences and facts relating to Christianity. Many, however, who *did* inquire, doubtless became Christians; their testimony therefore is not to be reckoned in this place.

---

§ 3.—Collateral Testimonies to the Truth of the Facts recorded in the Scriptures, from ancient Coins, Medals, and Marbles.

These are confessedly among the most important proofs of ancient history in general; and the confirmation which they afford of many particulars recorded in the Scriptures, is not less important and decisive than the series of evidence, furnished by profane historians in the preceding sections. Thus,

I. *The* MOSAIC NARRATIVE *of the* DELUGE

Is confirmed by a coin, struck at Apamea in the reign of Philip the elder; which commemorates the sending forth of the dove by Noah. (Gen. viii. 7—11.) On one of the front pannels of the chest or ark, which is represented on the reverse of this medal, is the word NOE in ancient Greek characters.

II. *The account of* PHARAOH-NECHO'S WAR *against the Jews and Babylonians, which is related in* 2 Chron. xxxv. 20—24, *and* xxxvi. 1—4,

Is confirmed by Herodotus, (Hist. lib. ii. c. 159,) and especially by the discoveries of the late Mr. Belzoni, in the tombs of the Egyptian sovereigns. (See his Narrative of Operations in Egypt, &c. pp. 242, 243. 4to. edit. and Nos. 4, 5, and 6, of his folio Atlas of Plates.)

III. *The* INVASION *of the Kingdom of Israel, by Shalmaneser, King of Assyria, and the carrying of the ten tribes into captivity, which are narrated in* 2 Kings, xvii. 6, *and* xviii. 10,

Are confirmed by certain ancient sculptures on the mountains of Be-Sitoon, near the borders of the ancient Assyria, which are described in Sir Robert Ker Porter's Travels in Georgia, Persia, &c. vol. ii. pp. 154—162.

IV. ACTS xiii. 7, *is confirmed by a coin, proving that the island of Cyprus was at that time under the government of a proconsul.*

On this coin the same title ΑΝΘΥΠΑΤΟΣ, or Deputy, is given to Proclus, which St. Paul gave to his predecessor, Sergius Paulus.

V. *In* Acts xvi. 11, 12, *the evangelist Luke says, "We came.........to Philippi, which is the chief city of that part of Macedonia, and a colony."—This passage may more correctly be rendered—"Philippi, a city of the first part of Macedonia, or of Macedonia Prima."*

The province of Macedonia had undergone various changes, and had been divided into various portions, particularly into *four*, while under the Roman government. Many medals of the first province, or Macedonia Prima, are extant, with the inscription ΜΑΚΕΔΟΝΩΝ ΠΡΩΤΗΣ, or the "*first* part *of Macedonia*," which confirm the accuracy of Luke, and show his attention to the minutest particulars. Further, by using the term ΚΟΛΩΝΙΑ, (which was originally a Latin word, *Colonia*,) instead of the corresponding Greek word ἀποικία, the historian plainly intimates that it was a Roman colony, which the twenty-first verse certainly proves it to have been. Now, among some coins that have been discovered, in which it is recorded under this character, there is one in particular, which explicitly states that Julius Cæsar himself bestowed the privileges of a Roman colony on the city of Philippi, which were afterwards confirmed by Augustus.

VI. *In* Acts xvi. 14, *we read that Lydia, a dealer in purple, from Thyatira, had settled at Philippi.*

Now, among the ruins of Thyatira, there is an inscription extant with the words ΟΙ ΒΑΦΕΙΣ (*the diers;*) whence we learn that the art and trade of dying purple were carried on in that city.

VII. *In* Acts xvii. 23, *Paul relates his having found an altar at Athens, with the inscription* ΑΓΝΩΣΤΩ ΘΕΩ, TO THE UNKNOWN GOD.

We know from the testimony of Lucian, that there was such an inscription: and the occasion of this altar being erected, in common with many others bearing the same inscription, is related at length by Diogenes Laertius (in Epimenide, lib. i. c. x. § 3.)

VIII. *In* Acts xix. 35, *the word* ΝΕΩΚΟΡΟΝ *(in the English version rendered* a worshipper) *is very emphatic.*

It properly signifies a person dedicated to the service of some god or goddess, whose peculiar office it was to attend the temple, and see that it was kept clean. At length the ΝΕΩΚΟΡΟΙ became persons of great consequence, and were those who offered sacrifices for the life of the emperor. Whole cities took this appellation, as appears on many ancient coins and medals. Ephesus is supposed to have been the first which assumed this title; and there is a medal extant, in which it is given to that city.

IX. *The* TRIUMPHAL ARCH *erected at Rome in honour of Titus*, (whereon are represented certain vessels used by the Jews in their religious worship, agreeably to the statements in the Old Testament,*) is an evidence to the truth of the historic accounts, which describe the dissolution of the Jewish State and Government, and relate the conquest of Jerusalem.

Further, there are extant numerous MEDALS of Judæa vanquished, struck by order of the Roman general Titus, (who was afterwards emperor,) in order to commemorate the conquest of Judæa and the subversion of the Jewish state and polity.

The following representation of the reverse of one of these is given from the original very rare coin, preserved in the cabinet of the British Museum.

It represents the conquered country as a desolate female sitting under a tree, and affords an extraordinary fnlfilment of Isaiah's prediction (iii. 26. *She being desolate* SHALL SIT *upon the ground,*) delivered at least *eight hundred* years before, as well as a striking illustration of the Lamentations of Jeremiah (ch. i. ver. 1.) *How doth the city* SIT *solitary*, that was *full of people! How is she*

* The vignettes, given in the subsequent part of this volume, are copied from this arch.

become as a widow! she that was great among the nations, princess among the provinces, how is she become tributary!

CHAPTER IV.

ALL THE BOOKS OF THE OLD AND NEW TESTAMENTS ARE OF DIVINE AUTHORITY, AND THEIR AUTHORS ARE DIVINELY INSPIRED.

Section I.—Preliminary Observations.

I. Inspiration defined.

It is the imparting of such a degree of divine influence, assistance, or guidance, as enabled the authors of the several Books of Scripture to communicate religious knowledge to others, without error or mistake.

II. Such Inspiration is both reasonable and necessary.

1. It is *reasonable* that the sentiments and doctrines delivered in the scriptures, should be suggested to the minds of the writers by the Supreme Being himself; since they relate to matters, concerning which the communication of information to men is worthy of God.

2. Further, Inspiration is *necessary;* for,

(1.) Some past facts are related in the Bible, which could not possibly have been known, had not God revealed them.

(2.) Some events are predicted, which God alone could foreknow.

(3.) Other things also are contained in the Scriptures which are far above the capacity of man.

(4.) The authoritative language of Scripture argues the necessity of inspiration, admitting the veracity of the writers. They do not present us with their own thoughts, but exclaim, ' *Thus saith the Lord;*" and on that ground they demand our assent.

III. The Scriptures could not have been the invention of men. Wicked men *would not* have produced books which condemn every thing that is unholy, even if they were capable of doing so; and good men *could not* deceive.

IV. Criteria of Inspiration.

These are twofold, viz. Miracles and Prophecy.

To these may be added other internal evidences for the divine inspiration of the Scriptures; viz.

The sublime doctrines and precepts which they contain;

The harmony and connexion subsisting between their various parts;

The miraculous preservation of the Scriptures; and

Their tendency to promote the present and eternal happiness of mankind, as evinced by the blessed effects which are invariably produced by a cordial belief of the doctrines of the Bible.

SECTION II.—The Miracles, related in the Old and New Testaments, are Proofs, that the Scriptures were given by Inspiration of God.

I. A MIRACLE defined.

A MIRACLE is an effect or event, contrary to the established constitution or course of things; or, a sensible suspension or controlment of, or deviation from, the known laws of nature, wrought either by the immediate act, or by the assistance or by the permission of God, and accompanied with a previous notice or declaration that it is performed according to the purpose and power of God, for the proof or evidence of some particular doctrine, or in attestation of the authority or divine mission of some particular person.

Nature is the assemblage of created beings: these beings act upon each other, or by each other, agreeably to certain laws, the result of which is, what we call the *course* or order of nature. These laws are invariable: it is by them God governs the world. He alone established them; He alone therefore can suspend them. Effects, which are produced by the regular operation of these laws, or which are conformable to the established course of events, are said to be *natural;* and every palpable deviation from the constitution of the natural system, and the correspondent course of events in that system, is called a *miracle.*

II. Nature of the EVIDENCE arising from Miracles.

OBJECTION.—Miracles are beyond comprehension, and therefore are contrary to reason.

ANSWER.—This is by no means the case: for the possibility of miracles is not contrary to reason. Every thing we see, indeed, is in one sense a miracle. How many of the most common phenomena in nature are beyond our comprehension! And yet, notwithstanding we cannot comprehend or solve the most common of these phenomena, they make no impression on us, because they *are* common, because they happen according to a stated course, and are seen every day. If they were out of the common course of nature, though in themselves not more difficult to comprehend, they would still appear more wonderful to us, and more immediately the work of God. Thus, when we see a child grow into a man, and, when the breath has left the body, turn to corruption, we are not in the least surprised, because we see it every day: but were we to see a man restored from sickness to health by a word, or raised to life from the dead by a mere command, though these things are not really more unaccountable, yet we call the uncommon event a miracle, merely because it *is* uncommon. We acknowledge, however, that both are produced by God, because it is evident that no other power can produce them.

Such, then, is the nature of the evidence which arises from miracles: and we have no more reason to disbelieve them, when well attested, and not repugnant to the goodness or justice of God, only because they were performed several ages ago, than we have to disbelieve the more ordinary occurrences of Providence which passed before our own time, because the same occurrences *may* never happen again during our lives. The ordinary course of nature proves the being and providence of God; these extraordinary acts of power prove the divine commission of that person who performs them.

III. Design of Miracles.

This is, not to prove the great doctrines and duties of natural religion, but to prove *new revealed* doctrines, which neither were nor could be known to the reason of man Consequently, believers in the Bible do not argue in a circle (as some modern objectors have asserted,) proving the doctrines first by the miracles, and then the miracles by the doctrines: because the doctrines which they *prove* by miracles, and the doctrines by which they *try* them, are not the same doctrines.

No miracles are related in the Scriptures to have been wrought in confirmation of falsehoods; yet this has been objected in the cases of the Egyptian Magicians, the Witch of Endor, and Satan in the time of Christ's temptation But this objection is utterly destitute of foundation: for,

1. The Magicians did *not* perform any miracle. All they did,—as the narrative of Moses expressly states,—was to busy

themselves in their enchantments; by which, every man knows, miracles cannot be accomplished.

2. The Witch of Endor neither wrought nor expected to work any miracle, being herself terrified at the appearance of Samuel, who was sent by God himself.

3. There was nothing miraculous in Satan's leading Christ, by his free consent, to a lofty mountain, whence he could discover,—not all the world, but all the four tetrarchies or kingdoms of οἰκουμενης, that is, the land of Judæa.

The proper effect of miracles is, to mark *clearly* the divine interposition; and the Scriptures intimate this to be their design; for both Moses and the Prophets, and Jesus Christ and his Apostles, appealed to them, in proof of their divine mission.

IV. Credibility of Miracles vindicated and proved.

Whatever miracles are wrought, they *are matters of fact*, and capable of being proved by proper evidence, as other historical facts are. The witnesses, however, must be supposed to be acquainted with the course of nature so as to be able to judge that the event in question was contrary to it; for an event is not miraculous merely because it is to us strange or unaccountable, but because it is contrary to the known course of nature. To those who beheld the miracles of Moses and Jesus Christ, the seeing of those miracles was sufficient evidence of their divine inspiration. But to other men, miracles, like other events, admit of the evidence of testimony: the credibility of the witnesses therefore is the only point now to be considered.

Hints for estimating the value of human testimony.

1. Any thing capable of being proved by mere testimony is credible, in proportion to the opportunity which the witness had of being well informed concerning it himself, and his freedom from any bias which might make him wish to impose upon others.

If the person, who gives us information of any fact, appears to be a competent judge of it,—and to have been in a situation in which he had the best opportunity of being rightly informed, and if there be no appearance of its being his interest to deceive us, we give our assent,—but we hesitate in proportion to the doubts we entertain on either of these heads.

2. The *more* persons there are, who relate the same transaction of which they are equally credible witnesses, the stronger is the evidence for it. But the more persons there are, through whose hands the *same narration* is conveyed to us, the weaker is the evidence.

In the latter case the witnesses are called *dependent* ones; but in the former they are said to be *independent.* Whatever imperfection there may be in any one of a number of independent witnesses, it is in part removed by the testimony of others: but every imperfection increases in proportion to the number of dependent witnesses, through whose hands the story is transmitted.

3. The proper mark or criterion of a story being related by a number of independent witnesses, of full credit, is their complete agreement in the principal arguments, and their disagreement with respect to things of less consequence, or, at least, variety or diversity, in their manner of relating the same story.

4. We likewise distinguish respecting the nature of the fact to which our assent is required. Miracles require stronger testimony than common facts; and such testimony they really have.

The greater part of our knowledge has no other foundation than testimony. Yet has it been laid down as a maxim, that no human testimony is sufficient to establish the truth of a miracle. This assertion was first made by the ablest and acutest of the deistical philosophers, and it has commonly been accounted the strong hold of infidelity. His argument, in substance, is this:—"Experience, which in some things is variable, in others is uniform, is our *only* guide in reasoning concerning matters of fact. Variable experience gives rise to probability only; an uniform experience amounts to proof. Our belief of any fact from the testimony of eye-witnesses is derived from no other principle, than our experience of the veracity of human testimony. If the fact attested be miraculous, there arises a contest of two opposite experiences, or proof against proof. Now, a miracle is a violation of the laws of nature: and as a firm and unalterable experience has established these laws, the proof against a miracle,—from the very nature of the fact,—is as complete as any argument from experience can possibly be imagined: and if so, it is an undeniable consequence, that it cannot be surmounted by any proof whatever, derived from human testimony."

To this specious reasoning it may be replied,

(1.) That the evidence arising from human testimony is *not* derived *solely* from experience: on the contrary, testimony has a natural influence on belief.

It is therefore more consonant to truth, to say, that our *diffidence* in testimony is the result of experience, than that our faith in it has this foundation. Besides, the uniformity of experience, in favour of any fact, is not a proof against its being reversed in any particular instance. The evidence, arising from the single testimony of a man of known veracity, will go further to establish a belief of its being reversed.

(2.) What is usually called the 'course of nature' is nothing but the will and pleasure of God acting continually upon matter, according to certain rules of uniformity, still bearing relation to contingencies. Now God is the governor of the *moral* as well as of the *physical* world: and, since the moral well-being of the universe is of more consequence than its physical order and regularity, it follows, that the latter may be subservient, and occasionally yield to the former.

(3.) The futility of this sophism may also be shown upon its own avowed principles. If the secret of compounding gunpowder had perished by the accidental death of its inventor, immediately after its extraordinary powers had been exhibited before a hundred competent witnesses, on the principles of the sophism now before us, the fact of its extraordinary powers must be rejected as a falsehood.

V. The Credibility of Miracles does NOT decrease with the lapse of years, as the antagonists of Christianity object.

There may be cases, in which credibility vanishes with time; but no testimony is really, in the nature of things, rendered less credible by any other cause than the loss or want of some of those conditions, which at first made it rationally credible. A testimony continues equally credible so long as it is transmitted with all those circumstances and conditions, which first procured it a certain degree of credit amongst men, proportionate to the intrinsic value of those conditions. But the evidence in favour of the facts of the Christian Religion has *increased* instead of diminishing; as recent inquiries of learned men have produced fresh testimonies.

VI. Criteria of Miracles:—they are six in number viz.:

1. A miracle should have an important end in view, worthy of its author.

2. It must be instantaneously and publicly performed, before credible witnesses.

3. It must be sensible and easy to be observed; in other words, the fact purporting to be miraculous must be such, that the senses of mankind can clearly and fully judge of it.

It ought to be independent of second causes.

OBJECTION.—In three of his miracles (John ix. 1—7. Mark viii. 23—26. Mark vii. 32—37.) Jesus made use of external applications.

ANSWER.—These applications were made only upon the blind or the deaf; and in these cases, the reason for using them seems to have been, to convey to the persons on whom the miraculous cures were performed, a clear assurance that Jesus Christ was the author of such cures.

5. Not only public monuments must be kept up, but some outward actions must also be constantly performed, in memory of the facts thus publicly wrought.

6. Such monuments must be set up, and such actions and observances instituted, at the very time when those

events took place, and be afterwards continued without interruption.

These two rules render it impossible that the belief of any facts should be imposed upon the credulity of after ages, when the generation asserted to have witnessed them had expired; for, whenever such facts come to be recounted, if not only monuments are said to remain of them, but public actions and observances had further been constantly used to commemorate them by the nation appealed to, ever since they had taken place, the deceit must be immediately detected, by no such monuments appearing, and by the experience of every individual, who could not but know that no such actions or observances had been used by them, to commemorate such events.

VII. Application of these Criteria to the Miracles related in the Sacred Writings.

1. With regard to the miracles recorded to have been wrought by Moses and Joshua :—

The posterity of Abraham, Isaac, and Jacob, being chosen by Jehovah to be his peculiar people for the preservation of true religion, the miracles performed on their behalf were unquestionably worthy of their Almighty Author. These miracles were instantaneously performed at the command of Moses, and before great numbers of Egyptians or Israelites, sometimes in the presence of both nations; as in the case of the plagues, and the destruction of Pharaoh's army, which were witnessed by the whole people of Israel, and were felt by the Egyptians. In commemoration of these and other miraculous occurrences, were instituted the three great festivals of the Hebrews —the Passover, the feast of Tabernacles, and the feast of Pentecost; all the first born of man and beast were solemnly consecrated to God; and the tribe of Levi was set apart, in special commemoration of the destruction of the first born of the Egyptians.

The memory of the miraculous supply of the Israelites with food was perpetuated by the pot of manna; and the twelve stones, taken out of the midst of Jordan at the time of the miraculous passage of the Israelites over that river, were set up by Joshua at Gilgal, as a perpetual memorial to them.

In all these instances, the preceding criteria are most decisively established.

2. With respect to the miracles related in the New Testament.

(1.) The NUMBER of Christ's miracles was very great.

About forty of them are narrated at length. The gospel history is full of them: and one of Christ's biographers informs us that he performed a greater number than are in any way recorded.

(2.) There was great VARIETY in the miracles recorded in the New Testament.

They were of a permanent nature, and might be reviewed and re-examined, as in many instances they actually were. We behold Christ giving sight to the born blind;—healing the obstinate leprosy;—making those who wanted a limb, perfect;—those who were bowed double, straight;—those who shook with palsy, robust;—nerving the withered arm with strength; —restoring the insane and demoniacs to reason;—and raising the dead to life. We behold the apostles also expelling demons, restoring the lame from his birth, giving sight to the blind, healing all manner of diseases, and giving life to the dead. All these supernatural works were performed, not in a *few* instances with hesitation and diffidence, but were very frequently repeated through a series of years; so that all suspicion of human management, compact, and imposture, was for ever precluded.

(3.) The DESIGN of Christ's miracles was important, and worthy of their Almighty Author.

The end and purpose, for which these miracles were wrought, was, to carry on one vast and consistent plan of Providence, extending from the creation to the consummation of all things· to establish a system of belief, hope, and practice adapted to the wants and conditions of mankind; which had been revealed in part to the Jews, and promised to the prophets, and which tended to destroy the four great moral evils, so prevalent and so pernicious, viz.—atheism, scepticism, immorality, and vice. In subservience to their grand object, (the confirmation of his divine mission,) the miracles of Christ were wrought for the most benevolent of all purposes,—the alleviation of misery in every form; and they carry in them the characters of the greatest goodness, as well as of the greatest power.

Only two of Christ's miracles bear any marks of severity; viz. his suffering the demons to enter the herd of swine (Matt. viii. 28—34. Mark v. 12—17.,) and his causing the fig-tree to wither away.

[i.] As to the destruction of the swine, though commonly regarded as a miraculous work, it was in point of fact not a miracle. He did not *command*, but only *permitted*, the demons to enter the swine; for which permission several satisfactory reasons may be assigned. For, if the owners of the swine were *Jews*, as there is every reason to believe, they were justly punished for their deliberate violation of their laws, which prohibited the keeping of swine: and if they were *Gentiles*, Christ might have permitted the demons to enter the swine, to convince them of the sanctity and divinity of the Jewish laws (which they were accustomed to ridicule,) and, further, it may be, to punish them for laying a snare in the way of the Jews.

[ii.] In causing the barren fig-tree to wither away, Jesus Christ neither invaded private property, nor did any injury to the community at large; but by this action he dictated an impressive and important moral lesson both to his disciples and to all mankind: viz.—That if we neglect or wilfully misemploy our opportunities of improvement in religious knowledge and in holiness, we must expect to be withered like the barren fig-tree before the displeasure of the Lord Jesus, when he shall come to judge the world.

Consider further the GREATNESS of Christ's Miracles.

The diseases which he healed were incurable, inveterate, and had baffled every attempt of art: and this greatness of Christ's miracles secures them against the suspicion of imposture. Impostors usually satisfy themselves with *little tricks*, because they are less open to suspicion, and usually gain credit.

(5.) Observe also the persons BY whom these miracles were accomplished.

They were wrought by persons, who were known to be poor, unlearned, of low condition, and destitute of great friends and powerful patrons; who gave other proofs of their mission, and did not rest the *whole* of their cause upon miracles, but likewise insisted upon the reasonableness of the doctrines which they offered to examination. Further, they were offered by persons, who appealed to God, and declared that they would perform them.

(6.) The persons, BEFORE whom the miracles were wrought, claim our especial notice.

They were wrought in a learned age, and before people who were not easily deluded, and they were stigmatised by the name of magic.

(7.) The MANNER too in which these miracles were performed is equally worthy of attention for its publicity, simplicity, and disinterestedness.

(8.) Another circumstance, which confirms the validity and truth of these miracles, is, the EFFECTS produced by them.

Numbers who were spectators of them yielded to conviction, and embraced the Gospel.

(9.) Lastly, the REALITY of the miracles of Christ and his apostles was never denied.

Both Jewish and Heathen opposers of the Christian faith were constrained, however reluctantly, to admit the reality of the miracles of Christ and his apostles; though they ascribed them to magic, and denied the divine commission of him who performed them.

VIII. A brief examination of a few of the principal Miracles related in the New Testament.

1. *The Conversion of Water into Wine.* (John ii. 1—10.)

The Jewish weddings continued seven days: during the nuptial feast, from the poverty of the bridegroom and bride, or perhaps from the number of guests being greater than was expected, there was a deficiency of wine. Jesus commanded the servants to fill the vessels with water *up to the brim;* it was therefore impossible to mix any wine. The servants alone were privy to the process; and the governor of the feast gives his attestation to the miraculous supply in so easy and natural a manner, that we cannot but esteem it beyond the reach of artifice.

2. *The miraculous Feeding of five thousand men, besides women and children.* (Matt. xiv. 15—21. Mark vi. 35—44. John vi. 5—13.)

The orderly disposition of the multitude, in ranks by hundreds and by fifties, exposed the miraculous operation to the view of all; so that deception was impossible. The gathering up of twelve baskets full of fragments is a proof that they had plenty of food; and the circumstance of the people being desirous to make Christ a King (for which he rebuked them on the following day,) is a further proof of the reality of the miracle, and of the impression which it had made.

3. *The Healing of the Paralytic.* (Matt. ix. 2—8. Mark ii. 4—12. Luke 5. 18—26.)

This miracle was wrought in the presence of many witnesses, some of whom were enemies to Jesus Christ. The manner in which the sick man was presented, is unparalleled, and shows the confidence which he and others had in Christ's power of healing him. The manner, too, in which Christ addressed him, is still more striking, beginning with the remission of his sins, without saying any thing concerning his malady.

4. *The giving of Sight to a man who had been born blind.* (John ix. 1—7.

There are many remarkable circumstances in this miracle. The man had not become blind by any accident, which admits of relief. He was *born blind.* He did *not* ask to be restored to sight: thus there was no room for suspicion on his part.

The question, proposed by the disciples (John ix. 1, 2,) proves that the man's blindness was from his birth; but the answer was so little in unison with their notions, that it never could have entered their minds if they had not heard it from Jesus. The mode employed for giving this man sight, was utterly *inadequate* to produce the effect which followed. Lastly, the miracle was performed in public, and immediately subjected to the strictest possible scrutiny.

5. *The Cure, by Peter and John, of a man who had been Lame from his Birth* (Acts iii. 1—10,) *is equally remarkable.*

The man's person and lameness were universally known in Jerusalem; a perfect cure was instantaneously wrought; and the transaction immediately underwent a severe examination, the effect of which was only to make the miracle still more widely known.

6. *The Raising of the Daughter of Jairus to life.* (Matt. ix. 18.—26. Mark v. 22—43. Luke viii. 41—56.)

Though all the circumstances in the account of this miracle have the aspect of the most natural and unexpected occurrences, (which could neither have been combined by human contrivance nor anticipated by human foresight,) no circumstance was wanting, either to ascertain the reality of the miracle, or without any apparent ostentation or design, to give it the most unquestionable publicity.

7. *The Raising of the Widow's Son from the Dead at Nain.* (Luke vii. 11—15.)

The fact of the young man's death was indisputable: a considerable number of her townsmen accompanied his mother who was following his remains to the grave: and in their presence the miracle was instantaneously and publicly performed.

8. *The Resurrection of Lazarus from the dead.* (John xi.)

The precise time of Christ's arrival at Bethany gave his enemies an opportunity of observing the transaction. "Many of the Jews had come to Martha and Mary:" and the restoring of Lazarus to life has every character of a miracle. For it was instantaneously and publicly performed before credible witnesses; it was independent of second causes; and the end for which it was performed, was important, for it was, to attest the divine mission of the Son of God.

IX. The most remarkable of all the miracles, related in the New Testament, is the RESURRECTION of Jesus Christ from the dead, and it demands a distinct examination.

1. As to Christ's PROPHETIC DECLARATIONS concerning his death and resurrection.

Jesus repeatedly predicted the circumstances of his death and resurrection to his disciples. Now, when he did this, he either did or did not foresee his resurrection. If he did *not* foresee it, with what hopes did he comfort his disciples? and why did he voluntarily offer himself to death, and actually endure the ignominious death of crucifixion? If he did foresee that he should rise again, he could not have believed it, but only on the experience he had already made of his power of giving sight to the blind, health to the sick, and (above all) life to the dead. His miracles therefore must be true; and, if so, he then possessed sufficient power to raise himself to life.

No one can doubt that Christ foretold his resurrection, who considers that it was *on this very account* that the chief priests and pharisees set a watch at the sepulchre.

2. Evidence of the REALITY of the resurrection.

It is an indisputed fact that Jesus died upon the cross and was interred in the sepulchre; at which the Jews took the precaution of placing a military guard. *After* the resurrection, the Jews reported that the disciples stole the body away while the guard were sleeping; a circumstance so manifestly improbable as well as false, that Matthew, though he faithfully records the report, does not offer a syllable to refute it.

Consider further,

(1.) The *terror* of the timid disciples, and the paucity of their number; the *season*,—that of the great annual festival, the Passover, when Jerusalem was full of people, and when also, it being the time of the full moon, the night was very light.

(2.) Is it probable that so many men, as composed the guard, would *all* fall asleep in the open air *at once*?

(3.) If the soldiers were *all* asleep, they could not know what was doing in the mean time; would not the noise, made in opening the sepulchre, have awakened some, if not the whole of them? and if *any* of them were awake, would they not soon have alarmed the rest, and prevented such an attempt?

(4.) Besides, are the appearances of composure and regularity in the tomb consistent with the hurry and trepidation of thieves, stealing when an armed guard is at hand, and in a moonlight night.

(5.) But, observe the conduct of the rulers. Why did not they order the Apostles to be seized? Why did they not command the soldiers to be punished? Why did they not bring the whole to a judicial determination? Why is this neglect in men who had been so anxious to have a guard placed upon the sepulchre? Why did they *never* after charge the disciples or apostles themselves with having stolen the body?

OBJECTION. Christ did not show himself to the Chief Priests and Jews.

ANSWER.—For this various satisfactory reasons may be assigned.

[*i.*] It is not probable that the Jews would have submitted to that evidence.

[*ii.*] If Jesus had appeared to them after his resurrection, and they had acknowledged him to be the Messiah, it is most probable that the persons who made this objection would not have been satisfied, but would have suspected, and would have represented, the whole as an artifice and imposture. Or, it might have been said that they were haunted with spectres, and consequently that their testimony was of no value.

[*iii.*] If they had remained unconvinced, the fact would have been questioned: if they had been convinced, without honesty or resolution to declare the truth, the fact would still have been doubtful; and, if they had been convinced, and had acknowledged Jesus to have been the Messiah or Christ, loud would have been the clamour of a combination, and the progress and prevalence of Christianity would have been ascribed to the secular influence of its advocates.

3. The CHARACTER OF THE WITNESSES also proves the truth of the Resurrection of Christ. Observe,

(1.) The *Condition* of these witnesses.

They were mean, despised, and unlearned men, and consequently were unequal to the task of imposing upon others.

(2.) Their *Number*, and also the number of the different appearances of Jesus Christ, which was more than sufficient to establish any fact.

Seven different JEWISH WRITERS have related or mentioned not fewer than *eleven* distinct appearances of Jesus Christ at different hours of the day and at different places; and on one occasion to "above five hundred" persons.

(3.) The *Incredulity* of the witnesses, and their slowness in believing the resurrection of Christ.

(4.) The *Moral Impossibility* of their succeeding in palming an imposition upon the world. Because,

[*i.*] It is inconceivable that a man should willingly expose himself to all sorts of punishment—even to death itself—on purpose to testify a matter of fact which he knew to be false.

[*ii.*] Although there should have been *one* person so disposed, it cannot be imagined—indeed it would be the height of absurdity to imagine,—that NUMBERS would have formed the *same* resolution.

[*iii.*] Though a great number of persons should have agreed together to attest a falsehood, yet it is incredible that *they* should bear witness to it, who considered perfidy and lying as sins utterly inconsistent with their salvation: neither could it be supposed or expected of those, who, if they allowed the resurrection of Jesus Christ to be a fiction, must also allow that they had followed an imaginary Messiah.

[*iv.*] Such a mutual concert or agreement could never have been so carried on, but that some of them, in order to avoid punishment, or to gain reward, would have disclosed the whole intrigue.

[*v.*] The very same principles, which had dissolved their mutual *fidelity*, would more probably break off their *mutual treachery.* It cannot reasonably be supposed that those disciples, who were scattered when their master was crucified, would afterwards conspire to affirm a bold and unprincipled falsehood.

(5.) Observe the *Facts*, which they themselves avow.

Their testimony relates to facts, in which it was impossible that they could have been deceived; such as the seeing, touching, sitting at table and conversing with, their risen master.

(6.) Consider further the *Agreement* of their evidence.

They all unanimously deposed that Christ rose from the dead.

Observe also the *Tribunals* before which they gave evidence, and the multitude of people by whom their testimony was scrutinised,—by Jews and heathens, philosophers and rabbis, and by a vast number of persons who went annually to Jerusalem: for Providence so ordered those circumstances, that the testimony of the apostles might be unsuspected.

(8.) Take notice also of the *Time*, when this evidence was given.

Only three days after the crucifixion, they declared that Christ was risen again, as he had foretold. Would impostors act thus?

(9.) Consider likewise the *Place*, where the apostles bore their testimony to the resurrection.

They preached a risen Saviour, in the synagogues, and in the prætorium, at Jerusalem, the very city where he had been ignominiously crucified.

(10.) Consider the *Motives*, which induced the apostles to publish the fact of Christ's resurrection.

It was, not to acquire fame, riches, or glory, but to found on this fact a series of exhortations to repentance, faith, and holiness:—topics these which were never proposed by an impostor. At the same time, they lived as no impostor ever did, and were enabled to appeal to their converts for the sanctity, justice, and unblamable tenour of their own lives.

(11.) Lastly, the MIRACLES performed by these witnesses in the name of Jesus Christ, after the effusion of the Holy Spirit on the day of Pentecost, and the success which attended their preaching throughout the world, are God's testimony to the fact of Christ's resurrection from the dead, as well as to their veracity in proclaiming it.

On the miraculous fact of Christ's resurrection, the first four of the Criteria above noticed (see p. 29. *supra*) are most clearly to be discerned. With regard to the last two, (see p. 30,) we may remark, that the Lord's Supper was instituted as a perpetual memorial of the death of Jesus Christ; and that the weekly festival of the Lord's Day (or Sunday) commemorates the miraculous fact of his resurrection. These memorials, it must be observed, were instituted at the *very time* when the circumstances to which they relate took place, and they have been observed throughout the Christian world, in all ages, to the present time.

X. A Comparison of the Scripture Miracles with pretended Pagan and Popish Miracles.

Counterfeit miracles are no proof that the miracles, related in the New Testament, are not real: the more strictly such pretended miracles are investigated, the more defective is the evidence adduced for them. For,

1. The scene of most of them is laid in remote countries and in distant ages.

2. They were performed in ages of gross ignorance, when the common people were likely to be deceived, and were wrought in secresy.

3. They were performed by persons of high rank, who were held in the profoundest veneration by the common people, and were never subjected to any scrutiny.

4. The heathen miracles were designed to support the established religion, and were engrafted upon the superstitious notions of the vulgar.

5. They are not vouched to us by any credible testimony.

6. They were not credited by the intelligent and judicious even among the heathen.

The same remarks are equally applicable to the pretended popish miracles.

But the contrary is the case with respect to the miracles recorded in the Scriptures, the reality of which is substantiated by the most positive and irresistible evidence.

Section III.—On Prophecy.

I. Prophecy defined.

Prophecy is a miracle of knowledge, a declaration, or description, or representation of something future, beyond the power of human sagacity to discern or to calculate; and it is the highest evidence, that can be given, of supernatural communion with the Deity, and of the truth of a revelation from God.

II. Difference be'ween the pretended predictions of Heathen Oracles, and the Prophecies contained in the Scriptures.

The oracles of the ancient heathens were delivered either for the purpose of satisfying some trivial curiosity, or to abet the designs of some ambitious leader. They uttered no spontaneous predictions. Those, who conducted them, threw various obstacles in the way of inquiry by sacrifices, &c. Sometimes, the gods were not in a humour to be consulted: at other times, when no means of evasion remained, the answers given were ambiguous or delusive; and whenever the oracles failed, there was always some subterfuge, to which the priests had recourse. If an evil event took place, when an auspicious one had been promised, this was ascribed to the fault of the inquirer. Something defective in the sacrifices was discovered, when too late; or the gods were averse to him. If the contrary proved to be the case, this was ascribed to the intercession of the priests.

Widely different are the prophecies contained in the Scriptures: for,

1. They were delivered without solicitation, and were pronounced openly before the people: and the prophet knew himself to be exposed to capital punishment, if any one of his predictions were to be overthrown. The events foretold were often complicated and remote; depending on the arbitrary will of man, and arising from a great variety of causes, which concurred to bring them to pass.

2. Some were accomplished shortly after they were delivered: others somewhat later; and others had a still more distant object. But the different events foretold were so connected with each other, that the most distant bordered pretty nearly upon some others, the accomplishment of which was preparatory to the fulfilment of the last. The fulfilment of the first served to raise an expectation of those which were distant, and the accomplishment of the last served to confirm the first.

3. A large portion of the scripture-prophecies was committed to writing, and left open to public examination: this is a test, which the spurious predictions of the heathens could never endure.

III. The Use and Intent of Prophecy was,—to raise expectation, and to soothe the mind with hope; to maintain the faith of a particular providence, and the assurance of a promised Redeemer; and to attest the divine inspiration of the Scriptures.

IV. Of the CHAIN of PROPHECY.

The scripture-prophecies respect contingencies too wonderful for the powers of man to conjecture or to effect. Many of those, which are found in the Old Testament, foretold unexpected changes in the distribution of earthly power: and, whether they announced the fall of flourishing cities, or the ruin of mighty empires, the event has minutely corresponded with the prediction. These prophecies form a regular chain or system, which may be reduced to four classes, viz.

1. Prophecies relating to the Jewish Nation in particular.

2. Prophecies relating to the neighbouring nations or empires.

3. Prophecies directly announcing the Messiah.

4. Prophecies delivered by Jesus Christ and his apostles.

CLASS I.—Prophecies relating to the Jewish Nation in particular.

1. *Predictions concerning the Posterity of Abraham* Gen. xii. 1. xlvi. 3.; Exod. xxxii. 13. Gen. xiii. 16. xv. 5. xvii. 2. 4—6. xxii. 17. xxvii. 4. xxviii. 14. xxxii. 12. xxxv. 11.

See the fulfilment of these predictions, as it respects the Jews (to omit the increase of Abraham's other posterity,) in Exod. i. 7. 9. 12 Numb. xxiii. 10. Deut. i. 10. x. 22. Ezek. xvi. 7. Heb. vi. 12. In less than five hundred years after the first of the above predictions was delivered, the number of the Israelites amounted to six hundred thousand men, besides women and children.

2. Prophecies concerning *Ishmael*.—Compare Gen. xvi. 10—12. xvii. 20, and xxv. 12—18.

From him descended the various tribes of Arabs, whose numbers and manner of living have ever since been, and to this very day are, a verification of the predictions respecting them.

3. It was foretold that the *Posterity of Abraham, Isaac, and Jacob*, should possess the land of Canaan: so that, though they should be expelled thence for their sins, yet their title should endure, and they should be resettled in it, and there continue in peace to the end of the world. (See Gen. xii. 7. xiii. 14, 15. 17. xv. 18—21. Exod. iii. 8. 17. Gen. xvii. 7, 8.)

Accordingly, the Jews enjoyed this land for above a thousand years: and when the two tribes of Judah and Benjamin were carried into captivity, it was announced that it should be for seventy years: which the event proved to be true, and they continued in possession of Canaan, for six hundred years, until the final subversion of their polity by Titus. Although the ten tribes carried captive by Shalmaneser, and the body of the two tribes who were carried into captivity by Titus, are not now in Canaan; yet since the time of their *final* restoration has not arrived, this is no objection against these ancient prophecies, but a fulfilment of others: besides we have reason to believe that the Jews will ultimately be restored to their native country.

4. The twenty-eighth chapter of Deuteronomy contains most striking ***Predictions concerning the Jews***, which have literally been fulfilled during their subjection to the Chaldæans and Romans, and in later times in all nations where they have been dispersed. To specify a very few particulars:—

(1.) Moses foretold that ***their enemies would besiege and take their cities:***

This prophecy was fulfilled by Shishak King of Egypt, Shalmaneser King of Assyria, Nebuchadnezzar, Antiochus Epiphanes, Sosius and Herod, and finally by Titus.

(2.) ***Moses foretold grievous famines during those sieges, so that they should eat the flesh of their sons and daughters.***

This was fulfilled six hundred years after the time of Moses, among the *Israelites*, when Samaria was besieged by the King of Assyria; again, about nine hundred years after Moses among the ***Jews***, during the siege of Jerusalem before the Babylonish captivity; and, finally, fifteen hundred years after his time, during the siege of Jerusalem by the Romans.

(3.) Moses predicted that the ***Jews should be few in number.***

This was literally fulfilled by immense numbers perishing by famine during the last siege of Jerusalem, after which many thousands were sold; and also after their final overthrow by Hadrian, when many thousands were sold, and those for whom purchasers could not be found (Moses had foretold that ***no man would buy them***) were transported into Egypt, where very many perished by shipwreck or famine; and others were massacred. Yet notwithstanding all their miseries and oppressions, they still continue a separate people, and have become "an astonishment and a bye-word among the nations."

5. ***Josiah*** was prophetically announced by name, (1 Kings xiii. 2,) three hundred and sixty-one years before the event.

The fulfilment of this prophecy was remarkable, plainly showing it to be, not from man, but from God. (2 Kings xxxiii. 15.)

6. The utter ***Subversion of Idolatry*** among the Jews, foretold by Isaiah (ii. 18—21,) was fulfilled after their return from the Babylonish Captivity.

The calamities, denounced against them by the same prophet, on account of their wickedness, within two hundred years afterwards overtook them. (Isa. iii. 1—14, compared with 2 Chron. xxxvi.) And, on the capture of Jerusalem by the Chaldæans, a few poor people were left to till the land, as Isaiah had prophesied. (Isa. xxiv. 13, 14, compared with Jer. xxxix. 10.)

7. Jeremiah foretold the *Conquests of Nebuchadnezzar*, and the consequent *captivity of the Jews.*

These were literally accomplished. Compare Jer. xxvii. 3—7, with xxxix. 11—14. And although the predictions of Jeremiah and Ezekiel concerning Zedekiah *appeared* to contradict each other, BOTH were fulfilled in the event; Zedekiah seeing the King of Babylon at Jerusalem, who commanded his eyes to be put out, and being carried to Babylon where he died.

8. While Ezekiel was a captive in Chaldæa, he prophesied (v. 12, and viii.) that the Jews, who remained in Judæa, should be punished for their wickedness. In a very few years all the evils predicted, literally came upon them by the Chaldæans.

9. The profanation of the temple by Antiochus Epiphanes, was foretold by Daniel (viii.) four hundred and eight years before the accomplishment of the prediction. The same prophet also foretold the destruction of Jerusalem, and the cessation of the Jewish sacrifices and oblations.

10. Hosea foretold the *present* state of the people of Israel in these words—"They shall be wanderers among the nations." (12. 17.)

CLASS II.—Prophecies relating to the Nations or Empires that were neighbouring to the Jews.

1. The once prosperous city of *Tyre*, as Ezekiel had foretold, (xxvi. 3—5. 14. 21,) is now become like "the top of a rock, a place for fishers to dry their nets on."

2. The prophecies concerning *Egypt*, (see Isai. xix. Jer. xliii. 8—13, and xlvi.; and Ezek. xxix.—xxxii., particularly Ezek. xxix. 10. 15, and xxx. 6. 12. 13,) have been signally fulfilled.

Not long after these predictions were delivered, this country was successively attacked and conquered by the Babylonians and Persians; next it became subject to the Macedonians, then to the Romans, after them to the Saracens, then to the Mamelukes, and is now a province of the Turkish empire. And the denunciation—"I will make her rivers dry," is fulfilled by the generally neglected state of the numerous canals with which Egypt was anciently intersected.

2. The doom of *Ethiopia* was foretold by Isaiah,

(xviii. 1—6, xx. 3—5, and xliii. 3,) and by Ezekiel, (xxx. 4—6.)

This country was invaded by Sennacherib, King of Assyria, or by Esarhaddon his son, and also by Cambyses, King of Persia. About the time of Christ's birth, it *was* ravaged by the Romans, and has *since* been ravaged successively by the Saracens, Turks, and Giagas.

4. Such an "utter end" has been made of *Nineveh*, agreeably to the predictions of Nahum, (i. 8, 9. ii. 8—13, iii. 17—19,) and Zephaniah, (ii. 13. 15,) that its very site cannot be ascertained.

5. *Babylon* is made "a desolation forever," as Isaiah (xiii. 4. 19—22. xliv. 27,) and Jeremiah (l. 38. li. 7. 36, 37. 64,] had severally foretold.

This city was taken, when Belshazzar and his thousand princes were drunk at a great feast, after Cyrus had turned the course of the Euphrates, which ran through the midst of it, and so drained its waters that the river became easily fordable for his soldiers to enter the city. Its site cannot now be exactly determined.

6. Daniel predicted the overthrow in succession of the *four great Empires of antiquity;* the Babylonian, Persian, Grecian, and Roman. (Dan. ii. 39, 40. vii. 17—24 viii.) This prediction has literally been fulfilled: but neither the rise of the last three, nor their fall, could have been foreseen by men.

Class III. Prophecies directly announcing the Messiah.

The great object of the prophecies of the Old Testament is the redemption of mankind. This, as soon as Adam's fall had made it necessary, the mercy of God was pleased to foretel. And as the time for its accomplishment drew near, the predictions concerning it gradually became so clear, that almost every circumstance in the life and character of the most extraordinary personage, that ever appeared among men, was most distinctly foretold.

The prophecies announcing the Messiah are numerous, pointed, and particular. They not only foretel that *a* Messiah should come; but they also specify the *precise Time* when he was to come; the *Dignity of his Character*, that he should be God and man together; *from whom* he was to be descended; the *Place* where he was to be born; the circumstances of his *Birth*, *Manner of*

Life and *Doctrine*, his *sufferings* and *Death; Resurrection* and *Ascension;* and the *Abolition of the Jewish Covenant* by the introduction of the Gospel.—See a Table of the Principal Prophecies relative to the Messiah, in the Appendix, No. VII.

The connexion of the predictions belonging to the Messiah, with those which are confined to the Jewish people, gives additional force to the argument from prophecy; affording a strong proof of the intimate union which subsists between the two dispensations of Moses and of Jesus Christ, and equally precluding the artful pretensions of human imposture, and the daring opposition of human power. The plan of prophecy was so wisely constituted, that the passions and prejudices of the Jews, instead of frustrating, fulfilled it, and rendered the person whom they regarded, the suffering and crucified Saviour, who had been promised. It is worthy of remark, that most of these predictions were delivered nearly, and some of them more than three thousand years ago. Any one of them is sufficient to indicate a prescience more than human; but the collective force of all taken together is such, that nothing more can be necessary to prove the interposition of Omniscience, than the establishment of their authenticity. And this, even at so remote a period as the present, we have already seen, is placed beyond all doubt.

CLASS IV.—Prophecies by Jesus Christ and his Apostles.

Jesus Christ foretold,

1. The *Circumstances of his own death;* Matt. xvi. 21. Mark x. 33, 34. Matt. xx. 18, 19. xxvi. 23. 31, all which were most minutely accomplished.

2. His *Resurrection;* Matt. xvi. 21. xxvi. 32, fulfilled in Matt. xxviii.

3. The *Descent of the Holy Spirit;* Luke xxiv. 49. Mark xvi. 17, 18, fulfilled in Acts ii.

4. The *Destruction of Jerusalem with all its preceding signs and its concomitant circumstances;* (Matt. xxiv. 1—28. Mark xiii. 1—23. Luke xxi. 5—24,) and the very generation that heard the prediction lived to be the miserable witnesses of its accomplishment.

5. The *Spread of Christianity;* and both sacred and profane historians bear testimony to the rapid propagation of the Gospel.

The character of the age, in which the Christian Faith was first propagated, must be considered.

It was not barbarous and uncivilized, but was remarkable for those improvements by which the human faculties were strengthened.

The profession of Christianity was followed by no worldly advantage, but, on the contrary, with proscriptions and persecutions.

Sceptics, particularly Mr. Gibbon, have endeavoured to account for the miraculous success of Christianity from causes merely human, viz.

(1.) *The inflexible and intolerant Zeal of the first Christians.*

This indeed might supply Christians with that fortitude which should keep them firm to their principles: but it could hardly be of service in converting infidels. *No* intolerance, however, existed among the primitive Christians; but, on the contrary, among their heathen persecutors.

(2.) *The Doctrine of a Future Life.*

The success which attended the preaching of this doctrine, was owing rather to the demonstration of the spirit and of the power that accompanied it, than to the doctrine itself, which was by no means suited either to the expectations or the wishes of the Pagans in general. Men must have believed the Gospel, generally, before they believed the doctrine of a future life on its authority.

(3.) *The Miraculous Powers ascribed to the Primitive Church.*

The actual possession of such powers by the apostles and first preachers of Christianity has already been proved. But when the numerous *pretended* miracles ascribed to the popular deities of the heathen, and the contempt in which they were held by the philosophers and by other thinking men, are considered, the miracles ascribed to the first propagators of Christianity, must have created a prejudice against their cause, which nothing could have subdued but miracles really and visibly performed.

(4.) *The Virtues of the first Christians.*

These Mr. Gibbon reduces to a mean and timid repentance for sins, and zeal in supporting the reputation of their society. But such virtues would have equally excited opposition to Christianity. The infidel historian does *not* account for the exemplary virtues of the first Christians; whose virtues arose from their faith, and not their faith from their virtues.

(5.) *The Union and Discipline of the Christian Republic*, as he terms the Christian Church.

But it is an incontrovertible fact, that the Gospel was propagated, before its professors were sufficiently numerous to establish a discipline, or to form themselves into a society.

V. Notwithstanding the variety and force of the evidence in favour of Christianity, its opposers continue to raise a variety of objections, viz.

OBJECTION 1.—*The rejection of Christianity by the unbelieving* JEWS, *in the time of Christ, and also by the greater part of the* GENTILES.

In reply to this objection, we may

ANSWER 1.—As to the Jews—That the Almighty does not *force* the judgment, and that their wickedness and strong *prejudices* blinded their understandings, and prevented them from receiving the evidences of the Gospel. Anger, resentment, self-interest, and worldly-mindedness induced the scribes and pharisees to reject Christ and cause him to be put to death, and to prevail upon the people at large to reject the Gospel. Such were the principal causes of the infidelity of the Jews and of their rejection of Christ at *first:* nor is it difficult to conceive what may be the reasons of their persisting in their infidelity *now*. For

(1.) In the first place, on the part of the *Jews*, most (if not all) the same reasons which gave birth to their infidelity, continue to nourish it, particularly their obstinacy, their vain hopes and expectations of worldly greatness, and the false Christs and false prophets who at different times have risen up among them. To which may be added their want of charitableness towards Christians, and their continuing to live insulated from the rest of mankind.

(2.) Secondly, on the part of the world, the obstacles are, the prevalence of Mohammedism, and other false religions, the schisms of Christians, the unholy lives of many nominal Christians, and the cruelties, which have at various times been inflicted on this unhappy people. So far, however, is the infidelity of the Jews from being an objection to the truth of the Gospel, that, on the contrary, it affords us a great number of unsuspected witnesses to the truth of the Old Testament: and many predictions of Moses and the prophets, of Christ and his apostles, are remarkably fulfilled. It is also a great advantage to the Christian Religion, to have been first preached and propagated in a nation of unbelievers: for nothing but divine truth could have stood the trial, and triumphed over all opposition.

ANSWER 2.—With regard to the rejection of the Gospel by the GENTILES, many of the preceding observations on the infidelity of the Jews are equally applicable to them. *Both* Jews and Gentiles were influenced by the prejudices of education,—by hatred of the pure morality of the Gospel,—by the temporal inconveniences which attended the profession of Christianity, and the temporal advantages to be obtained by rejecting or opposing it,—by the mean appearance, which Christ had made in the world,—and by his ignominious death, which they knew not how to reconcile with the divine power ascribed to him by his disciples.

The Gentiles also had other causes of unbelief peculiar to themselves, viz. the high notion, entertained by them, of the efficacy of magic, of charms and incantations, and of the power of demons and demi-gods;—their indifference about religion in general, the utter incompatibility of Christianity with the established worship of their several countries,—the bad opinion which they had of the Jews in general, of whom Christians were for some time accounted to be a sect,—the false doctrines and crimes of heretical teachers and vicious professors of Christianity,—and lastly, the antiquity of paganism.

Objection 2.—*The prevalence of Mohammedism over a considerable portion of the world.*

Answer.—The prophecies are fulfilled, when all parts of the world shall have *had the offer of Christianity;* but it by no means follows that it shall be upheld among them *by a miracle.* The present state of those countries, where the Koran is received, is an accomplishment of prophecy; inasmuch as it was foretold that such an apostacy would take place. The rapid progress of Mohammedism is not to be compared with the propagation of Christianity, for Mohammed came into the world at a time exactly suited to his purposes, when its policy and civil state were favourable to a new and ambitious conqueror: and he availed himself of every means, especially force of arms, to promote the diffusion of his pretended revelation.

Objection 3.—*Christianity is known only to a small portion of mankind.*

Answer.—For *one* who professes deism, we shall find in the world one thousand who profess Christianity.

The partial propagation of the Gospel, with the other objections brought against Christianity, having rendered its divine original a matter of dispute, the tendency of these disputes has been to separate the wheat from the chaff, and to make Christians draw their religion from the Scriptures alone.

The not having more evidence for the truth of the Gospel is not a sufficient reason for rejecting that which we already have. If such evidence were *irresistible,* it would restrain the voluntary powers too much, to answer the purpose of trial and probation. "Men's moral probation may be, whether they will take due care to inform themselves by impartial consideration; and afterwards, whether they will act as the case requires, upon the evidence they have." Further, if the evidence of the Gospel were irresistible, it would leave no room for internal evidence. They who sincerely act, or endeavour to act according to the just result of the probabilities in natural and revealed religion, seldom fail of proceeding further; while those, who act in a contrary manner, necessarily fail to perceive the force of the evidences for the truth of the Gospel.

VI. Objections have been made to the darkness and uncertainty of prophecy, which have been ascribed. 1. To its *Language;* and 2. To the *Indistinctness of its Representations.*

Answer 1.—With regard to prophetic *Language*, as prophecy is a peculiar species of writing, it is natural to expect a peculiarity in the language of which it makes use. Sometimes it employs plain terms, but most commonly figurative ones. It has symbols of its own, which are common to all the prophets; and these symbols have their appropriate rules of interpretation.

Answer 2.—With respect to the alleged *Indistinct Representations* of events predicted, it should be remembered, that, if some prophecies be obscure, others are clear: the latter furnish a proof of the inspiration of the Scriptures, the former contain nothing against it. Some predictions were to have their accomplishment in the early ages of the church, while others were designed for the benefit of those who lived in after ages.

Answer 3.—Another reason for throwing a veil over the face of prophecy will appear on considering the nature of the subject. Some of the events predicted are of such a nature, that the fate of nations depends upon them; and they are to be brought into existence by the instrumentality of men. In the present form of prophecy, men are left entirely to themselves; and they fulfil the prophecies without intending, or hinking, or knowing that they do so. The accomplishment strips off the veil, and then the evidence from prophecy appears in all its splendour.

CHAPTER V.

INTERNAL EVIDENCES OF THE INSPIRATION OF THE SCRIPTURES.

Section I.—The System of Doctrine and the Moral Precepts, which are delivered in the Scriptures, are so excellent and so perfectly holy, that the Persons who published them to the World, must have derived them from a purer and more exalted Source than their own Meditations.

The sacred volume opens with an account of the creation of the world by the Almighty, and of the formation of man in a happy state of purity and innocence. In this account there is nothing but what is agreeable to right reason, as well as the most ancient traditions which have obtained among the nations. We are further informed, that man fell from that state by sinning against his Maker; and that sin brought death into the world, together with all the miseries to which the human race is now obnoxious;

but that the merciful Parent of our being, in his great goodness and compassion, was pleased to make such revelations and discoveries of his mercy, as laid a proper foundation for the faith and hope of his offending creatures, and for the exercise of religion towards him. (Gen. iii.) Accordingly, the religion delivered in the Scriptures is the religion of man in his lapsed state: and every one, who *impartially* and carefully investigates and considers it, will find, that *one* scheme of religion and of moral duty, substantially the same, is carried throughout the whole, till it was brought to its full perfection and accomplishment by Jesus Christ. This religion may be considered principally under three periods, viz.

1. The Religion of the Patriarchal Times;
2. The Doctrines and Precepts of the Mosaic Dispensation; and
3. The Doctrines and Precepts of the Christian Revelation.

---

§ I.—A Concise View of the Religion of the Patriarchal Times.

The Book of Genesis exhibits to us a clear idea of the Patriarchal Theology, which taught

I. *Concerning the nature and attributes of God:*

That He is the Creator, Governor, and Preserver of all things; that He is eternal, omniscient, true, omnipotent, holy, and just, kind, supreme, merciful, long-suffering, gracious towards them that fear Him, and that He is not the Author of Sin.

II. *Concerning the Worship of God:*

The Patriarchs held that it was the duty of men to fear Him, to bless Him for mercies received, and to supplicate Him with profound humility; that the knowledge of God is to be promoted; vows made to Him are to be performed, and idolatry is to be renounced. With regard to the external rites of religion, the most ancient on record is that of offering sacrifice; and the Sabbath also appears to have been observed by the Patriarchs.

III. With regard to the *Moral Duties* between man and man:

These likewise are clearly announced, either by way of precept or by example; more particularly, the duties of children to honour their parents, of parents to instil religious principles into the minds of their offspring, and of servants to obey their masters. Wars may be waged in a *good* cause. Anger is sinful in the sight of God; strifes are to be avoided; murder is prohibited; hospitality is to be exercised; and injuries are to be forgiven. Matrimony is appointed by God, from whom a virtuous wife is to be sought by prayer; and a wife is to be subject to her husband. Children are the gift of God; and adultery and all impurity are to be avoided.

---

§ 2.—A Summary View of the Doctrines and Precepts of the Mosaic Dispensation.

The Mosaic Dispensation was substantially the same as that given to the Patriarchs, but with the addition of a special covenant made by the Almighty with a particular people, for wise and moral purposes worthy of the Supreme Being, and beneficial in its results to the whole human race.

I. In the Mosaic Law the essential Unity of God is most explicitly inculcated, no less than His underived self-existence, eternity, immutability, omnipotence, providence, justice, mercy, and other perfections. And the same sublime representations of the Divine Being and Perfections are made by the prophets and other inspired writers among the Jews.

II. Concerning the *Duty of Man towards God*,—both Moses and the Prophets enforce the obligation of loving Him, fearing Him, believing in Him, trusting in His promises, and obeying *all* His commandments; together with the duties of patience and resignation to the divine will, and the internal worship of the heart.

III. The belief of a *Future State*, which was held by the Patriarchs, (though not explicitly taught by Moses, whose writings pre-suppose it as a generally adopted article of religion,) was transmitted from them to the Israelites, and appears in various parts of the Old Testament.

The Book of Job is very explicit on this subject; David has spoken of it with great confidence, particularly in Psalms xxi. xxxvi. xlix. lxxiii. and cxxxix.; and Solomon expressly alludes to it in Proverbs v. 21—23. xiv. 32, and Eccles. iii. 16, 17, and viii. 11. 13. This doctrine is also inculcated, and pre-supposed as a matter of popular belief, by the prophets Isaiah (xiv. 19. xxvi. 19—21,) Hosea (xiii. 14,) Amos (iv. 12, 13,) and Daniel (viii. 9—14. xii. 1—3.)

IV. The *Expectation of a Redeemer*, which had been cherished by the Patriarchs, was also kept up by various predictions, delivered by Moses and the prophets.

V. The *Morality of the Jewish Code* exhibits a perfection and beauty in no respect inferior to its religious doctrines and duties. We owe to it the decalogue—a manual of duty to God and man, so pure and comprehensive, as to be absolutely without parallel: and the sanctions of the remaining enactments of the law are such as morality possessed in no other nation. More particularly,

1. It taught humility and meekness.

2. It prohibited *all* uncleanness and unnatural lusts, as well as drunkenness, gluttony, and all covetous desires.

3. Our duty towards our neighbour is also clearly set forth (Levit. xix. 18,) together with all the social and relative duties of life.

4. Every kind of justice was strictly required by the law of Moses. Murder was forbidden by the sixth commandment, adultery by the seventh, and theft by the eighth. All kinds of violence, oppression, and fraud were also forbidden.

5. All hatred and malice were prohibited; nor were kind offices to be confined to brethren and friends; they were also to be performed to enemies and to strangers. Nay, mercy was to be extended even to the brute creation.

VI. The Mosaic Dispensation was introductory to Christianity.

The Law of Moses, though not *absolutely* perfect, had a perfection suited to its kind and design. It was adapted to the genius of the people to whom it was given, and calculated to keep them distinct from the rest of mankind, and to prevent them from being involved in the idolatries common among other nations. It was at the same time ordained to pre-signify good things to come, and to bear a strong attestation to the truth of the Christian Religion.

But, however excellent in itself, and admirably adapted to the purposes for which it was designed, the Mosaic Dispensation was only of a local and temporary nature, and preparatory to that fuller manifestation of the divine will, which "in the fulness of time" was to be made known to the world under the Gospel Dispensation.

---

§ 3.—A Summary View of the Doctrines and Precepts of the Gospel Dispensation.

I. The whole CHARACTER and CONDUCT of the Founder of Christianity proved him to be a divine person. Never indeed was there so perfect a character, so godlike, venerable, and amiable, and so utterly remote from that of an enthusiast or an impostor.

II. The LEADING DOCTRINES of the Gospel are worthy of the character of the Almighty, and adapted to the necessities of mankind. More particularly,

1. The *Account of God and of his Perfections*, is worthy of the highest and most excellent of all beings. Of all the views of God which had ever been given, none was so calculated to endear Him to us, and to inspire our hearts with confidence, as this short but interesting description, of which the scheme of redemption affords a sublime illustration—"GOD is LOVE!"

2. What men had, in all ages, wished for in vain—*an Atonement for sin*, (which conscience and their natural notions of divine justice taught them to be necessary)—the Sacred Books point out in the death of Jesus, which, in consequence of the dignity of his person, our reason perceives to have been of sufficient value to expiate the guilt of innumerable millions.

3. The divine justice being satisfied, we are assured of the *Forgiveness of our Sins*, through Jesus Christ, upon sincere repentance; and our sins being forgiven, we are *justified*, or "accounted righteous before God, only for the merit of our Lord Jesus Christ, by faith, and not for our own merits or deservings."

4. In the Gospel we find the best principles of comfort and refreshment to the soul, under all the calamities and afflictions of life, as well as a rich magazine of all means proper for the sanctification of our souls, and our most successful advances in true piety. In the Scriptures we see that the *Holy Spirit* is ready with his mighty aids (which are promised to all who humbly pray for them,) to assist, enlighten, and strengthen our spirits in proportion to our sincere desires and endeavours after godliness; and there we are directed every day and at all times, to seek unto God, through Christ, by fervent and believing prayer, for his guidance and protection, and are assured that we shall never seek his face in vain.

5. In favour of the *Immortality of the Soul*, a point so important, but which to the wisest of the Gentiles seemed so doubtful, the Scriptures speak in the most decisive language, and hold out to the hopes and fears of mankind rewards and punishments suited to their nature, and which it is worthy of God to dispense.

6. Lastly, in the Gospel we see the dead both small and great restored to life, and appearing before the tribunal of God, to receive a sentence, "according to the deeds done in the body." The glories of heaven, which are reserved "for them that love him," and the everlasting miseries, which will be the terrible portion of all the wilfully impenitent workers of iniquity, are disclosed in the Scriptures: which alone set forth the true reason of our being in this world, viz. not for enjoyment but for trial; not to gain temporal pleasures or possessions, but that our souls may be disciplined and prepared for immortal honour and glory. While the divine displeasure is declared against all ungodliness and unrighteousness of men, and the most awful warnings are denounced against sinners, the means by which they may obtain mercy are clearly displayed and offered to them.

In all these doctrines we observe nothing low, or mean, or frivolous: every one of them is grand, sublime, and worthy of God; every one of them is most deeply interesting to man; and, altogether, they make up an infinitely more consistent and rational scheme of belief, than the most distinguished sages of antiquity ever *did* contrive, or the most cunning of modern unbelievers *can* possibly invent.

III. The Moral Precepts of the Gospel are admirably adapted to the actual state of mankind.

1. As to the Duties between man and man, the Gospel particularly enjoins integrity of conduct, charity, forgiveness of injuries.

2. It lays down the duties incumbent upon us in the several relations which we sustain in civil and social life; for instance, the mutual duties of governors and subjects, masters and servants, husbands and wives, parents and children.

3. It enforces, and recommends by various considerations, the personal duties of sobriety, temperance, chastity, humility, &c.; and guards us against an immoderate passion for transient worldly riches; while it affords us the best remedies against anxious cares, excessive sorrows, and desponding fears. While it enjoins trust in God, it directs us to the use of all honest and proper means and industry on our parts.

4. The Holiness of the moral precepts of the Gospel is another proof of its divine origin. All its precepts aim directly at the heart; teaching us to refer all our actions to the will of our Creator, and correcting all selfishness in the human character, by teaching us to have in view the happiness of those about us.

5. The Manner in which the morality of the Gospel is delivered attests its divine origin.

Among the heathen, no provision was made for the moral instruction of the unlettered multitude: but Christ taught *all* that would listen to him, with inimitable plainness and simplicity, and at the same time with the most perfect modesty and delicacy, blended with the utmost boldness and integrity.

The character of Christ forms an essential part of the morality of the Gospel. To the morality of almost every other teacher, some stain attaches: but he is charged by no vice either by friends or by enemies. In each of the four narratives of his life, besides the absence of every appearance of vice, we perceive traces of devotion, humility, patience, benignity, benevolence, mildness, and prudence. In short, the New Testament is replete with piety and devotional virtues, which were unknown to the ancient heathen moralists.

IV. Superiority of the Motives to duty presented by the Gospel.

However excellent and complete a rule of moral duty may be in itself, it will not and cannot answer the end proposed, unless it be enjoined by a proper authority, and enforced by the most powerful motives. Now in this respect the religious and moral precepts of the Gospel have an infinite advantage over every other system of doctrine or of morals; for they are urged upon us as the commands of the Eternal God himself, and are enforced by various motives, which are admirably adapted to influence the human heart. These motives are drawn,

1. From a consideration of the *Reasonableness of the Duty* recommended or enforced, or the infamy of the vice from which Christians are dissuaded. See instances of this in Rom. xii. 1. Acts iv. 19. Rom. x 12, 13, and Phil. iv. 8.

2. The singular *Favours* conferred upon us by God, as in Acts iii. 26. 1 Cor. vi. 20. Eph. iv. 32. Tit. ii. 14.

3. The *Example of Christ.* Matt. xi. 29. Eph. v. 2. Rom. xv. 2, 3 Phil. ii. 3—5. 1 Pet. i. 15.

4. *The Sanctions of Duty* which the civil relations among men have received from God: as in Rom. xiii. 2. 4, 5. Eph. vi. 5—7. 9. Col. iii. 22

5. The *Regard which Christians owe to their holy profession.* Eph. iv. 1—3. 1 Thess. ii. 12. Phil. i. 27. Tit. ii. 10.

6. The *Acceptableness of true Repentance,* and the assurance of pardon to the *really* penitent.

7. The *Divine Assistance,* offered to support men in the performance of their duty. John xiv. 16. 1 Cor. iii. 13. vi. 16. Luke xi. 13. 2 Cor xiii. 14. Heb. iv. 16.

8. Our *Relation to Heaven,* while upon earth. Phil. iii. 20. 1 Pet ii. 11.

9. The *Rewards and Punishments* proclaimed in the Gospel.

All these sublime lessons of morality are found in various parts of the New Testament. They enrich the divine sermon on the mount; and they are contained in the excellent parables delivered by Jesus Christ; they are also to be found in the discourses and epistles of the apostles. Wherever indeed we open the Christian volume, we may find some direction, which, if properly observed, would render us good neighbours, good members of society, good friends, and good men. Is it possible, then, to doubt the divine original of a system, which furnishes such rules, and contemplates so glorious an object?

All these sublime moral precepts and motives are found in various parts of the New Testament. How the writers of that volume should be able to draw up a system of morals, which the world, after the lapse of eighteen centuries, cannot improve, while it perceives numberless faults in those of the philosophers of India, Greece and Rome, and of the opposers of revelation, is a question of fact, for which the *candid* deist is concerned to account in a rational way. The Christian is able to do it with ease The Evangelists and the Apostles of Jesus Christ "spake as they were moved by the Holy Spirit."

---

§ 4.—On the Objections of Unbelievers to the Doctrines and Morality of the Bible.

OBJECTION I.—Some of the peculiar doctrines which the Scriptures propound to our belief, are mysterious and contrary to reason: and, where mystery begins, religion ends.

ANSWER.—This assertion is erroneous: for nothing is so mysterious as the eternity and self-existence of God; yet, to believe that God exists, is the foundation of all religion. We cannot comprehend the common operations of nature; and if we ascend to the higher departments of science —even to the science of demonstration itself, the mathematics—we shall find that mysteries exist there.

Mysteries in the Christian Religion, instead of being suspected, should rather be regarded as a proof of its divine origin: for, if nothing more were contained in the New Testament than we previously knew, or nothing more than we could easily comprehend, we might justly doubt if it came from God, and whether it was not rather a work of man's device.

Further, the mysteries which appear most contrary to reason, are closely connected with the truths and facts of which reason is convinced.

Though some of the truths revealed in the Scriptures are mysterious, yet the tendency of the most exalted of its mysteries, is practical. If, for instance, we cannot explain the influences of the Spirit, happy will it be for us, nevertheless, if we *experience* that the "fruits of the spirit are love, joy, peace, long-suffering, gentleness, goodness, faith, meekness, temperance."

Objection II.—The scripture doctrine of redemption is inconsistent with the ideas, which are now generally received concerning the magnitude of creation.

Answer.—The comparative dimension of our world is of no account if it be large enough for the accomplishment of events, which are sufficient to occupy the minds of all intelligences, that is all which is required.

Objection III.—The doctrine of a future judgment is improbable: and the two-fold sanction of rewards and punishments is of human invention.

Answer—It is but reasonable, that the same person, by whom God carried on his merciful design of recovering mankind from a state of sin, who felt our infirmities, and was tempted as we are, should be appointed the final judge of all men, and the dispenser of future retribution.

Lord Bolingbroke intimates, that the notion whereon the sanction of future rewards and punishment is founded, savours more of human passions than of justice or prudence; and that it implies, that the proceedings of God towards men in this life are unjust, if they need rectifying in a future one. But the present life is a state of trial, to fit us for a future and better condition of being. Though justice requires that rewards and punishments should, in this world, be proportioned to the different degrees of virtue and vice; facts prove that this is *not* the case. If therefore there be no recompense hereafter, injustice must characterise the divine government, and the Christian doctrine alone vindicates the ways of God to man.

Lord Shaftesbury argues against the doctrine of future rewards and punishments, as affording a mercenary and selfish motive to virtue, which ought to be practised because it is good and amiable in itself. It will however be seen, that this is not the case, if it be considered that the Christian looks for his reward, only to higher improvements in useful knowledge and moral goodness, and to the exalted enjoyments which result from these. But it is a proper reason to choose virtue, because it will make us happy; for man has a natural desire of life and happiness, and a fear of losing them; and a desire of well being may conspire with the rest in the discipline of the mind, and assist the growth of more liberal principles.

Further, when this respect to a future recompense is the effect of a deliberate trust in the Judge of the universe, an acquiescence in his government, and a belief that he is the rewarder of such as faithfully seek him, and disposes us to well-doing, it becomes religious faith, the first duty of rational beings, and a firm bond of virtue, private, social, and divine.

Objection IV.—Christianity establishes a system of priestcraft and spiritual despotism over the minds and consciences of men.

Answer.—Christianity establishes no such thing. That there should be teachers of religion, to instruct men in its principles, to enforce its precepts, and to administer its consolations, has nothing in it contrary to the fitness of things, and the public good. This argument acquires additional weight, when we consider the qualifications which the New Testament requires of the different orders of Christian ministers. See particularly 1 Tim. iii. 1—7. iv. 11, 12. 16. 2 Cor. vi. 3. 2 Tim. ii. 22. 24, 25. 1 Tim. iv 12, 13, 14. 1 Tim. iii. 8—10.

It has however been said, that the most extravagant claims to wealth and power have been made by men, who call themselves ministers of the Gospel. But with these claims Christianity is not chargeable. The New

Testament establishes the support of the ministers of religion on a reasonable footing. Is it thought equitable, that those who teach philosophy and the learned languages should be recompensed for their labour? The Gospel sets the maintenance of its ministers on the same footing (see Luke x. 7. 1 Cor. ix. 11—14;) but it does not countenance in them any claim of either power or wealth.

Objection V.—The Gospel prohibits free inquiry, and demands a full and implicit assent, without any previous examination.

Answer.—*The contrary is the fact.* The Gospel not only invites but demands investigation: free inquiry is not prejudicial, but in the highest degree beneficial to Christianity, whose evidences shine the more clearly, in proportion to the rigour with which they are examined.

Objection VI.—The Morality of the Bible is too strict, and lays mankind under too severe restraints.

Answer.—The contrary is the case: for the morality of the Bible restrains us only from what would be hurtful to ourselves or to others, while it allows of every *truly* rational, sober, and humane pleasure.

Objection VII.—Some of the Moral Precepts of Jesus Christ are unreasonable and impracticable.

Answer.—A candid examination of a few of the precepts objected to, will show how little foundation there is for such an assertion. For,

1. *The prohibition of anger*, in Matt. v. 22, condemns only implacable anger,—sinful anger unrepented of. The same restriction must be understood respecting other general assertions of Jesus, as Matt. x. 33, which cannot apply to Peter.

2. *The precept of Jesus Christ to forgive injuries, has been asserted to be contrary to reason and nature.*

A few of the most eminent heathen philosophers, however, have given the same direction; particularly Socrates, Cicero, Seneca, and Confucius.

It has further been objected that this precept is given in a general and indefinite way; whereas there are certain necessary restrictions.

Assuredly. But these exceptions are so plain, that they will always be supposed, and consequently need not to be specified. The Christian religion makes no alteration in the natural rights of mankind, nor does it forbid necessary self-defence, or seeking legal redress of injuries in cases where it may be expedient to restrain violence and outrage. The *substance* of what it recommends, relates chiefly to the temper of the mind.

3. *Against the injunction to love our enemies, it has been argued, "If love carry with it complacence, esteem, and friendship, and these are due to all men,—what distinction can we then make between the best and worst of men?"*

But, in this precept, as in all moral writings "love" signifies benevolence and good will; which may be exercised by kind actions towards those whom we cannot esteem, and whom we are even obliged to punish.

4. *The commandment to "love our neighbour as ourselves," is also objected to as unreasonable, and impossible to be observed.*

In moral writings, love (as we have just noticed) signifies good will expressing itself in the conduct. Now, this precept of Jesus Christ may be understood,

(1.) As enjoining the same *kind* of affection to our fellow creature as to ourselves, disposing us to avoid his misery, and to consult his happiness as well as our own. Or,

(2.) It may require us to love our neighbour in some certain *proportion* as we love ourselves. The love of our neighbour must bear some proportion to self-love, and virtue consists in the due proportion of it. Or,

(3.) The precept may be understood of an equality of affection. Moral obligation can extend no further than to natural possibility. Now, we have a perception of our own interests, like the consciousness of our own existence, which we always carry about with us; and which, in its continuation, kind, and degree, seems impossible to be felt with respect to the interests of others. Therefore, were we to love our neighbour in the same degree (so far as this is possible) as we love ourselves, yet the care of ourselves would not be neglected.

The precepts,—to "do to others as we would have them do to us," and to "love our neighbour as ourselves,"—are not merely intelligible and comprehensive rules: but they also furnish the means of determining the particular cases which are included under them: and they are likewise useful *means* of moral improvement, and afford a good test of a person's progress in benevolence.

5. The command to believe in Jesus Christ, and the sanctions by which it is enforced,—"he that believeth and is baptised, shall be saved, but he that believeth not shall be condemned," (Mark xvi. 16,)—have been objected against: and it has been said that "Faith, considered in itself, can neither be a virtue nor a vice, because men can no otherwise believe than as things appear to them."

Yet, that they appear in such a particular manner to the understanding of individuals, may be owing entirely to themselves. All threatenings, moreover, must be understood of unbelievers, who had *sufficient* light and evidence afforded them, and who, through inattention, neglect, wilful prejudice, or from corrupt passions and vices have *rejected* the Gospel, as Christ himself says in John iii. 19, and xv. 22.

Objection VIII.—Christianity produces a timid passive spirit, and also entirely overlooks the generous sentiments of friendship and patriotism.

Answer 1. Christianity omits precepts founded upon false principles, such as recommend fictitious virtues, which, however admired and celebrated, are productive of no salutary effects, and in fact are no virtues at all.

Valour, for instance, is for the most part constitutional; and, *when not under the control of true religion*, so far is it from producing any salutary effects by introducing peace, order, or happiness into society, that it is the usual perpetrator of all the violences, which, from retaliated injuries, distract the world with bloodshed and devastation. But, though Christianity exhibits no commendation of fictitious virtues, it is so far from generating a timid spirit, that, on the contrary, it forms men of a singular courage. It teaches them to be afraid of offending God, and of doing injury to man; but it labours to render them superior to every other fear. The lives of Christians have, in numberless instances, displayed the efficacy of its divine principles, which have enabled them to sustain unexampled active exertion, persevering labour, and patient suffering.

2. With regard to *Friendship*, various satisfactory reasons may be assigned why Jesus Christ did not enact any laws concerning it.

[i.] A pure and sincere friendship must be a matter of choice, and reluctant to the very appearance of compulsion.

[ii.] It depends upon similarity of disposition, and coincidence of sentiment and affection, and upon a variety of circumstances not within our control, or our choice.

[iii.] Partial attachments, which usually led persons to prefer their friends to the public, would NOT be favourable to the *general* virtue and happiness. But though the Gospel makes no provision for friendship, it does not prohibit that connexion, but rather sanctions it by the example of Christ himself; whose attachment to Lazarus and his family, and to

John the beloved disciple, may satisfy us of *his* approbation of friendship both as a duty and as an enjoyment.

3. With respect to *Patriotism*,—if by this be meant a bigoted, selfish, or fiery love of our country, which leads us to seek its aggrandisement, regardless of the morality of the means by which that is accomplished, it is no virtue.

But Jesus Christ virtually established the duty of patriotism, by establishing the principle from which it flows, viz. the *universal obligation of justice and love;* leading us to do good unto all men, but especially unto them who are of the household of faith, and enforcing more than ordinary affection between husbands and wives, parents and children, brethren and sisters. In all which cases he has decided that every additional tie, by which man is connected with man, is an obligation to additional love. Above all, Christ himself, by his own conduct, sanctioned, exemplified, and commanded patriotism.

Objection IX.—The Bible is the most immoral book in the world.

Answer.—A candid examination of the morality of the Scriptures, most completely refutes this assertion. If, indeed, the Bible *be* an immoral book, how is it that the reading of this book should have reclaimed millions from immorality?—a fact, too notorious to be denied by any impartial observer. Further, many of the immoral statements, which are *said* (but which cannot be proved) to exist in the Bible, are founded on a wilful inattention to the difference which exists between ancient and modern manners. The characteristic of modern manners is the free intercourse of the two sexes in the daily commerce of life and conversation. Hence the peculiar system of modern manners; hence that system of decorum, delicacy, and modesty (founded on the morality of Scripture) which belong entirely to this relation of the sexes, and to the state of society in which it exists. But in the ancient world there was nothing of this intercourse. Besides, the immoral actions which are recorded in Scripture, are not related for our imitation, but for our caution.

Objection. X. The Bible inculcates a spirit of intolerance and persecution.

Answer.—The religion of Jesus Christ has been represented as of an unsocial, unsteady, surly, and solitary complexion, tending to destroy every other but itself. It does, indeed, tend to destroy every other, but in the same manner as truth in every subject tends to destroy falsehood, that is, by *rational conviction.* Jesus Christ uniformly discountenanced bigotry and intolerance in his disciples. Distinctions of nations, sects, or parties, as such, to him were nothing: distinctions of truth and falsehood, right and wrong, were to him every thing.

The moderation and liberality of pagan governments have been eulogised by the opposers of Christianity, who have asserted that persecution for religion was indebted for its first rise to the Christian system. The very reverse is the fact. Ancient history records numerous instances of pagan governments that persecuted the professors of other religions.

Thus, the Athenians put Socrates to death, on account of his religious tenets; and Antiochus Epiphanes exercised the most horrid cruelties against the Jews for their religion. (1 Mac. i. 40—64,) Tiberius prohibited the Egyptian and Jewish worship, banished the Jews from Rome, and restrained the worship of the Druids in Gaul, while Claudius had recourse to penal laws, to abolish their religion. Domitian and Vespasian banished the philosophers from Rome, and the former confined some of them in the islands, and whipped or put others to death. The violent means and cruel persecutions, which were adopted by pagan governors to annihilate the Christian religion, for three hundred years after its first origin, are too well known to be controverted.

Men, indeed, *calling* themselves Christians, have cruelly persecuted others; but the Gospel does not authorise such a conduct, and therefore is not chargeable with it. And facts and experience have proved (particularly in France during the revolution,) that not the friends but the enemies of the Gospel,—not sincere believers, but apostates and atheists,—have been the most cruel oppressors and persecutors, and the greatest enemies both of civil and religious liberty.

SECTION II.—The wonderful Harmony and intimate Connexion subsisting between all the Parts of Scripture, are a further proof of its Divine Authority and Original.

Most of the writers of the Scriptures lived at very different times, and in distant places, through the long period of sixteen hundred years, so that there could be no confederacy or collusion: and yet their relations agree with, and mutually support, each other.

The same essential agreement, and the same dependency of one upon another, obtains also among the chief practical precepts, as well as between the doctrines and precepts of Christianity.

OBJECTION.—There are contradictions to morality as well as among the different writers themselves.

ANSWER.—These contradictions, as they are termed, are *seeming* only, and not real: they perplex only superficial readers. Nor is there a single instance, which does not admit of a rational solution, by attending to the original languages, and to the manners, customs, &c., that obtained in the countries where scenes mentioned in the Scriptures were situated.

SECTION III.—The Preservation of the Scriptures a Proof of their Truth and Divine Origin.

To nothing, indeed, but the mighty power of God, can we ascribe their preservation. amid all the attempts made to annihilate them.

SECTION IV.—The tendency of the Scriptures to promote the present and eternal Happiness of Mankind, constitutes another Proof of their Divine Inspiration.

Were all men sincerely and cordially to believe the Bible to be a divine revelation, and to obey its precepts, how would the moral face of the world be changed! Wherever it *has been* thus embraced, the most beneficial effects have been the result.

I. The Writings of the earliest Professors of Christianity prove, that the first converts were reformed characters.

1. For testimonies from the New Testament, compare Rom. vi. 21, 22. Cor. vi. 9—11. 1 Pet. iv. 3, 4.

2. The various Christian Apologists, who were compelled to vindicate their character, bear ample testimony to their exemplary lives and conversation. Among these, the attestations of Justin Martyr, Athenagoras, Tertullian, Minucius Felix, Origen, and Lactantius, are particularly worthy of notice.

Though we cannot expect, from PAGANS, *direct* testimonies to the virtues of men whom they persecuted; yet the works of heathen writers incidently furnish proofs of their innocence and worth. Pliny, for instance, in his memorable letter to Trajan, says, that the great crime of the Christians consisted,—not in the commission of any wickedness, but—in assembling together on a stated day before light, to sing hymns to Christ as God. The apostate emperor Julian, also, in his epistle to an heathen pontiff, commended their charity and other virtues to the imitation of the pagans. If the Gospel were merely the contrivance of man, the virtues and holiness of the first Christians would be an inexplicable fact.

II. A Summary of the beneficial effects of Christianity on SOCIETY IN GENERAL.

The benevolent spirit of the Gospel has served as a bond of union between independent nations, and has broken down the partition which separated Heathens and Jews; has abated their prejudices, and has rendered them more liberal towards each other. Further, it has checked pride and promoted humility and forgiveness; has rendered its *sincere* professors just and honest, and it has inspired them with firmness under persecution.

The benign influence of the Gospel has descended into families, and abolished polygamy; has diminished the pressure of private tyranny, has exalted and improved the female character; has improved every domestic endearment; given tenderness to the parent, humanity to the master, respect to superiors, and to inferiors ease: numberless charitable institutions unknown to the heathen world, have sprung from Christianity.

III. Beneficial Effects of Christianity on the POLITICAL STATE of the World.

A milder system of civil government, and a better administration of civil justice, have been introduced: the horrors of war have been mitigated; and the measures of governments have been directed to their proper objects.

IV. Beneficial Effects of Christianity on LITERATURE and the FINE ARTS.

Christianity has been the means of preserving and disseminating moral, classical, and theological knowledge in every nation where it has been established. The Law, the Gospel, the comments on them, and the works of the fathers, were written in Hebrew, Greek, or Latin, so that the knowledge of these languages became necessary to every man, who wished to become an intelligent Christian. The Christian doctrines and precepts being contained in books, the use of letters became necessary to its teachers; and by them was learning preserved. Modern opposers of revelation ascribe all our improvements to philosophy: but it was religion, the RELIGION OF CHRIST, *that took the lead*. The reformers opened to us the Scriptures, and broke all those fetters which shackled human reason. Philosophy crept humbly in her train, and now ungratefully claims all the honour and praise to herself. Luther, Melancthon, and Cranmer, preceded Lord Bacon, Boyle, Newton, and Locke.

Christianity is not to be charged with the crimes of those who have assumed the *name* of Christians, while their conduct has shown that they were utterly destitute of every Christian sentiment. It is not peculiar to the Christian revelation, that it has sometimes furnished a pretext for introducing the very evils and oppressions which it was designed to remedy. The mischiefs, which, through the corrupt passions of men, have been the *accidental* consequences of Christianity, ought not to be imputed to its spirit. Nothing is better calculated to diffuse real comfort, peace, and happiness throughout the world: and a *candid* comparison of the morals of professing Christians throughout the world, with those of heathen nations in a similar stage of society, will demonstrate the beneficial effects of Christianity.

V. Historical facts attest the benefits conferred by the Gospel on the world.

Wherever Christian Missionaries have gone, the most barbarous heathen nations have become civilised. The ferocious have become mild; those, who prowled about for plunder, have acquired settled property, as well as a relish for domestic happiness. Persons, who dwelt in caves or huts have learnt from missionaries the art of building; they who fed on raw flesh have applied to agriculture; men who were clothed in skins and were ignorant of manufactures, have become acquainted with the comforts of apparel; and the violent and rapacious have renounced their rapine and plunder.

The ancient inhabitants of Germany, Hungary, Scythia, Denmark, Sweden, and the aboriginal inhabitants of Britain and Ireland, as well as the modern inabitants of North and South America, the East and West Indies, Greenland, South and West Africa, are all illustrious monuments of the blessed effects produced by Christianity.

VI. The PRACTICAL EFFICACY of Christianity,

Especially when contrasted with the effects of infidelity, is seen more conspicuously and more satisfactorily in the holy, useful, and exemplary lives of real Christians in the private walks of life, and in the peculiar supports and consolations which they enjoy under adversity and afflictions, and in the prospect of futurity: while infidelity offers, and can offer, no ground or prospect of support to its unhappy professors.

SECTION V.—The peculiar Advantages, possessed by the Christian Religion over all other Religions, a demonstrative Evidence of its Divine Origin and authority.

It is the peculiar and distinguishing excellency of the Christian Religion, that it possesses advantages which no other religions or revelations have: at the same time it has none of the defects by which they are characterised.

No other religions are confirmed by ancient prophecies, or by the blood of an infinite number of *sensible and intelligent martyrs*, who voluntarily suffered death in defence of what they had seen and believed. And although other religions may pretend to be confirmed by signs and remarkable events, (as the Romans ascribed the success of their arms to their deities, and the Mohammedans consider the successes of their prophet as a proof of the divinity of his mission;) yet it is not prosperity or adversity *simply considered*, but prosperity or adversity *as foretold by God or his prophets*, which is a certain character of true religion.

Nor has the Christian Religion any of those defects, by which other religions are characterised. It is not designed for the satisfaction of the carnal and worldly appetites of men, as that of the Jews, who aspire after temporal prosperity and worldly pomp; nor is it a medley like that of the ancient Samaritans, made up of a mixture of the Jewish and Pagan religions; nor has it any of the faults or extravagant superstitions of the various religions of the heathen nations, ancient or modern.

The superiority of the Christian Religion over every other is particularly evident in the following respects:

I. In its Perfection.

Other religions, as being principally of human invention and institution, were formed, *by degrees*, from the different imaginations of several persons, who successfully made such additions or alterations as they thought convenient. But it is not so with the Christian Religion: which was wholly delivered by Christ, is entirely contained in each of the Gospels, and even in each epistle of the apostles.

II. In its Openness.

Other religions durst not show themselves openly, and therefore were veiled over with a mysterious silence, and an affected darkness. But the Christian Religion requires no veil to cover it, no mysterious silence, no dissimulation or disguise; although it proposes to us such objects as are contrary to our prejudices and received opinions.

III. In its Adaptation to the Capacities of all Men.

In heathen countries, the philosophers always derided the religion of the vulgar; and the vulgar understood nothing of the religion of the philosophers. But the Christian Religion is alike suited to the learned and to the unlearned, having a divine efficacy; and an agreeable power suitable to all hearts; and it is most wonderfully adapted to those habits and sentiments which spring up in proportion as knowledge and refinement advance.

IV. In the Spirituality of its Worship.

The heathen worship was corporeal and grossly sensual, both in its object and in its rites. But the Christian Religion gives us for the object of our worship,—not a God in human form,—but a God who is a Spirit, whom it teaches us to honour not with a carnal but with a spiritual worship. (John iv. 24.)

V. In its Opposition to the Spirit of the World.

While *all* other religions induce men to seek after the pleasures and profits of the world, in the worship of God; the Christian Religion makes us glorify God by renouncing the world, and teaches us that we must either glorify God, at the expense of worldly pleasures, or possess the advantages of the world with the loss of our religion.

VI. In its Humiliation of man, and Exaltation of the Deity.

All false religions debase the Deity and exalt man; but the Christian Religion debases man and exalts the Deity.

VII. In its Restoration of Order to the world.

The heathen religions degraded their deities to an equality with themselves, and elevated four-footed beasts, fowls of the air, and creeping things,—yea, even their own vices and imperfections, to the rank of gods. But the Christian Religion *alone* restores that order which ought to be established in the world, by submitting every thing to the power of man, that he might submit himself to the will of God.

VIII. In its Tendency to eradicate all evil passions from the heart.

Other religions chiefly tend to flatter the corrupt desires and propensities of men. But the Christian Religion tends to eradicate those desires and propensities from our hearts, and teaches us utterly to renounce them.

IX. In its Contrariety to the covetousness and ambition of mankind, and in its aversion to policy, and corruption, all of which were promoted by other religions.

X. In its Restoration of the Divine Image to Man.

Other religions would have God to bear the image of weak and sinful man; but the Christian Religion teaches us, that men ought to bear the image of God, which is a most powerful motive to holiness.

XI. In its Mighty effects.

False religions were the irregular, confused productions of the politest and ablest men of those times; whereas the Christian Religion is a wonderful composition, which seems to proceed only from the most simple and ignorant sort of people; and, at the same time, is such as evinces that it *must have* for its principle the God of holiness and love.

To conclude this argument:—if we contrast the advantages, which infidelity and Christianity respectively afford to those who embrace them, we shall perceive the evident superiority of the latter. The deist is not happier, or more useful, in society, than the real Christian, nor can he look into futurity with more composure. But the latter is both happy in himself, and useful in his day, and he looks forward to futurity with humble and holy tranquillity. At least, he is as safe in his death as any of the children of men. The deist, on the contrary, by rejecting all moral evidence, *forfeits all things*, and *gains nothing;* while the Christian *hazards* nothing, and GAINS ALL THINGS.

SECTION VI.—Inability to answer all Objections, no just Cause for rejecting the Scriptures.—Unbelievers in Divine Revelation more credulous than Christians.

EVEN though all the difficulties which are alleged to exist in the Sacred Writings could not be accounted for, yet this would be no just or sufficient cause, why we should reject the Scriptures; because objections are, for the most part, impertinent to the purpose for which they are adduced; and if they were pertinent, yet, unless they could confute that evidence, they ought not to determine us against the Bible. If the various arguments by which our Religion appears to be true, cannot be disproved (and disproved they cannot be,) all the objections which can be conceived must proceed from some mistake; and those arguments, together with the conclusions deduced from them, ought not to be rejected on account of the objections, but *such objections ought to be rejected on account of the arguments.* There is no science without its difficulties, and it is not pretended that theology is without them. But difficulties can never alter the nature of things, and make that which is true to become false.

To a *considerate* mind, all the objections which can be invented against the Scriptures, cannot seem nearly so great as that which arises from infidelity, from the supposition that God should not at all reveal himself to mankind; or that the heathen oracles, or the Koran of Mohammed should be of divine revelation.

Nothing is more frequent than the charge of superstition and credulity, which is brought by modern unbelievers against Christianity: and yet this charge attaches with no small force to the opposers of revelation. For it is much more easy to believe the facts recorded in the New Testament, than to suppose them false, and believe the absurd consequences which must follow from such a supposition. It is much more credible that God should work a miracle for the establishment of a useful system of religion, than that the first Christians should act against every principle that is natural to man.

They, who will not be convinced by the present evidence of the truth and certainty of the Christian Religion, would not be convinced by any other evidence whatever.

No man of reason can pretend to say, but that God *may* require us to take notice of *some* things at our peril, to inquire into them, and to consider them thoroughly. And the pretence of want of greater evidence, which is sometimes made, will not excuse carelessness or unreasonable prejudices, when God has vouchsafed to us all that evidence, which was either fit for him to grant, or reasonable for men to desire, or of which the nature of the thing itself, that was to be proved, was capable.

CHAPTER VI.

RECAPITULATION.—MORAL QUALIFICATIONS FOR THE STUDY OF THE SCRIPTURES.

I. Such are the principal proofs for the genuineness, authenticity, credibility, and inspiration of the Holy Scriptures: and taking the whole together, every candid inquirer must be convinced that we have every possible evidence for their truth and divinity, which can be reasonably expected or desired. How absolutely NECESSARY a revelation was, to make known to mankind the proper object of their worship, and to communicate to them a just rule of life, is manifest from the deplorable state of religion and morals in the Heathen world, both ancient and modern.

II. The manner in which the sacred Scriptures have been transmitted to us, their language and style, together with the minute circumstantiality of the facts and doctrines recorded in them, added to the moral impossibility of imposing forged writings upon mankind—are all indisputable proofs of their GENUINENESS and AUTHENTICITY.

III. Equally satisfactory is the evidence for the CREDIBILITY of the writers. For they had a perfect knowledge of the subjects which they have related, and their moral character was never impeached by their keenest opponents: their accounts were published among the people, who witnessed the events which they had recorded, and who could easily have detected falsehood if any such there had been, but who did not attempt to question either the reality of those facts or the fidelity of the narrators; there is an entire harmony between the Sacred Writers and profane history, both natural and civil; and the reality of the principal facts related in the Bible, is perpetuated and commemorated by monuments that subsist to this day in every country, where either Jews or Christians are to be found.

IV. And that the Scriptures are not merely entitled to be received as credible, but also as containing the revealed will of God,—in other words, that they are divinely inspired,—we have evidence of various kinds amounting to moral demonstration: for, on the one hand, their sacred origin is evinced by the most illustrious external attestations, viz. miracles and prophecy, which carry with them the most manifest proofs of a divine interposition; and which it cannot reasonably be supposed that God would ever give, or permit to be given, to an imposture. And, on the other hand, the Scriptures have the most excellent internal characters of truth and goodness, in the sublimity, excellence, and sanctity of the system of doctrines and morals which they announce,—in the harmony and connexion that subsist between all the parts of which they consist, in the preservation of the Sacred Scriptures, and in their admirable tendency (which is shown by its effects wherever the Scriptures are cordially and sincerely believed) to promote the glory of God and the good of mankind, and the cause of virtue and righteousness in the world, and to prepare men, by a life of faith and holy obedience upon earth, for the eternal enjoyment of God in Heaven;—together with the peculiar advantages possessed by the Christian Religion over all other religions.

On all these accounts the Holy Scriptures are thankfully to be received and embraced, as the word of God, and as the rule of Christian faith and practice. "And till I can see the evidence of them disproved, or the religion of Christ demonstrated to be irrational and absurd, I am determined, by the grace of God, to hold fast my profession to the end, seeking after the kingdom of glory by the practice of that righteousness which prepares for, and leads to it, in a firm dependence upon that comfortable declaration of Jesus Christ: *That God so loved the world that* WHOSOEVER *believeth in him should not perish, but have everlasting life.*"*

Since the Holy Scriptures contain all things necessary to salvation, it becomes the indispensable duty of all, carefully and constantly to peruse these sacred oracles, that through them we may become *perfect, thoroughly furnished to every good work*, (2 Tim. iii. 17.) This, indeed, is not only agreeable to the divine command—*Search the Scriptures*, (John v. 39,) and to the design of the Sacred Writings, but is further commended by the practice of the Church in every age, and by the divine promise to all true believers, that *they shall all be taught of God*, (Isa. liv. 13.) The circumstances of every individual must regulate the portion of time, that ought daily to be devoted to this important study; which should be undertaken with devout simplicity and humility, and prosecuted with diligence and attention, with a willingness to resort to all necessary helps for advancement in the truth, and for security against error. To these qualifications, especially, should be added prayer for divine aid and teaching, together with a sincere desire to know and perform the will of God, and, laying aside all prejudice, to follow the Scriptures wherever conviction may lead our minds: for it is indubitable that persons of piety, who are anxiously desirous of the knowledge of divine truth, are aided by the Spirit of God, in searching out the meaning of Scripture, particularly in such subjects as have a special reference to faith and religious practice.

* Bishop Watson's Tracts, vol. iii. p. 484.

PART II.

ON THE LITERARY HISTORY, CRITICISM, AND INTERPRETATION OF THE SCRIPTURES.

BOOK I.—ON THE LITERARY HISTORY AND CRITICISM OF THE SCRIPTURES.

CHAPTER I.

ON THE ORIGINAL LANGUAGES OF SCRIPTURE.

SECTION I.—On the Hebrew Language, and the Samaritan Pentateuch.

I. ANTIQUITY of the Hebrew Language.—In this language the Old Testament is written, with the exception of a few words and passages in the Chaldæan dialect, which occur in Jer. x. 11 Dan. ii. 4, to the end of vii. and Ezra iv. 8, to vi. 19, and vii. 12—17. It derived its name from the root עבר *(aber) to pass over:* whence Abraham was denominated the Hebrew, (Gen. xiv. 13,) having passed over the Euphrates, to come into the land of Canaan. The shortness of its words, the *descriptive* character of the names of places, of animals, and of nations, as well as of the names given to heathen deities, (as *Jove*, which is deduced from Jehovah, *Vulcan* from Tubal-cain, &c.) together with the traces of Hebrew, which are to be found in the Chaldee, Syriac, Arabic, Persian, and other languages;—all combine to prove that Hebrew is the original of all the languages or dialects which have been spoken in the world. The knowledge of this language was very widely diffused by means of the commercial connexions of the Phœnician merchants.

The Hebrew language has had its several ages or degrees of purity. Its *golden* age was the period from the time of Moses to that of David; its *silver* age was the interval between the reigns of Solomon and Hezekiah or Manasseh; the *iron* age, between that period and the

70 years' captivity in Babylon: after which the Jews for a short time spoke a mixed dialect of Chaldee and Hebrew, and ultimately lost it. The Priests and Levites, however, continued to cultivate it to the time of Christ, as a learned language, that they might be enabled to expound the law and the prophets to the people; which last period has been termed the *leaden* age.

II. ANTIQUITY of the Hebrew characters.—The twenty-two characters, now in use, are of a square form, and are generally ascribed to Ezra, who transcribed the ancient characters of the Hebrews into the square characters of the Chaldæans, since which time the Samaritan or ancient Hebrew character has fallen into disuse.

III. ORIGIN of the Samaritans.—

The Samaritans, mentioned in the New Testament, were descended from an intermixture of the ten tribes with the Gentile nations. This origin rendered them odious to the Jews, who refused to acknowledge them as Jewish citizens, or to permit them to assist in rebuilding the Temple, after their return from the Babylonish captivity. In consequence of this rejection as well as of other causes of dissension, the Samaritans erected a temple on Mount Gerizim, and instituted sacrifices according to the prescriptions of the Mosaic law. Hence arose that inveterate schism and enmity between the two nations, so frequently mentioned or alluded to in the New Testament. The Samaritans (who still exist but are greatly reduced in numbers) reject all the sacred books of the Jews except the PENTATEUCH, or five books of Moses, of which they preserve copies in the ancient Hebrew characters: these agree in all material points with our present copies, which were those of the Jews, and thus prove that the important books of Moses have been transmitted to us uncorrupted, in any thing material.

II. The few differences that actually exist between the Samaritan and Hebrew Pentateuchs, may be satisfactorily accounted for by the usual sources of various readings, viz. the negligence of copyists, the confounding of similar letters, transposition of letters, &c. The Samaritan Pentateuch is of great importance in establishing correct readings. Two versions of it are extant.

1. The Samaritan Version, made in the Aramæan dia-

lect (which is intermediate between the Chaldee and the Syriac languages,) by an unknown author in Samaritan characters before the schism took place between the Jews and Samaritans. It is close, and faithful to the original.

2. An Arabic Version, in Samaritan Characters, which was made by Abu Said in A. D. 1070, to supplant the Arabic translation of the Jewish Rabbi, Saadia Gaon, which had till that time been in use among the Samaritans.

Section II.—On the Greek Language.

I. The Septuagint Version of the Old Testament was executed in the Greek language; and as every Jew, who read Greek at all, would read the Greek Bible, the style of this operated in forming the style of the Greek Testament, to which, as well as to the Old Testament, the Septuagint is an important source of interpretation.

II. The New Testament was written in Greek, because it was the language best understood both by writers and readers, being spoken and written, read, and understood throughout the Roman Empire. Its style is characterised by the prevalence of Hebrew phraseology, the language of the New Testament being formed by a mixture of oriental idioms and expressions, with those which are properly Greek. Hence it has been termed Hebraic Greek: and, from the circumstance of the Jews having acquired the Greek language rather by practice than by grammar from the Greeks, among whom they resided, it has also been termed the Hellenistic-Greek. A large proportion of the phrases and constructions of the New Testament, however, is pure Greek, that is, of the same degree of purity as the Greek spoken in Macedonia, and that in which Polybius wrote his Roman History: whence the language of the New Testament will derive considerable illustration from consulting the works of classic authors, and particularly from the Septuagint Version of the Old Testament.

III. The popular Greek dialect was not spoken and written by the Jews, without some intermixtures of a foreign kind: in particular, they intermixed many idioms and the general complexion of their vernacular language. These peculiar idioms are termed Hebraisms; and their nature and classes have been treated at considerable length by various writers. A few examples will suffice to show the nature of these Hebraisms. Thus:

1. *To be called, to arise, and to be found,* are the same as *to be.* See Isa. lxi. 3. Matt. v. 9. 1 John iii. 1. Esth. iv. 14. Luke xxiv. 38. Dan. v. 12. Luke xvii. 18.

2. Verbs, expressive of a person's doing an action, are often used to signify his supposing the thing or discovering and acknowledging the fact, or his declaring and foretelling the event. Matt. x. 39. 1 Cor. iii. 18 Isa. vi. 9, 10. Acts x. 15.

3. Negative verbs are often put for a strong positive affirmation. Psal. lxxxiv. 11. Rom. iv. 19. John xiv. 8.

4. The privileges of the first born among the Jews being very great, the chief or most eminent thing of any kind is called the first born. Job. xviii. 13. The first born of death is the most fatal and cruel death.

5. The words *son*, and children, have various peculiar significations: as, *Sons of Belial*, wicked men; Children of disobedience (Eph. ii.) are disobedient persons, &c.

6. *Name* is frequently synonymous with *Persons.* John i. 12. iii. 18 Rev. iii. 4.

7. The Jews, having but few adjectives and no superlatives, in their language, had recourse to substantives to supply their place. Thus *kingdom and glory* denote a *glorious kingdom*, 1. Thess. ii. 12; *glory of his power*, denotes *glorious power*. 2. Thess. i. 9; *Mountains of God* are exceeding high mountains, Psal. xxxvi. 7, &c.

8. According to the Hebrew idiom, a sword has a *mouth;* or, the edge of a sword is called a mouth. Luke xxi. 24. Heb. xi. 34.

9. The verb to *know* frequently denotes to approve; as in Psal. i. 6. Matt. vii. 23.

10. To *hear* denotes to *understand*, to *attend to*, and to *regard what is said*, Deut. xviii. 15, with Acts iii. 23. Matt. xvii. 5. Luke viii. 8.

Besides these Hebraisms there are found in the New Testament various Syriac, Chaldee, Latin, and other idioms and words, which are respectively denominated Syriasms, Persisms, Latinisms, &c. &c.

1. *Syriasms* are the idioms peculiar to the Syriac or West-Aramæan dialect; and *Chaldaisms* are those peculiar to the Chaldee or East-Aramæan dialect. Instances of these idioms occur in Rom. viii. 15. Matt. xxvii. 46. Mark v. 41. vii. 34.

2. *Latinisms* are those Latin words and phrases, which occur in the New Testament, in consequence of the intercourse of the Jews with the Romans, after Judæa had been reduced into a Roman province. See Matt. x. 29. John ii. 15. Acts. vi. 9, &c.

3. The number of words used by St. Paul in peculiar senses, as well as words not ordinarily occurring in Greek writers, are considered to be provincial idioms at that time used in Cilicia: whence they have been termed *Cilicisms.*

CHAPTER II.

ON THE MANUSCRIRTS OF THE BIBLE.

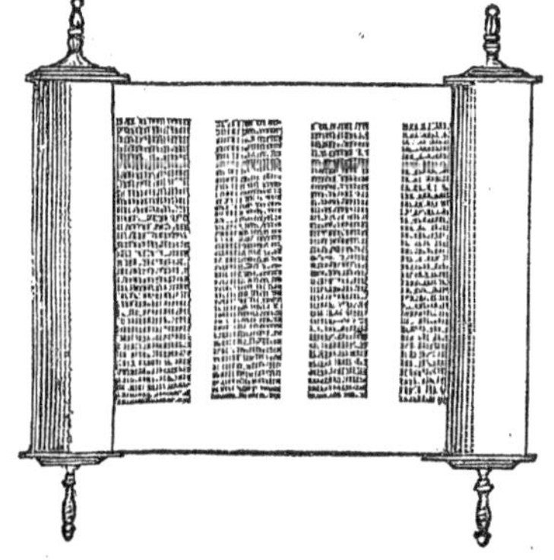

Form of a SYNAGOGUE ROLL of the Pentateuch.

SECTION I.—On the Hebrew Manuscripts of the Old Testament.

I. Hebrew Manuscripts are divided into two classes, viz. *autographs*, or those actually written by the inspired penmen, and *apographs*, or copies made from the originals, and multiplied by repeated transcription. The manuscripts still extant are of two descriptions; viz.

1. The ***Rolled Manuscripts*** used in the synagogues, which are transcribed with great care, and under various minute regulations designed to secure the purity of the sacred text. The form of one of these rolled manuscripts (from the original among the Harleian MSS. in the British Museum, No. 7619,) is given in the vignette at the head of this section. It is a large double roll, containing the Hebrew Pentateuch; written with very great care on forty brown African skins. These skins are of different breadths, some containing more columns than others. The columns are one hundred and fifty-three in number, each of which contains about sixty-three lines, is about twenty-two inches deep, and generally more than five inches broad. The letters have no points, apices, or flourishes about them. The initial words are not larger

than the rest; and a space equal to about four lines, is left between every two books. Altogether, this is one of the finest specimens of the synagogue-rolls that has been preserved to the present time.

2. The *Square Manuscripts*, which are in private use among the Jews, are written, after the manner of our printed books, on vellum, parchment, or paper of various sizes.

II. Among the Jews, five exemplars, or standard copies, have been particularly celebrated for their correctness; and from them all subsequent copies have been made. These are,

1. The *Codex of Hillel*, a manuscript seen by Rabbi Kimchi, in the 12th century, at Toledo.

2, 3. The *Codices of Aaron Ben Asher*, President of the Jewish Academy at Tiberias, and of *Jacob Ben Naphtali*, President of the Jewish Academy at Babylon; who, in the eleventh century, respectively collated the Manuscripts of the Oriental and Occidental Jews.

4, 5. The *Codex of Jericho* and the Codex of Sinai are both in high repute for their correctness. Of the Codex Sanbouki nothing certain is known.

III. Various criteria, furnished by external testimony as well as by internal marks, have been laid down by learned men, for ascertaining the AGE of Hebrew Manuscripts: but these criteria have been questioned by other distinguished critics, who have advanced strong reasons to prove that they are uncertain guides in determining the age of manuscripts.

IV. The ORDER in which the Sacred Books are arranged varies in different manuscripts. Few of those which have been preserved contain the Old Testament entire; the greater part, indeed, comprise only particular portions of it; and many have become mutilated by the consuming hand of time.

V. As the Hebrew Manuscripts, which have been in use since the 11th century, have all been corrected after some particular recension or edition, they have, from this circumstance, been classed into three or four families, according to the country where such recension has obtained; viz.

1. The *Spanish Manuscripts*, which were corrected after the Codex of Hillel, follow the Masoretic System with great accuracy. They are beautifully written, and highly valued by the Jews, though some critics hold them in little estimation.

2. The *Oriental Manuscripts* are nearly the same as the Spanish MSS., and may be referred to the same class.

3. The *German Manuscripts* are less elegantly written than the Spanish MSS. They do not follow the Masoretic Notation, and frequently exhibit important various readings, that are not to be found in the Spanish MSS. This class, though little esteemed by the Jews, is highly valued by Biblical critics.

4. The *Italian Manuscripts* hold a middle place, both in execution and critical value, between the Spanish and German MSS.

VI. The total number of manuscripts collated by Dr. Kennicott, for his edition of the Hebrew Bible, is about 630: the total number collated by M. De Rossi, for his Collection of Various Readings, is 479 MSS., besides 288 printed editions.

Almost all the Hebrew Manuscripts of the Old Testament, at present known to be extant, were written between the years 1000 and 1457; whence Dr. Kennicott infers that all the MSS. written before the years 700 or 800 were destroyed by some decree of the Jewish senate, on account of their numerous differences from the copies then declared genuine.

VII. Among the valuable biblical manuscripts brought from India, by the late Rev. Dr. Claudius Buchanan, and now deposited in the University Library, at Cambridge, there is a roll of the Pentateuch, which he procured from the black Jews in Malabar, who (there is every reason to believe) are descended from the remains of the first dispersion of that nation by Nebuchadnezzar. The date of this MS. cannot be ascertained; but it is supposed to be derived from those copies which their ancestors brought with them into India. It agrees in all material points with our common printed Hebrew text, and affords an additional argument for the integrity of the Pentateuch.

Section II.—Account of Greek Manuscripts containing the Old and New Testaments.

I. Materials of Greek Manuscripts.—These are two-fold: viz. 1. *Vellum*, of various thickness, which is either purple-coloured, or of its natural hue; and, 2. *Paper*, made of cotton or linen. MSS. on paper are of much later date than those on vellum.

II. Form of Letters.—The letters are either capital, which in the time of Jerome were called *uncial*, i. e. initial, or *cursive*, that is, small. Greek MSS. were written in capital letters till the seventh century; and a few so lately even as the ninth century: but the small letters were generally adopted towards the close of the tenth century. The most ancient MSS. were written without accents, spirits, or indeed any separations of the words, until the ninth century.

III. Numerous abbreviations exist in the earliest MSS. They are made by putting together the first and last letters, and sometimes also the middle letter: thus KC (KS) for Κυριος (*kurios*) Lord, ΣΗΡ (sēr) for Σωτηρ (*sotēr*,) *Saviour*, &c.

In the author's larger work, *fac-simile* specimens are given of some of the more ancient MSS. which could not be reduced within the size of this page, so as to convey an accurate idea of them: but the following literal rendering of Matt. v. 1—3., according to the Codex Bezæ, or Cambridge MSS. of the Four Gospels and Acts, (which is described in p. 78, *infra*,) will convey to the English reader some idea of the manner in which manuscripts were anciently written and printed:—

Matt. v. 1—3

ANDSEEINGTHEMULTITUDES·HEWENTUPINTOAMOUNTAIN
ANDWHENHEWASSETDOWN·CAMETOHIM
HISDISCIPLES·ANDOPENINGHISMOUTH
HETAUGHTTHEMSAYING

BLESSED*ARE*THEPOORINSPT*·FORTHEIRSIS
THEKINGDOMOFHEAVEN.

* SPT is contracted for spirit: the original Greek is ΠΝΙ (*pni*) for ΠΝΕΥΜΑΤΙ (PNeumatI.)

Very few MSS. contain the whole either of the Old or the New Testament; and almost all the more ancient manuscripts are imperfect.

Corrections and erasures occur in all MSS. Such corrections as were made *à primâ manu*, that is, by the copyist of a manuscript, are preferable to those made *à secundâ manu*, that is, by later hands. Erasures were made, either by drawing a line through a word, or with the penknife, or sometimes the old writing was obliterated with a sponge, and other words—treatises indeed—were written in lieu of it. Manuscripts thus re-written are termed Codices Palimpsesti, or Rescripti: many of them are of considerable antiquity. They may be easily known, as it rarely happens that the former writing is so completely erased, as not to exhibit some traces. In a few instances both writings are legible.

IV. Account of Greek Manuscripts, containing the Old and New Testaments.

No existing MSS. of the New Testament can be traced higher than the fourth century; and most of them are still later. Some contain the whole New Testament; others comprise particular books or fragments of books, and several contain only detached portions or lessons appointed to be read in the public service of the Church. Some are accompanied with a version, either interlined or in a parallel column. These are called *Codices Belingues:* the greatest number of them is in Greek and Latin; and the Latin version is in general one of those which existed before the time of Jerome.*

1. The Codex Alexandrinus, or Alexandrian Manuscript, is one of the most precious relics of Christian antiquity. It consists of four folio volumes: the three first containing the Old Testament and Apocryphal Books; the fourth comprising the New Testament, together with the first epistle of Clement to the Corinthians, the apocryphal psalms ascribed to Solomon, and some liturgical hymns. Athanasius's Epistle to Marcellus precedes the

* As the author found it impracticable to abridge the numerous bibliographical accounts of MSS., which are given in his larger Introduction to the Critical Study and Knowledge of the Holy Scriptures, so as to convey a *full idea* of their various contents, he has been obliged to confine the analysis contained in this section, to a notice of the three most important manuscripts; viz the Alexandrian, Vatican, and Cambridge, MSS.

Psalms, to which last are annexed the arguments of Eusebius, as his canons are, to the Gospels. In the New Testament there is wanting the beginning as far as Matt. xxv. 6; likewise, from John vi. 50, to viii. 52; and from 2 Cor. iv. 13, to xii. 7. This MS. was procured at Alexandria, by Cyrillus Lucaris, Patriarch of Constantinople, by whom it was sent as a present to King Charles I., in the year 1628. Since the year 1752, it has been deposited in the British Museum. It was most probably written between the middle and end of the fourth century: and tradition attributes the transcribing of it to one Thecla, a martyress, of whom nothing certain can now be known. It is written in uncial or capital letters. A fac-simile of the new Testament was published in 1786, in folio, by Dr. Woide, Assistant Librarian at the British Museum; and a fac-simile edition of the Old Testament is now in progress, under the editorial care of the Rev. H. H. Baber, keeper of the printed books in that noble library. The following passage, rendered rather more literally than the idiom of our language will admit, will enable the reader to form a correct idea of the manner in which the original Greek is written

John 1—14.

INTHEBEGINNINGWASTHEWORDANDTHEWORDWAS
WITHGOD'ANDGODWASTHEWORD'
HEWASINTHEBEGINNINGWITHGOD
ALLWEREMADEBYHIMANDWITH
OUTHIMWASMADENOTONE*THING*
THATWASMADEINHIMLIFEWAS
ANDTHELIFEWASTHELIGHTOFMEN
ANDTHELIGHTINDARKNESSSHIN
ETHANDTHEDARKNESSDIDNOTITCOMPRE
HEND' THEREWASAMANSE
NTFROMGODWHOSENAME*WAS*
JOHN'THIS*PERSON*CAME
ASAWITNESSTHATHEMIGHTTESTI
FYCONCERNINGTHELIGHTTHATA
LLMIGHTBELIEVETHROUGHHIM.

2. The Codex Vaticanus, or VATICAN MANUSCRIPT, which is preserved in the Vatican Library at Rome, is

also written on vellum in uncial characters, and most probably before the close of the fifth century, though some critics assign to it an earlier, and others a later date. It wants, in the Old Testament, from Gen. i. to xlvi. and from Psalm cv. to cxxxvii. inclusive; and in the New Testament, from Hebrews, ch. ix. 14, to the end of that epistle, as well as St. Paul's other epistles to Timothy, Titus, and Philemon, and the entire book of the Revelations. This last book, however, has been added, as well as the latter part of the epistle to the Hebrews, by a modern hand in the fifteenth century. In many places, the faded letters have been retouched by a modern but careful hand. Various defects, both in orthography and language, indicate that this MS. was written by an Egyptian copyist.

The following literal English version of the prophecy of Ezekiel, ch. i. ver. 1—3; will enable the reader to form a similarly correct idea of the manner in which the Codex Vaticanus was executed

IEZEKIEL.

\+ \+ \+

NNOWITCAMETOPASSINTHETHIR
INTHE
TIETHYEARFOURTH
MONTHONTHEFIFTHOFTHEMONTH
WHENIWASINTHEMIDST
OFTHECAPTIVESBYTHE
RIVERCHOBARAND
THEHEAVENSWEREOPENED
ANDISAWTHEVISIONSOFGDONTHEFI
FTHOFTHEMONTHTHIS
WASTHEFIFTHYEAROFTHE
CAPTIVITYOFTHEKI
NGJOACHIM ANDCA
METHEWORDOFTHELDTOE
ZEKIELTHESONOFBUZITHE
PRIESTINTHELANDOFTHECHALDEESB
YTHERIVERCHO
BARANDUPONMEWAS
THEHANDOFTHELDANDILOOKEDANDLO
AWHIRLWNDCAMEOUTOF
THENORTHANDAGREATCLOUD
WITHIT

This manuscript has been repeatedly collated by various critics: the Roman edition of the Septuagint, published in 1587, professes to exhibit the text of this manuscript, of which no fac-simile edition has ever been printed.

3. The Codex Cantabrigiensis was presented to the University of Cambridge by Theodore Beza, in 1531, after whom it is most commonly called the *Codex Bezæ*. It is a Greek-Latin manuscript; concerning its date, critics greatly differ, but it may most probably be referred to the fifth or sixth century. It contains the four Gospels and Acts of the Apostles: sixty-six leaves of it are much torn and mutilated, and ten have been supplied by a later transcriber. Notwithstanding its acknowledged antiquity, this MS. is deemed of comparatively little value, in consequence of the Greek text having been altered and readings introduced from some Latin version, which were warranted by no Greek manuscript. An elegant fac-simile edition of it was printed at the expense of the university of Cambridge, under the editorial care of the Rev. Dr. Kipling, in 2 vols. folio, 1793.

CHAPTER III.

ON THE DIVISIONS AND MARKS OF DISTINCTION OCCURRING IN MANUSCRIPTS AND PRINTED EDITIONS OF THE SCRIPTURES.

Section I.—Divisions and Marks of Distinction occurring in the Old Testament.

I. Different Appellations given to the Scriptures. The collection of writings, which is regarded by Christians as the rule of their faith and practice, has been variously termed,—the *Scriptures*, as being the most important of all *Writings;*—the *Holy* or *Sacred Scriptures*, because they were composed by divinely inspired persons;—the *Canonical Scriptures*, either because they are the rule of our faith and practice, or to distinguish them from apocryphal writings, (those of uncertain authority and of human origin;)—and, most frequently, the Bible, that is, The Book, by way of eminence, as being the Book of Books, infinitely superior to every unassisted production of the human mind.

II. The Canonical Books are usually divided into two parts: 1 The *Old Testament*, containing the revelations of the divine will before the Birth of Christ; and 2. The *New Testament*, which comprises the inspired writings of the Evangelists and Apostles.

III. The Old Testament was divided into three portions or classes; viz.:

1. The *Law*, including the Pentateuch, or five Books of Moses.

2. The *Prophets*, containing the Books of Joshua, Judges, 1 and 2 Samuel, and 1 and 2 Kings: these were termed the *Former Prophets;* and also the prophetical Books of Isaiah, Jeremiah, Ezekiel, and the twelve minor Prophets, who were called the *Latter Prophets*, with reference to the time when they flourished.

3. The *Cetubim*, or *Hagiographa*, that is, the *Holy Writings*, so called because the Jews affirm that they were written by holy men divinely inspired, but who had no public mission as prophets. This division comprehended the Psalms, Proverbs, Job, Song of Solomon, Ruth, Lamentations of Jeremiah, Ecclesiastes, Esther, Daniel. Ezra, and Nehemiah, and the two Books of Chronicles.

The Pentateuch is divided into fifty or fifty-four *Paraschioth*, or larger sections, according as the Jewish year is simple or intercalary, one of which is read in the synagogues every Sabbath day: and these Paraschioth are further subdivided into smaller sections termed *Siderim*, or orders. The reading of the law being prohibited during the persecution of Antiochus Epiphanes, the Jews substituted for it fifty-four *Haphtoroth* or sections from the prophets, which are further divided into *pesukim* or verses. After the restoration of the reading of the law, by the Maccabees, the section which had before been read from the law was used for the first, and that from the prophets for the second lesson.

IV. Origin and rise of the MASORA.—The sacred text was, originally, written without any divisions into chapters or verses, or even into words. In the lapse of ages, various readings having arisen in consequence of successive transcriptions, the Jews had recourse to a canon, which they judged to be infallible, in order to fix the reading of the Hebrew text. This rule they called MASORA, or Tradition, pretending that it was at first given by God to Moses, on Mount Sinai, when he taught him, first, its *true reading*, and, secondly, its *true interpretation*. The *former* is the subject of the Masora, the *latter* (or true interpretation) is that of the Misna, or Collection of Jewish Traditions and Expositions of Scripture Texts, and of the Gemara, or Commentary thereon.

The Masoretic criticisms relate to the divisions of the

books and sections of books, the number of verses, the notation of omissions, alterations, repetitions of words and verses, and other minutiæ. To this system also belong the marginal corrections found in Hebrew MSS. and printed editions of the Old Testament, termed *Ketib*, that is, *written*, and *Keri*, that is, *read* or *reading*, as if to intimate, "write in this manner," but "read in that manner;" for instance, instead of the sacred name JEHOVAH, the Jews substitute Adonai or Elohim. Learned men are greatly divided in sentiment concerning the date of the Masora; but the most probable opinion is that which refers its commencement to the *sixth* century, when it was invented by the learned Jews of Tiberias, and continued at different times by various authors. Their chief design in this undertaking, appears to have been the establishment or preservation of the Hebrew text, without variations.

V. The Old Testament is now divided into four parts; viz.:

1. The *Pentateuch*, or five Books of Moses.
2. The *Historical* Books, comprising Joshua to Esther, inclusive.
3. The *Doctrinal* or Poetical Books of Job, Psalms, Proverbs, Ecclesiastes, and the Song of Solomon; and
4. The *Prophetical* Books of Isaiah, Jeremiah, with his Lamentations, Ezekiel, Daniel, and the twelve Minor Prophets.

These are severally divided into chapters and verses. The former were invented by Cardinal Hugo de Sancto Caro, about the middle of the thirteenth century: who, having projected a concordance to the Latin Vulgate translation, divided the Old and New Testaments into chapters, which are the same we now have. These, again, he subdivided into smaller sections, distinguished by the letters A, B, C, D, E, F, and G. The facility of reference, afforded by these subdivisions, suggested the idea of a Hebrew concordance, upon the same plan, to Rabbi Mordecai Nathan, a celebrated Jewish teacher in the fifteenth century, who retained the divisions of chapters, but substituted numeral figures for the Cardinal's marginal letters. The introduction of verses into the Hebrew Bible was first made, in 1661, by Athias, a Jewish printer at Amsterdam: and from him the division of verses has been adopted in all copies of the Bible in other languages.

SECTION II.—On the Divisions and Marks of Distinction occurring in the New Testament.

I. ANCIENT DIVISIONS.—Before the fourth century the New Testament was divided into longer chapters, called τιτλοι (*titloi*,) and others which were shorter called κεφαλαια (*kephalaia*,) or heads, and also breves. The most celebrated division of the four Gospels into chapters was that of Ammonius, a learned Christian of Alexandria, in the third century, from whom they have been termed the *Ammonian Sections.* The Acts of the Apostles and the Catholic Epistles were similarly divided by Euthalius, an Egyptian Bishop, in the fifth century, after whom these divisions have been called the Euthalian Sections. Saint Paul's Epistles were divided in like manner, by some unknown author, in the fourth century. These divisions were superseded by Cardinal Hugo's chapters, in the thirteenth century.

II. PUNCTUATION and DIVISION OF VERSES.—Euthalius, who has just been mentioned, was the inventer of the division of the New Testament into ςιχοι (*stichoi*,) or lines regulated by the sense; so that each terminated where some pause was to be made in reading. The introduction of points or stops, to mark the sense, is a gradual improvement, commenced by Jerome in the fourth century, and continued and improved by succeeding critics. The verses at present found in the New Testament were invented (in imitation of those contrived by Rabbi Nathan) by Robert Stephens, a learned printer, who first introduced them into his edition of the New Testament published in 1551.

III. The Inscriptions, or TITLES, prefixed to the various books of the New Testament, are of great antiquity They were added, in order to distinguish one book from another, after the canon of the New Testament was formed, but the author of them is not known.

IV. But the SUBSCRIPTIONS annexed to the epistles are manifestly spurious, for some of them contradict both chronology and history. For instance, according to the subscriptions to 1 and 2 Thessalonians, those epistles were written at Athens, whereas they were written at Corinth. The subscription to 1 Corinthians states that it was written at Philippi; notwithstanding it appears from

xvi. 8, and 19, that the apostle was at that very time in Asia. The subscription to the epistle to the Galatians purports that epistle to have been written from Rome; whereas Saint Paul did not go to Rome until *ten* years AFTER the conversion of the Galatians. And the subscription to the first epistle to Timothy evidently was not, and indeed could not have been, written by the apostle Paul: for it states that epistle to have been written from Phrygia Pacatiana; whereas the country of Phrygia was not divided into the two provinces of ***Phrygia Pacatiana***, or ***Prima***, and ***Phrygia Secunda***, until the fourth century. The author of these subscriptions, it is evident was either grossly ignorant, or grossly inattentive.

CHAPTER IV.

ON THE ANCIENT VERSIONS OF THE SCRIPTURES.

To those who possess ability, means, and leisure of consulting them, the Ancient Versions of the Old Testament are a very important source of criticism and interpretation of the sacred writing; the value of them, however, varies according to the age and country of their respective authors, the purity of the text whence these versions were made, and the ability and fidelity of the translators.

SECTION I.—Of the Targums, or Chaldee Paraphrases.

TARGUM is a Chaldee word, signifying generally any version or explanation; but this appellation is particularly restricted to the versions or paraphrases of the Old Testament, which have been composed in the Chaldee Dialect. Ten of these expositions have been preserved to our times: viz.

I. The TARGUM of ONKELOS on the Pentateuch, or five books of Moses, was composed by a learned Jewish rabbi of the same name, who is supposed to have been contemporary with our Saviour. It is preferred to every other, on account of the purity of its style, and its general freedom from idle legends.

II. The TARGUM of the PSEUDO-JONATHAN, so called from being erroneously ascribed to Jonathan Ben Uzziel, is a more liberal paraphrase of the Pentateuch than the preceding, but abounds with the most idle Jewish legends. From internal evidence, learned men concur in referring its date to the seventh or eight century of the Christian Æra.

III. The JERUSALEM TARGUM, also on the five books of Moses, in many respects agrees with that of the Pseudo-Jonathan, in the impurity of its style, legendary tales, &c. It was most probably written in the eighth or ninth century.

IV. The TARGUM of JONATHAN BEN UZZIEL, on the Prophets (that is according to the Jewish Division of the sacred books mentioned in p. 79,) is held in the highest estimation. Its date cannot be exactly ascertained; some learned men making it nearly coeval with the time of Christ, while others place it three or four hundred years later.

V. The barbarous, and in many places, obscure TARGUM on the CETUBIM, or Holy Writings, though ascribed to Rabbi Joseph, surnamed the Blind, in the third century, is evidently a compilation of much later date.

VI. The TARGUM on the MEGILLOTH, or five books of Ecclesiastes, Song of Songs, Lamentations of Jeremiah, Ruth, and Esther, could not be written before the sixth century. It is of very little value. The same remark is applicable to

VII—IX. Three TARGUMS on THE BOOK of ESTHER; and X. a TARGUM on THE BOOKS of CHRONICLES; all of which are of very recent date.

XI. Of all these Chaldee Paraphrases, the Targums of Onkelos and Jonathan Ben Uzziel are held in the highest estimation by the Jews; but it is in establishing the genuine meaning of particular prophecies relative to the Messiah, in opposition to the false explications of the Jews and the erroneous expositions of Anti-Trinitarians, that these paraphrases are pre-eminently useful.

SECTION II.—Ancient Greek Versions of the Old Testament.

I. Among the Greek Versions of the Old Testament, the most ancient and valuable is that usually designated the SEPTUAGINT, from the tradition (now generally rejected) of one Aristeas, who related that it was made in seventy-two days, and by seventy learned Jews, who had been sent by the Jewish High Priest Eleazar to Alexandria, at the request of Ptolemy Philadelphus, King of Egypt. It is, however, most probable, that this version was really executed during the joint reigns of Ptolemy Lagus, and his son Philadelphus, and about 285 or 286 years before the Christian Æra.

II. The introduction of Coptic, or pure Egyptian words, and the rendering of Hebrew ideas in the Egyptian manner, clearly prove that the translators were natives of Egypt; as the difference of style and various ability, with which particular books have been rendered into Greek, evince this version to have been the work, not of one, but of several individuals.

III. The Septuagint Version, though originally made for the use of the Egyptian Jews, gradually acquired the highest authority among the Jews of Palestine, who were acquainted with the Greek language, and subsequently also among Christians. It retained its authority, even with the rulers of the Jewish Synagogue, until the commencement of the first century after Christ; when the Jews being unable to resist the arguments from prophecy which were urged against them by Christians, in order to deprive these of the benefit of that authority, began to deny that it agreed with the Hebrew Text, and, ultimately abandoning it they adopted the Greek Version of Aquila, which is noticed in p. 86, infra.

IV. Numerous errors having in the lapse of ages crept into the Septuagint, by the inaccuracy of transcribers and other circumstances, Origen, a learned Christian Father, in the early part of the third century, undertook the laborious task of collating the Greek Text then in use, with the original Hebrew, and with other Greek Translations then extant, and from the whole to produce a new recension or revisal. Twenty-eight years were devoted to this great critical work, which ancient writers have variously termed the *Tetrapla*, *Hexapla*, *Octaplu*, and *Enneapla*. *Tetrapla* contained the four Greek Versions of Aquila, Symmachus, the Septuagint, and Theodotion: when he subsequently added, in two columns, the Hebrew Text, in its original characters, and also in Greek characters, the six columns formed the *Hexapla.* The addition of two other Greek Versions of some parts of the Scriptures, in particular places, composed the *Octapla;* and a separate translation of the Psalms being afterwards subjoined, the entire work has by some been termed the *Enneapla* It is, however, most probable, that Origen edited only the Tetrapla and the Hexapla. As Origen's object was to correct the differences found in the existing copies of the Old Testament, he carefully noted the alterations made by him, with peculiar marks. Fifty years after his death, this great work was discovered in an obscure corner of the city of Tyre, by Eusebius and Pamphilus, by whom it was deposited in the Library of Pamphilus the Martyr, where Jerome saw it about the middle of the fourth century. It is supposed to have perished on the capture of that city by the Arabs, A. D. 653. A few fragments, retrieved from MSS. of the Septuagint and the writings of the Fathers, are all that remain of this noble undertaking in behalf of sacred literature.

V. The Septuagint continuing to be read in most of the Greek churches, the text, as corrected by Origen, was transcribed for their use together with his critical marks. In progress of time, from the introduction of numerous errors by copyists, a new revision became necessary: and as all the oriental churches did not receive Origen's labours with equal deference, three principal recensions were undertaken nearly at the same time, viz:

1. The edition, undertaken by Eusebius and Pamphilus, about A. D. 300, from the Hexaplar Text, with the whole of Origen's critical marks: by repeated transcriptions these marks soon became changed, and were finally omitted.

2. The recension of the Vulgate, or common Greek Text, by Lucian, a presbyter of the Church at Antioch, who suffered martyrdom A. D. 311. He took the Hebrew Text for the basis of his edition, which was received in all the eastern churches from Constantinople to Antioch. Contemporary with Lucian was

3. Hesychius, an Egyptian Bishop, who undertook a similar revision, which was generally adopted in the churches of Egypt.

All MSS. and printed editions of the Septuagint, now extant, are derived from these three recensions. The Septuagint Version is of great importance, in a critical point of view, not only for correcting the Hebrew text, but also for ascertaining the meaning of particular idiomatic expressions and passages in the New Testament.

VI. It remains to notice, briefly, some other ancient Greek Translations, which have been incidentally mentioned.

1. The Version of AQUILA, a native of Sinope, in Pontus, was executed about the year 160. He was of Jewish descent, and had apostatised from the Christian faith to Judaism. His version, which is very literal, was undertaken to gratify the Jews. Nearly contemporary with him was

2. THEODOTION, an Ebionite, or semi-christian: his version is a kind of revision of the Septuagint; it holds a middle place between the servile closeness of Aquila and the freedom of 4. SYMMACHUS, who lived about the year 200, and was also an Ebionite.

4—6. The three anonymous translations, usually called the ***fifth***, ***sixth***, and ***seventh*** versions, derive their names from the order in which Origen disposed them in his columns. Their authors are not known.

SECTION III.—Ancient Oriental Versions of the Old and New Testaments.

I. SYRIAC VERSIONS.—Christianity being very early preached in Syria, several versions of the Scriptures were made into the language of that country.

1. The most celebrated of these is the *Peschito*, (that is, right, literal, or exact,) also called the *Versio Simplex*, on account of its close adherence to the original sacred text. It was made early in the second, if not at the close of the first century: and, from some internal evidences furnished by the style, it is supposed to have been the work of several authors. The second epistle of Peter, the second and third epistles of John, and the epistle of

* In the larger edition of the author's Introduction to the Study and Knowledge of the Scriptures, he has treated the oriental versions of the Old and New Testaments in distinct sections. They are here condensed, in order to avoid repetitions, that would otherwise be necessary.

Jude, as well as the disputed passages in John viii. 2—11, and 1 John v. 7, are all wanting in the New Testament of this version; having been added in the sixth century by some unknown and indifferent translator. This version is much esteemed for its singular fidelity.

2. The *Philoxenian*, or *Syro-Philoxenian* Version, derives its name from Philoxenus or Xenayas, Bishop of Hierapolis in Syria, A. D. 488—518, who employed his rural bishop, Polycarp, to translate the New Testament from the original Greek into the vernacular Syriac of that time. Though inferior to the preceding, it is nevertheless of considerable value in a critical point of view, as well as for the interpretation of the New Testament.

3. The Syriac Translation of Jerusalem is known to have existed, from its having been discovered in a lectionarium, or book containing ecclesiastical lessons from the New Testament. It has never been published.

II. Egyptian Versions.—Two Translations of the Scriptures have been made in the Egyptian language,—one in the Coptic or ancient dialect of Lower Egypt, the other in the Sahidic, or dialect of Upper Egypt, and both from the Greek. The *Coptic* Version is by some eminent scholars referred to the second or third century, though others carry its date so low as the fifth century; the Sahidic Version was probably executed in the second century.

III. Several Arabic Translations have been made at different times between the seventh, and the tenth or eleventh centuries, for the inhabitants of those countries, where the Syriac and Egyptian languages have been supplanted by the Arabic. They were not all executed from the original text, but from those versions, which they were intended to accompany.

IV. The Ethiopic, or Abyssinian Version of the Old Testament was made from the Septuagint; some fragments of it only have been printed, but the entire New Testament, has been published. This version is of considerable antiquity, the Old Testament being referred to the second, and the New Testament to the fourth century

V. The Armenian Version of the Old Testament was

also made from the Septuagint; the New Testament has been twice translated, from the Syriac, and then from the Greek. This version is ascribed to Miesrob, the inventor of the Armenian Alphabet, towards the close of the fourth, or early in the fifth century

VI. Though the Scriptures are said to have been early translated into the PERSIAN language, no fragments of this ancient version are extant. The Pentateuch is all that has been printed of the Old Testament; it was translated by a Jew, and for the benefit of Jews. Of the New Testament, there are extant two versions of the four Gospels; the most ancient and valuable of which is printed in the London Polyglott, by bishop Walton, from a manuscript of the fourteenth century.

SECTION IV.—Ancient Western Versions of the Scriptures.

I. Many LATIN Versions of the Scriptures were made at the first introduction of Christianity, by unknown authors. One of these, called the Vetus Itala, or Old Italic, appears to have acquired a more extensive circulation than the others, to which it was preferred on account of its clearness and fidelity. It was translated from the Greek, both in the Old and New Testaments; and was made in the early part of the second century. In the progress of time, very numerous alterations, however, being made by transcribers, Jerome, towards the close of the fourth century, undertook to revise it, and make it more conformable to the original Greek. Some parts only of this revision have been preserved. But before it was completed, he undertook, and at length accomplished, a version of the Bible, which gradually acquired so great an authority in the West of Europe, that, ever since the seventh century, it has been exclusively adopted by the Romish Church; and in the sixteenth century, the assembly or council of Trent pronounced the Latin Vulgate (for so this version is termed) to be authentic, and to be exclusively used in the public service of the church. Various grave errors having crept into this version in the lapse of ages, several revisions were undertaken by learned men. Of these the most celebrated is the revision o.

Pope Sixtus V., published at Rome in 1590, but suppressed by Pope Clement VIII., whose authentic edition appeared in 1592. This edition has been followed in all subsequent impressions of the Latin Vulgate. Notwithstanding the variations between the Sixtine and Clementine editions, (both published by *infallible* pontiffs!) and that several passages are mistranslated in order to support the peculiar dogmas of the Romish Church, the Latin Vulgate preserves many true readings, where the modern Hebrew copies are corrupted.

II. The Gothic Version of the Bible was made from the Greek, both in the Old and New Testaments, by Ulphilas, Bishop of the Mæso-Goths, who invented the Gothic characters. A fragment of the Book of Nehemiah, the four Gospels, and some portions of the Epistles, are all that has been published, from this version; which, though interpolated from the Latin Vulgate, is nevertheless much esteemed for its general fidelity.

III. The Sclavonic or Old Russian translation was executed from the Greek, in the ninth century, by the two brothers, Cyril and Methodius. It is said to have undergone several revisions; and the New Testament is rendered with more perspicuity than the Old.

IV. The Anglo-Saxon Version is ascribed by Dr. Mill to several authors, and is supposed to have been executed in the eighth and ninth centuries. Having been made from the Old Latin, it may be of use in determining the readings of that version. Several portions of it have been published at different times.

Section V.—Use and Application of Ancient Versions.

As no one version can be absolutely free from error, reliance ought not to be implicitly placed on any one translation. Versions of Versions, that is, versions not made immediately from the Hebrew of the Old Testament, or the Greek of the New Testament, are of authority only to determine the meaning of the version from which they are taken.

I. The Alexandrian, or Septuagint Greek Version, from its very great antiquity, and its influence on the style of the New Testament, claims the first place. Next in order is,

II. The Syriac Peschito, which is particularly serviceable for the interpretation of the New Testament.

III. The Latin Vulgate, with the exception of the Psalms, claims the third place

IV. The Targums, or Chaldee Paraphrases, especially that of Jonathan Ben Uzziel, illustrate many difficult passages in the Old Testament, as well as in the New Testament.

V. Other versions made immediately from the Hebrew and Greek originals follow next in order.

Ancient versions need not to be consulted, except in passages that are really difficult, or unless an examination of them be instituted for some special object of inquiry.

CHAPTER V.

ON THE MODERN VERSIONS OF THE SCRIPTURES.

Numerous as were the ancient versions of the Sacred Scriptures, the publication of a version, being accomplished by the tedious process of transcription, was necessarily slow, while the high price of manuscripts enabled only the wealthy to procure them. The discovery of the art of printing in the fifteenth century, and the establishment of the glorious reformation throughout Europe in the following century, facilitated the circulation of the Scriptures, both in the original Languages and through the medium of translations. The Modern Versions of the Scriptures are two-fold, viz.: in the Latin Language, and in the vernacular languages of almost all the countries in which Christianity has been propagated: and both are made, either by persons in communion with the Church of Rome, or by Protestants.

Section I. On the Modern Latin Versions of the Old and New Testament.

I. Modern Latin Versions, executed in communion with the Church of Rome.

1. The Version of Sanctes Pagninus a Dominican monk, was undertaken under the patronage of several popes ; and,

after twenty-five years of unremitting labour, was published in 1528. Though it has been censured by one critic for its close adherence to the original text, all the later commentators and critics commend it for its exactness and fidelity. It contains only the Old Testament. This translation was revised by

2. Arias Montanus, who has from this circumstance been erroneously, considered as a new translator of the Bible into the Latin Language. Montanus's aim being to translate the Hebrew words by the same number of Latin words, his edition may rather be considered as a grammatical commentary than a true version, and is best adapted to suit young beginners in the Hebrew language.

3. The translations of Thomas Malvenda, and of Cardinal Cajetan (who was *not* the author of that which bears his name) have both fallen into oblivion.

4. Houbigant's Latin Version of the Old Testament is framed according to the corrected Hebrew Text, published by him in 1753, in 4 vols. folio; a work which has not answered the high expectations entertained of it.

II. Modern Latin Versions of the Bible, executed by Protestants

1. The translation of Sebastian Munster, first published in 1534, is considered, upon the whole, as very exact and conformable to the original.

2. The Version which bears the name of Leo Juda, though commenced by him, was finished by others: it is acknowledged to be very faithful. It was first published in 1543.

3. Sebastian Chatillon (better known by the name of Castalio) in 1551 published a version of the Bible, in which he aimed at rendering the Old and New Testaments into classical Latin. His style has been severely censured, as departing from the simple grandeur of the sacred originals

4. The Version of Francis Junius and Immanual Tremellius, first printed in 1575, is held in great estimation for its simplicity, perspicuity, and fidelity.

5. The Latin Translation of Sebastian Schmidt, published in 1696, is strictly literal.

6. The Version of Professor J. A. Dathe, printed be- veen the years 1779 and 1789, is deservedly in high pute for its general fidelity and excellence.

7. The Version of the Old Testament, commenced in 1816, by H. A. Schott and J. F. Winzer, professes to be very close. The Pentateuch only has been published.

III. Besides the preceding new modern Latin Versions, there have been several editions of the Latin Vulgate, so much corrected from the Hebrew and Greek originals, as in some degree to be considered new translations. Of this number are the Latin Bibles published by Isidore Clarius, in 1542; by Paul Eber, in 1565; and by Luke Osiander, in 1578, and Andrew Osiander in 1600. The edition of Clarius, who was a Romanist, is preferred to those of the other three Protestant scholars.

IV. Of the Latin Version of the New Testament the following are the principal:

1. Erasmus claims the first place. His version was published in 1516; and it is admitted that he succeeded in giving a clear and faithful version as far as it was possible, at that time. He varied but little from the Vulgate.

2. The Latin Version of Theodore Beza, published in 1556, has always been held in high estimation for its fidelity.

3. The Latin Version of Leopoldo Sebastiani, which appeared in 1817, professes to be formed after the text of the Alexandrian Manuscript, collated with other MSS. and critical helps. In all doctrinal points it agrees with the tenets of the Romish Church.

Section II.—Versions in the Modern Languages of Europe, Asia, Africa, and America.

The translations of the Scriptures into the different modern languages, which are spoken in the four quarters of the globe, are so numerous, that it is extremely difficult to obtain correct accounts of all of them, and still more difficult to compress those accounts into an analysis like the present. The following tables, however, will exhibit at one view the principal translations, together with the dates when they appeared, the authors by whom they were executed, and the places where they were severally printed. The first of these tables is taken from the second volume of the author's larger work, with a few additions; and the second and third are given. by permission, from the eighteenth volume of the Encyclopædia Metropolitana, for which work he originally composed them

Table I.

VERSIONS IN THE LANGUAGES OF MODERN EUROPE.

Translation.	N. T.	Bible.	Author.	Place of Printing
German	1522	1534	Martin Luther	Wittemberg
English	1526	1535	Tindal, and Coverdale	Uncertain
French	-	1535	Robert Olivetan	Geneva
Swedish	1534	1541	Olaus Petri	Upsal, Sweden
Danish	1524	1550	Palladius and others	Copenhagen
Dutch	-	1560		
Italian	-	1562	Antonio Brucioli's revised?	Geneva
Spanish	1556	1569	Cassiodorus de Reyna	Frankfort or Basil
Russian	1519	1581	Cyril and Methodius	Ostrog
Helvetian dialect	1525	1529		Zurich
Lower Saxon dialect	-	1533		Lubeck
Finnish	1548	1642		Stockholm
Croatian	1553	-		Tubinger
Basque	1571	-		Rochelle
Welsh	1567	1588		London
Hungarian	1574	1589		Vienna
Wendish	-	1584		Wittemberg
Icelandic	-	1584	Thorlack	Holum, Iceland
Pomeranian dialect	-	1588		Barth
Polish	1585	1596	Several	
Bohemian	-	1593	Several	Cralitz, Moravia
Hebrew	1599	-	Elias Hutter	Nuremberg
Modern Greek	1638	-	Maximus Calliergi	Geneva
Wallachian	1648	-		Belgrade
Romanese	-	1657		Schuol
Lithuanian	-	1660	Chylinsky	London
Turkish	1666	-	Lazarus Seaman	Oxford
Irish	1602	1685	Dr. Daniel, Bp. Bedell	London
Livonian	1685	1689		Riga
Esthonian	1685	1689		Riga
Esthonian, dialect of	1686	-		Riga
Dorpatian dialect	1727			
Grisons	-	1719		Coire
Upper Lusatian	1706	1728	Several	Bautzen
Lapponic	1755			
Manks	-	1763	Bishops Wilson and Hildesley,	
Gaelic	1767	1802	James Stewart and others	Edinburgh
Portuguese	1712	1748-53	Ferreira d'Almeida, Cath.	Amsterdam and Batavia
	1781	1783	Antonio Pereira, Cath.	Lisbon
Spanish	-	1793,4	Padre Scio, Cath.	Madrid
Maltese	1820	-	Rev. W. Jowett, M.A. and Signor Cannolo	Malta
Samogitian	1820			Petersburgh
Judæo-Polish	1821	-	N. Solomon	London
Modern Russ	1821			
Russian Dialects, viz				
Karelian (Gospel of Matthew)	1820	-	Russian Bible Society	Petersburgh
Mordwassian (4 Gospels)	1821			
Tcheremissian, (4 Gospels)	1821			

Table II.

VERSIONS IN THE LANGUAGES OF MODERN ASIA.

Language.	New Testament, or detached Books thereof.		Bible, or Old Testament, or detached Books thereof.		Author.	Place of Printing.
	New Test.	Detached Books.	Bible, or Old Tes.	Detached Books.		
1. Arabic, and its derivative languages.						
Arabic,	1816	—	—	—	N. Sabat and Rev. H. Martyn, B. D.	Calcutta
Persian	—	4 Gosp. 1804	—	—	Lt.Col. Colebrooke	Calcutta
	1815	—	—	—	Rev. H. Martyn	Petersburgh
Pushtoo	1818	—	—	Gen. Lev. 1822	John Leyden, M.D. and others.	Serampore
Bulocha	—	4 Gosp. 1816	—	—	Baptist Missionaries	Serampore
2. Sanscrit, and its derivative languages.						
Sanscrit,	1808	—	1811-18	—	Baptist Missionaries	Serampore
Sikh or Punjabee	1811	—	—	Pent. 1818	Baptist Missionaries	Serampore
Assamese	1819	—	—	—	Baptist Missionaries	Serampore
Kashmiree	1819	—	—	—	Baptist Missionaries	Serampore
Wutch, or Multanee	1819	—	—	—	Baptist Missionaries	Serampore
Guzerattee	1820	—	—	—	Baptist Missionaries	Serampore
Bikaneer	1819	—	—	—	Baptist Missionaries	Serampore
Kunkuna	1818	—	—	—	Baptist Missionaries	Serampore
Maruwar	1822	—	—	—	Baptist Missionaries	Serampore
Oojuvinee	1822	—	—	—	Baptist Missionaries	Serampore
Bundelkundee	1822	—	—	—	Baptist Missionaries	Serampore
Nepaulese	1822	—	—	—	Baptist Missionaries	Serampore
Mahratta	1807	—	—	Pent. and Hist. Bks. 1812-15	Baptist Missionaries	Serampore
Hindee	1812	—	—	Pnt. Hist. and Poet. Books, 1806-12	Baptist Missionaries	Serampore
Hindoostanhee	—	—	—	Ps. 1747	Danish Mission Benj. Schultz	Halle
Bengalee	1808--14	—	—	—	Rev. H. Martyn	Calcutta
	1801	—	1801-05	—	Baptist Missionaries	Serampore
Orissa	1807	—	1809-14	—	Baptist Missionaries	Serampore
Canarese	1820	—	—	—	Rev. W. Hands	
Tamul	1715	—	1723-28	—	Danish Miss. Ziegenbalg, and Schultz	Tranquebar
Telinga or Telogoo	—	Gosp. of Mark, 1812	—	—	M. Des Granges	Vizagapatam
Cingalese	1771-80	—	—	Gen. Ex. and Levit. 1771-83	Fybrantz and Phillipz	Colombo
	1820	—	—	—	Mr. W. Tolfrey and others	Colombo
Malay	1668	—	1731-33	·	Various Persons	Amsterdam & Batavia

Table II.—*continued.*

Language.	New Testament, or detached Books thereof.		Bible, or Old Testament, or detached Books thereof.		Author.	Place of Printing.
	New Test.	Detached Books.	Bible, or Old Tes.	Detached Books.		
3 Chinese	1809-14	—	1815-21	—	Rev. Dr. Marshman	Serampore
	1811-13-18	—	1815-20		Rev. Dr. Morrison & Rev. Mr. Milne	Canton
4. Other Asiatic Versions						
Formosan	—	Matt. and John 1661	—		Robert Junius	Amsterdam
Tartar	1813	—	—	Psal. 1815	Edin. Soc. Mission	Karass & Astrachan
Orenburg Tartar	1820	—	—	—	Ditto	Astrachan
Calmuc Tartar	1815-20	—	—	—	Morav. Mission	Petersburgh
Montgolian Tartar	—	Matt. and Luke 1815	—	—	Two Mongolian Chieftains	Petersburgh
Georgian	—	—	1743	—	Unknown	Moscow
Otaheitean or Tahitan	1818-25	—	—	—	Missionaries of the Lond. Soc.	Eimeo and Tahiti

Table III.

VERSIONS IN THE LANGUAGES OF MODERN AFRICA AND AMERICA

Language.	New Testament, or detached Books thereof.		Bible, or Old Testament, or detached Books thereof.		Author.	Place of Printing
	New Test.	Detached Books.	Bible, or Old Tes.	Detached Books.		
African.						
Bullom.	—	Gosp. of Matt. 1816	—	—	Rev. G. Nylander	London
Amharic, a dialect of Abyssinia	1822	—	—	—	M. Asselin de Cherville	London
American Indian.						
Virginian	1661	—	1663	—	Rev. John Eliot	Cambridge New Eng.
Delaware	—	3 Epist. of John 1818	—	—	C. F. Denke	New-York
Indian-Massachusett	—	Gosp. of John 1709	—	Psal. 1709	Experience Mayhew	Boston, New England
Mohawk	—	Matt. Mark, & John 1787, 1804	—	—	Rev. Mr. Freeman Capt. Brant Capt. Norton	London
Esquimaux	1809-13-19	—	—	—	Moravian Mission	
Greenlandish	1799	—	—	—	Ditto	
West Indian.						
Creolese	1781	—	—	—	Unknown	Copenhagen

Of the numerous versions noticed in the preceding tables, those are most interesting to the reader, which have been executed in our vernacular tongue : a few particulars, therefore, respecting the different translations into the English language, which have been made at different times, will appropriately conclude this section.

The earliest English translation, known to be extant, was made by an unknown individual, and is placed by Archbishop Usher to the year 1290. Of this there are three manuscript copies preserved in the Bodleian Library, and in the Libraries of Christ's Church and Queen's Colleges, Oxford. Towards the close of the following century, John de Trevisa, vicar of Berkeley, in Gloucestershire, is said to have translated the Old and New Testaments into the English tongue, at the request of his patron, Lord Berkeley : but as no part of this work appears ever to have been printed, the translation ascribed to him is supposed to have been confined to a few texts, which were painted on the walls of his patron's chapel, at Berkeley Castle, or which are scattered in some parts of his writings ; several copies of which are known to exist in manuscript. Nearly contemporary with him, was the celebrated John Wickliffe, who, about the year 1380, translated the entire Bible from the Latin Vulgate : the New Testament of Wickliffe was published in folio by Mr. Lewis in 1731 ; and was handsomely re-edited in quarto, in 1810, by the Rev. Henry Hervey Baber, one of the librarians of the British Museum, who prefixed a valuable memoir of this "Apostle of England," as Wickliffe has sometimes been called.

The first *printed* edition of any part of the Scriptures in English was of the New Testament, at Hamburgh, in the year 1526. It was translated by William Tindal, or Tyndale, with the assistance of John Fry and William Roye : the whole of this impression (with the exception, it is said, of a single copy,) being bought up and burnt by Tonstal, Bishop of London, and Sir Thomas More, Tindal put forth a new edition in 1527, and a third in 1528 ; and, two years after, his translation of the Pentateuch appeared at Hamburgh, with another edition of his Testament. In 1535 was published the translation of Miles Coverdale, great part of which was Tindal's ; and two years after, John Rogers, martyr, (who had assisted Tindal in his biblical labours,) edited a Bible, probably at Hamburgh, under the assumed name of Thomas Matthews, whence it is generally known by the name of Matthews's Bible. A revised edition of this translation, corrected by Cranmer and Coverdale, was printed at London, in 1539, by Grafton and Whitchurch, in large folio, and from its size is usually denominated the GREAT BIBLE. No new version was executed during the reign of Edward VI.; though several editions were printed both of the Old and New Testaments.

During the sanguinary reign of Queen Mary, Miles Coverdale, John Knox, Christopher Goodman, and other English exiles, who had taken refuge at Geneva, published a new translation, between the years 1557 and 1560, with short annotations, inculcating the doctrines espoused by Calvin. The New Testament of this edition was the first in English, which was divided into verses. The Geneva Bible was highly esteemed by the Puritans; and, in the course of little more than thirty years afterwards, not fewer than thirty editions of it were printed in various sizes, principally by the royal printers. This translation is allowed to possess considerable merit, for its general fidelity and perspicuity. Eight years after the completion of the Geneva Bible, a new version was published, with two prefaces, by Archbishop Parker, now generally termed the *Bishops' Bible*, from the circumstance of eight of the translators being bishops: although this translation was read in the churches, the Geneva Bible was generally preferred in families.

In 1582, the Roman Catholics published in 4to. an English translation of the New Testament at Rheims, and of the Old Testament at Douay, in 1609–10, in 2 volumes 4to. It was crowded with barbarous and foreign terms, calculated to perplex rather than to diffuse the light of truth.

The last English version, which remains to be noticed, is the translation now in use, which is commonly called King James's Bible. Shortly after his accession to the throne in 1603, several objections being made to the English Bible, the King, at the Conference held at Hampton Court in the following year, commanded that a new version should be undertaken, and fifty-four men, of distinguished learning and piety, were appointed to this important labour: but, before it was begun, seven of the persons were either dead, or had declined the task. Such of them as survived till the commencement of the work, being ranged under six divisions, entered upon their labour in 1607, and completed it in 1610; it was then revised by a committee of six of the translators, and finally reviewed by Bishop Bilson and Doctor Smith; the latter prefixed the arguments, and wrote the preface. This translation, generally known by the name of King James's Bible, was first printed in 1611, and is that now universally adopted wherever the English language is spoken. The edition, generally reputed to be the most correct, is that of Oxford, in quarto and folio, 1769, printed under the superintendence of the late Rev. Dr. Blayney: the text was carefully collated with several correct editions, and the punctuation amended; the summaries of chapters and running titles at the top of each page were also corrected, and 30,495 new references were inserted in the margin. From the singular pains bestowed, in order to render this edition as accurate as possible, it has hitherto been considered *the standard edition*, from which all subsequent impressions have been executed. Notwithstanding, however, the great labour and attention bestowed by Dr. Blayney, his edition must now yield the palm of accuracy to the very beautiful and correct editions published by Messrs. Eyre and Strahan, His Majesty's Printers, but printed by Mr. Woodfall in 1806, and again in 1813 in quarto; as not fewer than one hundred and sixteen errors were discovered in collating the edition of 1806 with Dr. B.'s, and one of these errors was an omission of considerable importance. Messrs. Eyre and Strahan's editions may therefore be regarded as approaching as near as possible to what bibliographers term an *immaculate text.*

Of all modern versions, the present authorised English translation is, upon the whole, undoubtedly the most accurate and faithful; the translators having seized the very spirit of the sacred writers, and having almost every where expressed their meaning with a pathos and energy that have never been rivalled by any subsequent versions either of the Old or the New Testament. "Its style is incomparably superior to any thing which might be expected from the finical and perverted taste of our own age. It is simple; it is harmonious; it is energetic; and, which is of no small importance, use has made it familiar and time has rendered it sacred."*

CHAPTER VI.

OF THE VARIOUS READINGS OCCURRING IN THE OLD AND NEW TESTAMENTS.

I. Origin and Nature of Various Readings.

The Old and New Testaments, in common with all other ancient writings, being preserved and diffused by transcription, the admission of mistakes was unavoidable: which, increasing with the multitude of copies, necessarily produced a great variety of different readings.

Among two or more different readings, one only can be the true reading; the rest must either be wilful corruptions, or the mistakes of the copyist. As it is often difficult to distinguish the genuine from the spurious, whenever the smallest doubts can be entertained, they all receive the appellation of *Various Readings:* but, where a transcriber has evidently written falsely, they receive the name of errata.

II. Sources of Various Readings.

As all manuscripts were either dictated to copyists, or transcribed by them: and, as all these persons were not supernaturally guarded against the possibility of error, different readings would naturally be produced, 1. By the negligence or mistakes of the transcribers; to which we may add, 2. The existence of errors or imperfections in the manuscript copied; 3. Critical emendations of the text made by the copyist without any authority; and 4. Wilful corruptions made to serve the purposes of a party. Mistakes thus produced in one copy, would of course be propagated through all succeeding copies made from it, each of which might have peculiar faults of its own; so that various readings would thus be increased, in proportion to the number of transcripts made.

* Bishop Middleton on the Greek article, p. 328.

III. The means by which the *true* reading is to be determined are, 1. Manuscripts; 2. The most ancient, and best Editions; 3. Ancient Versions; 4. Parallel Passages, (which, being an important help to interpretation, are noticed again in a subsequent page;) 5. Quotations made from the Scriptures in the Writings of the early Fathers of the Christian Church; and 6. Conjectural Criticisms. All these sources are to be used with great judgment and caution; and the common reading ought not to be rejected but upon the strongest evidence.

IV. Infidels have endeavoured to shake the faith of less informed Christians, by raising objections against the number of various readings. The unlettered Christian, however, need not be under any apprehension that they will diminish the certainty of his faith. Of all the many thousand various readings that have been discovered, none have been found that affect our faith, or destroy a single moral precept of the Gospel. They are mostly of a minute and trifling nature: and by far the greatest number make no alteration *whatever in the sense.* Such are Δαβιδ (D**a**B**id**) for Δαυιδ (*David*;) Σολομωντα (*Solomon*ΤA) for Σολομωνα (*Solomon*A) Solomon; καγω (*kagō*) for και εγω (*kai egō*) (&c for *and I*;) Ναζαρετ (*Nazare*T) for Ναζαρεθ (*Nazare*TH) Nazareth; which, with many others, may be used indifferently.

CHAPTER VII

ON THE QUOTATIONS FROM THE OLD TESTAMENT IN THE NEW.

A CONSIDERABLE difference of opinion exists among some learned men, whether the evangelists and other writers of the New Testament quoted the Old Testament from the Hebrew, or from the venerable Greek versions usually called the Septuagint. From an actual collation of the passages thus cited, (which is given at length in Hebrew, Greek, and English, in the author's larger work,) it appears, that, though the sacred writers of the New Testament have in many instances quoted from the Hebrew Scriptures; yet they have very frequently made their citations from the Septuagint, because it was generally known and read: and as the apostles wrote for the use of communities, whose members were ignorant of Hebrew, it was necessary on that account that they should refer to the Greek version. But where this materially varied from the meaning of the Hebrew Scriptures, they either gave the sense of the passage cited, in their own words, or took as much of the Septuagint as was necessary, introducing the requisite alterations.

Difficulty sometimes arises, with respect to the *application* of the quotations made by the apostles and evangelists; when they are applied to a purpose to which they seem to have no relation, according to their original design. This difficulty is occasioned by the writers of the New Testament making quotations from the Old, with very different views. It is, therefore, necessary to distinguish accurately between such quotations as, being merely borrowed, are used in the words of the writer himself, and such as are quoted in proof of a doctrine, or the completion of a prophecy

The quotations from the Old Testament in the New are generally introduced by certain formulæ, such as, *That it might be fulfilled — As it is written* — &c., and various rules have been framed in order to account for their application. They may, however, be referred to the four following classes, viz.:

I. Quotations from the Old Testament in the New, in which the things predicted are *literally* accomplished.

Direct Prophecies are those which relate exclusively to Christ and the Gospel, and cannot legitimately be taken in any other sense; and the Scripture is said to be *fulfilled* in the *literal* sense, when that event which it foretells is accomplished. The following table exhibits the principal quotations which belong to this class:

Gen. xii. 3. xviii. 18. xxii. 18. quoted in	Acts iii. 25. Gal. iii. 8.
Gen. xvii. 7. 19. xxii. 16, 17	Luke i. 55. 72, 73, 74.
Deut. xviii. 15. 19.	Acts iii. 22, 23.
Psalm ii. 1, 2.	Acts iv. 25, 26.
Psalm ii. 7.	Acts xii. 33. Heb. i. 5. v. 4.
Psalm viii. 2.	Matt. xxi. 16.
Psalm viii. 4.	Heb. ii. 6—8.
Psalm xvi. 8—11.	Acts ii. 25—28. 31.
Psalm xvi. 10.	Acts xiii. 35.
Psalm xxii. 1.	Matt. xxvii. 46. Mark xv. 34.
Psalm xxii. 18.	Matt. xxvii. 35. Mark xv. 34. Luke xxiii. 34. John xix. 24.
Psalm xxii. 22.	Heb. ii. 12.

Psalm xxxi. 5.	quoted in Luke xxiii. 46.
Psalm xli. 9.	John xiii. 18. Acts i. 16.
Psalm xlv. 6, 7.	Heb. i. 8, 9.
Psalm lxviii. 18.	Eph. iv. 7, 8.
Psalm lxix. 21.	John xix. 28, 29. Matt. xxvii. 48. Mark xv. 36. and Luke xxiii. 36.
Psalm lxix. 25, cix. 8.	Acts i. 20.
Psalm xcv. 7—11.	Heb. iii. 7—11, iv. 3. 5—7.
Psalm cii. 25—27.	Heb. i. 10—12.
Psalm cx. 1.	Matt. xxii. 44. Mark xii. 36. Luke xx. 42. Acts ii. 34 35. Heb. i. 13.
Psalm cx. 4.	Heb. v. 6.
Psalm cxviii. 22, 23.	Matt. xxi. 42. Mark xii. 10. Luke xx. 17. Acts iv. 11.
Psalm cxviii. 25, 26.	Matt. xxi. 9. Mark xi. 9. John xii. 13.
Psalm cxxxii. 11. 17.	Luke i. 69. Acts ii. 30.
Isa. vii. 14.	Matt. i. 23.
Isa. ix. 1, 2.	Matt. iv. 15, 16.
Isa. ix. 7. (with Dan. vii. 14. 27.)	Luke i. 32, 33.
Isa. xi. 10.	Rom. xv. 12.
Isa. xxv. 8.	1 Cor. xv. 54.
Isa. xxvii. 9, and lix. 20, 21.	Rom. xi. 26, 27.
Isa. xxviii. 16. (with Joel ii. 32.)	Rom. ix. 33. and 1 Pet. ii. 6.
Isa. xl. 3—5.	Matt. iii. 3. Mark i. 3. Luke iii. 4—6.
Isa. xliii. 1—4.	Matt. xii. 17—21.
Isa. xlix. 6.	Acts xiii. 47, and xxvi. 23. Luke ii. 32.
Isa. liii. 1.	John xii. 38. Rom. x. 16.
Isa. liii. 3—6.	Acts xxvi. 22, 23.
Isa. liii. 4—6. 11.	1 Pet. ii. 24, 25.
Isa. liii. 4.	Matt. viii. 17.
Isa. liii. 9.	1 Pet. ii. 22.
Isa. liii. 12.	Mark xv. 28. Luke xxii. 37.
Isa. liv. 13.	John vi. 45.
Isa. lv. 3.	Acts xiii. 34.
Jer. xxxi. 31—34.	Heb. viii. 8—12. x. 16, 17.
Hosea i. 10.	Rom. ix. 26.
Hosea ii. 23.	Rom. ix. 25. Pet. ii. 10.
Joel ii. 28—32. (in the Hebrew, iii. 1—4.)	Acts ii. 16—21.
Amos ix. 11, 12.	Acts xv. 16, 17.
Micah v. 2.	Matt. ii. 5, 6. John vii. 42.
Habak. i. 5.	Acts xiii. 40.
Haggai ii. 6.	Heb. xii. 26.
Zech. ix. 9.	Matt. xxi. 4, 5. John xii. 14. 16.
Zech. xi. 13.	Matt. xxvii. 9, 10.
Zech. xii. 10.	John xix. 37.
Zech. xiii. 7.	Matt. xxvi. 31. 56. Mark xiv. 27. 50.
Mal. iii. 1.	Matt. xi. 10. Mark i. 2. Luke vii. 27.
Mal. iv. 5, 6.	Matt. xi. 13, 14. xvii. 10—13. Mark ix. 11—13. Luke i. 16, 17.

II. Quotations from the Old Testament in the New, in which that is said to have been done, of which the Scriptures have not spoken in a literal, but in a *spiritual* sense.

There are citations out of the Old Testament in the New, in a mediate and typical, or spiritual sense, respecting Christ and his mystical body, the Church. The Scripture is therefore said to be fulfilled, when that is accomplished in the antitype which is written concerning the type. Thus, in John, xix. 36, we read, These things were done that the *Scripture should be fulfilled*, — "a bone of him shall not be broken." These words, which were originally written of the paschal lamb, (Exod. xii. 46. Numb. ix. 12.) are said to be fulfilled in Christ, who is the antitype of that lamb. Additional examples of the same kind will be found in the annexed passages

Gen. xiv. 18, 20. cited and applied in Heb. vii. 1—10.
Gen. xv. 5. - - - - - - Rom. iv. 18.
Gen. xvi. 15. - - - - - - Gal. iv. 22.
Gen. xvii. 4. - - - - - - Rom. iv. 17.
Gen. xviii. 10. - - - - - Rom. ix. 9.
Gen. xxi. 1—3. - - - - - Gal. iv. 22, &c.
Gen. xxi. 12. - - - - - - Rom. ix. 7.
Gen. xxv. 23. - - - - - - Rom. ix. 10.
Exod. xii. 46. Numb. ix. 12. - John xix, 36.
Exod. xvi. 13—15. - - - - John vi. 31. 49. 1 Cor. x. 3.
Exod. xvii. 6. Numb. xx. 11. - 1 Cor. x. 4.
Exod. xix. 6. - - - - - - 1 Pet. ii. 9.
Exod. xxiv. 8. - - - - - Heb. ix. 20.
Levit. xxvi. 11, 12. - - - 2 Cor. vi. 16.
Numb. xxi. 8, 9. - - - - John iii. 14.
Deut. xxi. 23. - - - - - Gal. iii. 13.
Deut. xxxii. 21. - - - - - Rom. x. 19.
2 Sam. vii. 14. - - - - - Heb. i. 5.
Psalm ii. 9. - - - - - - Rev. ii. 27.
Psalm viii. 4. - - - - - - Heb. ii. 6—8.
Psalm viii. 6. - - - - - - 1 Cor. xv. 27.
Psalm xviii. 49. - - - - - Rom. xv. 9.
Psalm xxxv. 19. lxix. 4. and cix. 3. John xv. 25.
Psalm xl. 6—8. - - - - - Heb. x. 6, 7.
Psalm lxix. 9. - - - - - John ii. 17.
Psalm civ. 4. - - - - - Heb. i. 7.
Isa. xl. 6, 7. - - - - - - 1 Pet. i. 24, 25.
Isa. lii. 7. and Nahum i. 15. - Rom. x. 15.
Isa. liv. 1. - - - - - - Gal. iv. 27.
Isa. lxiv. 4. - - - - - - 1 Cor. ii. 9.
Hosea, xi. 1. - - - - - - Matt. ii. 15.
Jonah i. 17. ii. 1. and iii. 5. Mat. xii. 40, 41. Luke xi. 30. 32.
Habak. ii. 3. - - - - - - Heb. x. 37.
Habak. ii. 4. - - - - - - Rom. i. 17. Gal. iii. 11. Heb. x. 38.

III. Quotations from the Old Testament in the New, in which a thing is done neither in a literal nor in a spiritual sense, according to the fact referred to in the Scriptures, but is *similar* to that fact; in other words, where the passages referred to, are cited in the way of illustration.

Numerous passages of the Old Testament are cited and applied by the writers of the New Testament to an occurrence, which happened in their time, merely on account of correspondence and similitude. These citations are not prophecies, though they are said sometimes to be fulfilled. This method of explaining Scripture by the way of illustration, will enable us to solve many difficulties relating to the prophecies. Similar instances, are to be found in some classic authors.

The following table presents a list of the passages, thus quoted from the Old Testament, by the writers of the New, in the way of illustration:

Old Testament	New Testament
Gen. xv. 5.	cited in Rom. iv. 18.
Gen. xv. 6.	Rom. iv. 3. Gal. iii. 6. and James ii. 23.
Gen. xviii. 10.	Rom. ix. 9.
Gen. xix. 15. 26.	Luke xvii. 28, 29. 32.
Gen. xxi. 12.	Rom. ix. 7.
Gen. xxv. 23.	Rom. v. 12.
Gen. xxv. 33.	Heb. xii. 16.
Gen. xxvii. 28, &c.	Heb. xi. 20. xii. 17.
Exod. ix. 16.	Rom. ix. 7.
Exod. xxxii. 6.	1 Cor. x. 7.
Exod. xxxiii. 19.	Rom. ix. 15.
Lev. xi. 45.	1 Pet. i. 16.
Lev. xviii. 5.	Rom. x. 5. Gal. iii. 12.
Deut. vi. 13.	Matt. iv. 10. Luke iv. 8.
Deut. vi. 16.	Matt. iv. 7. Luke iv. 12.
Deut. viii. 3.	Matt. iv. 4. Luke iv. 4.
Deut. xxv. 4.	1 Cor. ix. 9. 1 Tim. v. 18.
Deut. xxvii. 26.	Gal. iii. 10.
Deut. xxxii. 35.	Rom. xii. 19. Heb. x. 30.
Deut. xxxii. 36.	Heb. x. 30.
Deut. xxxii. 43.	Rom. xv. 10.
Josh. i. 5.	Heb. xiii. 5.
1 Sam. xxi. 6.	Matt, xii. 3, 4. Mark ii. 25, 26 Luke vi. 3, 4.
1 Kings xix. 14, 18.	Rom. xi. 3, 4.
Psalm v. 10. and cxl. 4.	Rom. iii. 13.
Psalm x. 7.	Rom. iii. 14.
Psalm xiv. 1—3. and liii. 1—3.	Rom. iii. 10—12.
Psalm xix. 4.	Rom, x. 18.
Psalm xxiv. 1.	1 Cor. x. 26.
Psalm xxviii. 16.	Rom. x. 11.
Psalm xxxii. 1, 2.	Rom. iv. 7, 8.
Psalm xxxiv. 12—16.	1 Pet. iii. 10—12.
Psalm xxxvi. 1.	Rom. iii. 18.
Psalm xliv. 22.	Rom. viii. 36.
Psalm li. 4.	Rom. iii. 4.
Psalm lxix. 9.	Rom. xv. 3.
Psalm lxix. 22, 23.	Rom. xi. 9, 10.
Psalm lxxviii. 2.	Matt. xiii. 35.
Psalm lxxxii. 6.	John x. 34.
Psalm cxii. 9.	2 Cor. ix. 9.
Psalm cxvi. 10.	2 Cor. iv. 13
Psalm cxvii. 1.	Rom. xv. 11.
Psalm cxviii. 6.	Heb. xiii. 6.
Prov. i. 16. Isa. lix. 78.	Rom. iii. 15—17.
Prov. iii. 11, 12.	Heb. xii. 5, 6.
Prov. iii. 34.	James iv. 6.

Prov. x. 12. - - - cited in	1 Pet. iv. 8.
Prov. xxv. 21, 22.	Rom. xii. 20.
Prov. xxvi. 11.	1 Pet. ii. 22.
Isa. i. 9.	Rom. ix. 29.
Isa. vi. 9, 10.	John xii. 40. Matt. xiii. 14, 15 Luke viii. 10. Rom. xi. 8
Isa. viii. 12, 13.	1 Pet. iii. 14, 15.
Isa. viii. 17, 18.	Heb. ii. 13.
Isa. x. 22, 23	Rom. ix. 27, 28.
Isa. xxix. 10.	Rom. xi, 8.
Isa. xxix. 13.	Matt. xv. 8, 9. Mark vii. 6.
Isa. xxix. 14.	1 Cor. i. 9.
Isa. xxix. 16, and xlv. 9.	Rom. ix. 20, 21.
Isa. xlv. 23.	Rom. xiv. 11. Phil. ii. 10.
Isa. lii. 5. with Ezek. xxxvi. 20.	Rom. ii. 24,
Isa. lii. 7. and Nahum i. 15.	Rom. x. 15.
Isa. lii. 11, 12.	2 Cor. vi. 17.
Isa. lii. 15.	Rom. xv. 21.
Isa. lvi. 7. and Jer. vii. 11.	Matt. xxi. 13. Mark xi. 17. Luke xix. 46.
Isa. lxi. 1, 2,	Luke iv. 18, 19.
Isa. lxv. 1, 2.	Rom. x. 20, 21.
Isa. lxvi. 1, 2.	Acts vii. 49, 50.
Jer. xxxi. 15.	Matt. ii. 17, 18.
Jer. xxxi. 33. and xxxii. 38. with 2 Sam. vii. 14.)	2 Cor. vi. 18.
Hab. ii. 4.	Rom. i. 17.
Joel ii. 32.	Rom. x. 13.
Mal. i. 2, 3.	Rom. ix. 13.

IV. Quotations and other passages from the Old Testament which are *alluded to* in the New.

The following table presents a list of the *principal* passages of this description:

Gen. i. 6. 9, - alluded to in	2 Pet. iii. 5.
Gen. i. 27.	Matt. xix. 4. Mark x. 6. 1 Cor. xi. 7. James iii. 9.
Gen. ii. 2, 3.	Heb. iv. 4.
Gen. ii. 7.	1 Cor. xv. 45.
Gen. ii. 21, 22.	1 Cor. xi. 8. 1 Tim. ii. 13.
Gen. ii. 24.	Matt. xix. 5. Mark x. 7. 1 Cor. vi. 16. Eph. v. 31.
Gen. iii. 6.	1 Tim. ii. 14.
Gen. iii. 4, 13.	2 Cor. xi. 3.
Gen. iii. 16.	1 Cor. xiv. 34.
Gen. iv. 4.	Heb. xi. 4.
Gen. iv. 8.	Matt. xxiii. 35. Luke xi. 51. 1 John iii. 12. Jude verse 11.
Gen. v. 24.	Heb. xi. 5.
Gen. vi. vii.	Matt. xxiv. 37, 38. Luke xvii. 26, 27. Heb. xi. 7. 1 Pet. iii. 19, 20. 2 Pet. ii. 5. iii. 6.
Gen. xii. 1—4.	Acts vii. 5. Heb. xi. 8.
Gen. xiii. 15.	Rom. iv. 13.
Gen. xv. 13, 14.	Acts vii. 6, 7.
Gen. xvii. 10.	Acts vii. 8.
Gen. xviii. 3. xix. 2	Heb. xiii. 2.
Gen. xviii. 10.	Heb. xi. 11.
Gen. xviii. 12.	1 Pet. iii. 6.
Gen. xix. 12.	2 Pet. ii. 6. Jude verse 7.

Gen. xxi. 12.	alluded to in	Heb. xi. 18.
Gen. xlvi. 27.		Acts vii. 14
Gen. xlvii. 31.		Heb. xi. 21.
Gen. l. 24.		Heb. xi. 22.
Exod. ii. 2. 11.		Heb. xi. 23—27. Acts vii. 20—29.
Exod. iii. 6.		Mark xii. 26. Acts vii. 31, 32. Heb. xi. 16.
Exod. xii. 12. 18.		Heb. xi. 28.
Exod. xiv. 22.		1 Cor. x. 2. Heb. xi. 29.
Exod. xix. 12. 18, 19.		Heb. xii. 18—20.
Exod. xx. 12—16. Deut. v. 16—20.		Matt. xix. 18, 19. Mark x. 19. Luke xviii. 20. Rom. xiii. 0. James ii. 2.
Lev. xiii. 2. Numb. viii. 16, 17. xviii. 15. 17.		Luke ii. 23.
Lev. xiv. 3, 4. 10.		Matt. viii. 4. Mark i. 44. Luke v. 14.
Lev. xix. 12.		Matt. v. 33.
Lev. xix. 18.		Matt. v. 43. Gal. v. 14.
Numb. xi. 4.		1 Cor. x. 6.
Numb. xiv. 23. 29. 37. & xxvi. 64, 65.		Heb. iii. 16, 17. Jude verse 5.
Numb. xxi. 4—6.		1 Cor. x. 9.
Numb. xxii. 23. 39.		2 Pet. ii. 15, 16. Jude verse 11.
Deut. xviii. 1.		1 Cor. ix. 13.
Deut. xxiv. 1.		Matt. v. 31. Mark x. 4. Luke xvi. 28.
Josh. ii. 1. vi. 22, 23.		Heb. xi. 31. James ii. 25.
Josh. vi. 20.		Heb. xi. 30.
Judges, the whole book generally,		Acts xiii. 20. Heb. xi. 32.
1 Sam. viii. 5. and x. 1.		Acts xiii. 21.
1 Sam. xiii. 14. xv. 23. xvi. 12, 13.		Acts xiii. 22.
1 Kings xvii. 1. and xviii. 42—45		James v. 17, 18.
1 Chron. xxiii. 13.		Heb. v. 4.
Psalm xc. 4.		2 Pet. iii. 8.
Prov. xxvii. 1.		James iv. 13, 14.
Isa. xii. 3.		John vii. 38.
Isa. lxvi. 24.		Mark ix. 44.
Jer. vi. 16.		Matt. xi. 29.
Lam. iii. 45.		1 Cor. iv. 13.
Dan. iii. 23—25		Heb. xi. 34.
Dan. ix. 27. xii. 11.		Matt. xxiv. 15. Mark xiii. 14.
Hos. xiii. 14.		1 Cor. xv. 55.
Hos. xiv. 2.		Heb. xiii. 15.
Amos v. 26, 27.		Acts vii. 42, 43.

Concerning the class of quotations contained in the preceding table, it has been remarked, that when the inspired writers quote a passage from the Old Testament, *merely in the way of allusion*, it is enough that the words which they borrow, emphatically express their own meaning. It is not necessary that they be precisely the same with those of the passage alluded to, nor that they be there used, either of the same subject, or of a similar subject. Thus, Deut. xxx. 12—14, which was originally written concerning the law, is by Saint Paul accommodated to the Gospel, (Rom. x. 6—8,) with proper variations and explanations.

CHAPTER VIII.

ON THE POETRY OF THE HEBREWS.

I. NATURE of Hebrew Poetry.

The diversity of style, evident in the different books of Scripture, sufficiently evinces which of them were written in prose, and which are poetical compositions; though the nature of the Hebrew verse cannot now be exactly ascertained. The grand characteristic of Hebrew Poetry, is what Bishop Lowth terms ***Parallelism;*** that is, a certain equality, resemblance, or relationship, between the members of each period: so that, in two lines or members of the same period, things shall answer to things, and words to words, as if fitted to each other by a kind of rule, or measure. Such is the general strain of Hebrew Poetry, instances of which occur in almost every part of the Old Testament, particularly in the ninety-sixth psalm.

II. Gradations of the poetical parallelism.

The poetical parallelism has much variety and many gradations; which may be referred to four species, viz.: Parallel Lines Gradational, Parallel Lines Antithetic, Parallel Lines Synthetic, and Parallel Lines Introverted. An example or two of each of these shall be given, which will enable the attentive reader of our admirable authorised version readily to discover others as they arise: for, that version being strictly word for word after the original, the form and order of the original sentences are preserved; and this circumstance will account for its retaining so much of a poetical cast, notwithstanding it is executed in prose.

1. ***Parallel Lines Gradational*** are those in which the second or responsive clause so diversifies the preceding clauses, as generally to rise above it; sometimes by a descending scale, in the value of the related terms and periods, but in all cases with a marked distinction of meaning. This species of parallelism is of most frequent occurrence, particularly in the psalms and the prophecies of Isaiah. The following example is given from the evangelical prophet, ch. lv. 6, 7.:

Seek ye Jehovah [or, the LORD] while he may be found;
Call ye upon him while he is near;
Let the wicked forsake his way,
And the unrighteous man his thoughts:
And let him return unto Jehovah, and he will compassionate him;
And unto our God for he aboundeth in forgiveness.

"In the first line, men are invited to seek Jehovah, not knowing where he is, and on the bare intelligence that he *may be found;* in the second line, having found Jehovah, they are encouraged to call upon him by the assurance that he is NEAR. In the third line, the wicked, the positive and presumptuous sinner, is warned to forsake *his way*, his habitual course of iniquity; in the fourth line, the unrighteous, the negatively wicked, is called to renounce the *very thought of sinning*. While, in the last line, the appropriative and encouraging title, OUR GOD, is substituted for the awful name JEHOVAH, and simple compassion is heightened into overflowing *mercy and forgiveness*." (Bp. Jebb's Sacred Literature, pp. 37, 38.) See further instances in Isa. li. 1. 47. Joel ii. 7. Psalm i. 1. xxi. 1, 2. and xxiv. 3, 4.

2. *Parallel Lines Antithetic* are those in which two lines correspond one with another, by an opposition of terms and sentiments; when the *second* is contrasted with the *first*, sometimes in expressions, sometimes in sense only This is not confined to any particular form. Accordingly, the degrees of antithesis are various, from an exact contraposition of word to word, sentiment to sentiment, singulars to singulars, plurals to plurals, down to a general disparity, with something of a contrariety in the two propositions. Thus, Prov. ch. x. 1.

A *wise* son *rejoiceth* his father:
But a *foolish* son is the *grief* of his mother.

Here every word has its opposite, the terms "*father*" and "*mother*" being relatively opposite.

3. *Parallel Lines Constructive* are those in which the parallelism consists only in the similar form of construction; wherein word does not answer to word, and sentence to sentence, as equivalent, or opposite: but there is a correspondence and equality, between the different propositions in respect of the shape and turn of the whole sentence, and of the constructive parts; such as noun answering to noun, verb to verb, member to member, negative to negative, interrogative to interrogative. This form of parallelism admits of great variety, the parallelism being sometimes more, sometimes less exact, and sometimes hardly at all apparent. Psalm xix. 7—11, will furnish a beautiful instance of this description of poetical parallelism.

The law of JEHOVAH is perfect, restoring the soul;
The testimony of JEHOVAH is sure, making wise the simple
The precepts of JEHOVAH are right, rejoicing the heart:
The commandment of JEHOVAH is clear, enlightening the eyes:
The fear of JEHOVAH is pure, enduring for ever;
The judgments of JEHOVAH are truth, they are just altogether;
More desirable than gold, or than much fine gold,
And sweeter than honey or the dropping of honey combs.

4. *Parallel Lines Introverted*, or *Introverted Parallelisms*, are stanzas so constructed, that whatever be the number of lines, the *first* line shall be parallel with the *last;* the *second* with the penultimate, or *last but one;* and so throughout, in an order that looks inward, or, to borrow a military phrase, from flanks to centre. Dr. Jebb, Bishop of Limerick, has illustrated this definition with numerous apposite examples, from which the following has been selected.

"And it shall come to pass in that day;
Jehovah shall make a gathering of his fruit
From the flood of the river;
To the stream of Egypt:
And ye shall be gleaned up, one by one,
O ye sons of Israel.
"And it shall come to pass in that day;
The great trumpet shall be sounded
And those shall come, who were perishing in the land of Assyria;
And those who were dispersed in the land of Egypt·
And they shall bow themselves down before Jehovah
In the holy mountain, in Jerusalem. (Isa. xxvii. 12, 13.)

"In these two stanzas, *figuratively* in the *first*, and *literally* in the *second*, is predicted the return of the Jews from their several dispersions. The *first* line of each stanza is parallel with the *sixth;* the *second* with the *fifth;* and the *third* with the *fourth*. Also, on comparing the stanzas one with another, it is manifest, that they are constructed with the utmost precision of mutual correspondence; *clause* harmonizing with *clause*, and *line* respectively with *line;* the *first line* of the *first* stanza with the first line of the second, and so throughout." (Sacred Lit. pp. 54, 55.)

Until very recently, the poetical parallelism was supposed to be confined to the Books of the Old Testament: but Bishop Jebb has shown that this characteristic of Hebrew Poetry, also exists, to a considerable degree, in the New Testament.

III. DIFFERENT KINDS of Hebrew Poetry.

Bishop Lowth reduces the various productions of the Sacred Poets to the following classes.

1. *Prophetic Poetry*, or that peculiar *to the prophetic Books:* for, though some parts of them are evidently in prose, yet the remainder are clearly poetical.

2. *Elegiac Poetry*, of which many passages occur in

the prophetical Books, in the Book of Job, in the Psalms, and especially in the Lamentations of Jeremiah.

3. *Didactic Poetry*, or that which delivers moral precepts in elegant verses. To this class belongs the Book of Proverbs.

4. Of *Lyric Poetry*, or that which is designed to be accompanied with music, numerous instances occur in the Old Testament, especially in the Book of Psalms. See also Exod. xv. Deut. xxxii. and Habakkuk iii.

5. Of the *Idyl*, or short pastoral poem, the historical Psalms afford abundant instances. See particularly Psalms lxxviii. cv. cvi. cxxxvi. and cxxxix.

6. To *Dramatic Poetry*, Bishop Lowth refers the Book of Job, and the Song of Solomon: but this opinion has been questioned by later critics. Many of the Psalms however are a kind of dramatic ode, consisting of dia logues between persons sustaining certain characters.

7. *Acrostic*, or *Alphabetical Poems*, are those which consist of twenty-two lines, or twenty-two systems of lines, periods, or stanzas, according to the number of letters of the Hebrew alphabet; that is, the first line or first stanza begins with א *(aleph,)* the second with ב *(beth,)* and so on. Twelve of these poems are found in the Old Testament, viz. Psalms xxv. xxxiv. xxxvii. cxi. cxii. cxix. and cxlv. Prov. xxxi. 10—31. Lamentations of Jeremiah i. ii. iii. iv. Some of these poems are perfectly, and others more or less, alphabetical.

CHAPTER IX.

ON HARMONIES OF SCRIPTURE.

I. Occasion and Design of Harmonies.

The several Books of the Holy Scriptures, having been written at different times, and on different occasions, necessarily treat on a great variety of subjects, historical, doctrinal, moral, and prophetic. The sacred authors also, writing with different designs, have not always related the same events in the same order; some are introduced by anticipation; and others again are related first, which should have been placed last. Hence, seeming contradictions have arisen, which have been eagerly seized by the adversaries of Christianity, in order to perplex the minds and shake the faith of those who may not be able to detect their sophistries. These contradictions, however, are not *real:* for they disappear as soon as they are brought to the test of candid examination.

The manifest importance and advantage of comparing the sacred writers with each other, have induced many learned men to undertake the compilation of works, which, being designed to shew the perfect agreement of all parts of the sacred writings, are commonly termed *Harmonies.* Two classes of these principally claim to be noticed in this place, viz.: Harmonies of the Old, and Harmonies of the New Testament.

II. Harmonies of the OLD TESTAMENT.

The design of these is, to dispose the historical, poetical, and prophetical Books in Chronological Order, so that they may mutually explain and authenticate one another. Our learned countryman, Dr. Lightfoot, in the year 1647, published a "Chronicle," or Harmony of the Old Testament; on the basis of which the Rev. George Townsend constructed "The Old Testament arranged in Historical and Chronological Order;" but he has deviated from and improved upon the plan of Lightfoot very materially. His work is noticed in the Appendix.

III. Harmonies of the NEW TESTAMENT are of two sorts, viz.:

1. *Harmonies of the* ENTIRE *New Testament,* in which not only are the four Gospels chronologically disposed, but the Epistles are also placed in order of time, and interspersed in the Acts of the Apostles. Mr. Townsend's "New Testament arranged in Chronological and Historical Order" is the most complete work of this kind in the English language.

2. *Harmonies of the Gospels,* in which the narratives, or memoirs, of the four evangelists, are digested in their proper chronological order. These are very numerous, according to the plans which their several authors proposed to themselves. Among foreign authors, the Latin Harmony of Chemnitz (or Chemnitius) is the most esteemed: and among our British divines those of Drs. Doddridge and Macknight are most generally read, on account of their valuable expositions and commentaries.

BOOK II.—ON THE INTERPRETATION OF SCRIPTURE.

The Literary History of the Sacred volume having thus been considered, we now proceed to discuss its INTERPRETATION: and here the various subsidiary means for ascertaining the sense of the inspired writers, first demand attention. This is the subject of the first chapter of the present book: the remaining chapters will show in what manner the sense, when discovered, is to be communicated, expounded, and applied.

CHAPTER I.

ON THE LITERAL, GRAMMATICAL, OR HISTORICAL SENSE OF SCRIPTURE.

ALTHOUGH, in every language, there are very many words, which admit of several meanings, yet in common speech there is *only* ONE *true sense* attached to any word, which sense is indicated by the connexion and series of the discourse, by the design of the speaker or writer, or by some other circumstances, unless any ambiguity be purposely intended. The same usage obtains in the sacred writings.

The LITERAL SENSE of any place in Scripture is that which the words signify, or require in their natural and proper acceptation. Thus, in

Gen. i. 1. *God created the heavens and the earth*, the words mean what they literally import, and must be interpreted according to the letter. So, in John x. 30., the words, *I and the Father are one*, so distinctly and unequivocally assert the Deity of Christ, and his equality with God the Father, that it is difficult to conceive how any other than their proper and literal meaning could ever be given to them.

The literal sense has been termed the HISTORICAL SENSE, as conveying the meaning of the words and phrases used by a writer at a certain time.

Thus, in Gen. x. 5. Isa. xi. 11. and many other passages of Scripture, the word *isles* or *islands* signifies EVERY inhabited region, particularly all the Western Coasts of the Mediterranean Sea, and the seats of Japhet's posterity, viz.: the northern parts of Asia, Asia Minor, and Europe, together with some other regions.

SECTION I.—Rules for Investigating the Meaning of Words, generally.

Since words compose sentences, from which the meaning of Scripture is to be collected, it is necessary that the individual meaning of such words be ascertained, before we proceed further to investigate the sense of Holy Writ. As the same method and the same principles of interpretation are common both to the sacred volume and to the productions of uninspired man, the signification of words in the Holy Scriptures must be sought precisely in the same way in which the meaning of words in other works usually is, or ought to be sought. And since no text of Scripture has more than one meaning, we must endeavour to find out that *one true sense* precisely in the same manner as we would investigate the sense of any ancient writer; and in that sense, when so ascertained, we ought to acquiesce, unless, by applying the just rules of interpretation, it can be shown that the meaning of the passage has been mistaken, and that another is the only just, true, and critical sense of the place. The following general rules will be found useful for this purpose.

1. Ascertain the notion affixed to a word by the persons in general, by whom the language either is now or formerly was spoken, and especially in the particular connexion in which such notion is affixed.

The meaning of a word used by any writer, is the meaning affixed to it by those for whom he *immediately* wrote. For there is a kind of natural compact between those who write and those who speak a language; by which they are mutually bound to use words in a certain sense: he, therefore, who uses such words in a different signification, in a manner violates that compact, and is in danger of leading men into error, contrary to the design of God, "who will have all men to be saved, and to come unto the knowledge of the truth." (1 Tim. ii. 4.) The received signification of a word is to be retained, unless weighty and necessary reasons require that it should be abandoned or neglected.

We shall be justified in rejecting the received meaning of a word in the following cases, viz.:

(1.) If such meaning clash with any doctrine clearly revealed in the Scriptures.

(2.) If a certain passage *require* a different explanation from that which it appears to present: as Mal. iv. 5, 6, compared with Luke. i. 17, and Matt. xi. 14.

2. Where a word has several significations in common use, that must be selected which best suits the passage in question, and which is consistent with an author's known character, sentiments, and situation, and the known circumstances under which he wrote.

For instance, the word BLOOD, which on various accounts is very significant in the Sacred Writings, denotes—our *natural descent* from one common family, in Acts xvii. 26;—*death*, in Heb. xii. 4; *the sufferings and death of Christ*, considered as an atonement for the souls of sinners, in Rom. v. 9. and Eph. i. 7; and also as the procuring cause of our justification, in Rom. v. 9, and of our sanctification in Heb. ix. 14.

3. Although the force of particular words can only be derived from etymology, yet too much confidence must not be placed in that frequently uncertain science.

4. The distinctions between words, which are apparently synonymous, should be carefully examined and considered.

In the 119th Psalm there are *ten* different words, pointing out the word of God; viz.: Law, Way, Word, Statutes, Judgments, Commandments, Precepts, Testimonies, Righteousness, and Truth, or Faithfulness. Now all these words, though usually considered as synonymous, are not *literally* synonymous, but refer to some latent and distinguishing properties of the Divine Word, whose manifold excellencies and perfections are thus illustrated with much elegant variety of diction.

5. The epithets introduced by the sacred writers are also to be carefully weighed and considered, as all of them have either a declarative or explanatory force, or serve to distinguish one thing from another, or unite these two characters together.

6. General terms are used sometimes in their whole extent, and sometimes in a restricted sense, and whether they are to be understood in the one way, or in the other, must depend upon the scope, subject-matter, context, and parallel passages.

The word, *live*, in 1 Thess. iii. 8, it is evident, both from the subject matter and the context, *must* be taken in a restricted sense, and not as implying the apostle's natural life or existence.

SECTION II.—Aids for Investigating the Meaning of Words in combination.

§ 1.—Of the Scope, and Context.

1. The SCOPE defined.

A consideration of the *Scope*, or design which the inspired author of any of the books of Scripture had in view, essentially facilitates the study of the Bible: because, as every writer had some design in view, it is natural to conclude that he would express himself in terms adapted to his purpose. To be acquainted with the scope, therefore, is to understand the chief part of the book. The scope of an author is either *general*, or *special;* by the former, we understand the design which he proposed to himself in writing his book; by the latter, we mean that design which he had in view, when writing particular sections, or even smaller portions, of his book or treatise

II. Hints for ascertaining the Scope.

The means, by which to ascertain the scope of a ***particular*** section, or passage, being nearly the same with those which must be applied to the investigation of the *general* scope of a book, we shall briefly consider them together in the following observations.

1. When the scope of a whole book, or of any particular portion of it, is expressly mentioned by the sacred writer, it should be carefully observed.

The scope and end of the whole Bible collectively, is contained in its manifold utility, which St. Paul expressly states in 2 Tim. iii. 16, 17, and also in Rom. xv. 4. In like manner, the author of Ecclesiastes announces at the beginning of his book, the subject he intends to discuss, viz: to show that all human affairs are vain, uncertain, frail and imperfect; and such being the case, he proceeds to inquire, *What profit hath a man of all his labour which he taketh under the sun?* (Eccl. i. 2, 3.) And towards the close of the same book, (ch. xii. 8,) he repeats the same subject, the truth of which he had proved by experience. So, in the commencement of the book of Proverbs, Solomon distinctly announces their scope (ch. i. 1—4. 6.) St. John (xx. 31,) announces his object in writing his Gospel to be, that men *might believe that Jesus* IS THE CHRIST THE SON OF GOD, *and that believing,* they *might* have life through his name; therefore all those discourses of our Lord, which are recorded almost exclusively by this evangelist, are to be perused with reference to this particular design.

2. The scope of the sacred writer may be ascertained from the known occasion, upon which his book was written, and also from history.

We know from history that many persons disseminated errors and defended Judaism, during the time of the apostles; who therefore found it necessary to oppose and refute such errors. This was the occasion of Saint Peter's second Epistle: and the circumstance will enable us to ascertain the scope of many of the other apostolic letters.

3. The express conclusion, added by the writer at the end of an argument, demonstrates his general scope.

Thus in Rom. iii. 28, after a long discussion, St. Paul adds this conclusion:—*Therefore we conclude, that man is justified by faith without the deeds of the law:* Hence we perceive with what design the whole passage was written, and to which all the rest is to be referred. The conclusions interspersed through the epistles may easily be ascertained by means of the particles, "wherefore," "seeing that," "therefore," "then," &c. as well as by the circumstances directly mentioned or referred to.

II. CONTEXT defined.

Another most important assistance, for investigating the meaning of words and phrases, is the consideration of the *Context*, or the comparison of the preceding and subsequent parts of a discourse: as this alone, in many instances, can enable us to determine that signification which is best adapted to any word or passage.

(1.) The Hebrew word בשר (BE-SHER) literally signifies the *skin*, by a metonomy, the *flesh* beneath the skin; and by a synecdoche it denotes *every animal*, especially man, considered as infirm or weak; a. in Je.

xvii. 5—*Cursed be the man that trusteth in man, and maketh* FLESH *his arm;* but that the word *flesh* is to be understood of *man* only in Gen. vi. 12, will be evident on the slightest inspection of the context. *All flesh had corrupted his way*—that is all men had wholly departed from the rule of righteousness, or had made their way of life abominable throughout the world.

(2.) There is a difference of opinion whether the address of Job's wife (Job ii. 9,) is to be understood in a good sense, as, *Bless* (or ascribe glory to) *God and die;* or in a different signification, *Curse God and die*, as it is rendered in our authorized version. Circumstances show that the last is the proper meaning; because as yet Job had not sinned with his lips, and consequently his wife had no ground for charging him with indulging a vain opinion of his integrity.

1. The context of a discourse in the Scriptures, may comprise either one verse, a few verses, entire periods, or sections, entire chapters, or whole books. Thus,

(1.) If 1 Cor. x. 16, be the passage under examination, the preceding and subsequent parts of the epistle, which belong to it, are the eighth, ninth, and tenth chapters.

(2.) If Isa. li. be the chapter in question, the reader must not stop at the end of it, but continue his perusal to the 12th verse of ch. lii.; for these together form one subject or argument of prediction, in which the prophet is announcing to his countrymen the certainty of their deliverance and return from the Babylonish captivity. This entire portion ought therefore to be read at once, in order to apprehend fully the prophet's meaning.

(3.) In like manner, the verses from v. 13 of ch. lii. to the end of ch. liii. form a new and entire section relative to the sufferings of the Messiah. Here then is a wrong division of chapters, to which no regard should be paid in examining the context of a book. Ch. li. ought to include v. 12 of ch. lii. and ch. lii. ought to commence at v. 13, and be continued to the end of ch. liii.

(4.) In like manner, the first verse of the fourth chapter of St. Paul's Epistle to the Colossians ought to be joined to the third chapter: the slightest attention to this point will enable a diligent student to add numerous other examples.

III. Hints for examining the Context.

1. Investigate each word of every passage.

2. Next, examine the entire passage with minute attention. Sometimes a single passage will require a whole chapter, or several of the preceding and following chapters, or even the entire book, to be perused; and that not once, or twice, but several times.

For instance, that otherwise difficult passage, Rom. ix. 18—*Therefore hath he mercy on whom he will have mercy, and whom he will he hardeneth,* will become perfectly clear by a close examination of the context, beginning at verse 18, of chapter viii. and reading to the end of the eleventh chapter; this portion of the epistle being most intimately connected.

3. A verse, or passage must not be connected with a remote context, unless the latter agree better with it than a nearer context.

Thus Rom. ii. 16, although it makes a good sense if connected with the preceding verse, makes a much better when joined with verse 12, (the intermediate verses being read parenthetically as in the authorized version;) and this shows it to be the true and proper context.

9

4. Examine whether the writer continues his discourse, lest we suppose him to make a transition to another argument, when he in fact is prosecuting the same topic.

Rom. v. 12. will furnish an illustration of this remark. From tha verse to the end of the chapter St. Paul produces a strong argument tc prove, that as all men stood in need of the grace of God in Christ to redeem them from their sins, so this grace has been afforded equally to all, whether Jews or Gentiles. To perceive the full force, therefore, of the apostle's conclusion, we must read the *continuation* of his argument from verse 12. to the close of the chapter.

5. The Parentheses which occur in the sacred writings should be particularly regarded: but no parenthesis should be interposed without sufficient reason.

Parentheses, being contrary to the genius and structure of the Hebrew language, are, comparatively, of rare occurrence in the Old Testament. But in the New Testament, they are frequent, especially in the writings of St. Paul; who, after making numerous digressions, (all of them appropriate to, and illustrative of, his main subject,) returns to the topic which he had begun to discuss.

Thus, in Rom. ii., verses 13, 14, and 15 are obviously parenthetical; because the context evidently requires verses 12 and 16 to be read together. In Rom. v., verses 12, 18, 19 evidently form one continued sentence; and all the intermediate verses are undoubtedly to be read as a parenthesis, though they are not marked as such in the authorised translation. 1 Cor. viii. 1, beginning with the words, *Knowledge puffeth up*, &c. to the end of the first clause in verse 4, is in like manner parenthetical. The connexion, therefore, of the first with the fourth verse is this:—*Now, as touching things offered unto idols, we know that we have all knowledge.—We know that an idol is nothing*, &c. 1 Cor. x. 29, latter clause, and verse 30, are parenthetical; as also are 2 Cor. ix. 9, 10, which are so printed in our version. A still more signal instance of parenthesis occurs in Eph. iii. where the first and fourteenth verses are connected, the twelve intermediate verses, (2 to 13,) being parenthetical: as also is 1 Tim. i. verses 3 to 17, inclusive.

7. Where no connexion exists with the preceding and subsequent parts of a book, none should be sought.

This observation applies solely to the Proverbs of Solomon, and chiefly to the tenth and following chapters; which form the second part of that book, and are composed of sentences, or proverbs, totally distinct and unconnected, though each individual precept is pregnant with the most weighty instruction.

---

§ 2.—Analogy of Scripture, or Parallel Passages.

1. Nature and importance of PARALLEL PASSAGES.

Parallel Passages are those which bear some degree of resemblance in sentiment, language, or idiom: and the comparison of them is a most important help for interpreting such parts of Scripture as may appear to us obscure, or uncertain: for, on almost every subject, there will be found a multitude of phrases, that, when diligently collated, will afford mutual illustration and support to each other; the truth, which is more obscurely intimated in one place, being expressed with greater precision in others.

Parallelisms are either ***near***, or ***remote:*** in the former case, the parallel passages are sought from the same writer; in the latter, from different writers. They are further termed *adequate*, when they affect the whole subject proposed in the text: and ***inadequate***, when they affect it only in part: but the most usual division of the analogy of Scripture, or parallelisms, is into ***verbal***, or parallelisms of words; and ***real***, or parallelisms of things.

1. A *Verbal* ***Parallelism***, or ***Analogy***, is that in which, on comparing two or more places together, the same words and phrases, the same mode of argument, the same method of construction, and the same rhetorical figures, are respectively to be found.

2. A ***Real Parallelism***, or ***Analogy***, is where the same event, or thing is related, the same doctrine is taught, or the same subject is discussed. But besides these two species of parallelisms, there is,

3. A third, partaking of the nature of both, and which is of equal importance for understanding the Scriptures: This has been termed a ***Parallelism of Members:*** it consists chiefly in a certain equality resemblance, or parallelism, between the members of each period; so that in two lines, or members of the same period, things shall answer to things, and words to words, as if fitted to each other by a kind of rule, or measure.

The nature of this kind of parallelism, which is the grand characteristic of the poetical style of the Hebrews, has been already considered; and its critical uses have been illustrated. See pp. **108—110**, ***supra.***

A single example will suffice to show the importance of this help to the interpretation of the poetical parts of Scripture.

Psal. lxxxiv. **5—7.** is confessedly a difficult passage of Scripture, but by considering it as an ***introverted parallelism*** (the nature of which is defined in p. **110.**) Bishop Jebb has thrown much light upon those verses.

> "Blessed is the man whose strength is in Thee:
>   The passengers in whose heart are the ways,
>   In the valley of Baca make it a spring;
>   The rain also filleth the pools;
>   They go from strength to strength;
> He shall appear before God in Zion.

"The first and sixth lines are here considered, at once, as constructively parallel, and as affording a *continuous* sense: the intermediate four lines may be accounted parenthetical; the second, constructively parallel with the fifth; and the third with the fourth. The first line seems to contain the character of a confirmed proficient in religion,—*his strength is in God;* the sixth line, to describe his final beatification,—*he shall appear before God in Zion.* The intermediate quatrain may be regarded as descriptive of the intermediate course pursued by those who desire to be good and happy; they are passengers; but they know their destination, and they long for it; at a distance from the temple, they are anxious to arrive there; the very highways to Jerusalem are in their heart. And what is the consequence? Affection smooths all difficulties: the parched and sandy desert becomes a rich well-watered valley; and they cheerfully advance from strength to strength; from one degree of virtuous proficiency to another." (Sacred Literature, pp. 55, 56.)

II. Rules for COMPARING Parallel Passages.

1. Ascertain the primary meaning of the passage under consideration.

In 1 Cor. iv. 5, we read, *Judge nothing before the time, until the Lord come, who will both bring to light the hidden things of darkness, and will make manifest the counsels of the hearts.* Now here is a parallelism of members, but the fundamental meaning is, that *God judges the counsels of men;* he therefore judges without respect of persons, and with unerring impartiality. The Apostle's design was, to show that it is impossible for men to perceive and judge the counsels of one another.

2. Although the Sacred Scriptures, PRIMARILY coming from God, are perfectly consistent, and harmonize throughout; yet, as they were SECONDARILY written by different authors, on various topics, and in different styles, those books are in the first instance to be compared, which were composed by the same author, in the same language, and on a parallel subject.

By comparing Psal. xxxviii. 10, with 1 Sam. xiv. 26, 27, (in which Jonathan, having taken some honey for his refreshment, is said to have had *his eyes enlightened,*) we shall readily apprehend the force of the psalmist's complaint, that *the light of his eyes was gone from him;* for the eyes of a person in good health are so strong as to sparkle with the rays of light that fall upon them; whereas, when the constitution is worn by long sickness, or broken by grief, the eyes lose their vigour and brilliancy, and, in cases of incipient blindness, the light gradually fails the eyes.

3. Collect all those similar passages, in which the same forms of speech occur, and the same topics are proposed: and consider well, whether they are *really* parallel, that is, not only whether the same word, but also the same thing, answers together, in order to form a safe judgment concerning it.

It often happens that *one* word has several distinct meanings, one of which obtains in one place, and one in another place. When, therefore, words of such various meanings present themselves, all those passages where they occur are not to be immediately considered as parallel, unless they have a similar power. Thus, if any one were to compare Jonah iv 10, (where mention is made of the gourd which came up in a night, and perished in a night, and which, in the original Hebrew, is termed *the son of a night,*) with 1 Thess. v. 5, where Christians are called, not children of the night, but *children of the day,* it would be a spurious parallel.

4. Where two parallel passages present themselves, the clearer and more copious place must be selected to illustrate one that is more briefly and obscurely expressed.

5. No assistance is to be derived from similar passages, the sense of which is uncertain.

The method here indicated is the only *effectual* way by which to ascertain parallel words and phrases, as well as parallelisms of things: it will indeed require a considerable portion of time and study, which *every one* may not perhaps be able to give; but individuals thus circumstanced may advantageously facilitate their researches by having recourse to editions of the Bible with parallel references, and to concordances, the most useful of which are specified in the Appendix.

---

§ 3.— Of the Analogy of Faith.

I. Analogy of Faith defined.

The *Analogy of Faith* may be defined to be *the constant and perpetual harmony of Scripture in the fundamental points of faith and practice*, deduced from those passages, in which they are discussed by the inspired penmen, either directly, or expressly, and in clear, plain, and intelligible language. Or, more briefly, the analogy of faith may be defined to be that proportion, which the doctrines of the Gospel bear to each other, or the close connexion between the truths of revealed religion. It is one of the most important aids for ascertaining the sense of Scripture. The *Analogy of Faith* is an expression borrowed from Saint Paul's Epistle to the Romans, (xii. 6,) where he exhorts those who *prophesy* in the church (that is, those who exercise the office of authoritatively expounding the Scriptures,) to *prophesy according to the proportion*, or, as the word is in the original, *the Analogy of Faith.*

II. Hints for investigating the Analogy of Faith.

1. Whenever any doctrine is manifest, either from the whole tenor of divine revelation, or from its scope, it must not be weakened or set aside by a few obscure passages.

No truth is more certain in religion, or is more frequently asserted in the Bible than this, viz.: that God is good, not only to *some* individuals, but also towards ALL men. (See Psal. cxlv. 9. Ezek. xviii. 23. 32. John iii. 16. Tit. ii. 11, &c. &c.) If, therefore, any passages occur which at first sight *appear* to contradict the goodness of God, as, for instance, that He has created some persons that he might damn them, (as some have insinuated;) in such case the very clear and certain doctrine relative to the goodness of God is not to be impugned, much less set aside, by these obscure places, which, on the contrary, ought to be illustrated by such passages as are more clear. Thus Prov. xvi. 4, has, by several eminent writers, been sup posed to refer to the predestination of the elect, and the reprobation of the wicked, but without any foundation. The passage, however, *may* be more correctly rendered, *The Lord hath made all things to answer to themselves,* or aptly to refer to one another, *yea, even the wicked, for the evil day,* that is, to be the executioner of evil to others; on which account they are in Scripture termed the rod of Jehovah, (Isa. x. 5,) and his sword (Psal. xvii. 13.) But there is no necessity for rejecting the received version, the plain and obvious sense of which is that there is nothing in the world which does not contribute to the glory of God, and promote the accomplishment of his adorable designs.

2. No doctrine can belong to the analogy of faith, which is founded on a *single* text.

Every essential principle of religion is delivered in more than one place. Besides, single sentences are not to be detached from the places where they stand, but must be taken in connexion with the whole discourse.

From disregard of this rule, the *temporary* direction of the apostle James (v. 14, 15,) has been perverted by the church of Rome, and rendered a permanent institution, (by her miscalled a sacrament, for it was never instituted by Jesus Christ,) from a mean of recovery, to a charm, when recovery is desperate, for the salvation of the soul.

3. The WHOLE system of revelation must be explained, so as to be consistent with itself.—When two passages APPEAR to be contradictory, if the sense of the one can be clearly ascertained, in such case that must regulate our interpretation of the other.

4. An obscure, doubtful, ambiguous, or figurative text must never be interpreted in such a sense as to make it contradict a plain one.

In explaining the Scriptures, consistency of sense and principles ought to be supported in all their several parts; and if any one part be so interpreted as to clash with another, such interpretation cannot be justified. Nor can it be otherwise corrected than by considering every doubtful or difficult text, first by itself, then with its context, and then by comparing it with other passages of Scripture; and thus bringing what may seem obscure into a consistency with what is plain and evident.

The doctrine of transubstantiation, inculcated by the church of Rome, is founded on a strictly literal interpretation of figurative expressions, "This is my body," &c. (Matt. xxvi. 26, &c.) and (which has no relation to the supper,) "Eat my flesh, drink my blood," (John vi. 51—58.) But independently of this, we may further conclude that the sense put upon the words, "This is my body," by the church of Rome, cannot be the true one, being contrary to the express declaration of the New Testament history, from which it is evident that our Lord is ascended into heaven, where he is to continue "till the time of the restitution of all things;" (Acts iii. 21,) that is, till his second coming to judgment. How then can his body be in ten thousand several places on earth at one and the same time? We may further add that, if the doctrine of transubstantiation be true, it will follow that our Saviour, when he instituted the Sacrament of the Lord's Supper, did actually eat his own flesh, and drink his own blood: a conclusion this, so obviously contradictory both to reason and to Scripture, that it is astonishing how any sensible and religious man can credit such a test.

5. Such passages as are expressed with BREVITY are to be expounded by those, where the same doctrines or duties are expressed MORE LARGELY and fully.

i. The doctrine of justification, for instance, is briefly stated in Phil. iii., but that momentuous doctrine is professedly discussed in the Epistle to the Galatians, and especially in that to the Romans: and according to the tenor of these, particularly Rom. iii., all the other passages of Scripture that treat of justification, should be explained.

ii. Even slight variations will frequently serve for the purpose of reciprocal illustration. Thus, the beatitudes, related in Luke vi., though delivered at *another time*, and in a *different place*, are the same with those delivered by Jesus Christ, in his sermon on the mount, and recorded in Matt. v. Being, however, epitomised by the *former* evangelist, they may be explained by the latter.

6. "Where several doctrines of equal importance are proposed, and revealed with great clearness, we must be careful to give to each its full and equal weight."

"Thus, that we are saved by the free grace of God, and through faith in Christ, is a doctrine too plainly affirmed by the sacred writers, to be set aside by any contravening position. (Eph. ii. 8.) But so, on the other hand, are the doctrines of repentance unto life, and of obedience unto salvation. (Acts iii. 19. Matt. xix. 17.) To set either of these truths at *variance* with the others, would be to frustrate the declared purpose of the Gospel, and to make it of none effect. Points thus clearly established, and from their very nature indispensable, must be made to correspond with each other: and the exposition, which best preserves them unimpaired and undiminished, will, in any case, be a safe interpretation, and most probably the true one. The analogy of faith will thus be kept entire, and will approve itself, in every respect, as becoming its Divine Author, and *worthy of all acceptation*." (Bp. Vanmildert's Bampton Lectures, p. 294.)

It must, however, be ever borne in mind, that, valuable as this aid is, it is to be used only *in concurrence* with those which have been discussed and illustrated in the preceding sections. But, by a due attention to these principles, accompanied by humility and sincerity, with a desire to know and obey the revealed will of God, and, above all, with fervent supplication to the throne of Grace for a blessing on his labours, the diligent inquirer after Scripture truth, may confidently hope for success, and will be enabled to perceive the design of every portion of holy writ, its harmony with the rest, and the divine perfection of the whole.

---

§ 4. Historical Circumstances.

Historical Circumstances are an important help to the correct understanding of the sacred writers. Under this term are comprised:—1. The *Order*; 2. The *Title*; 3. The *Author*; 4. The *Date* of each of the several books of Scripture; 5. The *Place* where it was written; 6. The *Occasion* upon which the several books were written; 7. *Ancient Sacred and Profane History*; 8. The *Chronology*, or period of time embraced in the Scriptures generally, and of each book in particular; 9. *Biblical Antiquities*; (All these topics are adverted to, in the third and fourth parts of this volume :) and, 10. The knowledge of the *Affections*, or feelings of the Sacred writers, and of the sentiments of the persons whom they addressed.

I. A knowledge of the Order of the different Books, especially such as are historical, will more readily assist the student to discover the order of the different histories and other matters discussed in them, as well as to trace the divine economy towards mankind, under the Mosaic and Christian dispensations.

II. The Titles are further worthy of notice, because some of them announce the chief subject of the book—as *Genesis*, the generations of heaven and earth—*Exodus*, the departure of the Israelites from Egypt, &c.; while other titles denote the churches, or particular persons for whose more immediate use some parts of scripture were composed, and thus elucidate particular passages.

III. Where the name of the Author of a book is not distinctly stated, it may be collected from internal circumstances; as, his peculiar character, mode of thinking, and style of writing, as well as the incidental testimonies concerning himself, which his writings may contain. Thus,

The expressions in 2 Pet. i. 18, and iii. 1. 15, prove Saint Peter to have been the author of that epistle; and a comparison of the Epistles and Gospel of St. John proves also that they are the production of one and the same author.

IV. A knowledge of the Time when a book was written, also of the state of the Church at that time, will indicate the reason and propriety of things said in such book, as well as the author's scope, or intention in writing it. Thus,

(1.) The injunction in 1 Thess. v. 27, which may appear unnecessary, will be found to be a very proper one, when it is considered that that was the *first* epistle written by St. Paul; and that the apostle, knowing the plenitude of his divine commission, demands the same respect to be paid to his writings, which had been given to those of the ancient prophets, which, in all probability, were read in every assembly for Christian worship.

(2.) When St. James wrote his epistle, the Christians were suffering a cruel persecution, in consequence of which many were not only declining in faith, love, and a holy life, but also abused the grace of God to licentiousness, boasting of a faith destitute of its appropriate fruits; viz. : who boasted of a bare assent to the doctrines of the Gospel, and boldly affirmed that this inoperative and dead faith was alone sufficient to obtain salvation. (Chapter ii. verse 17, *et seq.*) Hence we may easily perceive, that the apostle's scope, was not to treat of the doctrine of justification; but, the state of the church requiring it, to correct those *errors in doctrine, and those sinful practices, which had crept into the church, and particularly to expose that fundamental error of a dead faith unproductive of good works.* This observation further shows the true way of reconciling the supposed contradiction between the apostles Paul and James, concerning the doctrine of salvation by faith.

V. The consideration of the PLACE where a Book was written, as well as of the nature of the place, and the customs which obtained there, is likewise of great importance.

The first Psalm being written in Palestine, the comparison (in ver. 4,) of the ungodly to chaff driven away by the wind, will become more evident, when it is recollected that the threshing-floors in that country were not under cover, as those in our modern barns are, but that they were formed in the open air, without the walls of cities, and in lofty situations, in order that the wheat might be the more effectually separated from the chaff by the action of the wind. (See Hosea xiii. 3.) In like manner, the knowledge of the nature of the Arabian desert, through which the children of Israel journeyed, is necessary to the correct understanding of many passages in the books of Exodus, Numbers, and Deuteronomy, which were written in that desert.

VI. A knowledge of the OCCASION on which a book was written, will greatly help to the understanding of the Scriptures, particularly the Psalms, many of which have no title. The occasion in this case, must be sought from internal circumstances.

Psalm xlii. was evidently written by David, when he was in circumstances of the deepest affliction: but, if we compare it with the history of the conspiracy of Absalom, aided by Ahithopel, who had deserted the councils of his sovereign, as related in 2 Sam. xv., and also with the character of the country whither David fled, we shall have a key to the meaning of that psalm, which will elucidate it with equal beauty and propriety.

VII. A knowledge of SACRED AND PROFANE HISTORY is of great importance to the interpretation of the Bible, not only as it enables us to trace the fulfilment of prophecy, but also because it enables us to explain many customs and institutions which the Jews borrowed from neighbouring heathen nations, notwithstanding they were forbidden to have any intercourse with them.

A judicious comparison of the notions that obtained among ancient, and comparatively uncultivated nations, with those entertained by the Hebrews or Jews, will, from their similitude, enable us to enter more fully into the meaning of the sacred writers. Thus many pleasing illustrations of patriarchal life and manners may be obtained by comparing the writings of Homer and Hesiod with the accounts given by Moses: such comparisons are to be found in the best of the larger philological commentaries.

In order, however, that we may correctly explain the manners, customs, or practices, referred to by the sacred writers at different times, it is necessary that we should investigate the laws, opinions, and principles of those nations among whom the Hebrews resided for a long time or with whom they held a close intercourse, and from whom it is probable they received some of them.

The Hebrews, from their long residence in Egypt, seem to have derived some expressions and modes of thinking from their oppressors. A single example will suffice to illustrate this remark. Under the Jewish theocracy, the judges are represented as holy persons, and as sitting in the place of Jehovah. The Egyptians regarded their sovereigns in this light. Hence it has been conjectured, that the Israelites, just on their exit from Egypt, called their rulers *gods*, not only in poetry, but also in the common language of their laws. See Exod. xxi. 6, where the word *judges* is, in the original Hebrew, *gods*.

VIII. Chronology, or the science of computing and adjusting periods of time, is of the greatest importance towards understanding the historical parts of the Bible, not only as it shows the order and connexion of the various events therein recorded, but likewise as it enables us to ascertain the accomplishment of many of the prophecies, and sometimes leads to the discovery and correction of mistakes in numbers and dates, which have crept into particular texts. The chronology in the margin of our larger English Bibles is called the Usserian Chronology, being founded on the Annales Veteris et Novi Testamenti of the eminently learned Archbishop Usher.

IX. To all these are to be added a knowledge of Biblical Antiquities; which include Geography, Genealogy, Natural History, and Philosophy, Learning and Philosophical Sects, Manners, Customs, and Private Life, of the Jews and other Nations mentioned in the Bible, A concise sketch of the *principal* topics comprised under this head, is given in the Third Part of this manual.

X. Lastly, in order to enter fully into the meaning of the sacred writers, especially of the New Testament, it is necessary that the reader in a manner identify himself with them, and invest himself with their Affections or feelings; and also familiarize himself with the sentiments, &c. of those to whom the different books or epistles were addressed.

This canon is of considerable importance, as well in the investigation of words and phrases, as in the interpretation of the sacred volume, and particularly of the prayers and imprecations related or contained therein. If the assistance, which may be derived from a careful study of the affections and feelings of the inspired writers, be disregarded or neglected, it will be scarcely possible to avoid erroneous expositions of the Scriptures. Daily observation and experience prove, how much of its energy and perspicuity familiar discourse derives from the affections of the speakers: and also that the same words, when pronounced under the influence of different emotions convey very different meanings.

§ 5.—Ancient Versions.

Of the Ancient Versions of the Holy Scriptures, and their uses in sacred criticism, an account has already been given in pages 83—90. It may here be remarked, that, to those who are able to consult them, these versions afford a very valuable aid in the interpretation of the Bible: for they were the works of men, who enjoyed several advantages above the moderns, for understanding the original languages and the phraseology of Scripture. A single instance will illustrate the propriety of this remark.

In the first promulgation of the Gospel to mankind, (Gen. iii. 15,) God said to the serpent that beguiled our first parents, *And I will put enmity between thee and the woman, and between thy seed and her seed, and* IT, (that is, the seed of the woman, as our authorized translation rightly expounds it,) *shall bruise thy head, and thou shalt bruise his heel.* But in the Anglo-Romish version, after the Latin vulgate, (which has IPSA *conteret caput tuum,*) it is rendered, SHE *shall bruise his head,* as if a woman should do it: which the Romanists interpreting of the Virgin Mary, ascribe to her this great victory and triumph over sin and Satan, and are taught to say, in their addresses to her, "Adoro et benedico sanctissimos pedes tuos, quibus antiqui serpentis caput calcâsti;" that is, "I adore and bless thy most holy feet, whereby thou hast bruised the head of the old serpent." That this rendering of the Romanists is erroneous is proved by the Septuagint Greek version, by the Chaldee paraphrase, and by the Syriac version, all of which refer the pronoun IT to the *seed* of the woman, and not to the woman herself. (Bp. Beveridge's Works, vol. ii. p. 193. vol. ix. pp. 233, 234. Agier, Prophéties concernant Jèsus Christ et l'Eglise, pp. 243, 244.)

---

§ 6.—On Commentators.

I. Nature and Classes of Commentators.

Commentators are writers of Books of Annotations on Scripture: they have been divided into the following classes, viz:

1. Wholly *spiritual,* or *figurative;*—this class of expositors proceed on the principle, that the Scriptures are every where to be taken in the fullest sense of which they will admit:—a principle, of all others the most unsafe, and most calculated to mislead the student.
2. *Literal* and *Critical;*—those who apply themselves to explain the mere letter of the Bible.
3. *Wholly practical;*—those who confine themselves to moral and doctrinal observations: and,
4. Those who unite critical, philological, and practical observations

Expository writings may also be classed into *Scholiasts,* or writers of short explanatory notes, who particularly aim at brevity;—Commentators, or authors of a series of perpetual annotations, in which the train of their thoughts, and the coherence of their expressions, are pointed out;—and *Paraphrasts*, who expound a sacred writer by rendering his whole discourse, as well as every expression, in equivalent terms.

II. Use of Commentators, and in what manner they are to be consulted.

The use of Commentators is two-fold: first, that we may acquire from them a method of interpreting the Scriptures correctly; and second, that we may understand obscure and difficult passages. The best commentators only should be consulted; and, in availing ourselves of their labours, the following hints will be found useful:

1. We should take care that the reading of commentators does not draw us away from studying the Scriptures for ourselves, from investigating their real meaning, and meditating on their important contents.

This would be to frustrate the very design for which commentaries are written, namely, to *facilitate* our labours, to direct us aright where we are in danger of falling into error, to remove doubts and difficulties which we are ourselves unable to solve, to reconcile apparently contradictory passages, and, in short, to elucidate whatever is obscure or unintelligible to us. No commentators, therefore, should be consulted until we have previously investigated the sacred writings for ourselves, making use of every grammatical and historical help, comparing the scope, context, parallel passages, the analogy of faith, &c.: and even then, commentaries should be resorted to, only for the purpose of explaining what was not sufficiently clear, or of removing our doubts. This method of studying the sacred volume will, unquestionably, prove a slow one; but the student will proceed with certainty; and, if he have patience and resolution enough to persevere in it, he will ultimately attain greater proficiency in the knowledge of the Scriptures, than those who, disregarding this method, shall have recourse wholly to assistances of other kinds.

2. We should not inconsiderately assent to the interpretation of any expositor or commentator, or yield a blind and servile obedience to his authority.

3. Where it does not appear that either ancient or modern interpreters had more knowledge than ourselves respecting particular passages; and where they offer only conjectures,—in such cases their expositions ought to be subjected to a strict examination. If their reasons are then found to be valid, we should give our assent to them: but, on the contrary, if they prove to be false, improbable, and insufficient, they must be altogether rejected.

4. Lastly, as there are some commentaries, which are either wholly compiled from the previous labours of others, or which contain observations extracted from their writings, if any thing appear confused and perplexed in such commentaries, the original sources whence they were compiled must be referred to, and diligently consulted.

CHAPTER II.

ON THE INTERPRETATION OF THE FIGURATIVE LANGUAGE OF SCRIPTURE.

FIGURATIVE language had its rise in the first ages of mankind: the scarcity of words occasioned them to be used for various purposes: and thus figurative terms, which constitute the beauty of language, arose from its poverty; and it is still the same in all uncivilized nations. Figures, in general, may be described to be that language, which is prompted either by the imagination or by the passions. They are commonly divided into, 1. *Tropes*, or *Figures of Words*, which consist in the advantageous alteration of a word, or sentence, from its original and proper signification, to another meaning; and, 2. *Figures of Thought*, which suppose the words to be used in their literal and proper meaning, and the figure to consist in the turn of the thought; as is the case in exclamations, apostrophes, and comparisons; where, though we vary the words that are used, or translate them from one language into another, we may, nevertheless, still preserve the same figure in the thought. This distinction, however, is of no great use, as nothing can be built upon it in practice: neither is it always very clear. It is of little importance, whether we give to some particular mode of expression the name of a trope, or of a figure, provided we remember that figurative language always imports some colouring of the imagination, or some emotion of passion expressed in our style.

Disregarding, therefore, the technical distinctions, which have been introduced by rhetorical writers, we shall first offer some hints by which to ascertain and correctly interpret the tropes and figures occurring in the sacred writings; and in the following sections we shall notice the principal of them, with a few illustrative examples.

SECTION I.—General Observations on the Interpretation of Tropes and Figures.

In order to understand fully the figurative language of the Scriptures, it is requisite, *first*, to ascertain and determine what is really figurative, lest we take that to be literal which is figurative, as the disciples of our Lord and the Jews frequently did, or lest we pervert the literal meaning of words by a figurative interpretation ; and *secondly*, when we have ascertained what is really figurative, to interpret it correctly, and deliver its true sense. For this purpose the following hints will be found useful in addition to a consideration of historical circumstances,* parallel passages, and the context.

1. The literal meaning of words must be retained, more in the historical books of Scripture, than in those which are poetical

We are not, therefore, to look for a figurative style in the historical books: and still less are historical narratives to be changed into allegories and parables, unless these are obviously apparent. Those expositors, therefore, violate this rule, who allegorize the history of the fall of man, and that of the prophet Jonah.

2. The literal meaning of words is to be given up, if it be either improper, or involve an impossibility, or where words, properly taken, contain any thing contrary to the doctrinal or moral precepts delivered in other parts of Scripture. Thus,

(1.) The expressions in Jer. i. 18, are therefore necessarily to be understood figuratively. So, the literal sense of Isa. i. 25, is equally inapplicable; but in the following verse the prophet explains it in the proper words.

(2.) In Psal. xviii. 2, God is termed, a *rock*, a *fortress*, a *deliverer*, a *buckler*, a *horn of salvation*, and a *high tower;* it is obvious that these predicates are metaphorically spoken of the Almighty.

(3.) Matt. viii. 22—"*Let the dead bury their dead*, cannot possibly be applied to those who are really and naturally dead; and consequently must be understood figuratively. "Leave those who are spiritually dead to perform the rites of burial for such as are naturally dead."

(4.) The command of Jesus Christ, related in Matt. xviii. 8, 9, if interpreted literally, is directly at variance with the sixth commandment, (Exod. xx. 13,) and must consequently be understood figuratively.

(5.) Whatever is repugnant to natural reason, cannot be the true meaning of the Scriptures; for God is the original of natural truth, as well as of that which comes by particular revelation. No proposition, therefore, which is repugnant to the fundamental principles of reason, can be the sense of any part of the word of God; hence the words of Christ, *This is my body*, and, *This is my blood*, (Matt. xxvi. 26, 28,) are not to be understood in that sense which makes for the doctrine of transubstantiation; because it is impossible that contradictions should be true; and we cannot be more certain that any thing is true, than we are that *that* doctrine is false.

(6.) To *change day into night* (Job xvii. 12,) is a moral impossibility, contrary to common sense, and must be a figurative expression. In Isa. i. 5, 6, the Jewish nation are described as being sorely *stricken*, or chastised, like a man mortally wounded, and destitute both of medicine as well as of the means of cure. That this description is figurative, is evident from the context; for in the two following verses the prophet delineates the condition of the Jews in literal terms.

It is not, however, sufficient to know whether an expression be figurative or not, but, when this point is ascertained, another of equal importance presents itself; namely, to interpret metaphorical expressions, by corresponding and appropriate terms. In order to accomplish this object, it is necessary,

3 *That we inquire* in what respects the thing compared, and that with which it is compared, respectively agree, and also in what respects they have any affinity or resemblance.

For, as a similitude is concealed in every metaphor, it is only by diligent study that it can be elicited, by carefully observing the points of agreement between the proper, or literal, and the figurative meaning. For instance, the prophetic writers, and particularly Ezekiel, very frequently charge the Israelites with having committed adultery, and played the harlot, and with deserting Jehovah, their husband. From the slightest inspection of these passages, it is evident that spiritual adultery, or idolatry, is intended. Now the origin of this metaphor is to be sought from one and the same notion, in which there is an agreement between adultery and the worship paid by the Israelites to strange gods. That notion, or idea, is unfaithfulness; by which, as a wife deceives her husband, so they are represented as deceiving God, and as violating their fidelity in forsaking him.

4. Lastly, in explaining the figurative language of Scripture, care must be taken that we do not judge of the application of characters from modern usage; because the inhabitants of the East have very frequently attached a character to the idea expressed, widely different from that which usually presents itself to our views.

In Deut. xxxiii. 17, the glory of the *tribe* of Joseph is compared to the firstling of a bullock; in like manner Amos (iv. 1.) compares the noble women of Israel to the kine of Bashan, and Hosea compares the Israelites to refractory kine that shake off the yoke. If we take these metaphors according to their present sense, we shall greatly err. The ox-tribe of animals, whose greatest beauty and strength lie in their horns, was held in very high honour among the ancient nations, and was much esteemed on account of its aptitude for agricultural labour: hence, in the East, it is not reckoned disgraceful to be compared with these animals. In the comparison of the tribe of Joseph to the firstling of a bullock, the point of resemblance is strength and power. In the comparison of the matrons of Samaria to the kine of Bashan, the point of resemblance is luxury and wantonness, flowing from their abundance.

Section II.—On the Interpretation of the Metonymies occurring in Scripture.

A metonymy is a trope, by which we substitute one appellation for another, as the *cause* for the *effect*, the *effect* for the *cause*, the *subject* for the *adjunct* or the *adjunct* for the *subject.*

A *Metonymy of the cause* is used in Scripture, when the person acting is put for the thing done, or the instrument by which a thing is done is put for the thing effected, or when a thing or action is put for the effect produced by that action.

A *Metonymy of the effect* occurs, when the effect is put for the efficient cause.

A *Metonymy of the subject* is, when the subject is put for the adjunct, that is, for some circumstance or appendage belonging to the subject when the thing or place *containing* is put for the thing *contained* or placed; when the *possessor* is put for the thing *possessed;* when the *object* is put for the thing conversant about it; or when the thing signified is put for its sign.

A *Metonymy of the adjunct* is, when that which belongs to any thing serves to represent the thing itself.

---

§ 1.—Metonymy of the Cause.

I. Frequently the person acting is put for the thing done. Thus,

1. CHRIST is put for his *doctrine* in Rom. xvi. 9.

2. The HOLY SPIRIT for his *Effects* and *Operations*, in 2 Cor. iii. 6. Psalm li. 10; *Influences*, in Luke xi. 13, and 1 Thess. v. 19; a *Divine Power*, reigning in the soul of the renewed man, in Luke i. 46, 47, compared with 1 Thess. v. 23; the *Extraordinary Gifts* of the Spirit, in 2 Kings ii. 9. Dan. v. 12; and for revelations, visions, or ecstacies, whether really from the Holy Spirit, or pretended to be so, in Ezek. xxxvi. 1, 2 Thess. ii. 2, and Rev. i. 10.

3. *Parents*, or *Ancestors*, are put for their *Posterity;* as in Gen. ix. 27. Exod. v. 2, and very many other passages of holy writ.

4. The *Writer*, or *Author*, is put for his *Book* or *Work:* as in Luke xvi. 29. xxiv. 27. Acts xv. 21, xxi. 21, and 2 Cor. iii. 15, in which passages *Moses* and the *Prophets* respectively mean the Mosaic and Prophetic writings.

II. Sometimes the cause or instrument is put for the thing effected by it. Thus,

1. The *mouth*, the *lips*, and the *tongue*, are respectively put for the *speech*, in Deut. xvii. 6, xix. 15. Matt. xviii. 16, &c.

2. The *mouth* is also put for *commandment* in Gen. xlv. 21. (marginal rendering) (Heb. *mouth.*) Numb. iii. 16. 39, xx. 24, xxvii. 14. Deut. i. 26. 43. and in Prov. v. 3. the *palate* (marginal rendering) is also put for *speech.*

3. The *throat* is also put for *loud speaking*, in Isa. lviii. 1. *Cry aloud*, (Heb. with the throat.)

4. The *hand* is ordinarily put for its *writing*, 1 Cor. xvi. 21. Col. iv. 18.

5. The *sword, famine*, and *pestilence*, likewise respectively denote the effects of those scourges, as in Ezek. vii. 15.

---

§ 2.—Metonymy of the Effect.

III. Sometimes, on the contrary, the effect is put for the cause.

Thus *God* is called *Salvation*, that is, the Author of it, Exod. xv. 2, our *life* and the length of our days, Deut. xxx. 20, our *strength*, Psalm xviii. 1. So *Christ* is termed *Salvation*, Isa. xlix. 6. Luke ii. 30. *Life*, John xi. 25, and the *Resurrection* in the same place.

§ 3.—Metonymy of the Subject.

IV. Sometimes the subject is put for the adjunct, that is for some circumstance or appendage belonging to, or depending upon the subject. Thus,

The *heart* is frequently used for the *will* and *affection*, Deut. iv. 29, vi. 5, &c.: and for the *understanding*, Deut. iv. 39, vi. 6. Luke ii. 51, &c.

V. Sometimes the place or thing denotes that which is contained in such place or thing.

The *earth* and the *world* are frequently put for the men that dwell therein, as in Gen. vi. 11. Psalm xcvi. 13, &c. The *Houses of Israel* and *Levi* denote their several *families*, in Exod. ii. 1, and Ezek. iii. 1.

VI. Sometimes the possessor of a thing is put for the thing possessed.

Thus, Deut. ix. 1. *To possess nations greater and mightier than thyself*, means to possess the countries of the Gentiles. See also Psalm lxxix. 7, where *Jacob* means the *land of the Israelites*.

VII. Frequently the object is put for that which is conversant about it.

Thus *glory* and *strength* are put for the celebration of the divine glory and strength, in Psalm viii. 2; explained by Matt. xxi. 16; see also Psalm xcvi. 7, 8.

VIII. Sometimes the thing signified is put for its sign.

So, the *strength of God*, in 1 Chron. xvi. 11, and Psalm cv. 4, is the *ark*, which was a sign and symbol of the divine presence and strength.

IX. When an action is said to be done, the meaning frequently is, that it is declared, or permitted, or foretold, to be done: as in Gen. xli. 3. Jer. iv. 10. Matt. xvi. 9, &c.

X. An action is said to be done, when the giving of an occasion for it is only intended.

1 Kings xiv. 6. Jeroboam *made Israel to sin*, i. e. occasioned it by his example and command. See Acts i. 18, Rom. xiv. 15, and 1 Cor. vii. 16.

---

§ 4.—Metonymy of the Adjunct, in which the Adjunct is put for the Subject.

XI. Sometimes the accident, or that which is additional to a thing, is put for its subject in kind.

The abstract is put for the concrete. So *gray hairs* (Heb. *hoariness* or *gray-headedness*) in Gen. xlii. 38, denote me, who am now an old man and gray-headed; *abomination* for an abominable thing, in Gen. xlvi 34, and Luke xvi. 15.

XII. Sometimes the thing contained is put for the thing containing it, and a thing deposited in a place, for the place itself.

Thus Gen. xxviii. 22, means, this place where I have erected a pillar of stone, shall be God's house. Josh. xv. 19. Springs of water denote some portion of land, where there may be springs. Matt. ii. 11. *Treasures* are the cabinets or other vessels containing them.

XIII. Time is likewise put for the things which are done or happen in time, as in 1 Chron. xii. 32. John xii. 27.

XIV. In the Scriptures, things are sometimes named or described according to appearances, or to the opinion formed of them by men, and not as they are in their own nature.

Thus Hananiah, the opponent of Jeremiah, is called a *prophet*, not because he was truly one, but was *reputed* to be one, Jer. xxviii. 1. 5. 10. In Ezek. xxi. 3, the *righteous* mean those who had the semblance of piety, but really were not righteous. And in Luke ii. 48, Joseph is called the *Father* of Christ, because he was reputed so to be.

XV. Sometimes the action or affection, which is conversant about any object, or placed upon it, is put for the object itself.

Thus, the senses are put for the *objects* perceived by them, as *hearing* for doctrine or speech, in Isa. xxviii. 9, (marg. rend.) and liii. 1, (Heb.) In John xii. 38, and Rom. x. 16, the Greek word *ακοη*, translated *report*, literally means hearing, and so it is rendered in Gal. iii. 2. 5. Hearing is also put for fame or rumour in Psalm cxii. 7. (Heb.) Ezek. vii. 26 Obad. 1. Hab. iii. 2. (Heb.) Matt. iv. 24, xiv. 1, and xxiv. 6. Mark i. 28, and xiii. 7, &c.

The *eye,* in the original of Numb. xi. 7. Lev. xiii. 55. Prov. xxiii. 31 Ezek. i. 4, viii. 2, and x. 9, is put for colours which are seen by the eye.

XVI. Sometimes the sign is put for the thing signified as in Gen. xlix. 10. Isa. xxii. 22. Matt. x. 34.

XVII. Lastly, the names of things are often put for the things themselves, as in Psalm xx. 1, cxv. 1. Acts ii. 21. Rom. x. 13, &c.

Section III.—On the Interpretation of Scripture Metaphors and Allegories.

I. Nature and sources of Metaphors.

A metaphor is a trope, by which a word is diverted from its proper and genuine signification to another meaning, for the sake of comparison, or because there is some analogy between the similitude, and the thing signified. Of all the figures of rhetoric, the metaphor is that which is most frequently employed, not only in the Scriptures, but likewise in every language: for, independently of the pleasure which it affords, it enriches the mind with *two* ideas at the *same* time, the *truth* and the *similitude.* To illustrate this definition:—In Deut. xxxii. 42, we read, *I will make mine arrows drunk with blood, and my sword shall devour flesh.* Here, the *first* metaphor is borrowed from excessive and intemperate drinking, to intimate the very great effusion of blood, and the exceeding greatness of the ruin and destruction which would befall the disobedient Israelites: the *second* metaphor is drawn from the voracious appetite of a hungry beast, which in a lively manner presents to the mind the impossibility of their escaping the edge of the sword, when the wrath of God should be provoked. The foundation of them consists in a likeness, or similitude between the thing from which the metaphor is drawn, and that to which it is applied. When this resemblance is exhibited in one, or in a few expressions, it is termed a simple metaphor. When it is pursued with a variety of expressions, or there is a continued assemblage of metaphor, it is called an *allegory.* When it is couched in a short sentence, obscure and ambiguous, it is called a *riddle.* If it be conveyed in a short saying only, it is a *proverb;* and if the metaphorical representation be delivered in the form of a history, it is a *parable.* When the resemblance is far-fetched,—as *to see a voice,* (Rev. i. 12,) it is termed a *catachresis.* This last-mentioned species of figure, however, is of less frequent occurrence in the Bible than any of the preceding. Scripture Metaphors are variously derived from the works of nature—from the ordinary occupations and customs of life, as well as from such arts as were at that time practised;—from sacred topics, that is, the Religion of the Hebrews, and things connected with it, and also from their Natural History.

II. Nature of an Allegory.

The *Allegory* is another branch of the figurative language of Scripture; in which a foreign or distant meaning is concealed under the literal sense of the words. It differs from a metaphor, in that it is not confined to a word, but extends to a thought, or even to several thoughts. Of this species of figure Bishop Lowth has distinguished three kinds, viz.:

1. The *Allegory* properly so called, and which he terms a *continued metaphor;*—2. The *Parable,* or similitude, which is discussed in the following section:—and, 3. The *Mystical Allegory,* in which a double meaning is couched under the same words, or when the same prediction, according as it is differently interpreted, relates to different events, distant in time, and distinct in their nature. This case of allegory is exclusively derived from things sacred; and, while in those other forms of allegory, the exterior, or ostensible imagery, is fiction only, in

the mystical allegory each idea is equally agreeable to truth. As the mystical and typical interpretation of Scripture is discussed in a subsequent part of this volume, we shall, at present, consider allegory, or continued metaphor, properly and strictly so called.

III. The following rules may assist us to determine the meaning of an allegory.

1. The proper or literal meaning of the words must be ascertained, before we attempt to explain an allegory.

2. The design of the whole allegory must be investigated; and the point of comparison must not be extended to all the circumstances of an allegory.

For this purpose, the occasion that gave rise to it must be diligently examined and considered, together with historical circumstances, as well as the nature of the thing spoken of, and also the scope and context of the whole passage, in which it occurs; because the scope and interpretation of an allegory are frequently pointed out by some explanation that is subjoined.

3. We must not explain one part literally, and another part figuratively.

Thus the whole of 1 Cor. iii. 9—13, is allegorical: a comparison is there instituted between the office of a teacher of religion, and that of a builder. Hence a Christian congregation is termed a building; its ministers are the architects, some of whom lay the foundation on which others build; some erect a superstructure of gold and silver; others of wood, hay, and stubble. The sense concealed under the allegory is apparent: a Christian congregation is instructed by teachers, some of whom communicate the first principles, others impart further knowledge: some deliver good and useful things, (*the truth*,) while others deliver useless things, (*erroneous doctrines*, such as at that time prevailed in the Corinthian church.) That day (the great day of judgment) will declare what superstructure a man has raised; that is, whether what he has taught be good or bad. And as fire is the test of gold, silver, precious stones, wood, hay, stubble, so the great day will be the test of every man's work. Though the whole of this passage is obviously allegorical, yet it is understood literally by the church of Rome, who has erected upon it her doctrine of the fire of purgatory. How contrary this doctrine is to every rule of right interpretation, is too plain to require any exposition.

Section IV.—Interpretation of Scripture Parables.

I. Nature of a Parable.

The word *Parable* is of various import in Scripture, denoting a proverb, or short saying, a thing darkly, or figuratively expressed, and a similitude, or comparison. Strictly speaking, a parable is a similitude taken from things natural, in order to instruct us in things spiritual. This mode of instruction is of great antiquity, and an admirable means of conveying moral lessons: "by laying hold on the imagination, parable insinuates itself into the affections; and, by the intercommunication of the faculties, the understanding is made to apprehend the truth which was proposed to the fancy." In a word, this kind of instruction seizes us by surprise, and carries with it a force and conviction which are almost irresistible. It is no wonder, therefore, that parables were made the vehicle of natural instruction in the most early times; that the prophets, especially Ezekiel, availed themselves of the same impressive mode of conveying instruction or reproof; and that our Lord, following the same example, also adopted it for the same important purposes.

II. For the interpretation of a parable, (to which the rules belonging to the allegory may indeed be applied,) the following hints will be found useful:

1. The first excellence of a parable is, that it turns upon an image well known and applicable to the subject, the meaning of which is clear and definite: for this circumstance will give it that perspicuity which is essential to every species of allegory.

How clearly this rule applies to the parables of our Lord, is obvious to every reader of the New Testament. It may suffice to mention his parable of the *Ten Virgins* (Matt. xxv. 1—13,) which is a plain allusion to those things which were common at the Jewish marriages in those days. In like manner, the parables of the *lamp*, (Luke viii. 16,) of the *sower* and the seed, of the *tares*, of the *mustard seed*, of the *leaven*, of the *net cast into the sea*, all of which are related in Matt. xiii. as well as of the *householder* that planted a vineyard, and let it out to husbandmen, (Matt. xvi. 33,) are all representations of usual and common occurrences, and such as the generality of our Saviour's hearers were daily conversant with, and they were therefore selected by him as being the most interesting and affecting.

2. Further, the image must be not only apt and familiar, but must also be elegant and beautiful in itself; and all its parts must be perspicuous and pertinent; since it is the purpose of a parable, and especially of a poetic parable, not only to explain more perfectly some proposition, but frequently to give it animation and splendour.

Of all these excellencies there cannot be more perfect examples than the parables which have just been specified: to which we may add, the well known parables of Jotham, (Judges ix. 7—15;) of Nathan, (2 Sam. ii. 1—4;) and of the woman of Tekoah, (2 Sam. xiv. 4—7.)

3. As every parable has two senses, the LITERAL, or external, and the MYSTICAL, or internal sense; the literal sense must be first explained, in order that the correspondence between it and the mystical sense may be the more readily perceived. And wherever words seem to be capable of different senses, particularly in the parables of Jesus Christ, we may with certainty conclude that to be the true sense which lies most

level to the apprehensions of those to whom the parable was delivered.

4. It is not necessary, in the interpretation of parables, that we should anxiously insist upon every single word; nor ought we to expect too curious an adaptation or accommodation of it, in every part, to the spiritual meaning inculcated by it; for many circumstances are introduced into parables, which are merely ornamental, and designed to make the similitude more pleasing and interesting.

Inattention to this obvious rule has led many expositors into the most fanciful explanations: resemblances have been accumulated, which are for the most part futile, or at best, of little use, and manifestly not included in the scope of the parable. In the application of this rule, the two following points are to be considered, viz.:

(1.) Persons are not to be compared with persons, but things with things; part is not to be compared with part, but the whole of the parable with itself. Thus, the similitude in Matt. xiii. 24, 25, is, not with the *men* there mentioned, but with the *seed* and the *pearl:* and the construction is to be the same as in verses 31 and 33, where the progress of the Gospel is compared to the grain of mustard seed, and to leaven.

(2.) In parables, it is not necessary that all the actions of men, mentioned in them, should be just actions, that is to say, morally just and honest: for instance, the unjust steward (Luke xvi. 1—8,) is not proposed either to justify his dishonesty, or as an example to us in cheating his lord, (for that is merely ornamental, and introduced to fill up the story;) but as an example of his care and prudence in providing for the future.

Section V.--On Scripture Proverbs.

I. Nature of Proverbs.

Proverbs are concise and sententious common sayings, founded on a close observance of men and manners. They were greatly in use among the inhabitants of Palestine, in common with other oriental nations: and the teachers of mankind who had recourse to this mode of instruction, in order to render it the more agreeable, added to their precepts the graces of harmony; and decorated them with metaphors, comparisons, allusions, and other elegant embellishments of style.

II. Different kinds of Proverbs.

Proverbs are divided into two classes, viz.: 1. *Entire Sentences;* and 2. *Proverbial Phrases,* which by common usage are admitted into a sentence.

1. Examples of *Entire Proverbial Sentences* occur in Gen. x. 9, and xxii. 14. 1 Sam. x. 12, and xxiv. 13. 2 Sam. v. 8, and xx. 18. Ezek. xvi 44, and xviii. 2. Luke iv. 23. John iv. 37, and 2 Pet. ii. 22; in which passages the inspired writers expressly state the sentences to have passed into proverbs.

2. Examples of *Proverbial Phrases,* which indeed cannot be correctly termed proverbs, but which have acquired their form and use, are to be

found in Deut. xxv. 4. 1 Kings xx. 11. 2 Chron. xxv. 9. Job. vi. 5, xiv. 19, and xxviii. 18. Psal. xlii. 7, and lxii. 9. The Book of Proverbs likewise contains many similar sentences; examples of which may also be seen in the Book of Ecclesiastes, in some of the Prophets, as well as in the New Testament.

III. Interpretation of the Proverbs in the New Testament.

The Proverbs occurring in the New Testament are to be explained, partly by the aid of similar passages from the Old Testament, and partly from the ancient writings of the Jews; whence it appears how much they were in use among that people, and that they were applied by Christ and his apostles, agreeably to common usage.

SECTION VI.—Concluding Observations on the Figurative Language of Scripture.

Besides the figures discussed in the preceding sections, there are many others dispersed throughout the sacred Scriptures, the infinite superiority of which over all uninspired compositions, they admirably elucidate. Two or three of these, from their importance and frequent occurrence, claim to be noticed in this place.

1. A *Synecdoche* is a trope in which, 1. The *whole* is put for a *part*; 2. A *part* is put for the whole; 3. A certain number for an uncertain one; 4. A *general* name for a *particular* one; and, 5. *Special* words for *general* ones.

[i.] The whole is sometimes put for a part:

As, the *world* for the *Roman empire*, which was but a small, though very remarkable part of the world, in Acts xxiv. 5, and Rev. iii. 10. The *world* for the *earth* which is a part of it, 2 Pet. iii. 6. Rom. i. 8. 1 John v. 19.

[ii.] Sometimes the part is put for the whole.

Thus in Gen. i. 5. 8. 13. 19. 23. 31, the *evening and morning*, being the principal parts of the day, are put for the entire day. So the *soul* comprehends the *entire man*, Acts xxvii. 37. *Tree*, in Gen. iii. 8, is in the original put for *trees*; and *man*, in Gen. xlix. 6, for *men*.

[iii.] A certain number for an uncertain number, as *twice* for *several times*, in Psal. lxii. 11. *Ten*, for many, in Gen. xxxi. 7; and *seven* for an *indefinite* number, in Gen. iv. 15, and very many other passages of Scripture.

[iv.] A *general name* is put for a *particular* one.

As in Mark xvi. 15, where every creature means all mankind; as flesh also does in Gen. vi. 12. Psal. cxlv. 21. Isa. xl. 5, 6, lxvi. 23. Matt. xxiv 22. Luke iii. 6, and Rom. iii. 20.

[v.] Sometimes special words, or particular names, are put for such as are general:

Thus, *father* is put for any *ancestor* in Psal. xxii. 4; *father*, for *grandfather*, in 2 Sam. ix. 7, and Dan. v. 11. 18; *father* and *mother* for *all superiors*, in Exod. xx. 12.

2. An *Irony* is a figure, in which we speak one thing and de-

sign another, in order to give the greater force and vehemence to our meaning. An irony is distinguished from the real sentiments of the speaker, or writer, by the accent, the air, the extravagance of the praise, the character of the person, or the nature of the discourse.

Instances of irony may be seen in 1 Kings xviii. 27, 1 Kings xxii. 15. Job xii. 2, and 1 Cor. iv. 8.

Under this figure we may include the *Sarcasm* which may be defined to be an irony in its superlative keenness and asperity. See examples of this figure in Matt. xxvii. 29, and Mark xv. 32.

3. *Hyperbole*, in its representation of things, or objects, either magnifies, or diminishes them beyond or below their proper limits; it is common in all languages, and is of frequent occurrence in the Scripture.

Thus, a great quantity, or number, is commonly expressed by the *sand of the sea, the dust of the earth*, and *the stars of heaven*, Gen. xiii. 16, xli. 49. Judges vii. 12. 1 Sam. xiii. 5. 1 Kings iv. 29. 2 Chron. i. 9. Jer xv. 8. Heb. xi. 12. In like manner we meet, in Numb. xiii. 33, with *smaller than grasshoppers*, to denote extreme diminutiveness: 2 Sam. i. 23 *swifter than eagles* to intimate extreme celerity.

CHAPTER III.

ON THE SPIRITUAL INTERPRETATION OF SCRIPTURE.

SECTION I.—General Observations on the Spiritual or Mystical Sense of Scripture.

WHERE, besides the direct or immediate signication of a passage, whether literally or figuratively expressed, there is attached to it a more remote or hidden meaning, this is termed the SPIRITUAL or mystical sense: and this sense is founded not on a transfer of words from one signification to another, but on the entire application of the matter itself to a different subject. Thus,

Exod. xxx. 10, and Levit. xvi. What is here said concerning the high priest's entrance into the most holy place, on the day of atonement, we are taught by St. Paul to understand spiritually of the entrance of Jesus Christ into the presence of God, with his own blood. (Heb. ix. 7—20.)

The spiritual sense of Scripture has frequently been divided into allegorical, typical, and parabolic.

1. The *Allegorical Sense* is, when the Holy Scriptures, besides the literal sense, signify any thing belonging to faith, or *spiritual* doctrine.

Such is the sense which is required rightly to understand Gal. iv. 24, in our version rendered, *which things are an allegory;* literally, *which things are allegorically spoken*, or, *which things are thus allegorized* by me; that is, under the veil of the literal sense they further contain a spiritual or mystical sense.

2. The *Typical Sense* is, when, under external objects, or prophetic visions, secret things are represented, whether present or future; especially when certain transactions, recorded in the Old Testament, presignify, or shadow forth those related in the New Testament.

Thus, in Psal. xcv. 11, the words, *they should not enter into my rest*, literally understood, signify the entrance of the Israelites into the Promised Land; but, typically, the entering into rest, and the enjoyment of heaven, through the merits and mediation of Jesus Christ, as is largely shown in the third and fourth chapters of the Epistle to the Hebrews.

3. The *Parabolic Sense* is, when, besides the plain and obvious meaning of the thing related, an occult or spiritual sense is intended. As this chiefly occurs in passages of a moral tendency, the parabolic has by some writers been termed the *moral*, or tropological sense.

Of this description is the parable of the talents: the design of which is to show that the duties which men are called to perform, are suited to their situations, and the talents which they severally receive; that, whatever good a man possesses, he has received from God, as well as the ability to improve that good; and that the grace and temporal mercies of God are suited to the power which a man has of improving them. Thus, also, the injunction in Deut. xxv. 4, relative to muzzling the ox, while treading out the corn, is explained by St. Paul, with reference to the right of maintenance of ministers of the Gospel. (1 Cor. ix. 9—11.)

SECTION II.—Rules for the Spiritual or Mystical Interpretation of Scripture.

Some injudicious expositors having unduly preferred the spiritual, or mystical sense, to the literal sense, which is undoubtedly first in point of *nature* as well as in order of signification; others have been induced to conclude that no such interpretation is admissible. "A principle," however, "is not therefore to be rejected, because it has been abused: since human errors can never invalidate the truth of God." The following hints will be found useful for the spiritual interpretation of Scripture.

In this department of sacred literature it may be considered as an axiom, that the spiritual meaning of a passage is *there only* to be sought, where it is evident, from *certain* criteria, that such meaning was designed by the Holy Spirit.

The criteria, by which to ascertain whether there is a latent spiritual meaning in any passage of Scripture, are two-fold: either they are seated in the text itself, or they are to be found in some other passages.

1. Where these criteria are seated in the text, vestiges of a spiritual meaning are discernible, when the things, which are affirmed concerning the person or thing immediately treated of, are so august and illustrious that they cannot in any way be applied to it, in the fullest sense of the words.

The writings of the prophets, especially those of Isaiah, abound with instances of this kind. Thus, in the 14th, 40th, 41st, and 49th chapters of that evangelical prophet, the return of the Jews from the Babylonish captivity is announced in the most lofty and magnificent terms. If we compare this description with the accounts actually given of their return to Palestine by Ezra and Nehemiah, we shall not find any thing corresponding with the events so long and so beautifully predicted by Isaiah. In this description, therefore, of their deliverance from captivity, we must look beyond it to that infinitely higher deliverance, which, in the fulness of time, was accomplished by Jesus Christ.

2. Where the spiritual meaning of a text is latent, the Holy Spirit (under whose direction the sacred penman wrote) sometimes clearly and expressly asserts, that one thing or person was divinely constituted or appointed to be a figure or symbol of another thing or person: in which case the indisputable testimony of eternal truth removes and cuts off every ground of doubt and uncertainty.

For instance, if we compare Psalm cx. 4, with Heb. vii. 1, we shall find that *Melchisedec* was a type of Messiah, the great high priest and king. So *Hagar* and *Sarah* were types of the Jewish and Christian Churches. (Gal. iv. 22—24.)

3. Sometimes, however, the mystical sense is intimated by the Holy Spirit in a more *obscure* manner: and, without excluding the practice of sober and pious meditation, we are led by various intimations (which require very diligent observation and study) to the knowledge of the spiritual or mystical meaning.

This chiefly occurs in the following cases:

1. When the antitype is proposed under figurative names taken from the Old Testament.

Thus, in 1 Cor. v. 7, Christ is called the paschal lamb;—in 1 Cor. xv. 45, he is called the *last* Adam; the first Adam, therefore, was in some respect a type or figure of Christ.

[ii.] When, by a manifest allusion of words and phrases, the inspired writers refer one thing to another.

Thus, from Isa. ix. 4, which alludes to the victory obtained by Gideon (Judges vii. 22,) we learn that this represents the victory which Christ should obtain by the preaching of the Gospel, as Vitringa has largely shown on this passage.

So, when St. Paul is arguing against the Jews from the types of Sarah, Hagar, Melchisedec, &c. he supposes that in these persons there were *some* things in which Christ and his church were delineated, and that these things were admitted by his opponents: otherwise, his arguments would be inconclusive.

Section III.—On the Interpretation of Types.

I. Nature of a Type, and its different species.

A type, in its primary and literal meaning, simply denotes a rough draught, or less accurate model, from which a more perfect image is made: but, in the sacred or theological sense of the term, a type may be defined to be a symbol of something future and distant, or an example prepared and evidently designed by God to prefigure that future thing. What is thus prefigured is called the *antitype*.

In the examination of the sacred writings three species of types present themselves to our notice, viz.:

1. *Legal Types*, or those contained in the Mosaic law. On comparing the history and economy of Moses with the whole of the New Testament, it evidently appears, that the ritual law was typical of the Messiah and of Gospel blessings: and this point has been clearly established by the great apostle of the Gentiles, in his Epistle to the Hebrews.

2. *Prophetical Types* are those by which the divinely inspired prophets prefigured or signified things either present or future, by means of external symbols. Of this description is the prophet Isaiah's going naked (that is, without his prophetic garment,) and barefoot, (Isa. xx. 2,) to prefigure the fatal destruction of the Egyptians and Ethiopians.

3. *Historical Types* are the characters, actions, and fortunes of some eminent persons recorded in the Old Testament, so ordered by Divine Providence as to be exact prefigurations of the characters, actions, and fortunes of future persons who should arise under the Gospel dispensation.

Great caution is necessary in the interpretation of types; for unless we have the authority of the sacred writers themselves for it, we cannot conclude with certainty that this or that person or thing, which is mentioned in the Old Testament, is a type of Christ on account of the resemblance which we may perceive between them: but we may admit it as probable.

II. Hints for the interpretation of Types.

1. There must be a fit application of the Type to the Antitype

This canon is of great importance: and inattention to it has led fanciful expositors into the most unfounded interpretations of holy writ. In further illustration of this rule, it may be remarked,

[i.] The *type itself* must, in the first instance, be explained according to its literal sense; and if any part of it appear to be obscure, such obscurity must be removed: as in the history of Jonah, who was swallowed by a great fish, and cast ashore on the third day.

[ii.] *The analogy* between the thing prefiguring, and the thing prefigured must be *soberly* shown in all its parts.

2. There is often more in the type than in the antitype.

God designed one person or thing in the Old Testament to be a type or shadow of things to come, not in all things, but only in respect to *some particular thing*, or things; hence we find many things in the type, that are inapplicable to the antitype. The use of this canon is shown in the epistle to the Hebrews, in which the ritual and sacrifices of the Old Testament are fairly accommodated to Jesus Christ, the antitype, although there are many things in that priesthood which do not accord. Thus the priest was to offer sacrifice for his own sins, (Heb. v. 3) which is in no respect applicable to Christ. (Heb. vii. 27.)

3. Frequently there is more in the antitype than in the type.

The reason of this canon is the same as that of the preceding rule: for, as no single type can express the life and particular actions of Christ, there is necessarily more in the antitype than can be found in the type itself; so that one type must signify one thing, and another type another thing.

4. In types and antitypes, an enallage or change sometimes takes place; as when the thing prefigured assumes the name of the type or figure; and, on the contrary, when the type of the thing represented assumes the name of the antitype.

Of the first kind of enallage we have examples in Ezek. xxxiv. 23, xxxvii. 24, 25, and Hos. iii. 5; in which descriptions of Messiah's kingdom he is styled David; because as he was prefigured by David in many respects, so he was to descend from him.

Of the second kind of enallage we have instances:—1. *Prophetical Types*, in which the name of a person or thing, properly agreeing with the antitype, and for which the type was proposed, is given to any one, as in Isa. vii. 3, and viii. 1—3. 2. In *Historical Types;* as, when hanging was called in the Old Testament the curse of the Lord, because it was made a type of Christ, who was made a curse for our sins, as St. Paul argues in Gal. iii. 13.

5 That we may not fall into extremes in the interpretation of types, we must, in every instance, proceed cautiously, "with fear and trembling," lest we imagine mysteries to exist where none were ever intended.

No mystical or typical sense, therefore, ought to be put upon a plain passage of Scripture, the meaning of which is obvious and natural; unless it be evident from some other part of Scripture that the place is to be understood in a double sense. When St. Paul says, (Gal. iii. 24. Col. ii. 17,) that the *law was a schoolmaster to bring men to Christ*, and a *shadow of things to come*, we must instantly acknowledge that the ceremonial law in general, was a type of the mysteries of the Gospel.

CHAPTER IV

ON THE INTERPRETATION OF SCRIPTURE PROPHECIES.

PROPHECY, or the prediction of future events, is justly considered as the highest evidence that can be given of supernatural communion with the Deity. The force of the argument from prophecy, for proving the divine inspiration of the sacred records, has already been exhibited; and the cavils of objectors have been obviated. (See pp. 37—47, *supra*.) Difficulties, it is readily admitted, do exist in understanding the prophetic writings: but these are either owing to our ignorance of history, and of the Scriptures, or because the prophecies themselves are yet unfulfilled. The latter can only be understood when the events foretold have actually been accomplished: but the former class of difficulties may be removed in many, if not in all cases; and the knowledge, sense, and meaning of the prophets may, in a considerable degree, be attained by prayer, reading, and meditation, and by comparing Scripture with Scripture, especially with the writings of the New Testament, and particularly with the book of the Revelation. With this view, the following general rules will be found useful in investigating, first, the *sense and meaning* of the prophecies, and, secondly, their *accomplishment*.

I. Rules for ascertaining the SENSE of the Prophetic Writings.

1. As not any Prophecy of Scripture is of self-interpretation (2 Pet. i. 20,) or is its own interpreter, "the sense of the prophecy is to be sought in the events of the world, and in the harmony of the prophetic writings, rather than in the bare terms of any single prediction."

In the consideration of this canon, the following circumstances should be carefully attended to.

[i.] Consider well the times when the several prophets flourished, in what place and under what kings they uttered their predictions, the duration of their prophetic ministry, and their personal rank and condition, and, lastly, whatever can be known respecting their life and transactions.

[ii.] As the prophets treat not only of past transactions and present occurrences, but also foretell future events, in order to understand them, we must diligently consult the histories of the following ages, both sacred and profane, and carefully see whether we can trace in them the fulfilment of any prophecy.

[iii.] The words and phrases of a prophecy must be explained, where they are obscure; if they be very intricate, every single word should be expounded; and, if the sense be involved in metaphorical and emblematic expressions, (as very frequently is the case,) these must be explained according to the principles already considered.

[iv.] Similar prophecies of the same event must be carefully compared, in order to elucidate more clearly the sense of the sacred predictions.

For instance, after having ascertained the subject of the prophet's discourse and the sense of the words, Isa. liii. 5, (*He was wounded*, literally, *pierced through*, for our transgressions,) may be compared with Psal. xxii. 16, (*They pierced my hands and my feet*,) and with Zech. xii. 10,

(*They shall look on me whom they have pierced.*) In thus paralleling the prophecies, regard must be had to the predictions of former prophets, which are sometimes repeated with abridgment, or more distinctly explained by others; and also to the predictions of subsequent prophets, who sometimes repeat, with greater clearness and precision, former prophecies, which had been more obscurely announced.

2. In order to understand the prophets, great attention should be paid to the prophetic style, which is highly figurative, and particularly abounds in metaphorical and hyperbolical expressions.

By images borrowed from the natural world, the prophets often understand something in the world politic. Thus, the sun, moon, stars, and heavenly bodies, denote kings, queens, rulers, and persons in great power; and the increase of splendour in these luminaries denotes increase of prosperity, as in Isa. xxx. 26, and lx. 19. On the other hand, their darkening, setting, or falling, signifies a reverse of fortune, or the entire destruction of the potentate or kingdom to which they refer.

3. As the greater part of the prophetic writings was first composed in verse, and still retains much of the air and cast of the original, an attention to the division of the lines, and to that peculiarity of Hebrew poetry by which the sense of one line or couplet so frequently corresponds with another, will frequently lead to the meaning of many passages; one line of a couplet, or member of a sentence, being generally a commentary on the other.

Of this rule we have an example in Isa. xxxiv. 6:

> The Lord hath a sacrifice in Bozrah,
> And a great slaughter in the land of Idumea.

Here, the metaphor in the first verse is expressed in the same terms in the next: the sacrifice in Bozrah means the great slaughter in the land of Idumea, of which Bozrah was the capital.

4. Particular names are often put by the prophets for more general ones, in order that they may place the thing represented, as it were, before the eyes of their hearers: but in such passages they are not to be understood literally.

Thus, in Joel iii. 4, *Tyre and Sidon, and all the coasts of Palestine,* are put, by way of poetical description, for all the enemies of the Jews.

5. The order of time is not always to be looked for in the prophetic writings: for they frequently (particularly Jeremiah and Ezekiel) resume topics of which they have formerly treated, after other subjects have intervened, and again discuss them.

6. The prophets often change both persons and tenses, sometimes speaking in their own persons, at other times representing God, his people, or their enemies, as respectively speaking, and without noticing the change of persons; sometimes taking things past or present for things future, to denote the certainty of the events.

Isa. ix. 6, liii. throughout, lxiii. throughout, Zech. ix. 9, and Rev xviii. 2, to cite no other passages, may be adduced as illustrations of this remark.

7. When the prophets received a commission to declare any thing, the message is sometimes expressed as if they had been appointed to do it themselves.

Isa. vi. 9, 10, is merely a prediction of what the Jews would do: for when the prophetic declaration was fulfilled, Jesus Christ quoted the passage and explained its general sense in Matt. xiii. 15.

8. As symbolic actions and prophetic visions greatly resemble parables, and were employed for the same purpose, viz.: more powerfully to instruct and engage the attention of the people, they must be interpreted in the same manner as parables. (For which, see pp. 136—138, *supra*.)

II. Observations on the Accomplishment of Scripture Prophecies.

A prophecy is demonstrated to be fulfilled, when we can prove from unimpeachable authority, that the event has actually taken place, precisely according to the manner in which it was foretold.

1. The same prophecies frequently have a double meaning, and refer to different events, the one near, the other remote, the one temporal, the other spiritual, or perhaps eternal. The prophets thus having several events in view, their expressions may be partly applicable to one, and partly to another, and it is not always easy to mark the transitions. What has not been fulfilled in the first, we must apply to the second; and what has already been fulfilled, may often be considered as typical of what remains to be accomplished.

The following examples, out of many which might be offered, will illustrate this rule:

[i.] The second psalm is primarily an inauguration hymn, composed by David, the anointed of Jehovah, when crowned with victory, and placed triumphant on the sacred hill of Sion. But, in Acts iv. 25, the inspired apostles with one voice declare it to be descriptive of the exaltation of the Messiah, and of the opposition raised against the Gospel, both by Jews and Gentiles.

[ii.) Isa. xi. 6.—What is here said of the wolf dwelling with the lamb, &c., is understood as having its *first* completion in the reign of Hezekiah, when profound peace was enjoyed after the troubles caused by Sennacherib; but its *second* and full completion is under the Gospel, whose power in changing the hearts, tempers, and lives of the worst of men, is here foretold and described by a singularly beautiful assemblage of images. Of this blessed power there has in every age of Christianity been a cloud of witnesses.

Thus, it is evident that many prophecies *must be taken in a double sense*, in order to understand their full import; and as this twofold application of them was adopted by our Lord and his apostles, it is a full authority for us to consider and apply them in a similar way.

2. Predictions, denouncing judgments to come, do not in themselves speak the absolute futurity of the event, but only declare what is to be expected by the persons to whom they are made, and what will certainly come to pass, unless God in his mercy interpose between the threatening and the event.

Of these conditional comminatory predictions we have examples in Jonah's preaching to the Ninevites (Jonah iii. 4—10,) and in Isaiah's denunciation of death to Hezekiah. (Isa. xxxviii. 1.) See also a similar instance in Jer. xxxviii. 14—23.

III. Observations on the accomplishment of Prophecies concerning the MESSIAH in particular.

1. Jesus Christ being the great subject and end of Scripture revelation, we ought every where to search for prophecies concerning him.

We have the united testimony of Christ (John v. 39. Luke xxiv. 25—27. 44,) and of an inspired apostle, (Acts x. 43,) that he is the subject of Scripture prophecy. Whatever therefore is emphatically and characteristically spoken of some other person, not called by his own name, in the psalms or prophetical books, so that each predicate can be fully demonstrated in no single subject of that or any other time, must be taken and said of the Messiah. Psalm xxii. and Isa. liii. may be adduced as an illustration of this rule.

2. The interpretation of the word of prophecy, made by Jesus Christ himself, and by his inspired apostles, is a rule and key by which to interpret correctly the prophecies cited or alluded to by them.

The prophecy (in Isa. viii. 14,) that the Messiah would prove a stone of stumbling and a rock of offence, is more plainly repeated by Simeon (Luke ii. 34,) and is shown to have been fulfilled by St. Paul (Rom. ix. 32, 33,) and by St. Peter, (1 Pet. ii. 8;) and the sixteenth psalm is expressly applied to Jesus Christ by the latter of these apostles. (Acts ii. 25—31.)

3. Where the prophets describe a golden age of felicity, they clearly foretell Gospel times.

Many passages might be adduced from the prophetic writings in confirmation of this rule. It will however suffice to adduce two instances from Isaiah, ch. ix. 2—7, and xi. 1—9. In the former of these passages, the peaceful kingdom of the Messiah is set forth, its extent and duration; and in the latter, the singular peace and happiness which should then prevail, are delineated in imagery of unequalled beauty and energy.

4. Things, foretold as universally or indefinitely to come to pass under the Gospel, are not to be understood,—as they respect the duty,—of all persons; but,—as they respect the event,—only of God's people.

The highly figurative expressions in Isa. ii. 4, xi. 6, and lxv. 25, are to be understood of the nature, design, and tendency of the Gospel, and what is the duty of all its professors, and what would actually take place in the Christian world, if all who profess the Christian doctrine did sincerely and cordially obey its dictates.

5. As the ancient prophecies concerning the Messiah are of two kinds, some of them relating to his first coming to suffer, while the rest of them concern his second coming to advance his kingdom, and restore the Jews; in all these prophecies, we must carefully distinguish between his first coming in humiliation to accomplish his mediatorial work on the cross, and his second coming in glory to judgment.

In studying the prophetic writings, the two following cautions should uniformly be kept in view, viz.:

1. That we do not apply passing events, as actually fulfilling particular prophecies.

2. That we do not curiously pry beyond what is expressly written, or describe, as fulfilled, prophecies which are yet future. What the Bible hath declared, that *we* may without hesitation declare: beyond this all is mere vague conjecture.

CHAPTER V

ON THE DOCTRINAL, MORAL, AND PRACTICAL INTERPRETATION OF SCRIPTURE.

SECTION I.—On the Doctrinal Interpretation of Scripture.

As the Holy Scriptures contain the revealed will of God to man, they not only offer to our attention the most interesting histories and characters for our instruction by example, and the most sublime prophecies for the confirmation of our faith, but they likewise present, to our serious study, *doctrinal truths* of the utmost importance. Some of these occur in the historical, poetical, and prophetical parts of the Bible: but they are chiefly to be found in the apostolic epistles, which, though originally designed for the edification of particular Christian churches or individuals, are nevertheless of *general application, and designed for the guidance of the universal church in every age.* For many of the fundamental doctrines of Christianity are more copiously treated in the epistles, which are not so particularly explained in the gospels: and as the authors of the several epistles, wrote under the same divine inspiration as the evangelists, the epistles and gospels must be taken together, to complete the rule of Christian faith. The doctrinal interpretation, therefore, of the sacred writings is of paramount consequence: as by this means we are enabled to acquire a correct and saving knowledge of the will of God concerning us. In the prosecution of this important branch of sacred literature, the following observations are offered to the attention of the student:

1. The meaning of the sacred writings is not to be determined according to modern notions and systems: but we must endeavour to carry ourselves back to the very times and places in which they were written, and realize the ideas and modes of thinking of the sacred writers.

This rule is of the utmost importance for understanding the Scriptures but is too commonly neglected by commentators and expositors, who, when applying themselves to the explanation of the sacred writings, have a preconceived system of doctrine, which they seek in the Bible, and to which they refer every passage of Scripture. Thus they rather draw the Scriptures to *their* system of doctrine, than bring their doctrines to the standard of Scripture; a mode of interpretation which is altogether unjust, and utterly useless in the attainment of truth. The only way by which to understand the meaning of the sacred writers, and to distinguish between true and false doctrines, is, to lay aside all preconceived modern notions and systems, and to carry ourselves back to the very times and places in which the prophets and apostles wrote. In perusing the Bible, therefore, this rule must be most carefully attended to. It is only an unbiassed mind that can attain the true and genuine sense of Scripture.

2. In order to understand any doctrinal book or passage of Scripture, we must attend to the controversies which were agitated at that time, and to which the sacred writers allude: for a key to the apostolic epistles is not to be sought in the modern controversies that divide Christians, and which were not only unknown but, also, were not in existence at that time.

The controversies, which were discussed in the age of the apostles, are to be ascertained, partly from their writings, partly from the existing monuments of the primitive Christians, and likewise from some passages in the writings of the Rabbins. The most important passages of this kind are to be found in almost all the larger commentators.

3. The doctrinal books of Scripture, for instance, the Epistles, are not to be perused in detached portions or sections; but they should be read through at once, with a close attention to the scope and tenor of the discourse, regardless of the divisions into chapters and verses, precisely in the same manner in which we would peruse the letters of Cicero, Pliny, or other ancient writers.

Want of attention to the general scope and design of the doctrinal parts of Scripture, particularly of the epistles, has been the source of many and great errors: the reading, however, which is here recommended, should not be cursory or casual, but frequent and diligent; and the Epistles should be repeatedly perused, until we become intimately acquainted with their contents. On the investigation of the Scope, see p. 116, *supra*.

4. Where any doctrine is to be deduced from the Scriptures, it will be collected better, and with more precision, from those places in which it is professedly discussed, than from those in which it is noticed only incidentally, or by way of inference.

For instance, in the Epistles to the Romans and Galatians, the doctrine of justification by faith is fully treated: and in those to the Ephesians and Colossians, the calling of the Gentiles and the abrogation of the ceremonial law are particularly illustrated. These must therefore be diligently compared together, in order to deduce those doctrines correctly.

5. Distinguish figurative expressions from such as are proper and literal; and when easy and natural interpretations offer themselves, avoid all those interpretations which deduce astonishing and incredible doctrines.

6. It is of great importance to the understanding of the doctrinal books of the New Testament, to attend to and distinctly note the transitions of persons which frequently occur, especially in Saint Paul's Epistles.

The pronouns *I*, *We*, and *You*, are used by the apostles in such a variety of applications, that the understanding of their true meaning is often a key to many difficult passages. Thus, by the pronoun *I*, Saint Paul sometimes means himself, sometimes any Christian; sometimes a Jew; and sometimes any man, &c. To discover these transitions requires great attention to the apostle's scope and argument; and yet, if it be neglected or overlooked, it will cause the reader greatly to mistake and misunderstand his meaning, and will also render the sense very perplexed. Mr. Locke, and Dr. Macknight, in their elaborate works on the Epistles, are particularly useful in pointing out these various transitions of persons and subjects.

7. No article of faith can be established from metaphors, parables, or single obscure and figurative texts.

Instead of deriving our knowledge of Christianity from parables and figurative passages, *an intimate acquaintance with the doctrines of the Gospel is necessary, in order to be capable of interpreting them.* The beautiful parable of the man who fell among thieves, (Luke x. 30—37,) is evidently intended to influence the Jews to be benevolent and kind like the good Samaritan, and nothing more. And yet, regardless of every principle of sound interpretation, that parable has by some writers been considered as a representation of Adam's fall, and of man's recovery, through the interposition and love of Jesus Christ!

SECTION II.—On the Moral Interpretation of Scripture.

The moral Parts of Scripture are replete with the most important instructions for the government of life. They are to be interpreted precisely in the same manner as all other moral writings; regard being had to the peculiar circumstances of the sacred writers, viz.: the age in which they wrote, the nation to which they belonged, their style, genius, &c. In the examination of the moral parts of Scripture, the following more particular rules will be found useful.

1. Moral propositions or discourses are not to be urged too far, but must be understood with a certain degree of latitude, and with various limitations.

For want of attending to this canon, how many moral truths have been pushed to an extent, which causes them altogether to fail of the effect they were designed to produce! It is not to be denied that universal propositions may be offered: such are frequent in the Scriptures as well as in profane writers, and also in common life; but it is in explaining the expressions by which they are conveyed, that just limits ought to be applied, to prevent them from being urged too far. The nature of the thing, and various other circumstances, will always afford a criterion by which to understand moral propositions with the requisite limitations.

2. Principals include their accessaries, that is, whatever approaches or comes near to them, or has any tendency to them.

Thus, where any sin is forbidden, we must be careful not only to avoid it, but also every thing of a similar nature, and whatever may prove an occasion of it, or imply our consent to it in others: and we must endeavour to dissuade or restrain others from it. Compare Matt. v. 21—31. 1 Thess. v. 22. Jude 23. Ephes. v. 11. 1 Cor. viii. 13. Levit. xix. 17

James v. 19, 20. So, where any duty is enjoined, all means and facilities, enabling either ourselves or others to discharge it, according to our respective places, capacities, or opportunities, are likewise enjoined.

3. Negatives include affirmatives, and affirmatives include negatives: in other words, where any duty is enjoined, the contrary sin is forbidden; and where any sin is forbidden, the contrary duty is enjoined.

Thus, in Deut. vi. 13, where we are commanded to serve God, w[illegible]re forbidden to serve any other. Therefore, in Matt. iv. 10, it is said, [illegible]m *only* shalt thou serve.

4. Negatives are binding at all times, but not affirmatives; that is, we must never do that which is forbidden, though good may ultimately come from it. (Rom. iii. 8.) We must not speak wickedly for God. (Job xiii. 7.)

5. When an action is either required or commended, or any promise is annexed to its performance; such action is supposed to be done from proper motives and in a proper manner.

The giving of alms may be mentioned as an instance; which, if done from ostentatious motives, we are assured, is displeasing in the sight of God. Compare Matt. vi. 1.—4.

6. When the favour of God, or salvation, is promised to any deed or duty, all the other duties of religion are supposed to be rightly performed.

7. When a certain state or condition is pronounced blessed, or any promise is annexed to it, a suitable disposition of mind is supposed to prevail.

Thus, when the poor or afflicted are pronounced to be blessed, it is because such persons, being poor and afflicted, are free from the sins usually attendant on unsanctified prosperity, and because they are, on the contrary, more humble and more obedient to God. If, however, they be not the *characters* described, (as unquestionably there are many to whom the characters do not apply,) the promise in that case does not belong to them. *Vice versa*, when any state is pronounced to be wretched, it is on account of the sins or vices which generally attend it.

8. Some precepts of moral prudence are given in the Scriptures, which nevertheless admit of exceptions, on account of some duties of benevolence or piety that ought to preponderate.

We may illustrate this rule by the often-repeated counsels of Solomon respecting becoming surety for another. (See Prov. vi. 1, 2, xi. 15, xvii. 18, and xx. 16.) In these passages he does not condemn suretyship, which, in many cases, is not only lawful, but, in same instances, even an act of justice, prudence, and charity; but Solomon forbids his disciple to become surety *rashly*, without considering for whom, or how far he binds himself, or how he could discharge the debt, if occasion should require it.

Section III.—On the Interpretation of the Promises and Threatenings of Scripture.

1. Distinction between Promises and Threatenings

A promise, in the Scriptural sense of the term, is a

declaration or assurance of the divine will, in which God signifies what particular blessings or good things he will freely bestow, as well as the evils which he will remove. The *promises*, therefore, differ from the *threatenings* of God, inasmuch as the former are declarations concerning good, while the latter are denunciations of evil only: at the same time it is to be observed, that promises seem to include threats, because, being in their very nature *conditional*, they imply the bestowment of the blessing promised, only on the condition being performed, which blessing is *tacitly* threatened to be withheld on non-compliance with such condition. Further, promises differ from the *commands* of God, because the latter are significations of the divine will concerning a *duty* enjoined to be performed, while promises relate to *mercy* to be received.

There are four classes of promises mentioned in the Scriptures, particularly in the New Testament; viz.: 1. Promises relating to the Messiah; 2. Promises relating to the church; 3. Promises of blessings, both temporal and spiritual, to the pious; and, 4. Promises encouraging to the exercise of the several graces and duties that compose the Christian character. The two first of these classes, indeed, are many of them *predictions* as well as promises; consequently the same observations will apply to them, as are stated for the interpretation of Scripture prophecies: but in regard to those promises which are directed to particular persons, or to the performance of particular duties, the following remarks are offered to the attention of the reader.

1. "We must receive God's promises in such wise as they be generally set forth in the Holy Scripture." (Art. xvii.)

To *us* the promises of God are general and conditional: if, therefore, they be not fulfilled towards us, we may rest assured that the fault does not rest with Him, "who cannot lie," but with ourselves, who have failed in complying with the conditions, either tacitly, or expressly, annexed to them.

2. Such promises as were made in one case, may be applied in other cases of the same nature, consistently with the analogy of faith.

It is in promises as in commands; they do not exclusively concern those to whom they were first made; but being inserted in the Scriptures, they are made of public benefit: for, "whatsoever things were written aforetime, were written for our use; that we, through patience, and comfort of the Scriptures, might have hope." (Rom. xv. 4.) Thus, what was spoken to Joshua, (ch. i. 5,) on his going up against the Canaanites, lest he should be discouraged in that enterprise, is applied by St. Paul to the believing Hebrews, (Heb. xiii. 5,) as a remedy against covetousness, or inordinate cares concerning the things of this life; it being a very comprehensive promise, that God will never fail us, nor forsake us. But if we were to apply the promises contained in Psal. xciv. 14, and Jer. xxxii. 40, and John x. 28, as promises of *indefectible* grace, to believers, we should violate every rule of sober interpretation, as well as the analogy of faith.

3. God has suited his promises to his precepts.

By his *precepts* we see what is our *duty*, and what should be the *scope of our endeavours;* and by his *promises* we see what is our *inability*, what should be the *matter, or object of our prayers*, and where we may be supplied with that grace which will enable us to discharge our duty. Compare Deut. x. 16, with Deut. xxx. 6. Eccles. xii. 13, with Jer. xxxii. 40. Ezek. xviii. 31, with Ezek. xxxvi. 37, and Rom. vi. 12, with v. 14.

4. Where any thing is promised in case of obedience, the threatening of the contrary is implied in case of disobedience: and where there is a threatening of any thing in case of disobedience, a promise of the contrary is implied, upon condition of obedience.

In illustration of this remark, it will be sufficient to refer to, and compare Exod. xx. 7, with Psal. xv. 1—4, and xxiv. 3, 4, and Exod. xx. 12, with Prov. xxx. 17.

Section IV.—On the Practical Reading of Scripture.

The sense of Scripture having been explained and ascertained, it only remains that we apply it to purposes of practical utility; which may be effected either by deducing inferences from texts, or by practically applying the Scriptures to our personal edification and salvation: for, if serious contemplation of the Scriptures and *practice* be united together, our real knowledge of the Bible must necessarily be increased, and will be rendered, progressively, more delightful. This practical reading may be prosecuted by *every one*, with advantage: for the application of Scripture, which it recommends is connected with our highest interest and happiness.

The simplest practical application of the word of God, will, unquestionably, prove the most beneficial; provided it be conducted with a due regard to those moral qualifications which have already been stated and enforced, as necessary to the right understanding of the Scriptures. Should, however, any hints be required, the following may, perhaps, be consulted with advantage.

1. In reading the Scriptures, then, with a view to personal application, we should be careful that it be done with a pure intention.

He, however, who peruses the sacred volume, merely for the purpose of amusing himself with the histories it contains, or of beguiling time, or to tranquillize his conscience by the discharge of a mere external duty, is deficient in the *motive* with which he performs that duty, and cannot expect to derive from it either advantage, or comfort, amid the trials of life. Neither will it suffice to read the Scriptures, with the mere design of becoming intimately acquainted with sacred truths, unless such reading be accompanied with a desire, that, through them, he may be convinced of his self-love, ambition, or other faults, to which he may be peculiarly exposed; and that by the assistance of divine grace, he may be enabled to eradicate them from his mind.

2. In reading the Scriptures for this purpose, it will be advisable to select some appropriate lessons from its most useful parts; not being particularly solicitous about the exact connexion, or other critical niceties that may occur, (though at other times, as ability and opportunity offer, these are highly proper objects of inquiry,) but simply considering them in a devotional, or practical view.

After ascertaining, therefore, the plain and obvious meaning of the lesson under examination, we should first consider the present state of our minds, and carefully compare it with the passage in question: next, we should inquire into the causes of those faults, which such perusal may have disclosed to us; and should then look around for suitable remedies to correct the faults we have thus discovered.

3. In every practical reading, and application of the Scriptures to ourselves, our attention should be fixed on Jesus Christ, both as a *gift* to be received by faith, for salvation, and also as an *exemplar*, to be copied and imitated in our lives.

We are not, however, to imitate him in all things. Some things he did by his divine power, and in those we *cannot* imitate him: other things he performed by his sovereign authority, in those we *must not* imitate him: other things also he performed by virtue of his office as a Mediator; and in these, we *may not*, we *cannot* follow him. But, in his early piety, his obedience to his reputed earthly parents—his unwearied diligence in doing good, his humility, his unblameable conduct, his self denial, his contentment under low circumstances, his frequency in private prayer, his affectionate thankfulness, his compassion to the wretched, his holy and edifying discourse, his free conversation, his patience, his readiness to forgive injuries, his sorrow for the sins of others, his zeal for the worship of God, his glorifying his heavenly Father, his impartiality in administering reproof, his universal obedience, and his love and practice of holiness—in all these instances, Jesus Christ is the most perfect pattern for our imitation.

4. We should carefully distinguish between what the Scripture itself says, and what is only said in the Scripture, and also, the times, places, and persons, when, where, and by whom any thing is recorded as having been said or done.

In Mal. iii. 14, we meet with the following words: "It is in vain to serve God; and what profit is it that we have kept his ordinance?" And in 1 Cor. xv. 32, we meet with this maxim of profane men—"Let us eat and drink, for to-morrow we die." But, when we read these, and similar passages, we must attend to the characters introduced, and remember that the persons who spoke thus were wicked men. Even those, whose piety is commended in the sacred volume, did not always act in strict conformity to it. Thus, when David vowed that he would utterly destroy Nabal's house, we must conclude that he sinned in making that vow: and the discourses of Job's friends, though in themselves extremely beautiful and instructive, are not, in *every* respect, to be approved; for we are informed by the sacred historian, that God was wroth with them, because they had not spoken of him the thing that was right. (Job xlii. 7.)

5. As every *good* example, recorded in the Scriptures, has the force of a rule, so when we read therein of the *failings*, as well as of the sinful actions of men, we may see what is in our own nature: for there are in us the seeds of the same sin, and similar tendencies to its commission, which would bring forth similar fruits, were it not for the preventing and renewing grace of God. And as many of the persons, whose faults are related in the volume of inspiration, were men of infinitely more elevated piety than ourselves, we should learn from them not only to "*be not high-minded, but fear*," (Rom. xi. 20;) but further, to avoid being rash in censuring the conduct of others.

The *occasions* of their declensions are likewise deserving of our attention, as well as the temptations to which they were exposed; and whether they did not neglect to watch over their thoughts, words, and actions, or trust too much to their own strength (as in the case of Peter's denial of Christ;) what were the means that led to their penitence and recovery, and how they demeaned themselves after they had repented. By a due observation, therefore, of their *words and actions*, and of the *temper of their minds*, so far as this is manifested by words and actions, we shall be better enabled to judge of our *real* progress in religious knowledge, than by those characters which are given of holy men, in the Scriptures, without such observation of the tenor of their lives, and the frame of their minds.

6. In reading the promises and threatenings, the exhortations and admonitions, and other parts of Scripture, we should apply them to ourselves, in such a manner as if they had been personally addressed to us.

For instance, are we reading any of the prophetic Sermons? Let us so read and consider them, and, as it were, identify ourselves with the times and persons, when, and to whom such prophetic discourses were delivered, as if they were our fellow-countrymen, fellow-citizens, &c., whom Isaiah, Jeremiah, Ezekiel, and other prophets rebuke, in some chapters, while in others they labour to convince them of their sinful ways, and to convert them, or in the event of their continuing disobedient, denounce the divine judgments against them. So, in all the precepts of Christian virtue, recorded in Matt. v. vi. and vii, we should consider ourselves to be as nearly and particularly concerned, as if we had personally heard them delivered by Jesus Christ on the Mount. Independently, therefore, of the light which will thus be thrown upon the prophetic, or other portions of Scripture, much *practical* instruction will be efficiently obtained; for, by this mode of reading the Scriptures, the promises addressed to others, will encourage us; the denunciations against others, will deter us from the commission of sin; the exhortations delivered to others, will excite us to the diligent performance of our duty, and, finally, admonitions to others will make us walk circumspectly.

7. The words of the passage selected for our private reading, after its import has been ascertained, may beneficially be summed up, or comprised in very brief prayers or ejaculations.

The advantage resulting from this simple method has been proved by many, who have recommended it. If we pray over the substance of Scripture, with our Bible before us, it may impress the memory and heart the more deeply. Should any references to the Scriptures be required, in confirmation of this statement, we would briefly notice, that the following passages, among many others that might be cited, will, by addressing them to God, and, by a slight change also in the person, become admirable petitions for divine teaching; viz.: Col. i. 9, 10. Eph. i. 17, 18, 19. 1 Pet. ii. 1, 2. The hundred and nineteenth Psalm contains numerous similar passages.

8. In the practical reading of the Scriptures, all things are not to be applied at once, but gradually and successively; and this application must be made, not so much with the view of supplying us with materials for talking, as with matter for practice.

Finally, this practical reading and application must be diligently continued through life; and we may, with the assistance of divine grace, reasonably hope for success in it, if to reading we add constant *prayer*, and *meditation* on what we have read. With these we are further to conjoin a perpetual comparison of the sacred writings; daily observation of what takes place in ourselves, as well as what we learn from the experience of others; a strict and vigilant self-examination; together with frequent conversation with men of learning and piety, who have made greater progress in saving knowledge; and lastly, the diligent cultivation of internal peace.

Other observations might be offered; but the preceding hints, if duly considered and acted upon, will make us "neither barren nor unfruitful in the knowledge of our Lord Jesus Christ." (2 Pet. i. 8.) And if, to some of his readers, the author should *appear* to have dilated too much on so obvious a topic, its *importance* must be his apology. Whatever relates to the confirmation of our faith, the improvement of our morals, or the elevation of our affections, ought not to be treated lightly or with indifference.

PART III.

A COMPENDIUM OF BIBLICAL GEOGRAPHY AND ANTIQUITIES.

BOOK I.—1. A SKETCH OF THE GEOGRAPHY OF THE HOLY LAND.

CHAPTER I.

HISTORICAL GEOGRAPHY OF THE HOLY LAND

Grotto *at* Nazareth, *said to have been the House of* Joseph and Mary.

THIS country has, in different ages, been called by various NAMES, which have been derived either from its inhabitants, or from the extraordinary circumstances attached to it. Thus in Jer. iv. 20, it is termed generally the *land:* and hence, both in the Old and New Testament, the original word, which is sometimes rendered *earth, land*, or *country*, is by the context, in many places, determined to mean the promised land of Israel; as in Josh. ii. 3, Matt. v. 5, and Luke iv. 25. But the country occupied by the Hebrews, Israelites, and Jews, is, in the sacred volume, more particularly called

1. The *Land of Canaan*, from Canaan, the youngest son of Ham, and grandson of Noah, who settled here after the confusion of Babel, and divided the country among his eleven children. (Gen. xi. 15. *et seq.*)

2. The *Land of Promise*, (Heb. xi. 9,) from the pro mise made by Jehovah to Abraham, that his posterity should possess it, (Gen. xii. 7, and xiii. 15;) who being termed Hebrews, this region was thence called the *Land of the Hebrews*. (Gen. xl. 15.)

3. The *Land of Israel*, from the Israentes, or posterity of Jacob, having settled themselves there. This name is of most frequent occurrence in the Old Testament: it is also to be found in the New Testament, (as in Matt. ii. 20, 21.) Within this extent lay all the provinces or countries visited by Jesus Christ, except Egypt, and consequently almost all the places mentioned, or referred to in the four Gospels. After the separation of the ten tribes, that portion of the land which belonged to the tribes of Judah and Benjamin, who formed a separate kingdom, was distinguished by the appellation of Judæa, or the land of *Judah*, (Psal. lxxvi. 1;) which name the whole country retained during the existence of the second temple, and under the dominion of the Romans.

4. The *Holy Land*, which appellation is to this day conferred on it by all Christians, as having been hallowed by the presence, actions, miracles, discourses, and sufferings of Jesus Christ. This name is also to be found in the Old Testament, (Zech. ii. 12,) and in the Apocryphal books of Wisdom (xii. 3,) and 2 Maccabees, (i. 7.) The whole world was divided by the ancient Jews into two general parts, *the land of Israel*, and the *land out of Israel*, that is, all the countries inhabited by the *nations of the world*, or the Gentiles; to this distinction there seems to be an allusion in Matt. vi. 32. All the rest of the world, together with its inhabitants, (Judæa excepted,) was accounted as profane, *polluted*, and *unclean*, (see Isa. xxxv. 8, lii. 1, with Joel iii. 17, Amos vii. 7, and Acts x. 1;)

but, though the whole land of Israel was regarded as *holy*, as being the place consecrated to the worship of God, and the inheritance of his people, whence they are collectively styled *saints*, and a holy nation or people, (in Exod. xix. 6. Deut. vii. 6, xiv. 2, xxvi. 19, xxxiii. 3. 2 Chron. vi. 41. Psal. xxxiv. 9, l. 5. 7, lxxix. 2, and cxlviii. 4,) yet the Jews imagined particular parts to be vested with more than ordinary sanctity, according to their respective situations. Thus the parts situated beyond Jordan were considered to be less holy than those on this side; walled towns were supposed to be more clean and holy than other places, because no lepers were admissible into them, and the dead were not allowed to be buried there. Even the very dust of the land of Israel was reputed to possess such a peculiar degree of sanctity, that when the Jews returned from any heathen country, they stopped at its borders, and wiped the dust of it from their shoes, lest the sacred inheritance should be polluted with it; nor would they suffer even herbs to be brought to them, from the ground of their Gentile neighbours, lest they should bring any of the mould with them, and thus defile their pure land. To this notion, our Lord unquestionably alluded when he commanded his disciples to shake off the dust of their feet, (Matt. x. 14,) on returning from any house or city that would neither receive nor hear them; thereby intimating to them, that when the Jews had rejected the Gospel, they were no longer to be regarded as the people of God, but were on a level with heathens and idolaters.

5. The appellation of ***Palestine***, by which the whole land appears to have been called, in the days of Moses, (Exod. xv. 14,) is derived from the Philistines, a people who migrated from Egypt, and, having expelled the aboriginal inhabitants, settled on the borders of the Mediterranean; where they became so considerable as to give their name to the whole country, though they in fact possessed only a small part of it. The Philistines were, for a long time, the most formidable enemies of the children of Israel; but about the year of the world 3841, (B. C. 159,) the illustrious Judas Maccabeus subdued their country; and about sixty-five years afterward Jannæus burnt their city Gaza, and incorporated the remnant of the Philistines with such Jews as he placed in their country.

The BOUNDARIES of the land promised to Abraham are, in Gen. xv. 18, stated to be *from the river of Egypt unto the great river, the river Euphrates.* Of this tract, however, the Israelites were not immediately put in possession: and although the limits of their territories were extended under the reigns of David and Solomon, (2 Sam viii. 3. et seq. 2 Chron. ix. 26,) yet they did not always retain that tract. It lies far within the temperate zone, and between 31 and 33 degrees of north latitude, and was bounded on the west by the Mediterranean or Great Sea, as it is often called in the Scriptures; on the east by Arabia; on the south by the river of Egypt, (or the river Nile, whose eastern branch was reckoned the boundary of Egypt, towards the great desert of Shur, which lies between Egypt and Palestine,) and by the Desert of Sin, or Beersheba, the southern shore of the Dead Sea, and the river Arnon; and on the north by the chain of mountains termed Antilibanus, near which stood the city of Dan: hence, in the sacred writings we frequently meet with the expression, "*from Dan to Beersheba,*" to denote the whole length of the land of Israel.

The land of Canaan, previously to its occupation by the Israelites, was possessed by the descendants of Canaan, the youngest son of Ham, and grandson of Noah; who divided the country among his eleven sons, each of whom was the head of a numerous clan or tribe. (Gen. x. 15—19.) Here they resided upwards of seven centuries, and founded numerous republics and kingdoms. In the days of Abraham, this region was occupied by ten nations; the Kenites, the Kenizzites, and the Kadmonites, to the east of Jordan; and westward, the Hittites, Perizzites, Rephaims, Amorites, Canaanites, Girgashites, and the Jebusites. (Gen. xv. 18—21.) These latter, in the days of Moses, were called the Hittites, Girgashites, Amorites, Canaanites, Perizzites, Hivites, and Jebusites. (Deut. vii. 1. Josh. iii. 10, xxiv. 11.) Besides these devoted nations there were others, either settled in the land, at the arrival of the Israelites, or in its immediate environs, with whom the latter had to maintain many severe conflicts: they were six in number, viz.: the Philistines, the Midianites, or descendants of Midian, the fourth son of Abraham, by Keturah, (Gen. xxv. 2;) the Moabites and Ammonites, who sprang from the incestuous offspring of Lot; (Gen xix. 30—38;) the Amalekites, who were descended from Amalek, the son of Ham, and grandson of Noah; and the Edomites, or descendants of Esau or Edom.

On the conquest of Canaan by the children of Israel, Joshua divided it into twelve parts, which the twelve tribes drew by lot. The tribe of Levi, indeed, possessed no lands: God assigned to the Levites, who were appointed to minister in holy things, without any secular incumbrance, the tenths and first-fruits of the estates of their brethren. Forty-eight cities were appropriated to their residence, thence called Levitical cities; these were dispersed among the twelve tribes, and had their respective suburbs, with land surrounding them. Of these cities the Kohathites received twenty-three, the Gershomites thirteen, and the Merarites twelve; and six of them, three on each side of Jordan, were appointed to be cities of refuge, whither the inadvertant man-slayer might flee, and find an asylum from his pursuers, and be secured from the effects of private revenge, until cleared by a legal process. (Numb. xxxv. 6—15. Deut. xix. 4—10. Josh. xx. 7, 8.) In this division of the land into twelve portions, the posterity of Ephraim and Manasseh (the two sons of Joseph) had their portions as distinct tribes, in consequence of Jacob having adopted them; and these two are reckoned instead of Joseph and Levi. The tribes of Reuben, Gad, and half tribe of Manasseh, had their portion beyond Jordan; the rest settled on this side of the river. Dan was reputed to be the furthest city to the north of the Holy Land, as Beersheba was to the south.

Another division of the Holy Land took place after the death of Solomon, when ten tribes revolted from Rehoboam, and erected themselves into a separate kingdom under Jeroboam. This was called the kingdom of Israel, and its metropolis was Samaria. The other two tribes of Benjamin and Judah, continuing faithful to Rehoboam, formed the kingdom of Judah, whose capital was Jerusalem. But this division ceased on the subversion of the kingdom of Israel by Shalmaneser king of Assyria, after it had subsisted two hundred and fifty-four years, from the year of the world 3030 to 3283. (B. C. 717.)

In the time of Jesus Christ, the whole of this country

was divided into four separate regions, viz. : Judæa, Samaria, Galilee, and Peræ, or the country beyond Jordan.

I. JUDÆA.—Of these regions, Judæa was the most distinguished, comprising the territories which had formerly belonged to the tribes of Judah, Benjamin, Simeon, and part of the tribe of Dan. The southern part of it was called Idumæa, and it extended westward from the Dead Sea to the Great (or Mediterranean) Sea. Its metropolis was Jerusalem, of which a separate notice will be found in a subsequent number: and of the other towns or villages of note, contained in this region, the most remarkable were Arimathea, Azotus, or Ashdod, Bethany, Bethlehem, Bethphage, Emmaus, Ephraim, Gaza, Jericho, Joppa, Lydda, and Rama.

II. SAMARIA.—This division of the Holy Land derives its name from the city of Samaria, and comprises the tract of country which was originally occupied by the two tribes of Ephraim and Manasseh, within Jordan, lying exactly in the middle, between Judæa and Galilee ; so that it was absolutely necessary for persons, who were desirous of going expeditiously from Galilee to Jerusalem, to pass through this country. This sufficiently explains the remark of St. John (iv. 4.) The three chief places of this division noticed in the Scriptures are, Samaria, Sichem, or Schechem, and Antipatris.

III. GALILEE.—This portion of the Holy Land is very frequently mentioned in the New Testament; it exceeded Judæa in extent, but its limits probably varied at different times. It comprised the country formerly occupied by the tribes of Issachar, Zebulun, Naphtali, and Asher, and part of the tribe of Dan ; and is divided by Josephus into Upper and Lower Galilee. Upper Galilee abounded in mountains ; and, from its vicinity to the Gentiles who inhabited the cities of Tyre and Sidon, it is called *Galilee of the Gentiles* (Matt. iv. 15,) and the *coasts of Tyre and Sidon.* (Mark vii. 31.) The principal city in this region was Cæsarea Philippi, through which the main road lay to Damascus, Tyre, and Sidon. Lower Galilee was situated in a rich and fertile plain between the Mediterranean Sea and the lake of Gennesareth ; and, according to Josephus, this district was very populous, containing upwards of two hundred cities and towns.

This country was most honoured by our Saviour's presence. The principal cities of lower Galilee, mentioned in the New Testament, are Tiberias, Capernaum, Chorazin, Bethsaida, Nazareth, Cana, Nain, Cæsarea of Palestine, and Ptolemais.

IV. PERÆA.—This district comprised the six following provinces or cantons, viz.: Abilene, Trachonitis Ituræa, Gaulonitis, Batanea, and Peræa, strictly so called, to which some geographers have added Decapolis. 1. ABILENE was the most northern of these provinces, being situated between the mountains of Libanus and Antilibanus, and deriving its name from the city Abila. It is one of the four tetrarchies mentioned by Saint Luke (iii. 1.) 2. TRACHONITIS was bounded by the desert Arabia on the east, Batanea on the west, Ituræa on the south, and the country of Damascus on the north. It abounded with rocks, which afforded shelter to numerous thieves and robbers. 3. ITURÆA anciently belonged to the half tribe of Manasseh, who settled on the east of Jordan: it stood to the east of Batanea and to the south of Trachonitis. Of these two cantons Philip, the son of Herod the Great, was tetrarch at the time John the Baptist commenced his ministry. (Luke iii. 1.) It derived its name from Jetur, the son of Ishmael, (1 Chron. i. 31,) and was also called Auranitis from the city of Hauran. (Ezek. xlvii. 16. 18.) 4. GAULONITIS was a tract on the east side of the lake of Gennesareth, and the river Jordan, which derived its name from Gaulan or Golan the city of Og, king of Bashan. (Josh. xx. 8.) This canton is not mentioned in the New Testament. 5. BATANEA, the ancient kingdom of Bashan, was situated to the north-east of Gaulonitis: its limits are not easy to be defined. It was part of the territory given to Herod Antipas and is not noticed in the New Testament. 6. PERÆA, in its restricted sense, includes the southern part of the country beyond Jordan, lying south of Ituræa, east of Judeæ and Samaria; and was anciently possessed by the two tribes of Reuben and Gad. Its principal place was the strong fortress of Machærus, erected for the purpose of checking the predatory incursions of the Arabs. This fortress, though not specified by name in the New Testament, is memorable as the place where John the Baptist was put to death. (Matt

xiv. 3—12.) The canton of DECAPOLIS, (Matt. iv. 25. Mark v. 20, and vii. 31,) which derives its name from the ten cities it contained, was part of the region of Peræa. Concerning its limits, and the names of its ten cities, geographers are by no means agreed : among them, however, we may safely reckon Gadara, where our Saviour wrought some miracles, and perhaps Damascus, chiefly celebrated for the conversion of Saint Paul, which took place in its vicinity. Of the whole country thus described, JERUSALEM was the metropolis during the reigns of David and Solomon; after the secession of the ten tribes, it was the capital of the kingdom of Judah, but during the time of Christ, and until the subversion of the Jewish polity, it was the metropolis of Palestine.

Jerusalem is frequently styled in the Scriptures the *Holy City*, (Isa. xlviii. 2. Dan. ix. 24. Nehem. xi. 1. Matt. iv. 5. Rev. xi. 2,) because *the Lord chose it out of all the tribes of Israel to place his name there*, his temple and his worship; (Deut. xii. 5, xiv. 23, xvi. 2, xxvi. 2;) and to be the centre of union in religion and government for all the tribes of the commonwealth of Israel. It is held in the highest veneration by Christians for the miraculous and important transactions which happened there and also by the Mahommedans, who to this day never call it by any other appellation than *El-Kods*, or the Holy, sometimes adding the epithet *El-Sheriff*, or The Noble. The original name of the city was *Salem*, or Peace: (Gen. xiv. 18:) the import of Jerusalem is, the vision or inheritance of peace; and to this it is not improbable that our Saviour alluded in his beautiful and pathetic lamentation over the city. (Luke xix. 41.) It was also formerly called Jebus from one of the sons of Canaan. (Josh. xviii. 28.) After its capture by Joshua, (Josh. x.) it was jointly inhabited both by Jews and Jebusites (Josh. xv. 63,) for about five hundred years, until the time of David; who, having expelled the Jebusites, made it his residence, (2 Sam. v. 6—9,) and erected a noble palace there, together with several other magnificent buildings, whence it is sometimes styled the *City of David*. (1 Chron. xi. 5.)

Jerusalem, after its destruction by the Chaldæans, was rebuilt by the Jews, on their return from the Babylonish captivity. The city was built on three principal hills; viz.: 1. *Sion*, on the southern side, which was the highest, and contained the citadel, the king's palace, and the upper city. 2. *Moriah*, on which was the temple, a smaller eminence on the east of the northern part of Sion, and separated from it by a valley, over which was a bridge; and 3. *Acra*, so called in a later age, lying north of Sion, and covered by the lower city, which was the most considerable portion of the whole metropolis.

On the south side stood the mount of Corruption, where Solomon, in his declining years, built temples to Moloch, Chemosh, and Ashtaroth. (1 Kings. xi. 7. 2 Kings xxiii. 13.)

Towards the west, and without the walls of the city, agreeably to the law of Moses, (Levit. iv,) lay mount Calvary or Golgotha, that is, the place of a skull. (Matt. xxvii. 33.)

During the time of our Saviour, Jerusalem was adorned with numerous edifices, some of which are mentioned or alluded to in the New Testament; but its chief glory was the Temple, (described in a subsequent page,) which magnificent and extensive structure occupied the northern and lower eminence of Sion, as we learn from the Psalmist, (xlviii. 2.) *Beautiful for situation, the delight of the whole earth, is Mount Sion. On her north side is the city of the great king.*

Next to the temple in point of splendour, was the very superb palace of Herod, which is largely described by Josephus; it afterwards became the residence of the Roman procurators, who for this purpose generally claimed the royal palaces in those provinces which were subject to kings. These dwellings of the Roman procurators in the provinces were called *prætoria:* Herod's palace therefore was Pilate's prætorium: (Matt. xxvii. 27. John xviii. 28:) and in some part of this edifice was the armoury or barrack of the Roman soldiers that garrisoned Jerusalem, whither Jesus was conducted and mocked by them. (Matt. xxvii. 27. Mark xv. 16.) In the front of this palace was the tribunal, where Pilate sat in a judicial capacity to hear and determine weighty causes: being a raised pavement of Mosaic work, (λιθοςρωτον, *lithostrotōn*,) the evangelist informs us, that in the Hebrew language it was on this account termed *gabbatha*, (John xix. 13,) i. e. an elevated place. On a steep rock, adjoining the north-west corner of the Temple, stood the *Tower of Antonia*, a strong citadel, in which a Roman legion was always quartered. It overlooked the two outer courts of the temple, and communicated with its cloisters by means of secret passages, through which the military could descend and quell any tumult that might arise during the great festivals. This was the guard to which Pilate alluded in Matt. xxviii. 65. The tower of Antonia was thus named by Herod, in honour of his friend Mark Antony: and this citadel is the castle into which St. Paul was conducted, (Acts xxi. 34, 35,) and of which mention is made in Acts xxii. 24. As the temple was a fortress that guarded the whole city of Jerusalem, so the tower of Antonia was a guard that entirely commanded the temple. According to the Jewish Historian, Josephus, the circumference of Jerusalem, previously to its being besieged and destroyed by the Roman army, was thirty-three furlongs, or nearly four miles and a half: and the wall of circumvallation, constructed by order of the Roman general, Titus, he states to have been thirty-nine furlongs, or four miles eight hundred and seventy-five paces.

During the reigns of David and Solomon, Jerusalem was the metropolis of the land of Israel; but, after the defection of the ten tribes under Jeroboam, it was the capital of the kings of Judah, during whose government it underwent various revolutions. It was captured four times without being demolished, viz.: by Shishak, sovereign of Egypt, (2 Chron. xii,) from whose ravages it never recovered its former splendour; by Antiochus Epiphanes, who treated the Jews with singular barbarity; by Pompey the Great, who rendered the Jews tributary to Rome; and by Herod, with the assistance of a Roman force under Sosius. It was first entirely destroyed by Nebuchadnezzar, and again by the emperor Titus, the repeated insurrections of the turbulent Jews having filled up the measure of their iniquities, and drawn down upon them the implacable vengeance of the Romans Titus ineffectually endeavoured to save the temple: it was involved in the same ruin with the rest of the city, and, after it had been reduced to ashes, the foundations of that sacred edifice were ploughed up by the Roman soldiers. Thus literally was fulfilled the prediction of our Lord, that not one stone should be left upon another that should not be thrown down. (Matt. xxiv. 2.) On his return to Rome, Titus was honoured with a triumph; and, to commemorate his conquest of Judæa, a triumphal arch was erected, which is still in existence. Numerous medals of Judæa vanquished were struck in honour of the same event. A representation of one of these is given in page 23. *supra.*

The emperor Adrian erected a city on part of the former site of Jerusalem, which he called Ælia Capitolina: it was afterwards greatly enlarged and beautified by Constantine the Great, who restored its ancient name. During that emperor's reign, the Jews made various efforts to rebuild their temple, which, however, were always frustrated; nor did better success attend the attempt made A. D. 363, by the apostate emperor Julian. An earthquake, a whirlwind, and a fiery eruption, compelled the workmen to abandon their design.

From the destruction of Jerusalem by the Romans to the present time, that city has remained, for the most part, in a state of ruin and desolation; "and has never been under the government of the Jews themselves, but oppressed and broken down by a succession of foreign masters—the Romans, the Saracens, the Franks, the Mamelukes, and last by the Turks, to whom it is still subject. It is not, therefore, only in the history of Josephus, and in other ancient writers, that we are to look for the accomplishment of our Lord's predictions:—we see them verified at this moment before our eyes, in the desolate state of the once celebrated city and temple of Jerusalem, and in the present condition of the Jewish people, not collected together into any one country, into one political society, and under one form of government, but dispersed over every region of the globe, and every where treated with contumely and scorn." (Bp. Porteus.)

Mount Tabor, *as seen from the* Plain of Esdraelon.

CHAPTER II.

PHYSICAL GEOGRAPHY OF THE HOLY LAND.

The surface of the Holy Land being diversified with mountains and plains, its CLIMATE varies in different places; though in general it is more settled than in our more western countries. Generally speaking, however, the atmosphere is mild; the summers are commonly dry and extremely hot: intensely hot days, however, are frequently succeeded by intensely cold nights; and it is to these sudden vicissitudes, and their consequent effects on the human frame, that Jacob refers, when he says that *in the day the* DROUGHT *consumed him, and the* FROST *by night.* (Gen. xxxi. 40.)

Six several SEASONS of the natural year are indicated in Gen. viii. 22. viz.: *seed-time* and *harvest*, *cold* and *heat*, *summer* and *winter;* and as agriculture constituted the principal employment of the Jews, we are informed by the rabbinical writers, that they adopted the same division of seasons, with reference to their rural work. These divisions also exist among the Arabs to this day.

1. SEED-TIME comprised the latter half of the Jewish month Tisri, the whole of Marchesvan, and the former half of Kisleu or Chisleu, that is, from the beginning of October to the beginning of December. During this sea-

son the weather is various, very often misty, cloudy, with mizzling or pouring rain.

2. WINTER included the latter half of Chisleu, the whole of Tebeth, and the former part of Shebeth, that is, from the beginning of December to the beginning of February. In this season, snows rarely fall, except on the mountains, but they seldom continue a whole day; the ice is thin and melts as soon as the sun ascends above the horizon. As the season advances, the north wind and the cold, especially on the lofty mountains, which are now covered with snow, is intensely severe, and sometimes even fatal: the cold is frequently so piercing, that persons born in our climate can scarcely endure it. The cold, however, varies in the degree of its severity, according to the local situation of the country.

3. The COLD SEASON comprises the latter half of Shebeth, the whole of Adar, and the former half of Nisan, from the beginning of February to the beginning of April. At the commencement of this season, the weather is cold, but it gradually becomes warm and even hot, particularly in the plain of Jericho. Thunder, lightning, and hail are frequent. Vegetable nature now revives; the almond tree blossoms, and the gardens assume a delightful appearance. Barley is ripe at Jericho, though but little wheat is in the ear.

4. The HARVEST includes the latter half of Nisan, the whole of Jyar (or Zif,) and the former half of Sivan, that is, from the beginning of April to the beginning of June. In the plain of Jericho the heat of the sun is excessive, though in other parts of Palestine the weather is most delightful; and on the sea-coast the heat is tempered by morning and evening breezes from the sea

5. The SUMMER comprehends the latter half of Sivan, the whole of Thammuz, and the former half of Ab, that is, from the beginning of June to the beginning of August. The heat of the weather increases, and the nights are so warm that the inhabitants sleep on their house-tops in the open air.

6. The HOT SEASON includes the latter half of Ab, the whole of Elul, and the former half of Tisri, that is, from the beginning of August to the beginning of October. During the chief part of this season the heat is intense,

though less so at Jerusalem than in the plain of Jericho: there is no cold, not even in the night, so that travellers pass whole nights in the open air without inconvenience. Lebanon is for the most part free from snow, except in the caverns and defiles where the sun cannot penetrate.

During the hot season, it is not uncommon in the East Indies for persons to die suddenly, in consequence of the extreme heat of the solar rays, (whence the necessity of being carried in a palanquin.) This is now commonly termed a *coup-de-soleil* or stroke of the sun. The son of the woman of Shunem appears to have died in consequence of a coup-de-soleil; (2 Kings iv. 19, 20;) to which there is an allusion in Psalm cxxi. 2.

Rain falls but rarely, except in autumn and spring; but its absence is partly supplied by the very copious dews which fall during the night. The *early* or autumnal rains and the *latter* or spring rains are absolutely necessary to the support of vegetation, and were consequently objects greatly desired by the Israelites and Jews. The early rains generally fall about the beginning of November, when they usually ploughed their lands and sowed their corn; and the latter rains fall sometimes towards the middle, and sometimes towards the close of April; that is, a short time before they gathered in their harvest. These rains, however, were always chilly (Ezra x. 9, and Song ii. 11,) and often preceded by whirlwinds, (2 Kings iii. 16, 17,) that raised such quantities of sand as to darken the sky, or, in the words of the sacred historian, to make *the heavens black with clouds and wind.* (1 Kings xviii. 45.) In the figurative language of the Scripture, these whirlwinds are termed the *command* and the *word* of God: (Psalm cxlvii. 15. 18:) and as they are sometimes fatal to travellers who are overwhelmed in the deserts, the rapidity of their advance is elegantly employed by Solomon to show the certainty as well as the suddenness of that destruction which will befall the impenitently wicked. (Prov. i. 27.) The rains descend in Palestine with great violence; and as whole villages in the east are constructed only with palm-branches, mud, and tiles baked in the sun, (perhaps corresponding to and explanatory of the untempered mortar noticed in Ezek. xiii. 11,) these rains not unfrequently dissolve the cement, such as it is, and the houses fall to the ground. To these effects our Lord probably alludes in Matt. vii. 25—27. Very small clouds are likewise the forerunners of violent storms and hurricanes in the east as well as in the west: they rise *like a man's hand,* (1 Kings xviii. 44,) until the whole sky becomes black with rain, which descends in torrents. In our Lord's time, this phenomenon seems to have become a certain prognostic of wet weather. See Luke xii. 54.

In consequence of the paucity of showers in the east, WATER is an article of great importance to the inhabitants. Hence, in Lot's estimation, it was a principal recommendation of the plain of Jordan that it was *well watered every where:* (Gen. xiii. 10:) and the same advantage continued in later ages to be enjoyed by the Israelites, whose country was intersected by numerous brooks and streams.

Although *rivers* are frequently mentioned in the sacred writings, yet, strictly speaking, the only river in the Holy Land is the Jordan, which is sometimes designated in Scripture as *the river* without any addition; as also is the Nile, (Gen. xli. 1. Exod. i. 22, ii. 5, iv. 9, vii. 18, and viii. 3. 9. 11,) and, occasionally, the Euphrates: (as in Jer. ii. 18:) in the passages here referred to, the tenor of the dis course must determine which is the river actually intended by the sacred writers. The name of river is also given to inconsiderable streams and rivulets, as to the Kishon (Judges iv. 7, and v. 21,) and the Arnon. (Deut. iii. 16.)

The principal river which waters Palestine is the JORDAN, or *Yar-Dan,* i. e. the river of Dan, so called because it takes its rise in the vicinity of the little city of Dan. Its true source is in the lake Phiala, near Cæsarea Philippi, at the foot of Antilibanus, or the eastern ridge of mount Lebanon, whence it passes under ground, and, emerging to the light from a cave in the vicinity of Paneas, it flows due south through the centre of the country, intersecting the lake Merom and the sea or lake of Galilee, and (it is said) without mingling with its waters; and it loses itself in the lake Asphaltites or the Dead Sea, into which it rolls a considerable volume of deep water, and so rapid as to prevent a strong, active and expert swimmer from swimming across it. The course of the Jordan is about one hundred miles; its breadth and depth are various.

All travellers concur in stating that its waters are turbid, from the rapidity with which they flow.

Anciently, the Jordan overflowed its banks about the time of barley harvest, (Josh. iii. 15, iv. 18. 1 Chron. xii. 15. Jer. xlix. 19,) or the feast of the passover; when, the snows being dissolved on the mountains, the torrents discharged themselves into its channel with great impetuosity. Its banks are covered with various kinds of bushes and shrubs, which afford an asylum for wild animals now, as they did in the time of Jeremiah, who alludes to them (Jer. xlix. 19.)

The other remarkable streams, or rivulets of Palestine, are the following, viz.: 1. The *Arnon*, which descends from the mountain of the same name, and discharges itself into the Dead Sea:—2. The *Sihor* (the Belus of ancient geographers, at present called the Kardanah,) has its source about four miles to the east of the heads of the river Kishon. It waters the plains of Acre and Esdraelon, and falls into the sea at the gulph of Keilah:—3. The brook *Jabbok* takes its rise in the same mountains, and falls into the river Jordan:—4. The *Kanah*, or brook of reeds, springs from the mountains of Judah, but only flows during the winter: it falls into the Mediterranean Sea, near Cæsarea:—5. The brook *Besor*, (1 Sam. xxx. 9,) falls into the same sea, between Gaza and Rhinocorura:—6. The *Kishon* issues from the mountains of Carmel, at the foot of which it forms two streams; one flows eastward into the sea of Galilee, and the other, taking a westerly course through the plain of Jezreel, or Esdraelon, discharges itself into the Mediterranean Sea. This is the stream noticed in 1 Kings xviii. 40:—7. *Kedron*, *Kidron*, or *Cedron*, as it is variously termed,* runs in the valley of Jehoshaphat, eastward of Jerusalem, between that city and the mount of Olives: except during the winter, or after heavy rains, its channel is generally dry, but, when swollen by torrents, it flows with great impetuosity.

Lakes, Seas, &c.

Of the Lakes mentioned in the Scriptures, two are particularly worthy of notice; that of Gennesareth, and the

* 2 Sam. xv. 23. 1 Kings xv. 13. 2 Kings xxiii. 6. 12. 2 Chron. xxix. 16. Jer. xxxi. 40. John xviii.

lake of Sodom, both of which are termed seas, agreeably to the Hebrew phraseology, which gives the name of sea to any large body of water.

The SEA of GALILEE, through which the Jordan flows, was anciently called the Sea of Chinnereth, (Numb. xxxiv. 11,) or Cinneroth, (Josh. xii. 3,) from its vicinity to the town of that name; afterwards, Genesar, (1 Mac. xi. 67,) and in the time of Jesus Christ, Genesareth, or Gennezareth, (Luke v. 1,) from the neighbouring land of the same name, (Matt xiv. 34. Mark xv. 53,) and also the sea of Tiberias, (John vi. 1, xxi. 1,) from the contiguous city of Tiberias. The waters of this lake are very sweet, and abound with fish: this circumstance marks the propriety of our Lord's parable of the net cast into the sea, (Matt. xiii. 47—49,) near the shore. Pliny states this lake to be sixteen miles in length, by six miles in breadth. Dr. D. E. Clarke, by whom it was visited rather more than twenty years since, describes it as longer, and finer than our Cumberland and Westmoreland lakes, although it yields in majesty to the stupendous features of Loch Lomond, in Scotland: like our Windermere, the lake of Gennezareth is often greatly agitated by winds. (Matt viii. 23—27.

The LAKE, or SEA OF SODOM, or the DEAD SEA, is about seventy-two English miles in length, and nearly nineteen in breadth. It was anciently called in the Scriptures, the *Sea of the Plain*, (Deut. iii. 17, iv. 49,) being situated in a valley, with a plain lying to the south of it; the *Salt Sea*, (Deut. iii. 17. Josh. xv. 5,) from the extremely saline, bitter, and nauseous taste of its waters; the *Salt Sea eastward*, (Numb. xxxiv. 3,) and the *East Sea*, (Ezek. xlvii. 18. Joel ii. 20.) By Josephus and other writers, it is called the lake *Asphaltites*, from the abundance of bitumen found in it; and also the *Dead Sea*, from ancient traditions, erroneously, though generally received, that no living creature can exist in its stagnant and sulphureous waters. Here formerly stood the cities of Sodom and Gomorrah, which, with two other cities of the plain, were consumed by fire from heaven: to this destruction, there are numerous allusions in the Scriptures.

Beside the preceding rivers and lakes, the Scriptures mention several *Fountains* and *Wells*: of these the most remarkable are the fountain, or pool, of Siloam, and Jacob's Well.

SILOAM was a fountain under the walls of Jerusalem, east, between the city and the brook Kedron: it is supposed to be the same as the fountain En-Rogel, or the Fuller's Fountain. (Josh. xv. 7, and xviii. 16. 2 Sam. xvii. 17, and 1 Kings i. 9.) "The spring issues from a rock, and runs in a silent stream, according to the testimony of Jeremiah."

JACOB'S WELL, or fountain, is situated at a small dis tance, from Sichem, or Shechem, also called Sychar, and at present Napolose: it was the residence of Jacob before his sons slew the Shechemites. It has been visited by pilgrims of all ages, but especially by Christians, to whom it has become an object of veneration from the me morable discourse of our Saviour with the woman of Samaria. (John iv. 5—30.)

In our own time, it is the custom for the oriental women, particularly those who are unmarried, to fetch water from the wells, in the mornings and evenings; at which times they go forth adorned with their trinkets. This will account for Rebecca's fetching water, (Gen. xxiv. 15,) and will further prove, that there was no impropriety in Abraham's servant presenting her with more valuable jewels, than those she had before on her hands. (Gen. xxiv. 22—47.)

MOUNTAINS, &c.

PALESTINE is a mountainous country, especially that part of it, which is situated between the Mediterranean, or Great Sea, and the river Jordan. The principal MOUNTAINS, not already mentioned, are those of Lebanon, Carmel, Tabor, the mountains of Israel and of Gilead.

1. *Lebanon*, by the Greeks and Latins termed Libanus, is a long chain of lime-stone mountains, extending from the neighbourhood of Sidon on the west, to the vicinity of Damascus eastward, and forming the extreme northern boundary of the Holy Land. It is divided into two principal ridges, or ranges parallel to each other, the most westerly of which is known by the name of Libanus, and the opposite, or eastern ridge, by the appella-

tion of Anti-Libanus. These mountains may be seen from a very considerable distance; and it rarely happens that some part or other of them, is not covered with snow throughout the year. They are by no means barren, but are almost all well cultivated and well peopled: their summits are, in many parts, level, and form extensive plains, in which are sown corn, and all kinds of pulse. They are watered by numerous springs, rivulets, and streams of excellent water, which diffuse on all sides freshness and fertility, even in the most elevated regions. To these Solomon has a beautiful allusion. (Song iv. 15.) Lebanon was anciently celebrated for its stately cedars, which are now less numerous than in former times; they grow among the snow near the highest part of the mountain, and are remarkable, as well for their age and size, as for the frequent allusions made to them in the Scriptures. (See 1 Kings iv. 33. Psalm lxxx. 10, and xcii. 12, &c. &c.)

Anti-Libanus, or *Anti-Lebanon*, is the more lofty ridge of the two, and its summit is clad with almost perpetual snow, which was carried to the neighbouring towns for the purpose of cooling liquors; (Prov. xxv. 13, and perhaps Jer. xviii. 14;) a practice which has obtained in the east to the present day.

2. Mount Carmel is a range of hills, about fifteen hundred feet in height, and extending six or eight miles nearly north and south. It is situated about ten miles to the south of Acre, or Ptolemais, on the shore of the Mediterranean Sea. Its summits abound with oaks and other trees; and among brambles, wild vines and olive trees are still to be found. On the side next the sea is a cave, to which some commentators have supposed that the prophet Elijah desired Ahab to bring Baal's prophets, when celestial fire descended on his sacrifice. (1 Kings xviii. 19—40.) There was another mount Carmel, with a city of the same name, situated in the tribe Judah, and mentioned in Joshua xv. 55. 1 Sam. xxv. 2, and 2 Sam iii 3.

3. Tabor, or Thabor, is a mountain of a conical form, entirely detached from any neighbouring mountain, and stands on one side of the great plain of Esdraelon: it is entirely covered with green oaks, and other trees, shrubs, and odoriferous plants. The prospects from this moun

tain, are singularly delightful and extensive; and on its eastern side there is a small height, which by ancient tradition, is supposed to have been the scene of our Lord's transfiguration. (Matt. xvii. 1—8. Mark ix. 2—9.)

4. The MOUNTAINS OF ISRAEL, also called the mountains of Ephraim, were situated in the very centre of the Holy Land, and opposite to the MOUNTAINS OF JUDAH. The soil of both is fertile, excepting those ridges of the mountains of Israel, which look towards the region of the Jordan, and which are both rugged and difficult of ascent, and also with the exception of the chain extending from the Mount of Olives near Jerusalem to the plain of Jericho, which has always afforded lurking-places to robbers. (Luke x. 30.) The most elevated summit of this ridge, which appears to be the same that was anciently called the rock of *Rimmon*, (Judg. xx. 45. 47,) is at present known by the name of *Quarantania*, and is supposed to have been the scene of our Saviour's temptation. (Matt. iv. 8.) It is described by Maundrel, as situated in a mountainous desert, and being a most miserably dry and barren place, consisting of high rocky mountains, torn and disordered, as if the earth had here suffered some great convulsion. The MOUNTAINS OF EBAL (sometimes written *Gebal*) and GERIZIM (Deut. xi. 29, xxvii. 4. 12. Josh. viii. 30—35,) are situate, the former to the north, and the latter to the south of Sichem or Napolose, whose streets run parallel to the latter mountain, which overlooks the town. In the mountains of Judah, there are numerous caves, some of a considerable size: the most remarkable of these is the cave of Adullam, mentioned in 1 Sam. xxii. 1, 2.

5. The MOUNTAINS OF GILEAD are situated beyond the Jordan, and extend from Hermon southward to Arabia Petræa. The northern part of them, known by the name of Bashan, was celebrated for its stately oaks, and numerous herds of cattle pastured there, to which there are many allusions in the Scriptures. (See, among other passages, Deut. xxxii. 14. Psalm xxii. 12, and lxviii. 15. Isa. ii. 13. Ezek. xxxix. 18. Amos iv. 1.) The middle part, in a stricter sense, was termed *Gilead;* and in the southern part, beyond Jordan, were the *Mountains of Abarim*, the northern limits of the territory of Moab,

which are conjectured to have derived their name from the passes between the hills of which they were formed. The most eminent among these are *Pisgah* and *Nebo*, which form a continued chain, and command a view of the whole land of Canaan. (Deut. iii. 27, xxxii. 48—50, xxxiv. 1, 2, 3.) From Mount Nebo, Moses surveyed the promised land, before he was *gathered to his people*. (Numb. xxvii. 12, 13.) The Hebrews frequently give the epithet of *everlasting* to their mountains, because they are as old as the earth itself. See, among other instances, Gen. xlix. 26, and Deut. xxxiii. 15.

The Mountains of Palestine were anciently places of refuge to the inhabitants when defeated in war, (Gen. xiv. 10,) and modern travellers assure us that they are still resorted to for the purpose of shelter. The rocky summits found on many of them, appear to have been not unfrequently employed as altars, on which sacrifices were offered to Jehovah; (Judg. vi. 19—21, and xiii. 15—20;) although they were afterwards converted into places for idol worship, for which the prophets Isaiah (lvii. 7,) and Ezekiel (xviii. 6,) severely reprove their degenerate countrymen. And as many of the mountains of Palestine were situated in desert places, the *shadow* they project has furnished the prophet Isaiah with a pleasing image of the security that shall be enjoyed under the kingdom of Messiah. (xxxii. 2.)

Valleys, Plains, &c.

Numerous Valleys are mentioned in Scripture: the three most memorable of these are,

1. The Vale of Siddim, in which Abraham discomfitted Chedorlaomer, and his confederate emirs, or kings, Gen. xiv. 2—10.

2. The Valley of Elah, which lies about three miles from Bethlehem, on the road to Jaffa: it is celebrated as the spot where David defeated and slew Goliath. (1 Sam. xvii.) "Nothing has ever occurred to alter the appearance of the country. The very brook whence David *chose him five smooth stones* has been noticed by many a thirsty pilgrim, journeying from Jaffa to Jerusalem; all of whom must pass it in their way."

3. The narrow Valley of Hinnom lies at the foot of

Mount Sion, and is memorable for the inhuman and barbarous, as well as idolatrous worship, here paid to Moloch; to which idol parents sacrificed their smiling offspring, by making them pass through the fire. (2 Kings xxiii. 10. 2 Chron. xxviii. 3.) To drown the lamentable shrieks of the children thus immolated, musical instruments (in Hebrew termed *Tuph)* were played; whence the spot where the victims were burnt, was called Tophet. From the same circumstance, Ge-Hinnom (which in Hebrew denotes the *Valley of Hinnom*, and from which the Greek word Γεέννα, *Gehenna*, is derived,) is sometimes used ,to denote hell, or hell-fire.

The country of Judæa, being mountainous and rocky, is full of CAVERNS; to which the inhabitants were accustomed to flee for shelter from the incursions of their enemies. (Judg. vi. 2. 1 Sam. xiii. 6, xiv. 11.) Some of these caves were very capacious: that of Engedi was so large, that David and six hundred men, concealed themselves in its sides; and Saul entered the mouth of the cave without perceiving that any one was there.

Numerous fertile and level tracts, are mentioned in the sacred volume, under the title of PLAINS. Three of these are particularly worthy of notice, viz.:

1. The PLAIN OF THE MEDITERRANEAN SEA, which reached from the river of Egypt to Mount Carmel.

2. The Tract between Gaza and Joppa, was simply called the PLAIN: in this stood the five principal cities of the Philistine satrapies, Ascalon, Gath, Gaza, Ekron, or Accaron, and Azotus, or Ashdod.

3. The Plain of Jezreel, or Esdraelon, also called the GREAT PLAIN, (the Armageddon of the Apocalypse:) it extends from Mount Carmel and the Mediterranean, to the place where the Jordan issues from the Sea of Tiberias, through the middle of the Holy Land. This plain is enclosed on all sides by mountains, and is cultivated.

WILDERNESSES, OR DESERTS.

FREQUENT mention is made in the Scriptures of WILDERNESSES, OR DESERTS, by which we usually, though erroneously, understand desolate places, equally void of cities and inhabitants: for the Hebrews gave the name of desert, or wilderness, to all places that were not cultivated, but which were chiefly appropriated to the feeding of cattle, and in many of them trees and shrubs grew wild. Some of them are mountainous and well watered, while others are sterile sandy plains, either destitute of water, or affording a very scanty supply from the few springs that are occasionally to be found in them; yet even these afford a grateful, though meagre pasturage to camels, goats, and sheep. In this latter description of deserts, it is that the weary traveller is mocked by the distant appearance of white vapours, which are not unlike those white mists we often see hovering over the surface of a river in a summer evening, after a hot day. When beheld at a distance, they resemble an expanded lake; but, upon a nearer approach, the thirsty traveller perceives the deception. To this phenomenon the prophet Isaiah alludes, (xxxv. 7,) where, predicting the blessings of the Redeemer's kingdom, he says, *The glowing sand shall become a pool, and the thirsty soil bubbling springs.*

The deserts of the Hebrews frequently derived their appellations, from the places to which they were contiguous. The most celebrated is the ***Great Desert***, called the ***Wilderness***, or ***Desert of Judah.*** (Psal. lxiii. title.) The desert of Judæa, in which John the Baptist abode till the day of his showing unto Israel, (Luke i. 80,) and where he first taught his countrymen, (Matt. iii. 1. Mark i. 4. John x. 39,) was a mountainous, wooded, and thinly inhabited tract of country, but abounding in pastures; it was situated adjacent to the Dead Sea, and the River Jordan. In the time of Joshua it had six cities, with their villages. (Josh. xv. 61, 62.)

This country also produced some WOODS, or FORESTS mentioned in holy writ, such as those of ***Hareth*** in the tribe of Judah, to which David withdrew from Saul; (1 Sam. xxii. 5;) of ***Ephraim***, where Absalom received the due reward of his unnatural rebellion (2 Sam. xviii. 6—9;) that of *Lebanon*, where Solomon erected a sumptuous palace (1 Kings vii. 2;) the forest of *Bethel*, supposed to have stood near the city of that name; (2 Kings ii. 24;) and the *Forest of* ***Oaks***, on the hills of Bashan (Zech. xi. 2.)

The FERTILITY of the soil of the Holy Land, so often mentioned in the sacred writings, (and especially in Deut. viii. 7—9, xi. 10—12. Gen. xxvi. 12. and Matt. xiii. 8,) is confirmed by the united testimonies of ancient writers, as well as by all modern travellers. We are assured that under a wise and beneficent government, the produce of the Holy Land, would exceed all calculation. Its perennial harvest; the salubrity of its air; its limpid springs; its rivers, lakes, and matchless plains; its hills and vales —all these, added to the serenity of its climate, prove this land to be indeed "a field which the Lord hath blessed:" (Gen. xxvii. 28:) "God hath given it of the dew of heaven, and the fatness of the earth, and plenty of corn and wine."

Such being the state of the Holy Land, at east of that part of it which is properly cultivated, we can readily account for the vast population it anciently supported. Its present forlorn condition is satisfactorily explained by the depredations and vicissitudes to which it has been exposed in every age: and so far is this from contradicting the assertions of the sacred writings, that it confirms their authority; for, in the event of the Israelites proving unfaithful to their covenant engagements with Jehovah, all these judgments were predicted, and denounced against them; (Lev. xxvi. 32. Deut. xxix. 22. *et seq.;*) and the exact accomplishment of these prophecies affords a permanent comment on the declaration of the royal psalmist, that God "turneth a fruitful land into barrenness for the wickedness of them that dwell therein." (Psal. cvii. 34.)

BOOK II.—POLITICAL ANTIQUITIES OF THE JEWS.

CHAPTER I.

DIFFERENT FORMS OF GOVERNMENT FROM THE PATRIARCHAL TIMES, TO THE BABYLONIAN CAPTIVITY.

I. THE earliest FORM OF GOVERNMENT of which we read in Scripture, was the PATRIARCHAL; or that exercised by the heads of families over their households, without being responsible to any superior power. Such was that exercised by Abraham, Isaac, and Jacob. The patriarchal power, was a sovereign dominion, so that parents may be considered as the first kings, and children the first subjects: they had the power of life and death, of disinheriting their children, or of dismissing them from the paternal home without assigning any reason.

II. On the departure of the Israelites from the land of their oppressors, under the guidance of Moses, Jehovah was pleased to institute a new form of government, which has been rightly termed a THEOCRACY; the supreme legislative power being exclusively vested in GOD, or his ORACLE, who alone could enact, or repeal laws. Hence the judges, and afterwards the kings, were merely temporal viceroys, or the first magistrates in the state: their office was, to command the army in war, to summon and preside in the senate, or council of princes and elders, and in the general assembly of the congregation of Israel, and to propose public matters to the deliberation of the former, and to the ratification of the latter. During the life of Moses, the chief magistracy was lodged in him: but, his strength being inadequate to determine all matters of controversy between so numerous a nation, a council of seventy princes, or elders was instituted, at his request, to assist him with their advice, and to lighten the burden of government. (Exod. xviii. 13—26.)

III. On the death of Moses, the command of the children of Israel was confided to Joshua, who had been his minister, (Exod. xxiv. 13. Josh. i. 1,) and under whom the land of Canaan was subdued, and divided agreeably to the divine injunctions: but, his office ceasing with his life, the government of Israel was committed to certain supreme magistrates, termed JUDGES. Their dignity was for life; but their office was not hereditary, neither was their succession constant. Their authority was not inferior to that of kings: it extended to peace and war. They decided causes without appeal; but they had no power to enact new laws, or to impose new burdens upon the people. They were protectors of the laws, defenders of religion, and avengers of crimes, particularly of idolatry, which was high treason against Jehovah, their Sovereign.

IV. At length, the Israelites, weary of having God for their sovereign, desired a king to be set over them. (1 Sam. viii. 5.) Such a change in their government was foreseen by Moses, who accordingly prescribed certain laws for the direction of their future sovereigns, which are related in Deut. xvii. 14—20.

Though the authority of the kings was in some respects limited, by stipulation, yet they exercised very ample powers. They had the right of making peace, or war, and of life and death; and they administered justice, either in person, or by their judges. And though they exercised great power in reforming ecclesiastical abuses, yet this power was enjoyed by them, not as *absolute* sovereigns, in their own right. They were merely the viceroys of Jehovah, who was the sole legislator of Israel: and, therefore, as the kings could neither enact a new law, nor repeal an old one, the government continued to be a *theocracy*, as well under their permanent administration, as we have seen that it was under the occasional administration of the judges. They were inaugurated to their high office with great pomp, and were arrayed in royal apparel, with a crown and sceptre. The majesty of royalty was studiously maintained. It was accounted the highest possible honour to be admitted into the royal presence, and above all to sit down in his presence. The knowledge of this circumstance illustrates several passages of Scripture, particularly Luke i. 19. Matt. v. 8, xviii. 10, xx. 20—23. After the establishment of royalty among the Jews, it appears to have been a maxim in their law, that *the king's person was inviolable, even though he might be tyrannical and unjust*; (1 Sam. xxiv. 5—8;) a maxim which is necessary not only to the security of the king, but also to the welfare of the subject. On this principle, the Amalekite, who told David the improbable and untrue story of his having put the mortally wounded Saul to death, that he might not fall into the hands of the Philistines, was, merely on this, his own statement, ordered by David to be instantly despatched, *because he had laid his hand on the Lord's Anointed.* (2 Sam. i. 14.)

The eastern monarchs were never approached but with presents of some kind or other, according to the ability of the individuals, who accompanied them with expressions of the profoundest reverence, prostrating themselves to the ground; and the same practice continues to this day. Thus Jacob instructed his sons to carry a present to Joseph, when they went to buy food of him, as governor of Egypt. (Gen. xliii. 11. 26.) In like manner, the magi, who came from the east to adore Jesus Christ, as king of the Jews, brought him presents of gold, frankincense, and myrrh. (Matt. ii. 11.) Allusions to this practice occur in Gen. xxxii. 13. 1 Kings x. 2. 10. 25. 2 Kings v. 5; see also 1 Sam. ix. 7, and 2 Kings viii. 8. The prostrations were made, with every demonstration of reverence, to the ground. See an instance in 1 Sam. xxiv. 8.

Further, whenever the oriental sovereigns go abroad, they are uniformly attended by a numerous and splendid retinue: the Hebrew kings, and their sons, either rode on asses, or mules, (2 Sam. xiii. 29. 1 Kings i. 33. 38,) or in chariots, (1 Kings i. 5. 2 Kings ix. 21, x. 15,) preceded or accompanied by their royal guards, (who, in 2 Sam. viii. 18, and xv. 18, are termed Cherethites and Pelethites;) as the oriental sovereigns are to this day. And whenever the Asiatic monarchs entered upon an expedition, or took a journey through desert and untravelled countries, they sent harbingers before them, to prepare all things for their passage, and pioneers to open the passes, level the ways, and remove all impediments. To this practice there are allusions in Isa. xl. 3, and Matt. iii. 3.

The revenues of the kings arose from various sources, viz.: 1. *Voluntary offerings*, which were made to them, conformably to the oriental custom. (1 Sam. x. 27, xvi. 20.) 2. *The Produce of the Royal Flocks*, (1 Sam. xxi. 7. 2 Sam. xiii. 23. 2 Chron. xxxii. 28, 29,) and also of the royal demesnes, over which certain officers were appointed. 3. The *Tenth Part* of all the produce of the fields and vineyards, the collection and management of which seem to have been confided to the officers mention ed in 1 Kings iv. 7, and in 1 Chron. xxvii. 25. It is also probable from 1 Kings x. 14, that the Israelites likewise paid a tax in money. 4. A portion of the spoil of conquered nations, (2 Sam. viii.) upon whom tributes or imposts were also laid; (1 Kings iv. 21. Psal. lxxii. 10, compared with 1 Chron. xxvii. 25—31;) and, lastly, 5. The *Customs* paid to Solomon, by the foreign merchants who passed through his dominions, (1 Kings x. 15,) afforded a considerable revenue to that monarch: who, as the Mosaic laws did not encourage foreign commerce, carried on a very extensive and lucrative trade, (1 Kings x. 22,) particularly in Egyptian horses, and the byssus, or fine linen of Egypt. (1 Kings x. 28, 29.)

Besides the kings, there were some inferior magistrates, who, though their origin may be traced to the time of Moses, continued to retain some authority, after the establishment of the monarchy. Of this description were, 1. the *Heads*, or *Princes of Tribes*, who appear to have watched over the interest of each tribe; they were twelve in number; and, 2. *The Heads of Families*, who are sometimes called *Heads of Houses of Fathers*, and sometimes simply *heads*. These are likewise the same persons who, in Josh. xxiii. 2, and xxiv. 1, are called *Elders*. (Compare also Deut. xix. 12, and xxi. 1—9.) It does not appear in what manner these heads, or elders of families, were chosen, when any of them died. The princes of tribes do not seem to have ceased with the commencement, at least, of the monarchy: from 1 Chron. xvii. 16—22, it is evident that they subsisted in the time of David; and they must have proved a very considerable restraint upon the power of the king.

V. The kingdom which had been founded by Saul, and

carried to its highest pitch of grandeur and power by David and Solomon, subsisted entire for the space of one hundred and twenty years; until Rehoboam, the son and successor of Solomon, refused to mitigate the burdens of his subjects, when a division of the twelve tribes took place; ten of which, adhering to Jeroboam, formed the kingdom of Israel, while the tribes of Judah and Benjamin, continuing faithful in their allegiance to Rehoboam, constituted the kingdom of Judah. The *Kingdom of Israel* subsisted under various sovereigns, during a period of 264, or 271 years, according to some chronologers; its metropolis, Samaria, being captured by Shalmaneser, king of Assyria, B. C. 717, or 719, after a siege of three years, of the Israelites, whose numbers had been reduced by immense and repeated slaughters, some of the lower sort were suffered to remain in their native country; but the nobles, and all the more opulent persons, were carried into captivity beyond the Euphrates. The *Kingdom of Judah* continued 388, or according to some chronologers, 404 years; Jerusalem, its capital, being taken, the temple burnt, and its sovereign, Zedekiah, being carried captive to Babylon, by Nebuchadnezzar; the rest of his subjects (with the exception of the poorer classes, who were left in Judæa) were likewise carried into captivity, beyond the Euphrates, where they, and their posterity, remained seventy years, agreeably to the divine predictions.

CHAPTER II.

POLITICAL STATE OF THE JEWS, FROM THEIR RETURN FROM THE BABYLONISH CAPTIVITY, TO THE SUBVERSION OF THEIR CIVIL AND ECCLESIASTICAL POLITY.

I. Political State of the Jews under the Maccabees and the sovereigns of the Herodian Family.

After the return of the Jews from Babylon, they obeyed the High Priests, from whom the supreme authority subsequently passed into the hands of the Maccabean Princes. Mattathias was the first of these princes; and was succeeded by his three valiant sons, Judas, Jonathan, and Simon, the last of whom was succeeded by his son, John Hyrcanus. The name *Maccabees* is supposed to have been derived from the four letters, M. C. B. I. which are the initial letters of the Hebrew words *Mi Chamoka Baelim Jehovah*, that is, *who among the gods is like unto thee, O Jehovah ?* (Exod. xv. 11,) which letters were displayed on their standards. This illustrious house, whose princes united the regal and pontifical dignity in their own persons, administered the affairs of the Jews, during a period of one hundred and twenty-six years; until disputes arising between Hyrcanus II. and his brother, Aristobulus, the latter was defeated by the Romans, under Pompey, who captured Jerusalem, and reduced Judæa to a tributary province of the republic. (B. C. 59.)

Though Pompey continued Hyrcanus in the high priesthood, he bestowed the government of Judæa on Antipater, an Idumæan by birth, who was a Jewish proselyte, and the father of Herod, surnamed the Great, who was subsequently king of the Jews. Antipater divided Judæa between his two sons, Phasael and Herod, giving to the former the government of Jerusalem, and to the latter the province of Galilee ; which being at that time greatly infested with robbers, Herod signalized his courage by dispersing them, and shortly after attacked Antigonus, the competitor of Hyrcanus in the priesthood, who was supported by the Tyrians. In the mean time, the Parthians having invaded Judæa, and carried into captivity Hyrcanus, the high priest, and Phasael, the brother of Herod ; the latter fled to Rome, where Mark Antony, with the consent of the senate, conferred on him the title of king of Judæa. By the aid of the Roman arms, HEROD, a sanguinary and crafty prince, kept possession of his dignity ; and after three years of sanguinary and intestine war with the partizans of Antigonus, he was confirmed in his kingdom by Augustus.

Herod, misnamed the Great, by his will divided his dominions among his three sons, Archelaus, Herod Antipas, and Herod Philip.

To ARCHELAUS he assigned Judæa, Samaria, and Idumæa, with the regal dignity, subject to the approbation of Augustus, who ratified his will as it respected the territorial division, but conferred on Archelaus the title of *Ethnarch*, or chief of the nation, with a promise of the regal dignity, if he should prove himself worthy of it. His sub sequent reign was turbulent; and, after repeated complaints against his tyranny and mal-administration, he was deposed and banished by Augustus, and his territories were annexed to the Roman province of Syria.

HEROD ANTIPAS, (or Antipater,) another of Herod's sons, received from his father the district of Galilee and Peræa, with the title of Tetrarch. He is described by Josephus as a crafty and incestuous prince, with which character the narratives of the evangelists coincide; for, having deserted his wife, the daughter of Aretas king of Arabia, he forcibly took away and married Herodias the wife of his brother Herod Philip, a proud and cruel woman, to gratify whom he caused John the Baptist to be beheaded, (Matt. xiv. 3. Mark vi. 17. Luke iii. 19,) who had provoked her vengeance by his faithful reproof of their incestuous nuptials. Some years afterwards, Herod aspiring to the regal dignity in Judæa, was banished together with his wife, first to Lyons, in Gaul, and thence into Spain.

PHILIP, tetrarch of Trachonitis, Gaulonitis, and Batanæa, is mentioned but once in the New Testament, (Luke iii. 1:) on his decease without issue, after a reign of thirty-seven years, his territories were annexed to the province of Syria.

AGRIPPA, or Herod Agrippa, was the son of Aristobulus, and grandson of Herod the Great, and sustained various reverses of fortune previously to his attaining the royal dignity. He governed his dominions much to the satisfaction of his subjects, (for whose gratification he put to death the apostle James, and meditated that of St. Peter, who was miraculously delivered, Acts xii. 2—17;) but being inflated with pride on account of his increasing power and grandeur, he was struck with a noisome and painful disease, of which he died at Cæsarea in the manner related by St. Luke. (Acts xii, 21.—23.)

AGRIPPA junior, was the son of the preceding Herod Agrippa: being only seventeen years of age at the time of his father's death, he was judged to be unequal to the task of governing the whole of his dominions. These were again placed under the direction of a Roman procurator or governor, and Agrippa was first king of Chalcis, and afterwards of Batanæa, Trachonitis, and Abilene, to which other territories were subsequently added. It was before this Agrippa and his two sisters, Bernice and Drusilla the wife of the Roman governor Felix, that St. Paul delivered his masterly defence. (Acts xxvi.)

II. Political State of the Jews under the Roman Procurators.

The Jewish kingdom, which the Romans had created in favour of Herod the Great, was of short duration; expiring on his death, by his division of his territories, and by the dominions of Archelaus, (which comprised Samaria, Judæa, and Idumæa,) being reduced to a Roman province, annexed to Syria, and governed by the Roman procurators. These officers not only had the charge of collecting the imperial revenues, but also had the power of life and death in capital causes; and on account of their high dignity they are sometimes called *Governors.* Though the Jews did not enjoy the power of life and death, yet they continued to possess a large share of civil and religious liberty; and lived pretty much after their own laws. Three of these procurators are mentioned in the New Testament, viz.: Pilate, Felix, and Festus.

1. Pontius Pilate was sent to govern Judæa, A. D. 26 or 27. He was a cruel and unjust governor; and dreading the extreme jealousy and suspicion of Tiberius, he delivered up the Redeemer to be crucified, contrary to the conviction of his better judgment, and in the vain hope of conciliating the Jews whom he had oppressed. After he had held his office for ten years, having caused a number of innocent Samaritans to be put to death, that injured people sent an embassy to Vitellius, proconsul of Syria: by whom he was ordered to Rome, to give an account of his mal-administration to the emperor. But Tiberius being dead before he arrived there, his successor, Caligula, banished him to Gaul: where he is said to have committed suicide, about the year of Christ 41.

2. On the death of king Herod Agrippa, Judæa being again reduced to a Roman province, the government of it was confided to Antonius Felix: he liberated that country from banditti and impostors; (the *very worthy deeds* alluded to by Tertullus, Acts xxiv. 2;) but he was in other respects a cruel and avaricious governor, incontinent, intemperate, and unjust. So oppressive at length did his administration become, that the Jews accused him

before Nero, and he with difficulty escaped condign punishment. His wife, Drusilla, (mentioned Acts xxiv. 24,) was the sister of Agrippa junior, and had been married to Azizus king of the Emesenes: Felix, having fallen desperately in love with her, persuaded her to abandon her legitimate husband and live with him. The knowledge of these circumstances materially illustrates Acts xxiv. 25, and shows with what singular propriety St. Paul reasoned of righteousness, temperance, and a judgment to come. On the resignation of Felix, the government of Judæa was committed to

3. Portius Festus, before whom Paul defended himself against the accusations of the Jews, (Acts xxv,) and appealed from his tribunal to that of Cæsar. Finding his province overrun with robbers and murderers, Festus strenuously exerted himself in suppressing their outrages. He died in Judæa about the year 62.

The situation of the Jews under the two last-mentioned procurators was truly deplorable. Distracted by tumults, excited on various occasions, their country was overrun with robbers, that plundered all the villages whose inhabitants refused to listen to their persuasions, to shake off the Roman yoke. Justice was sold to the highest bidder; and even the sacred office of high priest, was exposed to sale. But, of all the procurators, no one abused his power more than Gessius Florus, a cruel and sanguinary governor, and so extremely avaricious, that he shared with the robbers in their booty, and allowed them to follow their nefarious practices with impunity. Hence, considerable numbers of the wretched Jews, with their families, abandoned their native country; while those who remained, being driven to desperation, took up arms against the Romans, and thus commenced that war, which terminated in the destruction of Judæa, and the *taking away of their name and nation.*

CHAPTER III.

COURTS OF JUDICATURE, LEGAL PROCEEDINGS, CRIMINAL LAW, AND PUNISHMENTS OF THE JEWS.

SECTION I.—Jewish Courts of Judicature, and Legal Proceedings.

On the settlement of the Israelites in the land of Canaan, Moses commanded them to *appoint judges and officers in all their gates throughout their tribes.* (Deut. xvi. 18.) The priests and Levites, who from their being devoted to the study of the law were consequently best skilled in its various precepts, and old men who were eminent for their age and virtue, administered justice to the people: in consequence of their age, the name of *Elders* became attached to them. Many instances of this kind occur in the New Testament: they were also called *Rulers.* (Luke xii. 58, where ruler is synonymous with judge.)

In the early ages of the world, the *Gate of th City* was the seat of justice; (Gen. xxiii. 10. Deut. xxi. 19, xxv. 6, 7,) on which account, in the time of Moses, the judges appear to have been termed the *Elders of the Gate.* (Deut. xxii. 15, xxv. 7. Isa. xxix. 21.)

From these inferior tribunals, appeals lay to a higher court, in cases of importance. (Deut. xvii. 8—12.

But the highest and most eminent tribunal of the Jews, after their return from the Babylonish captivity, was the *Sanhedrin,* or Great Council, so often mentioned in the New Testament. It consisted of seventy or seventy-two members, under the chief presidency of the high priest, under whom was a vice-president, called the *Father of the Council.* These assessors comprised three descriptions of persons, viz.: 1. The *Chief Priests,* who were partly such priests as had executed the Pontificate, and partly the princes or chiefs of the twenty-four *courses* or classes of priests, who enjoyed this honourable title;—2. The *Elders,* perhaps the princes of tribes or heads of families; —and 3. The *Scribes,* or men learned in the law. It does not appear that *all* the elders and scribes were members of this tribunal: most probably those only were assessors who were either elected to the office, or nominated to it by oyal authority.

Besides the Sanhedrin, the Talmudical writers assert that there were other smaller councils, each consisting of twenty-three persons who heard and determined petty causes: two of these were at Jerusalem, and one in every city containing one hundred and twenty inhabitants. Josephus is silent concerning these tribunals, but they certainly appear to have existed in the time of Jesus Christ: who, by images taken from these two courts, in a very striking manner represents the different degrees of future punishments, to which the impenitently wicked will be doomed according to the respective heinousness of their crimes. See Matt. v. 22.

These various tribunals had their inferior ministers or officers, who are alluded to in Matt. v. 25.

It appears from Jer. xxi. 12, that causes were heard, and judgment was executed in the morning; and at first every one pleaded his own cause; (1 Kings iii. 16—28;) though, in succeeding ages, the Jews seem to have had advocates, for Tertullus was retained against St. Paul. (Acts xxiv. 1, 2.)

On the day appointed for hearing the cause, the parties appeared before the judges; who, in criminal cases, exhorted the culprit to confess his crime. (Josh. vii. 19.) In matters of life and death, the evidence of two or three credible witnesses was indispensable. (Num. xxxv. 30. Deut xvii. 6, 7, xix. 15.) All perjury was most severely prohibited. (Exod. xx. 16, xxiii. 1—3.) Recourse was, in certain cases, had to the sacred lot, called Urim and Thummim, in order to discover the guilty party. (Josh. vii. 14—18. 1 Sam. xiv. 37—45.)

Sentences were only pronounced in the daytime, as appears from Luke xxii. 66. Where persons had rendered themselves obnoxious to the populace, it was usual (and the same practice still obtains in the East) for them to demand prompt justice on the supposed delinquents. This circumstance illustrates Acts xxii. 28—36. As soon as sentence of condemnation was pronounced against a person, he was immediately dragged from the court to the place of execution. Thus our Lord was instantly hurried from the presence of Pilate to Calvary: a similar instance of prompt execution occurred in the case of Achan; and the same practice obtains to this day, both in Turkey and Persia. So zealous were the Jews for the observance of their law, that they were not ashamed themselves to be the executioners of it, and to punish criminals with their own hands. In stoning persons, the witnesses threw the first stones, agreeably to the enactment of Moses. (Deut xvii. 7.) Thus the witnesses against the protomartyr Stephen, after laying down their clothes at the feet of Saul, stoned him: (Acts vii. 58, 59:) and to this custom there is an allusion in John viii. 7. As there were no public executioners in the more ancient periods of the Jewish history, it was not unusual for persons of distinguished rank themselves to put the sentence in execution upon offenders. See an instance in 1 Sam. xv. 33.

But in whatever manner the criminal was put to death, according to the Talmudical writers, the Jews always gave him some wine with incense in it, in order to stupify and intoxicate him. This custom is said to have originated in the precept, recorded in Prov. xxxi. 6, which sufficiently explains the reason why wine mingled with myrrh, was offered to Jesus Christ when on the cross. (Mark xv. 23.

SECTION II.—Roman Judicature, Manner of Trial, and Treatment of Prisoners.

Wherever the Romans extended their power, they also carried their laws; and though, as we have already seen, they allowed their conquered subjects to enjoy the free performance of their religious worship, as well as the exercise of some inferior courts of judicature, yet in all cases of a capital nature the tribunal of the Roman prefect or president was the last resort. Without his permission no person could be put to death at least in Judæa.

The Roman law forbade any one especially Roman citizens, to be scourged or condemned, unheard and without a trial. To this St. Paul alludes in Acts xxii. 25. Neither could a Roman citizen be legally bound, in order to be examined by scourging, or by any other mode of torture, for the purpose of obtaining a confession. When therefore, the tribune, Lysias, not knowing that the apostle enjoyed the citizenship of Rome, had commanded that he should be bound and examined with thongs, and was subsequently informed that he was a citizen, the sacred historian relates that he *was afraid, after he knew that he was a Roman, and because he had bound him.* (Acts xxii 29.) Further, Roman citizens had the privilege of appealing to the imperial tribunal; and this privilege the same apostle exercised. (Acts xxv. 9—12.

"The Roman method of fettering and confining criminals was singular. One end of a chain, that was of commodious length, was fixed about the right arm of the prisoner, and the other end was fastened to the left arm of a soldier. Thus a soldier was coupled to the prisoner, and every where attended and guarded him. This manner of confinement is frequently mentioned, and there are many beautiful allusions to it in the Roman writers. Thus was St. Paul confined. Fettered in this manner, he delivered his apology before Festus, king Agrippa, and Bernice." (Acts xxvi. 29.)

Sometimes the prisoner was fastened to two soldiers, one on each side, wearing a chain both on his right and left hand. St. Paul at first was thus confined. When the tribune received him from the hands of the Jews, he commanded him to be bound with two chains. (Acts xxi. 33.) In this manner was Peter fettered and confined by Herod Agrippa. *The same night Peter was sleeping between two soldiers, bound with two chains.* (Acts xii. 6.) If these soldiers appointed to guard criminals, and to whom they were chained, suffered the prisoner to escape, they were punished with death; (Acts xii. 19;) and the same punishment appears to have awaited gaolers, who permitted their prisoners to escape. (Acts xvi. 27.)

Though not strictly a Roman tribunal, yet as its sittings were permitted by the Roman government, the senate and court of *Areopagus*, at Athens, claims a concise notice in this place. It took cognizance, among other things, of matters of religion, the consecration of new gods, the erection of temples and altars, and the introduction of new ceremonies into divine worship. On this account, Saint Paul was brought before the tribunal of the Areopagus, as a *setter forth of strange gods, because he preached* unto the Athenians Jesus and Αναςασις, *(Anastasis,)* or *the Resurrection.* (Acts xvii. 19.) Its sittings were held on the Αρειος Παγος, (*Areïos Pagos*, or *Hill of Mars*, whence its name was derived,) which is situated in the midst of the city of Athens.

Section III.—On the Criminal Law of the Jews.

I. Crimes against God.—The government of the Israelites being a *Theocracy*, that is, one in which the supreme legislative power was vested in the Almighty, who was regarded as their king, it was to be expected that, in a state confessedly religious, crimes against the Supreme Majesty of Jehovah should occupy a primary place in the statutes given by Moses to that people. Accordingly

1. *Idolatry*, that is, the worship of other gods, in the Mosaic law occupies the first place in the list of crimes. An Israelite therefore was guilty of idolatry,

(1.) When he actually worshipped other gods besides Jehovah, the only true God. This crime is prohibited in Exod. xx. 3.

(2.) *By worshipping images*, whether of the true God under a visible form, to which the Israelites were but too prone, (Exod. xxxii. 4, 5. Judg. xvii. 3, xviii. 4—6. 14—17. 30, 31, vi. 25—33, viii. 24—27. 1 Kings xii. 26—31,) or of the images of the gods of the Gentiles, of which we have so many instances in the sacred history. All *image-worship* whatever is expressly forbidden in Exod xx. 4, 5; and a curse is denounced against it in Deut. xxvii. 15.

(3.) *By prostration before, or adoration of, such images*, or of any thing else revered as a god, such as the sun, moon, and stars. (Exod. xx. 5, xxxiv. 14. Deut. iv. 19.) This prostration consisted in falling down on the knees, and at the same time touching the ground with the forehead.

(4.) *By having altars or groves dedicated to idols, or images thereof;* all which the Mosaic law required to be utterly destroyed; (Exod xxxiv. 13. Deut. vii. 5, xii. 13;) and the Israelites were prohibited, by Deut. vii. 25 26.

from keeping, or even bringing into their houses, the gold and silver that had been upon any image, *lest it should prove a snare*, and lead them astray.

(5.) *By offering sacrifices to idols*, which is forbidden in Levit. xviii. 1—7, especially human victims, which is prohibited in Levit. xviii. 21. Deut. xii. 30. and xviii. 10.

(6.) *By eating of offerings made to idols, made by other people*, who invited them to their offering-feasts. Though no special law was enacted against thus attending the festivals of their gods, it is evidently presupposed as unlawful in Exod. xxxiv. 15.

Idolatry was punished by stoning the guilty *individual.* When a whole city became guilty of idolatry, it was considered in a state of rebellion against the government and was treated according to the laws of war. Its inhabitants, and all their cattle, were put to death ; no spoil was made, but every thing which it contained was burnt, together with the city itself; nor was it ever allowed to be rebuilt. (Deut. xiii. 13—19.) This law does not appear to have been particularly enforced: the Israelites, from their proneness to adopt the then almost universally prevalent polytheism, in most cases overlooked the crime of a city that became notoriously idolatrous ; whence it happened, that idolatry was not confined to any one city, but soon overspread the whole nation. In this case, when the people, *as a people*, brought guilt upon themselves by their idolatry, God reserved to himself the infliction of the punishments denounced against that national crime ; which consisted in wars, famines, and other national judgments. (Lev. xxvi. Deut. xxviii., xxix., xxxii.) For the crime of seducing others to the worship of strange gods, the appointed punishment was stoning to death. (Deut. xiii. 2—12.) In order to prevent the barbarous immolation of infants, Moses denounced the punishment of stoning upon those who offered human sacrifices; which the by-standers might instantly execute upon the delinquent, when caught in the act, without any judicial inquiry whatever. (Levit. xx. 2.)

2. God being both the sovereign and the legislator of the Israelites, *Blasphemy*, that is, the speaking injuriously of his name, his attributes, his government, and his reve-

lation, was not only a crime against Him, but also against the state; it was therefore punished capitally by stoning. (Lev. xxiv. 10—14.)

3. It appears from Deut. xviii. 20—22, that a *False Prophet* was punished capitally, being stoned to death.

4. *Divination,* or the conjecturing of future events, from things supposed to presage them, is expressly prohibited in Levit. xix. 26. 31, xx. 6. 23. 27, and Deut. xviii. 9—12. The punishment of the party *consulting* a diviner, was reserved to God himself; (Levit. xx. 6;) but the diviner himself was to be stoned. (Levit. xx. 27.)

5. *Perjury* is, by the Mosaic law, most peremptorily prohibited as a most heinous sin against God, to whom the punishment of it is left.

II. Crimes against Parents and Magistrates constitute an important article of the criminal law of the Hebrews.

1. In the form of government among that people, we recognise much of the patriarchal spirit; in consequence of which, fathers enjoyed great rights over their families. The *cursing* of parents, that is, not only the imprecation of evil on them, but probably also all *rude* and *reproachful language* towards them, was punished with death; (Exod. xxi. 17. Levit. xx. 9;) as likewise was the *striking* of them. (Exod. xxi. 15.) An example of the crime of cursing a parent, which is fully in point, is given by Jesus Christ in Matt. xv. 4—6, or Mark vii. 9—12. Both these crimes are included in the case of the stubborn, rebellious, and drunkard son; whom his parents were unable to keep in order, and who, when intoxicated, endangered the lives of others. Such an irreclaimable offender was to be punished with stoning. (Deut. xxi. 18—21.) Severe as this law may *seem,* we have no instance recorded of its being carried into effect; but it must have had a most salutary operation in the prevention of such crimes.

2. Civil government being an ordinance of God, provision is made in all well regulated states for respecting the persons of magistrates. All reproachful words, or curses, uttered against persons invested with authority, are prohibited in Exod. xxii. 28. No punishment, how-

ever, is specified; probably it was left to the discretion of the judge, and was different, according to the rank of the magistrate and the extent of the crime.

III. The CRIMES, or Offences AGAINST PROPERTY, mentioned by Moses, are theft, man-stealing, and the denial of any thing taken in trust, or found.

1. On the crime of *Theft*, Moses imposed the punishment of double (and in certain cases still higher) restitution; and if the thief was unable to make it, he was ordered to be sold for a slave, and payment was to be made to the injured party, out of the purchase money. (Exod. xxii. 1. 3.) The same practice obtains, according to Chardin, among the Persians. If, however, a thief, after having denied, even upon oath, any theft with which he was charged, had the honesty, or conscience, to retract his perjury, and to confess his guilt, instead of double restitution, he had only to repay the amount stolen, and one-*fifth* more. (Levit. vi. 2. 5.) In case of debt also, the creditor might seize the debtor's person, and sell him, together with his wife and children, if he had any. This is inferred from the words of the statute, in Levit. xxv. 39. There is an allusion to this custom in Job xxiv. 9; and a case in point is related in 2 Kings iv. 1. This practice also obtained among the Jews, in the days of Nehemiah, (v. 1—5,) and Jesus Christ refers to it in Matt. xviii. 25.

2. *Man-stealing*, that is, the seizing, or stealing of the person of a free-born Israelite, was absolutely and irremissibly punished with death. (Exod. xxi. 16. Deut. xxiv. 7.)

3. Where a person was judicially convicted of having *denied any thing committed to his trust*, or found by him, his punishment, as in the case of theft, was double restitution. If the person accused of this crime had sworn himself guiltless, and afterwards, from the impulse of his conscience, acknowledged the commission of perjury, he had only one-fifth beyond the value of the article denied, to refund to its owner. (Levit. vi. 5.)

IV. Among the CRIMES which may be committed AGAINST THE PERSON,

1. *Murder* claims the first place. As this is a crime

of the most heinous nature, Moses has described four necessary circumstances, or marks, by which to distinguish it from simple homicide, or manslaughter, viz.: 1. When it proceeds from *hatred*, or enmity. (Numb. xxxv. 20, 21. Deut. xix. 11.) 2. When it proceeds from *thirst* of blood, or a desire to satiate revenge with the blood of another. (Numb. xxxv. 20.) 3. When it is committed *premeditatedly and deceitfully*. (Exod. xxi. 14.) 4. When a man lies in wait for another, falls upon him, and slays him. (Deut. xix. 11.) The punishment of murder was death, without all power of redemption.

2. *Homicide*, or *Manslaughter*, is discriminated by the following adjuncts, or circumstances: 1. That it takes place *without* hatred or enmity. (Numb. xxxv. 22. Deut. xix. 4—6.) 2. *Without* thirst for revenge. (Exod. xxi. 13. Numb. xxxv. 22.) 3. When it happens by mistake. (Numb. xxxv. 11. 15.) 4. By *accident*, or (as it is termed in the English law) *chance-medley*. (Deut. xix. 5.) The punishment of homicide was confinement to a city of refuge.

3. For other corporal injuries of various kinds, different statutes were made, which show the wisdom and humanity of the Mosaic laws. See Exod. xxi. 18, 19, 22—27, and Levit. xxiv. 19—22.

4. *Adultery*, and another crime not to be named, were both punished with death. (Levit. xx. 10, xviii. 22, 23, and xx. 13. 15, 16.)

V. Crimes of Malice were punished with equal justice and severity.

Malicious informers were odious in the eye of the law; (Levit. xix. 16—18;) and the publication of false reports, affecting the characters of others, is expressly prohibited in Exod. xxiii. 1; as also is all manner of false witness, even though it were to favour a poor man. But where a person was convicted of having borne false testimony against an innocent man, he suffered the very same punishment which attended the crime of which he accused his innocent brother. (Deut. xix. 16—21.)

Section IV.—On the Punishments mentioned in the Scriptures.

The Punishments, mentioned in the sacred writings, are usually divided into two classes,—*non-capital*, and *capital*.

I. The *non-capital*, or inferior punishments, were as follow:

1. *Scourging;* this was the most common corporal punishment under the Mosaic law. It is frequently mentioned, both in the Old and New Testaments; and in order that the legal number of forty stripes might not be exceeded, it was inflicted with a scourge consisting of three lashes, so that the party received only thirteen blows, or *forty stripes, save one.*

2. *Retaliation,* (Exod. xxi. 24,) or returning like for like, was the punishment of corporal injuries to another. It is expressly forbidden by Jesus Christ, in Matt. v. 38, 39.

3. *Restitution* of things stolen, and for various other injuries done to the property of another person. (Exod. xxi. 32, 33, 34. 36, xxii. 6. Levit. xxiv. 18.)

4. *Compensation* to an injured party, to induce him to depart from his suit, was permitted, at least in one case, (Exod. xxi. 30,) but was forbidden in the case of murder and homicide. (Num. xxxv. 31, 32.)

5. *Sin and Trespass Offerings* were also in the nature of punishments: the various cases for which they were to be made, are specified in Levit. iv. 2, v. 1. 4—7. 14, 15, vi. 1—7, and xix. 22.

6. *Imprisonment,* though not enjoined by Moses, was practised, both during the Jewish monarchy, and in the time of Christ. In Gen. xli. 14, Jer. xxxviii. 6, Zech. ix., and Acts v. 18, there are allusions to inner prisons or dungeons, where the persons confined were very harshly treated; especially as the ancient gaolers (like those in the East to this day) had a discretionary power to treat the prisoners just as they pleased. To this painful situation of prisoners, there are allusions in Psal. lxxix. 11, and Jer. xxxvii. 16—20.

7. *Banishment* was not introduced among the Jews until after the captivity. It also existed among the Ro-

mans. St. John was banished to the isle of Patmos. (Rev. i. 9.)

8. In the East, anciently, as well as in modern times, prisoners were deprived of their eyes. See instances in Judg. xvi. 21, and 2 Kings xxv. 7.

9. *Plucking off the hair*, with great violence, was both a painful and ignominious punishment. It is alluded to in Neh. xiii. 25.

10. *Excommunication*, or exclusion from sacred worship, was a civil, as well as an ecclesiastical punishment, which varied in the degrees of its severity. The first, called *Nidui*, was simply casting out of the synagogue. (John ix. 22, xvi. 2, &c.,) and was in force for thirty days, which might be shortened. In the second, termed *Cherem*, or anathema, the excommunicated party was delivered over to Satan, and devoted by a solemn curse. To this St. Paul alludes in 1 Cor. v. 5, and Rom. ix. 2. The third degree was called *Sham-Atha*, or *Maran-Atha*, i. e. the *Lord cometh*, or *may the* Lord come; and intimated that the party had nothing more to expect but the terrible day of judgment. The effects of excommunication were dreadful: the individuals against whom it was fulminated were debarred of all social intercourse, and the privilege of divine worship, and were subjected to various civil disabilities.

II. Eleven different sorts of Capital Punishments are mentioned in the Scriptures, viz.:

1. *Slaying with the sword*, which appears to have been inflicted in any way in which the executioner thought proper. This was the punishment of murder: but in the case of homicide, if the next of kin, called *Goël*, or the *Blood-avenger*, overtook and slew the unintentional man-slayer, before he reached an asylum, he was not considered to be guilty of blood. The man-slayer was therefore enjoined to flee to one of the six cities of refuge, which, if he reached, he was immediately protected; and an inquiry was instituted, whether he had *deliberately*, or *accidentally* caused his neighbour's death. In the *former* case he was judicially delivered to the goël, who might put him to death in any way that he chose; in the *latter*, the homicide continued to reside in the place of refuge until the high priest's death: yet, if the goël found him

without the city, or its suburbs, he might slay him, without being guilty of blood. (Numb. xxxv. 26, 27.) There is a beautiful allusion to the goël in Heb. vi. 17, 18.

2. *Stoning* was denounced against idolaters, blasphemers, Sabbath-breakers, and other criminals, mentioned in Levit. xx. 2. 27, xxiv. 14. Deut. xiii. 10, xvii. 5, xxi. 21, and xxii. 21. 24. The witnesses threw the first stones, and the rest of the people followed. The frequent taking up of stones, by the Jews, against our Saviour, mentioned in the New Testament, and also the stoning of Stephen, (Acts vii. 59,) and of Paul, (Acts xiv. 19,) have been referred, erroneously, to this punishment: it belonged to what was, in the later times of the Jewish commonwealth, called the *rebels' beating*. It was often fatal, and was inflicted by the populace on those who had either transgressed, or were supposed to have transgressed, any prohibition of the scribes.

3. *Burning alive* was the punishment denounced against certain criminals, mentioned in Levit. xx. 14, and xxi. 9. It is also mentioned in Gen. xxxviii. 24. Jer. xxix. 22, and Dan. iii. 6.

The preceding are the only capital punishments denounced in the Mosaic Law: in subsequent times others were introduced among the Jews, as their intercourse increased with foreign nations; viz.:

4. *Beheading*. It is mentioned in Gen. xl. 19, Matt. xiv. 8—12, and Mark vi. 27.

5. *Precipitation*, or casting headlong from a window, though rarely used, yet was practised on certain occasions. See instances in 2 Kings ix. 30—33, and 2 Chron. xxv. 12.

6. *Drowning* is alluded to in Matt. xviii. 6, but we have no proof that it was practised by the Jews.

7. *Bruising*, or *Pounding in a mortar*, is alluded to in Prov. xxvii. 22. It is still in use among the Turks.

8. *Dichotomy*, or *cutting asunder*, was a punishment inflicted in the countries contiguous to Judæa, (see Dan. ii. 5, and iii. 29,) as it still is in Barbary and Persia

9. *Beating to death* was in use among the Greeks: it was practised by Antiochus towards the Jews, (2 Macc. vi. 19. 28. 30,) and is referred to by St. Paul, in Heb. xi. 35. (Gr. in our version rendered *tortured*.)

10. *Exposing to wild Beasts* was a punishment among

the Medes and Persians; (Dan. vi. 7. 12. 16—34;) from them it passed to the Romans, who either cast slaves and vile persons, to wild beasts, to be devoured by them, or sent armed men into the theatre to fight with the animals. If they conquered, they had their lives and liberty; but if not, they fell a prey to the beasts. To this latter usage St. Paul refers in 2 Tim. iv. 17, and 1 Cor. xv. 32.

11. CRUCIFIXION was a punishment which the ancients inflicted only upon the most notorious criminals and malefactors; and it included every idea and circumstance of lingering torture, odium, disgrace, and public scandal. Hence St. Paul takes occasion to magnify the exceeding great love of our Redeemer, *in that, while we were yet sinners, Christ died for us, and, for the joy that was set before him, endured the cross, despising the shame* and ignominy attached to it. (Rom. v. 8. Heb. xii. 2.) In this punishment, the cross was made of two beams, either crossing at the top at right angles, or in the middle of their length, like an X. Our Lord appears to have been crucified on a cross of the former kind. The horror of crucifixion will be evident, when it is considered that the person was permitted to hang (the whole weight of his body being borne up by his nailed hands and feet, and by the projecting piece in the middle of the cross,) until he perished through agony and want of food. There are instances of crucified persons living in this exquisite torture several days. The rites of sepulture were denied them. Their dead bodies were generally left on the crosses on which they were first suspended, and became a prey to every ravenous beast, and carnivorous bird. This mode of executing criminals, obtained among various ancient nations, especially among the Romans, by whom it was inflicted chiefly on vile, worthless, and incorrigible slaves. In reference to this, the apostle, describing the condescension of Jesus, and his submission to this most opprobrious death, represents him as taking upon him the form of a servant, (Phil. ii. 7, 8,) and becoming obedient to death, even the death of the cross. All the circumstances attending the crucifixion of Jesus Christ, as related in the four gospels, agree with the accounts given of this punishment by Greek and Roman authors.*

* For a full detail of these circumstances, which do not admit of abridgment, see the author's larger Introduction, vol. iii. pp 150—160.

CHAPTER IV.

JEWISH AND ROMAN MODES OF COMPUTING TIME, MENTIONED IN THE SCRIPTURES.

A KNOWLEDGE of the different divisions of time mentioned in the Scriptures, will elucidate the meaning of a multitude of passages with regard to seasons, circumstances, and ceremonies.

I. The Hebrews computed their DAYS from evening to evening, according to the command of Moses. (Lev. xxiii. 32.)

The Romans had two different computations of their days, and two denominations for them. The one they called the *civil*, the other the *natural* day: the first was the same as ours; the second, which was the vulgar computation, began at six in the morning, and ended at six in the evening. The *civil* day of the Jews varied in length, according to the seasons of the year. This portion of time was, at first, divided into *four* parts, (Nehem. ix. 3;) which, though varying in length according to the seasons, could nevertheless be easily discerned from the position, or appearance of the sun in the horizon. Afterwards, the civil day was divided into twelve hours, which were measured either from the position of the sun, or from dials constructed for that purpose.

II. These HOURS were equal to each other, but unequal with respect to the different seasons of the year; thus the twelve hours of the longest day in summer were much longer than those of the shortest day in winter. The Jews computed their hours of the civil day, from six in the morning, till six in the evening; thus their *first* hour corresponded with our *seven* o'clock; their *second* to our *eight;* their *third* to our *nine*, &c.

The night was originally divided into *three* parts, or WATCHES, (Psal. lxiii. 6, xc. 4. Lam. ii. 19. Jud. vii. 19. Exod. xiv. 24,) which probably were of unequal length. In the time of Jesus Christ, it was divided into *four* watches; a fourth watch having been introduced among the Jews from the Romans. The *hour* is frequently used with great latitude in the Scriptures, and sometimes implies the space of time occupied by a whole watch. (Matt.

xxv. 13, xxvi. 40. Mark xiv. 37. Luke xxii. 59. Rev. iii. 3.)

The Jews reckoned two evenings: the former began at the ninth hour of the natural day, or three o'clock in the afternoon; and the latter at the eleventh hour. Thus the paschal lamb was required to be sacrificed *between the evenings.* Exod. xii. 6. Lev. xxiii. 4.)

III. Seven nights and days constituted a WEEK; six of these were appropriated to labour, and the ordinary purposes of life, and the *seventh* day, or *Sabbath*, was appointed by God to be observed as a day of rest. Besides weeks of days, the Jews had *weeks of seven years*, (the seventh of which was called the *sabbatical year*,) and weeks of seven times seven years, or of forty-nine years, which were reckoned from one jubilee to another. The fiftieth, or *jubilee* year was celebrated with singular festivity and solemnity.

IV. The Hebrews had their MONTHS, which like those of all other ancient nations, were lunar ones, being measured by the revolutions of the moon, and consisting alternately of twenty-nine and thirty days. While the Jews continued in the land of Canaan, the commencement of their months and years was not settled by any astronomical rules, or calculations, but by the *phasis* or actual appearance of the moon. As soon as they saw the moon, they began the month; but since their dispersion throughout all nations, they have had recourse to astronomical calculations and cycles, in order to fix the beginning of their months and years.

Originally, the Jews had no particular names for their months, but called them the first, second, &c. In Exod. xiii. 4, the *first* month is termed Abib; in 1 Kings vi. 1, the *second* is named Zif; in 1 Kings viii. 2, the *seventh* is named Ethanim; and the *eighth*, Bul, in 1 Kings vi. 38: but concerning the origin of these appellations, critics are by no means agreed. On their return from the Babylonish captivity, they introduced the names which they had found among the Chaldeans and Persians, and some of which are mentioned in the sacred writings.

V. The Jews had four sorts of years; one for *plants*, so called, because they paid tithe-fruits of the trees which budded at that time; another for *beasts*, in which they paid tithes of the beasts that fell within the year: a third for *sacred* purposes, and the fourth was *civil* and common to all the inhabitants of Palestine. The two last as being most known, require briefly to be noticed.

1. The *Ecclesiastical*, or *Sacred Year*, began in March, or on the first day of the month Nisan, because at that time they departed out of Egypt. From that month they computed their feasts, and the prophets also occasionally dated their oracles and visions. (See Zech. vii. 1.) The following table presents the months of the Jewish ecclesiastical year, compared with our months:

1. Nisan or Abib (Neh. ii. 1. Esth. iii. 7.) answering to part of	March and April.
2. Jyar or Zif	April and May.
3. Sivan (Esth. viii. 9.)	May and June.
4. Thammuz	June and July.
5. Ab	July and August.
6. Elul (Neh. vi. 15.)	August and September.
7. Tisri	September and October.
8. Marchesvan	October and November.
9. Kisleu or Chisleu (Zech. vii. 1. Neh. i. 1.)	November and December.
10. Thebet	December and January.
11. Sebat (Zech. i. 7.)	January and February.
12. Adar (Ezr. vi. 15. Esth. iii. 7.)	February and March.

2. The *Civil Year*, commenced on the fifteenth of our September, because it was an old tradition that the world was created at that time. From this year the Jews computed their jubilees, dated all contracts, and noted the birth of children, and the reigns of kings. The annexed table exhibits the months of the Jewish civil year with the corresponding months of our computation:

1. Tisri corresponds with part of	September and October.
2. Marchesvan	October and November.
3. Chisleu or Kisleu	November and December
4. Thebet	December and Janaury.
5. Sebat	January and February.
6. Adar	February and March.
7. Nisan or Abib	March and April.
8. Jyar or Zif	April and May
9. Sivan	May and June.
10. Thammuz	June and July.
11. Ab	July and August.
12. Elul	August and September.

Some of the preceding names are still in use in Persia.

As the Jewish years, being regulated by the phases, or appearances of the moon, were lunar years, consisting of three hundred and fifty-four days and eight hours, it be came necessary to accommodate them to solar years, in order that their months, and consequently their festivals, might always fall at the same season. For this purpose, the Jews added a whole month to the year, as often as it was necessary; which occurred commonly once in three years, and sometimes once in two years. This intercalary month was added at the end of the ecclesiastical year, after the month Adar, and was therefore called Ve-Adar, or the second Adar.

VI. In common with other nations, the Jews reckoned any *part* of a period of time for the whole, as in Exod. xvi. 35. Thus, a part of the day is used for the whole, and part of a year for an entire year. An attention to this circumstance will explain several apparent contradictions in the sacred writings; particularly the account of our Lord's resurrection, in Matt. xxvii. 63, and Mark viii. 31, *three days after*, with that of his resurrection *on the third day*, according to Matt. xvi. 21, and Luke ix. 22.

Besides the computation of years, the Hebrews first, and the Jews afterwards, were accustomed to reckon their time from some remarkable æras, or epochas: as, 1. The *Lives of the Patriarchs*, or other illustrious persons; (Gen. vii. 1, viii. 13;)—2. From their *Departure out of Egypt*, and the first institution of their polity; (Exod. xix. 1, xl. 17. Numb. i. 1, ix. 1, xxxiii. 38. 1 Kings vi. 1;)—3. Afterwards, from the *Building of the Temple*, (1 Kings ix. 10. 2 Chron. viii. 1,) and from the reigns of the kings of Judah and Israel;—4. Then from the commencement of the Babylonian Captivity. (Ezek. i. 1, xxxiii. 21, xl. 1.) In process of time they adopted, and for one thousand years employed, 5. The æra of the Selucidæ, which in the books of Maccabees is called the æra of the Greeks; in later times, (1 Macc. xiii.42, xiv.27,) they computed according to the years of the Maccabean princes; and since the compilation of their Talmud, they have reckoned their years from the foundation of the world.

CHAPTER V.

ON THE TRIBUTES AND TAXES MENTIONED IN THE SCRIPTURES.—CONTRACTS, HOW MADE.

I. Of Tributes and Taxes

On their first departure out of Egypt, the Israelites con tributed, upon any extraordinary occasion, according to their several ability : after the erection of the tabernacle, half a shekel was paid by every male of twenty years and upwards, (Exod. xxx. 13, 14,) when the census, or *sum of the people* was taken. On their return from the Babylonian captivity, an annual payment of the third part of a shekel was made towards the temple worship and service; (Neh. x. 32;) and in the time of our Saviour, two drachmæ were paid by EVERY Jew, whether he resided in Palestine or elsewhere: besides which, every one, who was so disposed, made voluntary offerings according as he or she was able. (Mark xii. 41—44.)

To supply the Jews, who came to Jerusalem from all parts of the Roman Empire, to pay the half-shekel above mentioned, with the current coins, money-changers stationed themselves at tables in the courts of the temple, and chiefly, it should seem, in the court of the Gentiles, for which they exacted a small fee. It was the tables on which these men trafficked for this unholy gain, which were overturned by Jesus Christ. (Matt. xxi. 12.)

While the Jews were in the height of their prosperity, the Moabites and other neighbouring nations were tributary to their sovereigns. Afterwards, however, the Jews became tributaries to other nations. For a short time they were freed from paying tribute under the Maccabean Princes; but after they were conquered by the Romans, they were subjected to the payment of a capitation tax of a denarius, as well as various other burdens, which they paid with great reluctance. This will account for their hatred of the PUBLICANS, or Tax gatherers. In the provinces of the Roman empire, the tributes were farmed by Roman knights, who had under them inferior officers. Some of these are called *chief publicans*, (as Zaccheus,) probably because they were receivers-general for large districts: others were receivers for some particular post, or place. Such was Matthew, who is simply termed a publican.

II. Of Contracts and bargains of Sale.

Among the Hebrews, and long before them, among the Canaanites, the purchase of any thing of consequence was concluded, and the price paid, at the gate of the city, as the seat of judgment, before all who went out and came in. (Gen. xxiii. 16—20. Ruth iv. 1, 2.) In process of time, the joining, or striking of hands was introduced as a ratification of a bargain and sale. This usage was not unknown in the days of Job, (xvii. 3,) and Solomon often alludes to it. (See Prov. vi. 1, xi. 15, xvii. 18, xx. 16, xxii. 26, xxvii. 13.) The earliest vestige of written instruments, sealed and delivered for ratifying the disposal and transfer of property, occurs in Jer. xxxii. 10—12, which the prophet commanded Baruch to bury in an earthen vessel in order to be preserved for production at a future period, as evidence of the purchase, (14, 15.) No mention is expressly made of the manner in which deeds were anciently cancelled. Some expositors have imagined, that in Col. ii. 14, Saint Paul refers to the cancelling of them by blotting, or drawing a line across them, or by striking them through with a nail; but we have no information whatever from antiquity to authorize such a conclusion.

CHAPTER VI.

OF THE MILITARY AFFAIRS OF THE JEWS, AND OTHER NATIONS MENTIONED IN THE SCRIPTURES.

I. Respecting the Military Discipline of the Jews, numerous particulars are incidentally dispersed through the Sacred Writings, for a *full* account of which the reader is necessarily referred to the author's larger work: from which the following leading circumstances are selected.

The earliest wars, noticed in the sacred writings, appear to have been nothing more than mere predatory excursions, like those of the modern Bedouin Arabs. The wars in which the Israelites were engaged, were of two kinds, either such as were expressly enjoined by divine command, or such as were voluntary, and entered upon by the prince for revenging some national affronts, and for the honour of his sovereignty. After their departure from Egypt, the whole of the men, from twenty years and upwards until the age of fifty, (when they might demand their discharge if they chose,) were liable to military service, the priests and Levites not excepted. (Numb. i. 3. 22. 2 Sam. xxiii. 20. 1 Kings ii. 35.) Like the militia in some countries, they were always ready to assemble at the shortest notice. If the occasion were extremely urgent, affecting their existence as a people, all were summoned to war; but ordinarily, when there was no necessity for convoking the whole of their forces, a selection was made. This mode of choosing soldiers, to which there are numerous allusions in the Scriptures, accounts for the rapid formation of the vast armies, of which we read in the Old Testament. There were, however, certain exemptions in favour of particular persons, which are specified in Deut. xx. 5—8, xxiv. 5. The officers, who were placed at the head of the Hebrew forces, appear not to have differed materially from those whom we find in ancient and modern armies. The most distinguished was the *Captain of the Host*, (2 Kings iv. 13,) who possessed great power and influence, sometimes indeed nearly equal to that of the sovereign, and who appears to have been of the same rank with him who is now termed the commander in chief of an army. After the establishment of the monarchy, this officer, and also the captains of thousands, hundreds, &c., received their commissions from the sovereign; (2 Sam. xviii. 1. 2 Chron. xxv. 5;) who at first went to war in person, and fought on foot, like the meanest of his soldiers, until David being exposed to great danger, his people would no longer allow him to lead them on to battle. (2 Kings xxi. 17.) There were no horse in the Israelitish army before the time of Solomon; nor, though mention is made in Scripture of the military chariots of other nations, does it appear that the Hebrews ever used war chariots. Solomon, indeed, had a considerable number, but no military expedition is recorded, in which he employed them. No information is given us in the Scriptures concerning the order of encampment adopted by the Israelites after their settlement in Canaan. During their sojourning in the wilderness, the form of their camp, according to the account given in

Numb. ii. appears to have been quadrangular, having three tribes placed on each side, under one general standard, so as to enclose the tabernacle, which stood in the centre. Between these four great camps and the tabernacle, were pitched four smaller camps of the priests and Levites, who were immediately in attendance upon it; the camp of Moses and of Aaron and his sons (who were the ministering priests, and had the charge of the sanctuary,) was on the east side of the tabernacle, where the entrance was. The following diagram, which is reduced from the author's larger work, will give the reader an idea of the beautiful order of the Israelitish Encampment, which extorted from the mercenary Balaam, the exclamation related in Numb xxiv. 2. 5. 6.

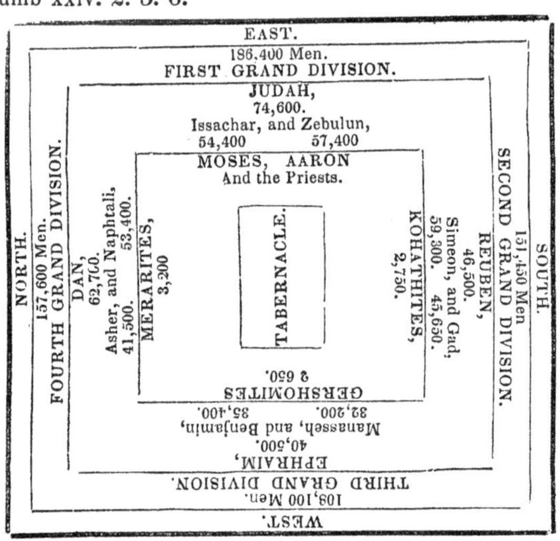

During the encampment of the Israelites in the wilderness, Moses made various salutary enactments, which are recorded in Deut. xxiii. 10—15. Anciently, the Hebrews received no pay for their military service: the Cherethites and Pelethites appear to have been the first stipendiary soldiers. During the monarchy, however, both officers and privates were paid by the sovereign, who rewarded them for distinguished achievements. (See 2 Sam.

xviii. 11. Jos. xv. 16. 1 Sam. xviii. 25. 1 Chron. xi. 6.) In the age of the Maccabees, the patriot Simon both armed and paid his brave companions in arms at his own expense. (1 Mac. xiv. 32.) Afterwards it became an established custom, that all soldiers should receive pay. (Luke iii. 14. 1 Cor. ix. 7.)

From various passages of Scripture, and especially from Isa. ii. 4, and Mic. iv. 3, it appears that there were military schools, in which the Hebrew soldiers *learned war*, or, in modern language, were trained by proper officers in those exercises which were in use among the other nations of antiquity. Swiftness of foot was an accomplishment highly valued, both for attacking and pursuing an enemy. The Hebrews do not appear to have had any peculiar military habit; as the flowing dress, which they ordinarily wore, would have impeded their movements, they girt it closely around them when preparing for battle, and loosened it on their return. They used the same arms as the neighbouring nations, both defensive and offensive; and these were made either of iron or of brass, but principally of the latter metal.

At first every man provided his own arms; but, after the establishment of regal government, the sovereigns formed depôts, whence they supplied their troops. (2 Chron. xi. 12, xxvi. 14, 15.) The *defensive* arms consisted of a helmet, breast-plate, shield, military girdle, and greaves, or boots to protect the feet and legs from stakes, which were stuck into the ground to impede the march of a hostile force. Their *offensive* arms were, the sword, spear, or javelin, bows and arrows.

The onset of battle was very violent, and was made with a great shout. (Numb. xxiii. 24. Exod. xxxii. 17. 1 Sam. xvii. 20, 52, &c.) When the victory was decided, the bodies of the slain were interred, (1 Kings xi. 15. 2 Sam. ii. 32. 2 Mac. xii. 39,) but sometimes the remains of the slain were treated with every possible mark of indignity; (1 Sam. xxxi. 9—12;) and various cruelties were inflicted upon the unhappy captives, from which not even women and children were exempted. (2 Sam. iv. 12. Judg. i. 7. Isai. iii. 17. 2 Kings viii. 12. Psal. cxxxvii. 9.)

On their return home, the victors were received with every demonstration of joy. (Exod. xv. 1—21. Judg

xi. 34. 1 Sam. xviii. 7, 8. 2 Chron. xx. 27, 28.) Besides a share of the spoil and the honours of a triumph, various rewards were bestowed on those warriors who had pre-eminently distinguished themselves: allusions to them occur in 1 Sam. xvii. 25. 2 Sam. v. 8, and xviii. 11. 1 Chron. xi. 6.

II. At the time the apostles and evangelists wrote, Judæa was subject to the dominion of the Romans, whose troops were stationed in different parts of the country. Hence numerous allusions are made to the MILITARY DISCIPLINE OF THE ROMANS, in the New Testament, particularly in the writings of Saint Paul. See especially Eph. vi. 11—17, in which the various parts of the armour of their heavy troops are distinctly enumerated and beautifully applied to those moral and spiritual weapons with which the true Christian ought to be fortified.

The strictest subordination and obedience were exacted of every Roman soldier, who was also inured to great hardships, and was not allowed to marry. To these circumstances there are allusions in Matt. viii. 8, 9, and 2 Tim. ii. 3, 4; and Rev. iii. 5, probably refers to the practice of expunging from the muster-roll the names of those who died, or were cashiered for misconduct. Upon those who pre-eminently distinguished themselves, were conferred rich and splendid crowns, frequently of gold, to which there are allusions in Rev. ii. 10, James i. 12, 1 Pet. v 4, and 2 Tim. iv. 8. But the highest military honour which any one could receive, was a *Triumph:* in which, besides great numbers of wagons full of the arms and the richest spoils which had been taken from the vanquished foe, the most illustrious captives—sovereigns not excepted—were led in fetters before the victorious general's chariot, through the streets of Rome, amidst the applause of the assembled multitudes. After the triumphal procession was terminated, the unhappy captives were generally imprisoned, and, if not put to death, were sold for slaves. The knowledge of these circumstances beautifully illustrates the allusions in 1 Cor. ii. 14—16, and Col. ii. 15.

BOOK III.—SACRED ANTIQUITIES OF THE JEWS, AND OF OTHER NATIONS MENTIONED IN THE SCRIPTURES

CHAPTER I.

OF SACRED PLACES.

THE Patriarchs, both before and after the flood, were accustomed to worship Almighty God, before altars, and also upon mountains, and in groves. (Gen. viii. 20, xii. 8, xxi. 33, and xxii. 2.) In the wilderness, where the Israelites themselves had no settled habitations, they had, by God's command, a moving tabernacle; and as soon as they were fixed in the land of promise, God appointed a temple to be built at Jerusalem, which David intended, and his son Solomon performed. After the first temple was destroyed, another was built in the room of it, (Ezra iii. 8,) which Christ himself owned for his *house of prayer*. (Matt. xxi. 13.) There were also places of worship, called in Scripture *High Places*, used promiscuously during the times of both the tabernacle and temple, until the captivity; and, lastly, there were *Synagogues* among the Jews, and other places used only for prayer, called *Proseuchæ*, or *oratories*, which chiefly obtained after the captivity: of these various structures some account will be found in the following sections.

SECTION I.—Of the Tabernacle.

Mention is made in the Old Testament of three different tabernacles, previously to the erection of Solomon's temple. The *first*, which Moses erected for himself, is called the *tabernacle of the congregation;* (Exod. xxxiii. 7;) here he gave audience, heard causes, and inquired of Jehovah; and here also at first, perhaps, the public offices of religion were solemnized. The *second* tabernacle was that erected by Moses, for Jehovah, and at his express command, partly to be a palace of his presence as the king of Israel, (Exod. xl. 34, 35,) and partly to be the medium of the most solemn public worship, which the people were to pay to him, (26—29.) This tabernacle was erected on the first day of the first month, in the second year after the departure of the Israelites from Egypt. The *third* public tabernacle was that erected by David in his own city, for the reception of the ark, when he received it from the house of Obed-edom. (2 Sam. vi. 7. 1 Chron. xvi. 1.) Of the second of these tabernacles we are now to treat; it was called the TABERNACLE, by way of distinction, and was a moveable chapel, so contrived as to be taken to pieces, and put together again at pleasure, for the convenience of carrying it from place to place. The materials of this tabernacle were provided by the people, who contributed each according to his ability, as related in Exodus, ch. xxxv. and xxxvi.

The tabernacle consisted, first, of a house, or tent, the form of which appears to have resembled that of our modern tents, but much larger; and, secondly, of an open court that surrounded it. Its constituent parts are minutely described in Exod. xxv.—xxx. and xxxv.—xl. from which the following particulars have been selected:

1. The tent itself was an oblong square, thirty cubits in length and ten in height and breadth; and the body of it was composed of forty-eight boards, or planks, each of which was a cubit and a half wide, and ten cubits high, and its roof was a square frame of planks. The inside of it was divided by a veil, or hanging, made of rich embroidered linen, which separated the *Holy Place* from the *Holy of Holies.* In the former stood the altar of incense, overlaid with gold, the table of shewbread, consisting of twelve loaves, and the great candlestick of pure gold, containing seven branches: none of the people were allowed to go into the holy place, but only the priests. The Holy of Holies, so called because it was the most sacred place of the tabernacle, into which none went but the high priest, contained in it the ark, called the ark of the testimony, (Exod. xxv. 22,) or the ark of the covenant. (Josh. iv. 7.) This was a small chest, or coffer, made of shittim wood, overlaid with gold, into which were put the two tables of the law, as well the broken ones, say the Jews,

as the whole, with the pot of manna, and Aaron's rod that budded. (Heb. ix. 4.)

The lid, or covering of this ark, was wholly of solid gold, and called the mercy-seat: at the two ends of it were two cherubim, or hieroglyphic figures, the form of which it is impossible now to ascertain, looking inwards towards each other, with wings expanded, which, embracing the whole circumference of the mercy-seat, met on each side in the middle. Here the Shechinah, or Divine Presence, rested, both in the tabernacle and temple, and was visibly seen in the appearance of a cloud over it. (Lev. xvi. 2.) From this the divine oracles were given out by an audible voice, as often as Jehovah was consulted on behalf of his people. (Exod. xxv. 22. Numb. vii. 89.) And hence it is that God is so often said, in Scripture, *to dwell between the cherubim.* (2 Kings xix. 15. Psal. lxxx. 1.)

2. The Tabernacle was surrounded by an oblong court, separated by curtains from the camp of Israel. The priests, and other sacred ministers, alone were permitted to enter it; the people, who came to offer sacrifices, stopped at the entrance, opposite to which stood the brazen altar for burnt offerings; and nearly in the centre of the court stood a capacious brazen vessel, called the brazen laver, in which the priests washed their hands and feet previously to performing any of their sacred functions.

The tabernacle being so constructed as to be taken to pieces, and put together as occasion required, it accompanied the Israelites in all their progresses, until they arrived in the land of Canaan. There it was set up, first at Gilgal, and afterwards at Shiloh: on being restored by the Philistines, who had taken it and deposited it in the temple of one of their idols, as related in 1 Sam. iv. 10, 11, v., vi.; it remained for twenty years in the custody of Abinadab, of Gibeah, and afterwards, for three months, in the house of Obed-edom, whence David brought it with great solemnity into that part of Jerusalem, which was called the city of David. (2 Sam. vi. 17. 1 Chron. xv. 25, xvi. 1.) Here it remained until it was deposited in the temple of Solomon, where, having been subsequently removed, it was again replaced by order of the pious King Josiah. (2 Chron. xxxv. 3.) It is supposed to have been consumed in the destruction of Jerusalem by Nebuchadnezzar.

SECTION II.—Of the Temple.

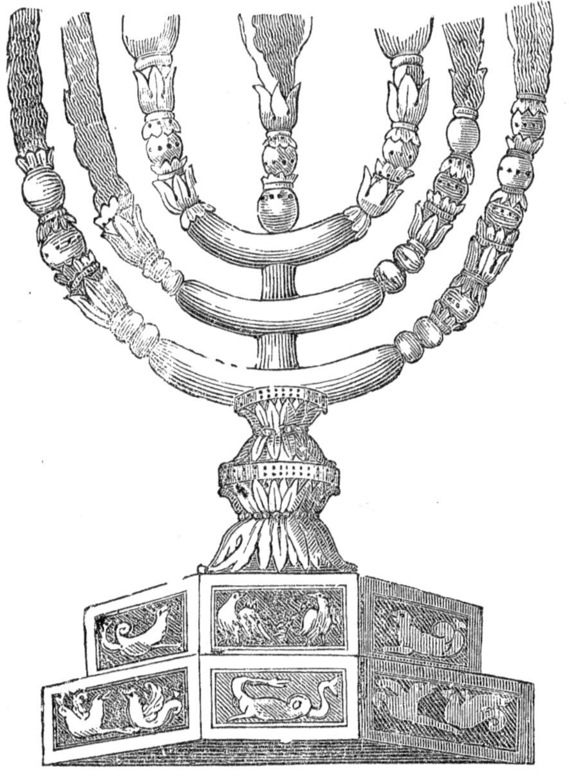

Representation of the GOLDEN CANDLESTICK, from the Triumphal Arch of Titus.

Two Temples are mentioned in the Scriptures, 1. That of Solomon; and 2. That erected after the Captivity.

I. The FIRST TEMPLE is that which usually bears the name of Solomon; the materials for which were provided by David before his death, though the edifice was raised by his son. It stood on Mount Moriah, an eminence of the mountainous ridge, in the Scriptures termed Mount Sion, (Psal. cxxxii. 10, 14,) which had been purchased of Araunah, or Ornan, the Jebusite. (2 Sam. xxiv. 23, 24. 1 Chron. xxi. 25.) The plan, and whole model of this superb structure, were formed after that of the tabernacle, but of much larger dimensions. It was dedicated by Solomon with great solemnity. Various attempts have been made to describe the proportions, and several parts of this structure: but as no two writers, scarcely, agree on this subject, a minute description of it is designedly omitted. It retained its pristine splendour only thirty-three or thirty-four years, when Shishak, king of Egypt, took Jerusalem, and carried away the treasures of the temple; and, after undergoing subsequent profanations and pillages, this stupendous building was finally plundered and burnt by the Chaldæans, under Nebuchadnezzar, in the year of the world 3416, or before Christ, 584. (2 Kings xxv. 13—15. 2 Chron. xxxvi. 17—20.)

II. After the captivity, the temple emerged from its ruins, being rebuilt by Zerubbabel, but with vastly inferior and diminished glory; as appears from the tears of the aged men who had beheld the former structure in all its grandeur. (Ezra iii. 12.) The SECOND TEMPLE was profaned by order of Antiochus Epiphanes; (A. M. 387, B. C. 163;) who caused the daily sacrifice to be discontinued, and erected the image of Jupiter Olympus on the altar of burnt offering. In this condition it continued three years, (1 Macc. i. 62,) when Judas Maccabeus purified and repaired it, and restored the sacrifices and true worship of Jehovah. (A. M. 3840. B. C. 160.)

Some years before the birth of our Saviour, the repairing, or rather *gradual* rebuilding, of this second temple, which had become decayed in the lapse of five centuries, was undertaken by Herod the Great, who for nine years employed eighteen thousand workmen upon it, and spared no expense to render it equal, if not superior, in magnitude, splendour, and beauty, to any thing among mankind. But though Herod accomplished his original design, in the time above specified, yet the Jews continued to ornament and enlarge it, expending the sacred treasure in annexing additional buildings to it; so that they might with great propriety assert, that their temple had been forty and six years in building. (John ii. 20.)

The second temple, originally built by Zerubbabel, after the captivity, and repaired by Herod, differed in several respects, from that erected by Solomon, although they agreed in others.

The temple erected by Solomon was more splendid and magnificent than the second temple, which was deficient in five remarkable things that constituted the chief glory of the first: these were, the ark and mercy-seat, the shechinah, or manifestation of the divine presence in the holy of holies, the sacred fire on the altar, which had been first kindled from heaven, the urim and thummim, and the spirit of prophecy. The second temple, however, surpassed the first in glory; being honoured by the frequent presence of our divine Saviour, agreeably to the prediction of Haggai, (ii. 9.) Both, however, were erected upon the same site, a very hard rock, encompassed by a very frightful precipice; and the foundation was laid with incredible expense and labour. The superstructure was not inferior to this great work: the height of the temple wall, especially on the south side, was stupendous. In the lowest places it was three hundred cubits, or four hundred and fifty feet, and in some places even greater. This most magnificent pile was constructed with hard white stone of prodigious magnitude. Of its general disposition some idea may be formed from the plan annexed to the Map which faces page 163.

The temple itself, strictly so called, which comprised the portico, the sanctuary, and the holy of holies, formed only a small part of the sacred edifice on Mount Moriah; being surrounded by spacious courts, making a square of half a mile in circumference. It was entered through nine magnificent gates: one of which, called the *Beautiful Gate* in Acts iii. 2, was more splendid and costly than all the rest: it was composed of Corinthian brass, the most precious metal in ancient times. The first, or outer court, was called the *Court of the Gentiles;* because they were not permitted to advance any further, though they were allowed to enter it. Markets were held here for the sale of incense, salt, animals, and every other article necessary for the Jewish sacrifices. Here also sat the money-changers. (Matt. xxi. 12, 13. Mark xi. 15—17.) This court was surrounded by a range of porticoes, or cloisters, one of which was called *Solomon's Porch.* (John x. 23. Acts iii. 11.) The south-east corner of the roof of this portico is supposed to have been the pinnacle, whence Satan tempted Christ to precipitate himself. (Mat. iv. 5.)

Within the court of the Gentiles stood the *Court of the Israelites*, divided into two parts, or courts, the outer one being appropriated to the women, and the inner one to the men. The *Court of the Women* was separated from that of the Gentiles, by a low stone wall, or partition, of elegant construction, on which stood pillars at equal distances, with inscriptions in Greek and Latin, importing that no alien should enter into the holy place. To this wall Saint Paul most evidently alludes in Eph. ii. 13, 14. In this court was the Treasury, mentioned in Mark xii. 41, and John viii. 20.

From the court of the women, which was on higher ground than that of the Gentiles, there was an ascent of fifteen steps into the inner, or men's court; and so called because it was appropriated to the worship of the male Israelites. In these two courts, collectively termed the court of the Israelites, were the people praying, each apart by himself, for the pardon of his sins, while Zechariah was offering incense within the sanctuary. (Luke i. 10.)

Within the court of the Israelites was that of the priests, who alone were permitted to enter it: thence twelve steps ascended to the *Temple*, strictly so called, which consisted of three parts, viz.: the Portico, the outer Sanctuary, and the Holy Place.

1. In the *Portico* were suspended the splendid votive offerings, made by the piety of various individuals, which are alluded to in Luke xxi. 5. Similar offerings were common in the temples of the heathen. From this porch,

2. The *Sanctuary*, or Holy Place, was separated from the holy of holies by a double veil, which is supposed to have been the veil that was rent in twain at our Saviour's

crucifixion; thus emblematically pointing out that the seperation between Jews and Gentiles was abolished, and that the privilege of the high priest was communicated to all mankind, who might thenceforth have access to the throne of grace through the one great Mediator, Jesus Christ. (Heb. x. 19—22.)

This corresponded with the Holy Place in the Tabernacle. In it were placed the Golden Candlestick, the Altar of Incense, and the Table of Shew-Bread, which consisted of twelve loaves, according to the number of the tribes of Israel. In the Hebrew, these loaves are collectively termed, *Bread of the faces;* because each loaf, being square, had, as it were, *four faces* or sides. Various fanciful delineations have been given of these articles: in the vignette at the head of this section, is represented the form of the *Golden Candlestick*, as it was actually carried in the triumphal procession of the Roman General, Titus; and the following engraving exhibits the table of shew-bread, with a cup upon it, and with two of the sacred

trumpets, which were used to proclaim the year of Jubilee, as they were also carried in the same triumph. They are copied from the plates in Reland's Treatise on he

Spoils of the Temple of Jerusalem,* the drawings for which were made at Rome, upwards of a century since, when the triumphal arch of Titus (which has been mentioned in p. 23, *supra*,) was in a much better state of preservation than it now is.

3. The *Holy of Holies* was twenty cubits square. No person was ever admitted into it but the high priest, who entered it once a year on the great day of atonement. (Exod. xxx. 10. Levit. xvi. 2. 15. 34. Heb. ix. 2—7.)

This most magnificent temple, for which the Jews cherished the highest veneration, was utterly destroyed by the Romans, A.M. 4073, (A.D. 73,) on the *same day* of the *same month* in which Solomon's temple had been razed to the ground by the Babylonians

---

Section III.—Of the High Places, Proseuchæ, or Oratories, of the Jews.

I. The High Places, which are frequently mentioned in the Old Testament, were places appropriated to divine worship, in groves, woods, or mountains, first by the patriarchs, and afterwards by the heathen idolaters, by whom they were made the scenes of the most diabolical and impure rites. As the Canaanites, among whom the Israelites lived, were eminently addicted to this idolatrous worship, *after* a place had been assigned for the worship of God, it became unlawful to offer sacrifices upon these high places, or any where else, but in the place that God did choose. Hence it is that the conduct of the Israelites, both kings and people, in offering sacrifices even after the erection of the temple, is so frequently reprobated in the books of Kings and Chronicles. They were indeed removed by several pious kings, and particularly by Josiah, after whose time they are not mentioned in sacred history.

II. Though public worship was forbidden to be offered in any but the appointed place, yet mention is made, in Scripture, of places built for *private devotion*, and resorted to for that purpose only. These have been termed

* De Spoliis Hierosolymitani in Arcu Titiano Romæ Conspicuis. The first edition was printed at Utrecht, in 1716, 8vo.; the second, with a preliminary dissertation and notes, by Professor Schultze, in 1765, 8vo.

PROSEUCHÆ, or Oratories. From the proseucha, (so it should be rendered in Luke vi. 12,) where our Lord spent a whole night in prayer, being erected on a mountain, it is probable that these edifices were the same as the High Places already noticed. The Jews, who were resident in heathen countries, appear to have erected them in sequestered retreats, commonly on the banks of rivers, or on the sea-shore. The proseucha, or oratory at Philippi, where *the Lord opened the heart of Lydia, that she attended unto the things which were spoken by Paul*, was *by a* RIVER SIDE; (Acts xvi. 13, 14. 16;) the Jews being accustomed, before prayer, to perform an ablution.

SECTION IV.—On the Synagogues of the Jews.

The SYNAGOGUES were buildings in which the Jews assembled for prayer, reading and hearing the sacred Scriptures, and other instructions. Though frequently mentioned in the historical books of the New Testament, their origin is not very well known; and many learned men are of opinion that they are of recent institution. In the time of the Maccabees, synagogues became so frequent that they were to be found in almost every place in Judæa. Maimonides says, that wherever any Jews were, they erected a synagogue. Not fewer than four hundred and eighty are said to have been erected in Jerusalem, previously to its capture and destruction by the Romans. In the evangelical history we find, that wherever the Jews resided, they had one or more synagogues, constructed after those at Jerusalem. It does not appear that the synagogues had any peculiar *form* of structure: there were, however, various officers whose business it was to see that the duties of religion were decently performed therein. These were, 1. The RULERS OF THE SYNAGOGUE, (Luke xiii. 14. Mark v. 22,) of whom there appear to have been several: they regulated all its concerns, and gave permission to persons to preach. 2. Next to the Ruler of the Synagogue was an officer, whose province it was to offer up public prayers to God for the whole congregation; hence he was called *Sheliach Zibbor*, or the ANGEL OF THE CHURCH, because, as their messenger, he spoke to God for them. Hence also, in Rev. ii., iii. the ministers of the Asiatic churches are termed *angels.* 3. The *Chazan* appears to have been a different officer from the *Sheliach Zibbor*, and inferior to him in dignity. He seems to have been the person, who, in Luke iv. 20, is termed the MINISTER, and had the charge of the sacred books; and whose office it was to hand the book of the law to the person who was to read it, and return it to its place.

The service performed in the synagogue consisted of three parts, viz.: prayer, reading the Scriptures, and preaching, or exposition of the Scriptures.

1. The first part of the Synagogue service is PRAYER; for which some learned men have thought that the Jews had liturgies, in which are all the prescribed forms of synagogue-worship. Though the eighteen prayers, used by the modern Jews, are of great antiquity, yet they cannot be referred to the time of Jesus Christ.

2. For the more commodious READING OF THE SCRIPTURES, the Law was divided into Paraschioth, or Sections, and the Prophets into Haphtoroth, or Portions; of which a brief notice has already been given in page 79.

3. The third and last part of the synagogue service is, EXPOSITION OF THE SCRIPTURES, and PREACHING to the people. The first was performed *at* the time of reading them, and the other *after* the reading of the law and the prophets. In Luke iv. 15—22, we have an account of the service of the synagogue in the time of Christ; who appears to have taught the Jews in both these ways. From this passage we learn that when Jesus Christ came to Nazareth, his own city, he was called out, as a member of that synagogue, to read the haphtoroth, that is, the section or lesson out of the prophets for that day; which appears to have been the fifty-first haphtoroth, and to have commenced with the *first* verse of Isa. lxi. Further, he stood up (as it was customary, at least for the officiating minister to do, out of reverence for the word of God) to read the scriptures; and unrolled the manuscript (or *opened the volume*, as it is rendered in Luke iv. 17,), until he came to the lesson appointed for that day; which having read, he rolled it up again (or *closed the book*, verse 20,) and gave it to the proper officer; and then he sat down and expounded it, agreeably to the usage of the Jews. The ancient books, being written on parchment, or vellum, and similar flexi-

ble materials, were rolled round a stick, and, if they were very long, round two, from the extremities. This is the case in the vignette inserted in page 71,* which will convey some idea of the manner in which the Synagogue Rolls are unrolled. It is taken from the original and very valuable manuscript in the British Museum, which is described at length in p. 71, *supra*.

Those who had been guilty of any notorious crime, or were otherwise thought unworthy, were cast out of these synagogues, that is excommunicated, and excluded from partaking with the rest in the public prayers and religious offices there performed; so that they were looked upon as mere Heathens, and shut out from all benefit of the Jewish religion, which exclusion was esteemed scandalous.

CHAPTER II.

SACRED PERSONS.

SECTION I.—Of the Jewish Church and its Members.

FROM their covenant relation to Almighty God, the whole Jewish nation are, in the scriptures, frequently termed holy; and the apostles, being Jews by birth, (though they wrote in Greek,) have often applied to Christians the phraseology of the Old Testament, in order to convey to them accurate ideas of the magnitude of God's love to them in Christ.

The first members of the Jewish Church were the immediate and lineal descendants of Abraham, Isaac, and Jacob; who professed the Jewish religion and used the national language wherever they might reside, and whom St. Paul (Phil. iii. 5,) terms *Hebrews of the Hebrews*, as opposed to the *Hellinists*, or those Jews who lived among the Greeks and spoke their language, and many of whom (as Timothy, Acts xvi. 1,) were descended from parents, *one* of whom only was a Jew. They did not, however, exclude such persons as were willing to qualify themselves for participating in their sacred rites. Hence they admitted Gentile converts to Judaism, who are often termed strangers and sojourners, or proselytes. The *Libertines*,

* Hence is derived the term *volume*, or thing rolled up, from the Latin word *volvo*, to roll.

mentioned in Acts vi. 9, were the descendants of the *Liberti*, or those Jews, who, having been taken captive at different times and carried into Italy, had subseqently acquired their liberty. The *Devout men who feared God*, of whom we frequently read in the New Testament, were Gentiles; who, though they did not qualify themselves for full communion with the Jewish church, had, nevertheless, acquired a better knowledge of the Most High than the Pagan Theology furnished, and who, in some respects, conformed to the Jewish religion. Of this description was Cornelius the Centurion. (Acts x.)

All these persons, with the exception of the last class, were members of the Jewish church, participated in its worship, and regulated themselves by the law of Moses, (or at least professed to do so,) and by the other inspired Hebrew books, whence their sacred rites and religious instruction were derived. No person, however, was allowed to partake of the sacred ordinances until he had undergone the rite of circumcision: which sacrament was enjoined to be observed on the eighth day after the birth of a male child, who then received a name. (Gen. xvii. 12. Luke i. 59, ii. 22.)

In the initiation of proselytes to the Jewish religion, according to the rabbinical writers, the three following observances were appointed, namely, circumcision, baptism, and the offering of sacrifice.

All these rites, except circumcision were performed by the women, as well as the men, who became proselytes; and it was a common notion among the Jews, that every person, who had duly performed them all, was to be considered as a new-born infant.

Section II.—On the Ministers of the Temple, and other Ecclesiastical, or Sacred Persons.

On the establishment of the Jewish Commonwealth, the tribe of Levi was specially devoted to the service of God, instead of the first-born of the tribes of Israel, and was disengaged from all secular labours. The honour of the priesthood, however, was reserved to the family of Aaron alone, the rest of the tribe being employed in the inferior offices of the temple: so that all the priests were Levites, but all the Levites were not priests.

Originally, the LEVITES, or tribe of Levi, were divided into the three families and orders of Gershomites, Kohathites, and Merarites; (1 Chron. vi. 16, &c.;) but afterwards they were divided by David (1 Chron. xxiii.) into four classes.

Their principal office was to wait upon the priests, and be assisting to them in the service of the tabernacle, with its utensils, (which, during the migrations of the Israelites in the wilderness, they alone were permitted to carry and to set up when the camp rested,) and afterwards in the service of the temple; so that they were properly the ministers and servants of the priests, and obliged to obey their orders. (Numb. iii. 9. 1 Chron. xxiii. 28.) It was their duty to open, close, and guard the temple, to cleanse the sacred vessels, to have the charge of the sacred loaves, &c. &c. Some of them also sang psalms, while others played on instruments, but all were divided into companies, over whom a president was placed. The Levites had under them persons called *Nethinims*, who performed various laborious services in the temple.

In order to enable the Levites to devote themselves to that service, forty-eight cities were assigned to them for their residence, on the division of the land of Canaan; thirteen of these were appropriated to the priests, to which were added the tithes of corn, fruit, and cattle. (Numb. xviii. 21—24.) The Levites, however, paid to the priests a tenth part of all their tithes; and as they were possessed of no landed property, the tithes which the priests received from them were considered as the first fruits which they were to offer to God.

Next to the Levites, but superior to them in dignity, were the ordinary PRIESTS, who were chosen from the family of Aaron exclusively. They served immediately at the altar, prepared the victims, and offered the sacrifices. They kept up a perpetual fire on the altar of the burnt sacrifices, and also in the lamps of the golden candlestick in the sanctuary; in short, performed, first in the tabernacle, and afterwards in the temple, every thing directly connected with the service of God. And, as the number and variety of their functions required them to be well read in their law, in order that they might be able to judge of the various *legal* uncleannesses, &c.; this circumstance caused them to be consulted as interpreters of the Law, (Hos. iv. 6. Mal. ii. 7, &c. Lev. xiii. 2. Numb. v. 14, 15,) as well as judges of controversies. (Deut. xxi. 5, xvii. 8—13.) In the time of war, their business was to carry the ark of the covenant, to sound the holy trumpets, and animate the army to the performance of its duties. To them also it belonged publicly to bless the people in the name of the Lord.

The priests were divided by David into twenty-four classes, (1 Chron. xxiv. 7—18,) which order was retained by Solomon, (2 Chron. viii. 14,) and at the revivals of the Jewish religion by the kings Hezekiah and Josiah. (2 Chron. xxxi. 2, xxxv. 4, 5.) As, however, only four classes returned from the Babylonish captivity, (Ezra ii. 36—39. Neh. vii. 39—42, xii. 1,) these were again divided into twenty-four classes, each of which was distinguished by its original appellation. One of these classes went up to Jerusalem every week to discharge the sacerdotal office, and succeeded one another on the Sabbath-day, till they had all attended in their turn. To each order was assigned a president, (1 Chron. xxiv. 6—31. 2 Chron. xxxvi. 14,) whom some critics suppose to be the same as the *chief priests*, so often mentioned in the New Testament. The prince, or prefect of each class appointed an entire family to offer the daily sacrifices; and at the close of the week, they all joined together in sacrificing. And as each family consisted of a great number of priests, they drew lots for the different offices which they were to perform. It was by virtue of such lot, that the office of burning incense was assigned to Zacharias, the father of John the Baptist, *when he went into the temple of the Lord.* (Luke i. 9.)

For the residence of the priests, thirteen of the Levitical cities, already mentioned, were assigned, around each of which they had three thousand cubits of land: their maintenance was derived from tithes, and various other offerings enumerated in Levit. vii. 6. 10. 33, 34, Deut. xviii. 3, Numb. xviii. 13. 15, 16, Levit. xix. 23, 24, and Numb. xxxi. 28—41.

Over all the priests was placed the High Priest, who

enjoyed peculiar dignities and influence. He alone could enter the Holy of Holies in the tabernacle, and afterwards in the temple: the supreme administration of sacred things was confided to him; he was the final arbiter of all controversies; in later times he presided over the sanhedrin, and held the next rank to the sovereign, or prince. His authority, therefore, was very great at all times, especially when he united the pontifical and regal dignities in his own person. In the Old Testament he is sometimes called *the priest*, by way of eminence, (Exod. xxix. 30. Neh. vii. 65,) and sometimes the head, or chief of the high priests, because the appellation of high priests was given to the heads of the sacerdotal families, or courses.

The pontifical dignity, in its first institution, was held for life, provided the high priests were not guilty of crimes that merited deposition. During this period the high priesthood is supposed to have been elective.

The first high priest, after the return from the captivity, was Joshua, the son of Josedek, of the family of Eleazar; whence the succession went into a private Levitical family. The office was then filled by some of the princes of the Maccabean family. According to the law, it was, or ought to have been held, for life; but this was very ill obeyed under the Roman government, especially during the time of our Saviour, and in the latter years of the Jewish polity, when election and the right of succession were totally disregarded. The dignity, sanctity, and authority of the high priest were then almost annihilated; and this office was not unfrequently sold to the highest bidder, to persons who had neither age, learning, nor rank to recommend them; nay, even to individuals who were not of the sacerdotal race; and sometimes the office was made annual. The knowledge of this fact will explain the circumstance of several high priests being in existence at the same time, or rather of their being several pontifical men, (Annas and Caiphas, for instance,) who, having once held the office for a short time, seem to have retained the dignity originally attached to the name.

The high priest, who was the chief man in Israel, and appeared before God, in behalf of the people, in their sacred services, and who was appointed for sacrifice, for blessing, and for intercession, was a type of Jesus Christ, that great high priest, who offered himself a sacrifice for sin, who blesses his people, and who *evermore liveth to make intercession for them.* The term *priest* is also applied to every true believer, who is enabled to offer up himself a spiritual sacrifice acceptable to God through Christ. (1 Pet. ii. 5. Rev. i. 6.)

Next to the Levites, priests, and high priests, the OFFICERS OF THE SYNAGOGUE may be mentioned here, as being, in some degree, sacred persons; since to them was confided the superintendence of those places which were set apart for prayer and instruction. Their functions and powers have been stated in pp. 223, 224, *supra*.

The NAZARITES, or NAZARENES, (as the Hebrew word Nazir implies,) were persons separated from the use of certain things, and sequestered, or consecrated to Jehovah. They are commonly regarded as sacred persons: a notice of their institute will be found *infra*, in page 243.

The RECHABITES, are by many writers considered as a class of holy persons, who, like the Nazarites, separated themselves from the rest of the Jews, in order that they might lead a more pious life. But this is evidently a mistake: for they were not Israelites, or Jews, but Kenites, or Midianites, who used to live in tents, and traverse the country in quest of pasture for their cattle, as the Nabathæan Arabs anciently did, and as the modern Arabians, and Crim-Tartars still do. Their manner of living was not the result of a religious institute, but a mere civil ordinance grounded upon a national custom. They derived their name from Jonadab, the son of Rechab, a man of eminent zeal for the pure worship of God against idolatry, who assisted king Jehu in destroying the house of Ahab and the worshippers of Baal. (2 Kings x. 15, 16. 23.) The Rechabites flourished, as a community, about one hundred and eighty years; but were dispersed after the destruction of Jerusalem by Nebuchadnezzar. Some of their descendants are said to have been lately discovered in Arabia.

The PROPHETS were eminently distinguished among the persons accounted holy by the Jews: they were raised up by God in an extraordinary manner for the performance of the most sacred functions. Originally, they were called *Seers:* they discovered things yet future, declared the will of God, and announced their divine messages, both to kings and people, with a confidence and freedom that could only be produced by the conviction that they were indeed authorized messengers of Jehovah. The gift of prophecy was not always annexed to the priesthood; there were prophets of all the tribes, and sometimes even among the Gentiles. The office of a prophet was not confined to the prediction of future events; it was their province to instruct the people, and they interpreted the law of God; hence the words *prophet* and *prophecy* are, in many passages of the Scriptures, synonymous with interpreter, or teacher, and interpretation, or teaching. They also had seminaries, termed *Schools of the Prophets*, where religious truths, or the divine laws, were particularly taught. It is unanimously agreed, both by Jews and Christians, that Malachi was the last of the prophets under the Old Testament dispensation: and it is a remarkable fact, that so long as there were prophets among the Jews, they were not divided by sects, or heresies, although they often fell into idolatry. This circumstance may thus be accounted for. As the prophets received their communications of the divine will *immediately* from God himself, there was no alternative for the Jews; either the people must obey the prophets, and receive their interpretation of the law, or no longer acknowledge that God who inspired them. When, however, the law of God came to be explained by weak and fallible men, who seldom agreed in their opinions, sects and parties were the unavoidable result of such conflicting sentiments.

CHAPTER III.

SACRED THINGS.—ON THE SACRIFICES AND OTHER OFFERINGS OF THE JEWS.

THE offerings prescribed to the Israelites have been divided into four classes, viz.: Bloody Offerings, Unbloody Offerings, Drink Offerings, and Oblations of different kinds.

I. BLOODY OFFERINGS were sacrifices properly and strictly so called; by which we may understand the infliction of death on a living creature, generally by the effusion of its blood, in a way of religious worship, and the presenting of this act to God as a supplication for the pardon of sin, and as a supposed mean of compensation for the insult and injury offered by sin to his majesty and government. In all sacrifices of this class, it was required that the victims should be *clean*, that is, such as might be eaten. Of the bird tribe, the dove was the most common offering; of quadrupeds, oxen, sheep, and goats were the *only* kinds destined for the altar. Further, the victim was to be without blemish, (Levit. xxii. 22,) and one which had never borne the yoke. Being found immaculate, it was led to the altar by the person offering the sacrifice, who laid his hands upon its head; by which act he acknowledged the sacrifice to be his own, and that he offered it as an atonement for his own sins, by which he had forfeited his life to the violated law of God. The animal being immolated, the blood was caught in a vessel. and partly sprinkled round about upon the altar; by which the atonement was made. (Levit. i. 5—7.) The remainder of the blood was poured out at the foot of the altar; previously to laying the sacrifice thereon, it was salted for the fire. (Levit. ii. 13. Mark ix. 46.) At first, sacrifices were offered at the door of the tabernacle; but after the erection of the temple, it was not lawful to offer them elsewhere. The Jewish sacrifices were of three kinds, viz.:

1. The Burnt Offerings, or *Holocausts*, were free-will offerings, wholly devoted to God, according to the primitive patriarchal usage. The man himself was to bring them before the Lord, and they were offered in the manner just described. The victim to be offered was, according to the person's ability, a bullock without blemish, or a male of the sheep, or goats, or a turtle-dove, or pigeon. (Levit. i. 3. 10. 14.) If, however, he was too poor to bring either of these, he was to offer a mincha, or meat-offering, of which an account is given in page 234. It was a very expressive type of the sacrifice of Christ, as nothing less than his *complete* and full sacrifice could make atonement for the sins of the world.

2. The Peace Offerings (Levit. iii. 1,) were also free-will offerings, in token of peace and reconciliation between God and man; they were either eucharistical, that is,

offered as thanksgivings for blessings received, or were offered for the impetration of mercies. These offerings consisted either of animals, or of bread, or dough; if the former, part of them was burnt upon the altar, especially all the fat, as an offering to the Lord; and the remainder was to be eaten by the priest, and by the party offering. To this sacrifice of praise, or thanksgiving, Saint Paul alludes in Heb. xiii. 15, 16. In this kind of sacrifices the victims might be either male or female, provided they were without blemish. The same apostle has a fine allusion to them in Eph. ii. 14—19.

3. SIN OFFERINGS were offered for sins committed, either through ignorance, or wilfully against knowledge, and which were always punished unless they were expiated. In general they consisted of a sin offering to God, and a burnt offering, accompanied with restitution of damage. (Levit. v. 2—19, vi. 1—7.)

4. The TRESPASS OFFERINGS were made, where the party offering had just reason to doubt whether he had violated the law of God or not. (Levit. v. 17, 18.) They do not appear to have differed materially from sin offerings. In both these kinds of sacrifices, the person who offered them placed his hands on the victim's head, if a sin offering, and confessed his sin over it, and his trespass over the trespass offering; the animal was then considered as vicariously bearing the sins of the person who brought it.

All these sacrifices were occasional, and had reference to individuals; but there were others which were national and regular, daily, weekly, monthly, and annual.

The perpetual, or *Daily Sacrifice*, was a burnt offering, consisting of two lambs, which were offered every day, morning and evening, at the third and ninth hours. (Exod. xxix. 38—40. Levit. vi. 9—18. Numb. xxviii. 1—8.) They were burnt as holocausts, but by a small fire, that they might continue burning the longer. With each of these victims was offered a bread offering, and a drink offering of strong wine. The morning sacrifice, according to the Jews, made atonement for the sins committed in the night, and the evening sacrifice expiated those committed during the day.

The *Weekly Sacrifice*, on every Sabbath-day, was equal

to the daily sacrifice, and was offered in addition to it. (Numb. xxviii. 9, 10.)

The *Monthly Sacrifice*, on every new moon, or at the beginning of each month, consisted of two young bullocks, one ram, and seven lambs of a year old, together with a kid for a sin offering, and a suitable bread and drink-offering. (Numb. xxviii. 11—14.)

The *Yearly Sacrifices* were thus offered on the great annual festivals, which are noticed in the following chapter, viz.: 1. The paschal lamb at the passover, which was celebrated at the commencement of the Jewish *sacred* year; 2. On the day of Pentecost, or day of first-fruits: 3. On the New Moon, or first day of the seventh month, which was the commencement of their civil year; and 4. on the day of expiation.

II. The Unbloody Sacrifices, or Meat-offerings, were taken solely from the vegetable kingdom: they could not, regularly, be presented as sin-offerings, unless the person who had sinned was so poor that he could not afford to bring two young pigeons, or two turtle-doves. They were to be free from leaven, or honey, but to all of them it was necessary to add pure salt, that is, saltpetre.

III. Drink-Offerings were an accompaniment to both bloody and unbloody sacrifices: they were never used separately; and consisted of wine, which appears to have been partly poured upon the brow of the victim, in order to consecrate it, and partly allotted to the priests, who drank it, with their portions of both these kinds of offerings.

IV. Besides the preceding sacrifices, various other oblations are mentioned in the sacred writings, which have been divided into ordinary, or common, voluntary, or free oblations, and such as were prescribed.

1. The *Ordinary Oblations* consisted, 1. Of the *Shew-bread*, which has been already noticed in p. 221; the loaves were placed hot, every Sabbath-day, by the priests, upon the golden table of the sanctuary before the Lord, when they removed the stale loaves which had been exposed the whole of the preceding week; and, 2. Of *Incense*, which was composed of several fragrant spices, prepared according to the commands given in Exod. xxx. 34—36. It was offered twice, daily, by the

officiating priest, upon a golden altar, whereon no bloody sacrifice was to come, except on the day of atonement, when it was offered by the high priest. During this offering, the people prayed silently without; (Luke i. 10;) and to this solemn silence St. John alludes in Rev. viii. 1.

2. The *Voluntary*, or *Free* Oblations were, the fruits either of promises or of vows; but the former were not considered so strictly obligatory as the latter, of which there were two kinds: 1. The *vow of consecration*, when any thing was devoted to God, either for sacrifice or for the service of the temple, as wine, wood, salt, &c. To this class of vows belonged the Corban, reprobated by Jesus Christ, which the Pharisees carried so far as to exonerate children from assisting their indigent parents (Mark vii. 9—11. 13;) and, 2. The *vow of engagement*, when persons engaged to do something that was not in itself unlawful, as not to eat of some particular meat, not to wear some particular habits, not to drink wine, nor to cut their hair, &c.

3. The *Prescribed Oblations* were either First Fruits, or Tithes.

(1.) All the *First Fruits*, both of fruit and animals, were consecrated to God; (Exod. xxii. 29. Numb. xviii. 12, 13. Deut. xxvi. 2. Neh. x. 35, 36;) and the first fruits of sheep's wool were offered for the use of the Levites. (Deut. xviii. 4.) These first fruits were offered from the feast of Pentecost, until that of Dedication, because after that time the fruits were neither so beautiful, nor so good as before. Further, the Jews were prohibited from gathering in the harvest until they had offered to God the *omer*, that is, the new sheaf, which was presented the day after the great day of unleavened bread; neither were they allowed to bake any bread made of new corn, until they had offered the new loaves upon the altar on the day of pentecost; without which all the corn was regarded as unclean and unholy. To this St. Paul alludes in Rom. xi. 16.

2. Besides the first fruits, the Jews also paid the tenths, or *tithes*, of all they possessed; (Numb. xviii. 21;) they were, in general, collected from all the fruits of the earth, but chiefly of corn, wine, and oil, and were rendered every year, except the sabbatical year.

CHAPTER IV.

SACRED TIMES AND SEASONS OBSERVED BY THE JEWS.

In order to perpetuate the memory of the numerous wonders God had wrought in favour of his people, Moses by the divine command instituted various festivals, which they were obliged to observe : these sacred seasons were either weekly, monthly, or annual, or recurred after a certain number of years.

I. Every *seventh day* was appropriated to sacred repose, and called the SABBATH ; although this name is in some passages given to other festivals, as in Levit. xxv. 4 ; and sometimes it denotes a week, as in Matt. xxviii. 1, Luke xxiv. 1, and Acts xx. 7. It was originally instituted to preserve the memory of the creation of the world ; (Gen. ii. 3 ;) and when God gave the Israelites rest in the land of Canaan, he commanded the Sabbath to be statedly kept. (Exod. xx. 10, 11, xvi. 23.) Accordingly, it was observed with great solemnity ; the Jews religiously abstaining from all servile work. (Exod xx. 10, xxiii. 12, &c. &c.) It was therefore unlawful to gather manna on that day, (Exod. xvi. 22—30,) to light a fire for culinary purposes, and also to sow or reap. (Exod. xxxv. 3. Numb. xv. 32—36. Exod. xxxiv. 21.) The services of the temple, however, might be performed without profaning the sabbath, such as preparing the sacrifices ; (Lev. vi. 8—13. Numb. xxviii. 3—10. Matt. xii. 5 ;) and it was also lawful to perform circumcision on that day. (John vii. 23.) The sabbath commenced at sun-set, and closed at the same time on the following day. (Matt. vii. 16. Mark i. 32.) Whatever was necessary was prepared on the latter part of the preceding day, that is, of our Friday; whence the day preceding the Sabbath is termed the *preparation* in Matt. xxvii. 62, Mark xv. 42, Luke xxii. 54, and John xix. 14. 31. 42.

We know not with certainty from the Mosaic writings what constituted the most ancient worship of the Israelites on the Sabbath-day. It is, however, evident from the New Testament, that the celebration of this day chiefly consisted in the religious exercises which were then performed: though there is no injunction recorded, except that a burnt-offering of two lambs should on that day be added to the morning and evening sacrifices, (Numb. xxviii. 9,) and that the shewbread should be changed. (Levit. xxiv. 8,) In the synagogues, as we have already seen, the sacred writings were read and expounded; to which was sometimes added, a discourse, or sermon by some doctor, or eminent teacher. (Luke iv. 16. Acts xiii. 15.)

Prayer also appears to have formed a part of their sacred worship in the synagogue, and especially in the temple: (1 Sam. i. 9, 10. 1 Kings viii. 29, 30. 33. Psal. xxviii. 2. Luke xviii. 10:) the stated hours were at the time of offering the morning and evening sacrifice, or at the third and ninth hours; (Acts ii. 15, and iii. 1;) although it was the custom of the more devout Jews, as David (Psal. lv. 17,) and Daniel, (vi. 10.) to pray three times a day. Peter *went up to the house top to pray.* (Acts x. 9.)

II. The Jewish months being lunar, were originally calculated from the first appearance of the moon, on which the *Feast of the new moon*, or beginning of months, (as the Hebrews termed it,) was celebrated. (Exod. xii. 2. Numb. x. 10, xxviii. 11. Isa. i. 13, 14.) It seems to have been in use long before the time of Moses, who by the divine command prescribed what ceremonies were then to be observed. It was proclaimed with the sound of trumpets, (Numb. x. 10. Psal. lxxxi. 3,) and several additional sacrifices were offered. (Numb. xxviii. 11—15.)

Besides the Sabbath, Moses instituted other festivals: three of these, viz.: the passover, the feast of pentecost, and the feast of tabernacles, which are usually denominated the *Great Festivals*, were distinguished from the Sabbath, and indeed from all other holy days, by the circumstance of each of them lasting seven (one for eight) successive days; during which, the Jews were bound to rejoice before the Lord for all their deliverances and mercies. (Deut. xvi. 11—15.) All the males of the twelve tribes were bound to be present at these grand festivals; (Exod. xxxiv. 23. Deut. xvi. 16;) and for their encouragement to attend, they were assured that "no man should desire their land" during their absence: (Exod. xxxiv. 24:) in other words, that they should be secure from hostile invasion during their attendance on religious worship:—a manifest proof this of the divine origin of their religion, as well as of the power and particular providence of God, in working thrice every year an especial miracle for the protection of his people.

III. The first and most eminent of these festivals was the PASSOVER, instituted the night before the Israelites' departure from Egypt, for a perpetual memorial of their signal deliverance, and of the favour which God showed them in passing over, and sparing their first-born, when he slew the first-born of the Egyptians. (Exod. xii. 12—14. 29, 30—51.) This festival was also called the *feast, or the days of unleavened bread;* (Exod. xxiii. 15. Mark xiv. 1. Acts xii. 3;) because it was unlawful to eat any other bread during the seven days the feast lasted. The name was also, by a metonymy, given to the lamb that was killed on the first day of this feast, (Ezra vi. 20. Matt. xxvi. 17,) whence the expressions, to *eat the passover* (Mark xiv. 12. 14,) and to *sacrifice* the passover. (1 Cor. v. 7.) Hence also, St. Paul calls Jesus Christ our passover, (ibid.) that is our true paschal lamb. But the appellation, *passover*, belongs more particularly to the second day of the feast, viz.: the fifteenth day of the month Nisan. It was ordained to be celebrated on the anniversary of the deliverance of the Israelites. This was an indispensable rite, to be observed by every Israelite, except in particular cases enumerated in Numb. ix. 1—13, on pain of death; and no uncircumcised person was allowed to partake of the passover. In the later times of the Jewish Polity, the custom was introduced, of liberating some criminals, in order to render this festival the more interesting: and this custom had become so strong that Pilate could not deviate from it, and therefore reluctantly liberated Barabbas. (Matt. xxvii. 15. Luke xxiii. 17. John xviii. 39.) The particular rites with which this festival was to be celebrated, are specified in Exod. xii. The later Jews made some addition to the rites prescribed by Moses respecting the paschal sacrifice. They drank with it four cups of wine, of which the third was called *the cup of blessing*, (alluded to in 1 Cor. x. 16, compared with Matt. xxvi. 27.) After which they sang the hymn called the "Great Hallel," viz.: Psalm cxiii.—

cxviii. Sometimes, when, after the fourth cup, the guests felt disposed to repeat Psalms cxx.—cxxxvii. a fifth cup was also drunk. These ceremonies appear to have been in part imitated by Jesus Christ, in the institution of the Eucharist. The paschal victim typified Jesus Christ, his sufferings, and death: not a bone of it was to be broken: a circumstance, in which there was a remarkable correspondence between the type and the antitype. (Exod. xii. 46. John xix. 33—36.)

IV. The Second Great Festival, was the Feast of Pentecost, which was celebrated on the fiftieth day after the first day of unleavened bread. It was a festival of thanksgiving for the harvest, which commenced immediately after the passover. On this account two loaves made of the new meal were offered before the Lord as the first fruits: whence it is called the day of the first fruits. The form of thanksgiving is given in Deut. xxvi. 5—10.

V. The Feast of Tabernacles, was instituted to commemorate the dwelling of the Israelites in tents, while they wandered in the desert. (Lev. xxiii. 34—43.) Hence it is called by St. John, the *feast of tents*, (σκηνοπηγια, *skenopegia*, John vii. 2.) It is likewise termed the *feast of ingatherings*, (Exod. xxiii. 16, xxxiv. 22.) Further, the design of this feast was, to return thanks to God, for the fruits of the vine, as well as of other trees, which were gathered about this time, and also to implore his blessing upon those of the ensuing year. During the whole of the solemnity they were obliged to dwell in tents, which anciently were pitched on the flat terrace-like roofs of their houses. (Neh. viii. 16.) Besides the ordinary daily sacrifices, there were several extraordinary ones offered on this occasion, which are detailed in Numb. xxix. One of the most remarkable ceremonies performed at this feast, was the libation, or pouring out of water, drawn from the fountain, or pool of Siloam, upon the altar. As, according to the Jews themselves, this water was an emblem of the Holy Spirit, Jesus Christ manifestly alluded to it, when he "cried, saying, *If any man thirst, let him come unto me and drink.*" (John vii. 37—39.)

VI. To the three grand *annual* festivals above described, Moses added two others, which were celebrated with great solemnity, though the presence of every male Israelite was not absolutely required.

1. The first of these was the FEAST OF TRUMPETS: it was held on the first and second days of the month Tisri, which was the commencement of the civil year of the Hebrews. This feast derives its name from the blowing of trumpets in the temple with more than usual solemnity. (Numb. xxix. 1. Levit. xxiii. 24.) On this festival, they abstained from all labour, (Levit. xxiii. 25.) and offered particular sacrifices to God, which are described in Numb. xxix. 1—6.

2. The other feast alluded to, was the FAST, or FEAST OF EXPIATION, or DAY OF ATONEMENT; which day the Jews observed as a most strict fast, abstaining from all servile work, taking no food, and *afflicting their souls.* (Levit. xxiii. 27—30. Of all the sacrifices ordained by the Mosaic law, the sacrifice of the atonement was the most solemn and important: it was offered on the tenth day of the month Tisri, by the high priest alone, for the sins of the whole nation. On this day only, in the course of the year, was the high priest permitted to enter the sanctuary, and not even then without due preparation, under pain of death; all others being excluded from the tabernacle during the whole ceremony, which prefigured the grand atonement to be made for the sins of the whole world by Jesus Christ. The particulars incident to this solemnity are detailed in Levit. xvi.

VII. Besides these various annual festivals, which were instituted by divine command, the Jews in later times introduced several other feast and fast days, of which the following were the principal:—

1. The FEAST OF PURIM, or of LOTS, as the word signifies, is celebrated on the fourteenth and fifteenth days of the month Adar, (or of Ve-Adar, if it be an intercalary year,) in commemoration of the providential deliverance of the Jews from the cruel machinations of Haman, who had procured an edict from Artaxerxes to extirpate them. (Esth. iii.—ix.) On this occasion the entire book of Esther is read in the synagogues of the modern Jews, not out of a printed copy, but from a roll, which generally contains this book alone. All Jews, of both sexes, and

of every age, who are able to attend, are required to come to this feast, and to join in the reading, for the better preservation of the memory of this important fact.

2. The FEAST OF DEDICATION, mentioned in John x. 22, was instituted by Judas Maccabeus, to commemorate the purification of the second temple, after it had been profaned by Antiochus Epiphanes. (1 Macc. iv. 52—59.) It commenced on the 25th day of the month Cisleu, and was solemnized *throughout the country* with great rejoicings.

VIII. The preceding are the chief annual festivals noticed in the sacred writings, that are particularly deserving of attention: the Jews have various others, of more modern institution, which are here designedly omitted. We, therefore, proceed to notice those extraordinary festivals, which were only celebrated after the recurrence of a certain number of years.

1. The first of these was the SABBATICAL YEAR; for, as the seventh day of the week was consecrated as a day of rest to man and beast, so this gave rest to the land; which, during its continuance, was to lie fallow, and the "sabbath of the land," or its spontaneous produce, was dedicated to charitable uses, to be enjoyed by the servants of the family, by the way-faring stranger, and by the cattle. (Levit. xxv. 1—7. Exod. xxiii. 11.) This was also the year of release from personal slavery, (Exod. xxi. 2,) as well as of the remission of debts. (Deut. xv. 1, 2.)

2. The JUBILEE was a more solemn sabbatical year, held every seventh sabbatical year, that is, at the end of every forty-nine years, or the fiftieth current year. (Levit. xxv. 8—10.) It commenced on the evening of the day of atonement, and was proclaimed by the sound of trumpet throughout the whole land. All debts were to be cancelled; all slaves, or captives, were to be released. Even those who had voluntarily relinquished their freedom at the end of their six years' service, and whose ears had been bored in token of their perpetual servitude, were to be liberated at the jubilee: for then they were to *proclaim liberty throughout all the land, unto all the inhabitants thereof.* (Levit. xxv. 10.) Further, in this year all estates that had been sold reverted to their original proprieors, or to the families to which they had originally be-

longed ; thus provision was made, that no family should be totally ruined, and doomed to perpetual poverty ; for the family estate could not be alienated for a longer period than fifty years. The value and purchase-money of estates, therefore, diminished in proportion to the near approach of the jubilee. (Levit. xxv. 15.) From this privilege, however, houses in walled towns were excepted ; these were to be redeemed within a year, otherwise they belonged to the purchaser, notwithstanding the jubilee. (ver. 30.) During this year, as well as in the sabbatical year, the ground also had its rest, and was not cultivated.

CHAPTER V.

SACRED OBLIGATIONS AND DUTIES.—OF OATHS.—NATURE AND DIFFERENT SORTS OF VOWS.

1. Of Oaths.—The person who confirmed his assertion by a voluntary oath, pronounced the same with his right hand elevated : but when an oath was exacted, whether judically, or otherwise, the person to whom it was put, answered by saying, *Amen, Amen, (So let it be,)* or, *Thou hast said it.* (Numb. v. 19—22. Deut. xxvii. 15—26. Matt. xxvi. 64.) In the time of Christ, the Jews were in the habit of swearing by the altar, by Jerusalem, by themselves, &c. &c. ; and because the sacred name of God was not mentioned in such oaths, they considered them as imposing little, if any deception. Such fraudu lent conduct is severely censured by Jesus Christ in Matt. v. 33—37, and xxiii. 16—22.

II. Nature and different kinds of Vows.

A Vow is a religious engagement, or promise, voluntarily undertaken by a person towards Almighty God : to render it valid, Moses requires that it be actually uttered with the mouth, and not merely in the heart; (Numb xxx. 3. 7. 9. 13. Deut. xxiii. 24;) and in Deut. xxiii. 18, he prohibits the offering of what is acquired by impure means. Two sorts of Vows are mentioned in the Old Testament; viz.:

I. The Cherem, or *Irremissible Vow:* it was the most solemn of all, and was accompanied with a form of exe-

-cration. This vow is no where enjoined by Moses. The species of cherem with which we are best acquainted, was the previous devotement to God of hostile cities, against which they intended to proceed with extreme severity; and *that* with a view the more to inflame the minds of the people to war. In such cases, not only were all the inhabitants put to death, but also, according as the terms of the vow declared, no booty was made by any Israelite; the beasts were slain; what would not burn, as gold, silver, and other metals, was added to the treasure of the sanctuary; and every thing else, with the whole city, burnt, and an imprecation pronounced upon any attempt that should ever be made to rebuild it. Of this the history of Jericho (Josh. vi. 17—19. 21—24, and vii. 1. 12—26,) furnishes the most remarkable example.

2. The common vows were divided into two sorts, viz.: 1. Vows of dedication; and, 2. Vows of self-interdiction, or abstinence.

i. The NEDER, or vow, in the stricter sense of the word, was when a person engaged to do any thing, as, for instance, to bring an offering to God; or otherwise to dedicate any thing unto him. Things vowed in this way, were, 1. *Unclean beasts.* These might be estimated by the priest, and redeemed by the vower, by the addition of one-fifth to the value. (Lev. xxvii. 11—13.) 2. *Clean beasts used for offerings.* Here there was no right of redemption; nor could the beasts be exchanged for others, under the penalty of both being forfeited, and belonging to the Lord. (Lev. xxvii. 9, 10.) 3. *Lands and houses.* These had the privilege of valuation and redemption. (Lev. xxvii. 14—24.) To these we have to add, 4. *The person of the vower himself,* with the like privilege. (Lev. xxvii. 1—8.)

ii. Vows of SELF-INTERDICTION, or SELF-DENIAL, were, when a person engaged to abstain from wine, food, or any other thing. To this class of vows may be referred the *Nazareate*, or Nazariteship, the statutes respecting which are related in Numb. vi. The Nazarites were required to abstain from wine, fermented liquors, and every thing made of grapes, to let their hair grow, and not to defile themselves by touching the dead; and if any person had accidentally expired in their presence, the Nazarites of the second class were obliged to recommence their Naza riteship.

Similar to the Nazareate was the vow frequently made by devout Jews, on their recovery from sickness, or deliverance from danger, or distress: who, for thirty days before they offered sacrifices, abstained from wine, and shaved the hair of their head. This usage illustrates the conduct of St. Paul, as related in Acts xvii. 18.

III. The PURIFICATIONS of the Jews were various, and the objects of them were either persons, or things dedicated to divine worship. The Jews had two sorts of washing; one, of the whole body by *immersion*, which was used by the priests at their consecration, and by the proselytes at their initiation;—the other, of the hands, or feet, called *dipping*, or *pouring of water*, and which was of daily use, not only for the hands, and feet, but also for the cups and other vessels used at their meals. (Matt. xv. 2. Mark vii. 3, 4. John ii. 6.) To these two modes of purification, Jesus Christ seems to allude in John xiii. 10

IV. In the Mosaic law, those persons are termed *unclean*, whom others were obliged to avoid touching, or even meeting, unless they chose to be themselves defiled, that is, cut off from all intercourse with their brethren; and who, besides, were bound to abstain from frequenting the place where divine service and the offering-feasts were held, under penalties still more severe.

The duration and degrees of impurity were different. In some instances, by the use of certain ceremonies, an unclean person became purified at sunset; in others, this did not take place, until eight days after the physical cause of defilement ceased. Lepers were obliged to live in a detached situation, separate from other people, and to keep themselves actually at a distance from them. They were distinguished by a peculiar dress; and if any person approached, they were bound to give him warning, by crying out, *Unclean! unclean!* Other polluted persons, again, could not directly touch those that were clean, without defiling them in like manner, and were obliged to remain without the *camp*, that they might not be in their way. (Numb. v. 1—4.) Eleven different species of impurity are enumerated in the Levitical law, to which the later Jews added many others. But the severest of all was the

Leprosy, an infectious disease of slow, and imperceptible progress, beginning very insidiously and gently, until at length it became incurable, and most offensively loathsome. The Mosaic statutes respecting this malady, are recorded in Levit. xiii. xiv. Numb. v. 1—4, and Deut. xxiv. 8, 9. The leprosy has ever been considered as a lively emblem of that moral taint, or corruption of the nature of every man, *that naturally is engendered of the offspring of Adam*;* as the sacrifices, which were to be offered by the healed leper, prefigured that spotless *Lamb of God that taketh away the sin of the world.*

CHAPTER VI.

ON THE CORRUPTIONS OF RELIGION BY THE JEWS.

I. On the Idolatry of the Jews.—II. Jewish Sects, mentioned in the New Testament.—III. Extreme corruption of the Jewish People at the time f Christ's Birth.

I. Idolatry of the Jews.

Idolatry is the superstitious worship of idols, or false gods. From Gen. vi. 5, compared with Rom. i. 23, there is every reason to believe that it was practised before the flood; and this conjecture is confirmed by the apostle Jude, (ver. 4,) who, describing the character of certain men in his days, that *denied the only Lord God*, adds, in the eleventh verse of his epistle, *Wo unto them, for they are gone into the way of Cain;* whence it may be inferred that Cain and his descendants were the first who threw off the sense of a God, and worshipped the creature instead of the Creator. The heavenly bodies were the first objects of idolatrous worship, and Mesopotamia and Chaldæa were the countries where it chiefly prevailed after the deluge, whence it spread into Canaan, Egypt, and other countries. Although Moses, by the command and instruction of God, had given to the Israelites such a religion as no other nation possessed, and notwithstanding all his laws were directed to preserve them from idolatry, yet, so wayward were the Israelites, that, almost immedi-

* Article IX. of the Confession of the Anglican Church.

ately after their departure from Egypt, we find them worshipping idols. (Exod. xxxii. 1. Psal. cvi. 19, 20. Acts vii. 41—43.) Soon after their entrance into the land of Canaan, they adopted various deities that were worshipped by the Canaanites and other neighbouring nations; (Judg. ii. 13, viii. 33;) for which base ingratitude, they were severely punished. And, after the division of the two kingdoms, it is well known, that, with the exception of a few short intervals, both the sovereigns and people of Israel, were wholly given to idolatry: nor were the people of Judah, exempt from the worship of strange gods, as the frequent reproofs of the prophets abundantly testify. At length, however, become wiser by the severe discipline they had received, the tribes that returned into their native country from the Babylonian captivity, wholly renounced idolatry; and thenceforth, uniformly evinced the most deeply rooted aversion from all strange deities, and foreign modes of worship. This great reformation, was accomplished by Ezra and Nehemiah, and the eminent men who accompanied, or succeeded them; but, in the progress of time, though the exterior of piety was maintained, the "power of godliness" was lost; and we learn from the New Testament, that, during our Saviour's ministry, the Jews were divided into various religious parties, which widely differed in opinion, and pursued each other with the fiercest animosity, and with implacable hatred.

II. Of these Sects, and their respective tenets, to which there are frequent allusions in the New Testament, we are now to give a concise account.

. The sect of the Sadducees derived its name from Sadok, a pupil of Antigonus Sochæus, president of the sanhedrin, or great council; who flourished about two hundred and sixty years before the Christian æra. They disregarded all the traditions and unwritten laws, which the Pharisees prized so highly, and professed to consider the Scriptures, as the only source and rule of the Jewish religion. They denied the existence of angels and spirits, considered the soul as dying with the body, and consequently admitted of no future state of rewards and punishments. The tenets of this sect, which was small in point of numbers, were not so acceptable to the people as those of the Pharisees.

2. The PHARISEES are supposed to have appeared not long after the Sadducees. They were the most numerous, distinguished, and popular sect among the Jews. They derived their name from the Hebrew word *Pharash*, which signifies *separated*, or *set apart*, because they *separated* themselves from the rest of the Jews, to superior strictness in religious observances. They boasted that, from their accurate knowledge of religion, they were the favourites of heaven; and thus, trusting in themselves that they were righteous, despised others. (Luke xi. 52, xviii. 9. 11.)

Though they professed to esteem the written books of the Old Testament as the sources of the Jewish religion, yet they also attributed great and equal authority to traditional precepts, relating principally to external rites. They held the soul to be immortal, and the doctrine of the resurrection of the body; but they believed that all things were controlled by fate. They rigidly interpreted the Mosaic Law, but not unfrequently violated its spirit by their traditional and philosophical expositions. They were zealous in making proselytes; and their professed sanctity gave them great influence among the common people, especially with the female part of the community Their general hypocrisy and profligacy, are severely arraigned by Jesus Christ.

3. The ESSENES, who were the third principal sect among the Jews, differed in many respects from the Pharisees and Sadducees, both in doctrines and in practice. They were divided into two classes: 1. The *practical* who lived in society, (and some of whom were married,) though, it appears, with much circumspection. These dwelt in cities and their neighbourhoods, and applied themselves to husbandry, and other innocent occupations 2. The *contemplative* Essenes, who were also called Therapeutæ, or Physicians, from their application principally to the cure of the diseases of the soul, devoted themselves wholly to meditation, and avoided living in great towns, as unfavourable to a contemplative life. But both classes were exceedingly abstemious, exemplary in their moral deportment, averse from profane swearing, and most rigid in their observance of the Sabbath. They held, among other tenets, the immortality of the soul,

(though they denied the resurrection of the body,) the existence of angels, and a state of future rewards and punishments. They believed every thing to be ordered by an eternal fatality, or chain of causes. Though they are not mentioned in the New Testament, they are supposed to be referred to in Col. ii. 18. 21. 23: and the contemplative Essenes, are supposed to have been intended by those who in Matt. xix. 12, are said to have made themselves eunuchs, for the kingdom of God's sake.

4. The SCRIBES and LAWYERS, who are frequently mentioned in the Gospels, are usually classed among Jewish sects. The Scribes had the charge of transcribing the sacred books, of publicly interpreting the more difficult passages, and of deciding in cases which grew out of the ceremonial law. They possessed great influence, as well as the lawyers, or private teachers of the law.

5. The SAMARITANS, are generally considered as a Jewish sect: their origin and tenets, have already been noticed in p. 68.

6. The HERODIANS, were a political faction, the partisans of Herod, misnamed the Great, from whom they derived their name, and with whom they co-operated in all his political and time-serving schemes, to conciliate the favour of the Romans.

7. The GALILÆANS, were the followers of Judas the Gaulonite, or Galilæan, whose tenets they embraced, and acted upon. They held, that tribute was due to God alone, and consequently, ought not to be paid to the Romans; and that religious liberty, and the authority of the divine laws, were to be defended by force of arms. In other respects, their doctrines appear to have been the same as those of the Pharisees.

The ZEALOTS, so often mentioned in Jewish history, appear to have been the followers of this Judas: and it has been supposed, that the JUST MEN, whom the Pharisees and Herodians sent to entangle Jesus in his conversation, were members of this sect. (Matt. xxii. 15, 16. Mark xii. 13, 14. Luke xx. 20.)

8. The SICARII, noticed in Acts xxi. 38, were assassins, who derived their name from their using poniards, bent like the Roman *sicæ*, which they concealed under

their garments, and privately stabbed the objects of their malice.

III. The Corruption of the Jewish People, both in religion and morals, in the time of Christ, sufficiently appears from the censures of Jesus Christ, which are to be found in the four Gospels. The evidence of the sacred writers is confirmed by the testimony of profane writers, especially Josephus, the Jewish Historian, from whom we learn, that the corruption and profligacy of the chief priests, and other distinguished leaders, pervaded the priests; and that from them, the moral and religious contamination had spread to the lowest classes of the people, who were immersed in ignorance and vice, and cherished the most supercilious contempt, and bitter hatred towards the Gentiles. So great was their profligacy in the last period of their commonwealth, that Josephus has recorded it as his opinion, that if the Romans had delayed any longer to have come against them, the city (Jerusalem) would either have been swallowed up by an earthquake, overwhelmed by a deluge, or destroyed by fire from heaven, as Sodom was: for that generation was far more enormously wicked, than those who suffered these calamities.*

* De Bell. Jud. lib. v. c. 13. § 6.

BOOK IV.—DOMESTIC ANTIQUITIES OF THE JEWS AND OTHER NATIONS, INCIDENTALLY MENTIONED IN THE SCRIPTURES.

CHAPTER I.

ON THE DWELLINGS OF THE JEWS.

THE earliest dwellings of mankind, after they began to multiply, are supposed to have been CAVES: thus Lot and his daughters abode in a cave after the destruction of Sodom: and both ancient and modern travellers attest, that, in some parts of the East, caves have been employed for the purposes of habitation. In succeeding ages, they abode in tents; (Gen. xviii. 4;) and, in progress of time, houses were erected; those of the rich were formed of stone, or bricks, but the dwellings of the poor, were formed of wood, or more frequently of mud, (as they are to this day, in various parts of the East,) a material which is but ill calculated to resist the effects of the impetuous torrents, that descended from the mountains of Palestine. Our Lord alludes to this circumstance at the close of his sermon on the mount. (Matt. vii. 26, 27.) In the East Indies also, nothing is more common than for thieves to dig, or break through these mud walls, while the unsuspecting inhabitants are overcome by sleep, and to plunder them. To similar depredations, Jesus Christ appears to allude, when he exhorts his disciples, not to lay up their treasure where thieves break through and steal. (Matt. vi. 19, 20.) In the holes and chinks of these walls, serpents sometimes concealed themselves. (Amos v. 19.)

The following diagram will convey some idea of the form of an oriental house.

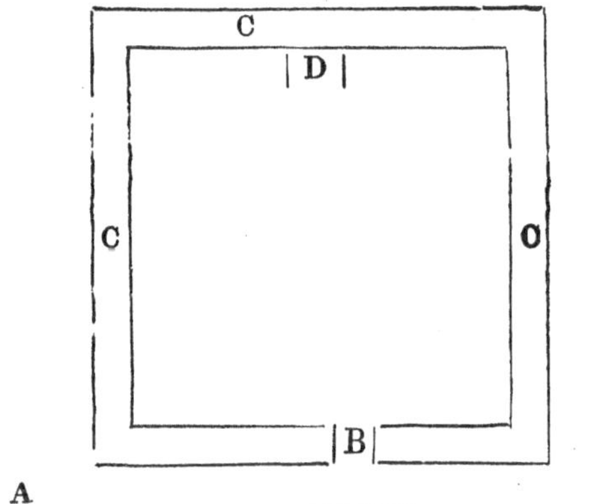

As the style of Architecture and manners of the East have remained unaltered, the description of a modern oriental house will enable us to form a tolerably correct notion of the structure of the Jewish houses. In the East, the streets are usually narrow, the better to shade them from the sun, and sometimes they have a range of shops on each side. If, then, we enter a house from the street, A A, we shall pass through the outer porch, B, into a square court open to the weather. This court, strewed with mats or carpets, is the usual place for receiving large companies at nuptials, circumcisions, and on other occasions. The banquet of Ahasuerus was given in a court of the royal palace; (Esth. i. 5;) and in a court the multi tude was assembled to hear the discourse of Jesus Christ, mentioned in Luke v. 19, where it is termed τὸ μεσον, (*to meson,*) *the midst.* The court is, for the most part, sur rounded with a cloister, over which is a gallery, C C C with a balustrade, or piece of lattice, or carved work going round it, to prevent accidents: and from this cloister, we are led into apartments of the same length as the court. D, is an inner porch, at the entrance into the main building. The gates were always shut, and a servant acted the part of porter. (John xvii. 16, 17. Acts xii. 13.) The roofs were flat, (as they still are,) and were formed of earth, spread evenly along, and rolled very hard, to exclude the rain ; but upon this surface, grass and weeds grow freely, to which there is an allusion in Psal. cxxix. 6. and Isa. xxxvii. 27. These roofs are surrounded by a wall, breast high, to prevent persons from falling through: such a defence, or battlement, was required by Deut. xxii. 8. It was this parapet which the men demolished, in order to let the paralytic down into the court, or area of the house. (Mark ii. 4. Luke v. 19.) The back part of the house is allotted to the women: in Arabic it is called the Harem, and in the Old Testament the *Palace.* Manahem, king of Israel, was assassinated in his harem, or palace. (2 Kings xv. 25.) The harem of Solomon was an inner and separate building. (1 Kings vii. 8. 2 Chron viii. 11.)

The furniture of the oriental dwellings, at least in the earliest ages, was very simple: that of the poorer classes, consisted of but few articles, and those such as were absolutely necessary. Instead of chairs, they sat on mats, or skins; and the same articles on which they laid a mattress, served them instead of bedsteads, while their upper garment served them for a covering. (Exod. xxii. 25, 26. Deut. xxiv. 12.) This circumstance accounts for our Lord's commanding the paralytic to take up his bed and go unto his house. (Matt. ix. 6.) The more opulent had (as those in the East still have) fine carpets, couches, or divans, and sofas, on which they sit, lay, and slept. (2 Kings iv. 10. 2 Sam. xvii. 28.) In later times, their couches were splendid, and the frames inlaid with ivory, (Amos vi. 4,) and the coverlids rich and perfumed. (Prov. vii. 16, 17.) On these sofas, in the latter ages of the Jewish state, (for before the time of Moses, it appears to have been the custom to sit at table, Gen. xliii. 33.) they universally reclined when taking their meals, (Amos vi. 4. Luke vii. 36—38,) resting on their side, with their heads towards the table, so that their feet were accessible to one who came behind the couch.

CHAPTER II.

ON THE DRESS OF THE JEWS.

In the early ages, the dress of mankind was very simple. Skins of animals, furnished the first materials, which, as men increased in numbers and civilization, were exchanged for more costly articles, made of wool and flax, of which they manufactured woollen and linen garments; (Levit. xiii. 47. Prov. xxxi. 13;) afterwards, fine linen and silk, dyed with purple, scarlet, and crimson, became the usual apparel of the more opulent. (2 Sam. i. 24. Prov. xxxi. 22. Luke xvi. 19.) In the more early ages, garments of various colours were in great esteem: such was Joseph's robe, of which his envious brethren stripped him, when they resolved to sell him. (Gen. xxxvii. 23.) The daughters of kings, wore richly embroidered vests. (Psal. xlv. 13, 14.) It appears that the Jewish garments, were worn pretty long; for it is mentioned, as an aggravation of the affront done to David's ambassadors, by the king of Ammon, that he cut off their garments *in the middle, even to their buttocks*. (2 Sam. x. 4.)

The most simple and ancient garment, was a tunic; it was a piece of cloth, commonly linen, which encircled the whole body, was bound with a girdle, and descended to the knees. Those who are clothed with a tunic merely, are sometimes said to be naked, as in John xxi. 7. An under garment, or shirt, was worn under the tunic. To prevent the latter from impeding the person, girdles were worn round the loins, whence various figurative expressions are derived in the Scriptures, to denote preparation, active employment, and despatch. Sometimes, also, these girdles served as a pouch to carry money, and other necessary things. (Matt. x. 9. Mark vi. 8.) Over the tunic was worn an upper garment, or mantle: it was a piece of cloth nearly square, several feet in length and breadth, which was wrapped round the body, or tied over the shoulders. The feet were protected from injury, by sandals bound round the feet; to loose and bind them on, was the office of the lowest menial servants. The beard was considered a great ornament: to pluck, or mar it in any way, was considered a great disgrace. (2 Sam. x. 4.)

A heavy head of hair, was considered a great ornament, (2 Sam. xiv. 26,) as baldness was accounted a source of contempt. (2 Kings ii. 23.) The hair was combed, set in order, and anointed, especially on festive occasions. To this practice, there are very numerous allusions in the Scriptures. A sort of mitre, probably similar to the modern turbans, was worn to defend the head. A prodigious number of magnificent habits was, anciently, regarded as a necessary part of the treasures of the rich: and the practice of amassing them is alluded to in Job xxvii. 6, and Matt. vi. 19. It appears from Psal. xlv. 8, that the wardrobes of the East, were plenteously perfumed with aromatics.

The dress of the women differed from that of the men, chiefly in the quality of the materials, and in the women wearing a veil. Rings, necklaces, pendants, and other ornaments, still worn by the fair sex, formed part of the apparel of the Jewish ladies: and like the oriental women of our time, they tinged their eyelids with the powder of lead ore. Thus Jezebel did, who, in 2 Kings ix. 30, is said to have painted her face: and Job's youngest daughter (xli. 14,) had a name (Keren-happuch, that is, the horn of pouk, or *lead ore*,) in reference to this practice.

Mirrors formed an important accompaniment to the female wardrobe: anciently, they were made of molten brass polished, and were carried in the hand.

CHAPTER VII.

MARRIAGE CUSTOMS OF THE JEWS.

MARRIAGE, was regarded by the Jews, as a sacred obligation, and celibacy was accounted a great reproach. Polygamy was tolerated, but not authoritatively allowed. The concubines, of whom we read, were secondary, or inferior wives, whose children did not inherit the father's property, except on failure of issue by the primary, or more honourable wives. Thus, Sarah was Abraham's primary wife, by whom he had Isaac, who was the heir of his wealth. But besides her, he had two concubines, namely,

Hagar and Keturah; by these he had other children, whom he distinguished from Isaac: for it is said, *he gave them gifts, and sent them away while he yet lived.* (Gen. xxv. 5, 6.)

No formalities appear to have been used by the Jews —at least none were enjoined to them by Moses—in joining man and wife together. Mutual consent, followed by consummation, was deemed sufficient. The manner in which a daughter was demanded in marriage, is described in the case of Shechem, who asked Dinah, the daughter of Jacob, in marriage; (Gen. xxxiv. 6—12;) and the nature of the contract, together with the mode of solemnizing the marriage, is described in Gen. xxiv. 50, 51. 57. 67. There was indeed, a previous espousal, or betrothing, which was a solemn promise of marriage, made by the man and woman, each to the other, at such a distance of time as they agreed upon. This was sometimes done by writing, sometimes by the delivery of a piece of silver to the bride, in presence of witnesses, as a pledge of their mutual engagements. After such espousal was made, (which was generally when the parties were young,) the woman continued with her parents several months, if not some years, (at least till she was arrived at the age of twelve,) before she was brought home, and her marriage consummated. That it was the practice to betroth the bride sometime before the consummation of the marriage, is evident from Deut. xx. 7. Thus we find, that Samson's wife remained with her parents a considerable time after the espousal. (Judg. xiv. 8.) If, during the time between the espousal and the marriage, the bride was guilty of any criminal correspondence with another person, contrary to the fidelity she owed to her bridegroom, she was treated as an adulteress. Among the Jews, and generally throughout the East, marriage was considered as a sort of purchase, which the man made of the woman he desired to marry; and therefore, in contracting marriages, as the wife brought a portion to the husband, so the husband was obliged to give her or her parents money, or presents, in lieu of this portion. See instances in Gen. xxxiv. 12, xxix. 18. 1 Sam xviii. 25. The nuptial solemnity, was celebrated with great festivity and splendour. The parable of the ten virgins in Matt. xxv. gives a good idea of the customs practised on these occasions.

Marriage was dissolved among the Jews by divorce as well as by death. Our Saviour tells us that Moses suffered this only because of the hardness of their heart, but from the beginning it was not so, (Matt. xix. 8,) meaning that they were accustomed to this abuse, and to prevent greater evils, such as murders, adulteries, &c., he permitted it; and he expressly limited the permission of divorce to the single case of adultery. (Matt. v. 31, 32.) Nor was this limitation unnecessary: for at that time it was common for the Jews, to dissolve this sacred union, upon verv slight and trivial pretensions.

CHAPTER IV.

BIRTH, EDUCATION, ETC. OF CHILDREN.

In the East, child-birth is, to this day, an event of but little difficulty, and mothers were originally the only assistants of their daughters, any further aid being deemed unnecessary, though midwives were sometimes employed. (Exod. i. 19. Gen. xxxv. 17, xxxviii. 28.) The birth of a son was celebrated as a festival, which was solemnized in succeeding years with renewed demonstrations of joy, especially those of sovereign princes. (Gen. xl. 20. Job i. 4. Matt. xiv. 6.) The birth of a son, or daughter, rendered the mother ceremonially unclean for a certain period.

On the eighth day after his birth, the son was circumcised, and received a name. The *first-born* son, enjoyed peculiar privileges. He received a double portion of the estate: he was the high priest of the whole family; and he enjoyed an authority over those who were younger, similar to that possessed by a father. The sons remained till the fifth year in the care of the women; after which, the father took charge of them, and instructed them, or caused them to be instructed, in the arts and duties of life, and in the law of Moses. (Deut. vi. 20—25, xi. 19.) The daughters rarely went out, unless sent for a specific purpose. Where there were no children, adoption—or the taking of a stranger into a family, in order to make him a part of it, acknowledging him as a son and heir to the estate—was practised. The elder Hebrews, indeed, do not appear to have had recourse to adoption, because Moses is silent concerning it in his laws. It was, however, common in the time of Jesus Christ; and St. Paul has many beautiful allusions to it in his epistles.

CHAPTER V.

ON THE CONDITION OF SLAVES, AND THE CUSTOMS RELATING TO THEM, MENTIONED, OR ALLUDED TO IN THE NEW TESTAMENT.

Slavery is of very remote antiquity. It existed before the flood: (Gen. ix. 25:) and when Moses gave his laws to the Jews, finding it already established, though he could not abolish it, yet he enacted various salutary laws and regulations.

Slaves were acquired in various ways, viz.: 1. By *Captivity;* (Gen. xiv. 14. Deut. xx. 14, xxi. 10, 11;) 2. By *Debt*, when persons, being poor, were sold for payment of their debts; (2 Kings iv. 1. Matt. xviii. 25;) 3. By committing a *Theft*, without the power of making restitution; (Exod. xxii. 2, 3. Neh. v. 4, 5;) and 4. By *Birth*, when persons were born of married slaves, These are termed *born in the house*, (Gen. xiv. 14, xv. 3, xvii. 23, xxi. 10,) *home-born*, (Jer. ii. 14,) and the *sons*, or children of *handmaids*. (Psal. lxxxvi. 16, cxvi. 16.)

Slaves received both food and clothing, for the most part of the meanest quality, but whatever property they acquired, belonged to their lords: hence, they are said to be worth double the value of a hired servant. (Deut. xv. 18.) They formed marriages at the will of their master, but their children were slaves, who, though they could not call him a father, (Gal. iv. 6. Rom. viii. 15,) yet they were attached and faithful to him as to a father; on which account, the patriarchs trusted them with arms. (Gen. xiv. 14, xxxii. 6, xxxiii. 1.) Their duty was to execute their lord's commands, and they were, for the most part, employed in tending cattle, or in rural affairs: and though the lot of some of them was sufficiently hard, yet under a mild and humane master, it was tolerable. (Job xiii. 13.) When the eastern people have no male issue, they frequently (as in Barbary) marry their daughters to their slaves: so Sheshan did, who gave his daughter to his Egyptian servant [slave] Jarha. (See 1 Chron. ii. 34, 35.) Various regulations were made by Moses to ensure the humane treatment of slaves, among which the three following, are particularly worthy of notice; 1. Hebrew slaves were to continue in slavery only till the year of jubilee, when they might return to liberty, and their masters could not detain them against their wills. If they were desirous of continuing with their master, they were to be brought to the judges; before whom they were to make a declaration, that, for this time, they disclaimed the privilege of the law: and they had their ears bored through with an awl, against the door-posts of their master's house, after which, they had no longer any power of recovering their liberty until the next year of jubilee, after forty-nine years. (Exod. xxi. 5, 6.) 2. If a Hebrew by birth, was sold to a stranger, or alien, dwelling in the vicinity of the land of Israel, his relations were to redeem him, and such slave was to make good the purchase money, if he were able, paying in proportion to the number of years that remained, until the year of jubilee. (Lev. xxv. 47—55.) 3. Lastly, if a slave of another nation fled to the Hebrews, he was to be received hospitably, and on no account to be given up to his master. (Deut. xxiii. 15, 16.)

Although Moses inculcated the duty of humane treatment towards slaves, and enforced his statutes by various strong sanctions, yet it appears from Jer. xxxiv. 8—22, that their condition was sometimes very wretched; and, in later times, among the Greeks and Romans, it was, in general, truly miserable. Being for the most part captives taken in war, they were bought and sold like beasts of burden; and were at the mercy of their owners, who had an absolute right over their lives, and who branded them, in order to mark their property. To the practice of buying, purchasing, and branding slaves, St. Paul has several fine allusions. See particularly, 1 Cor. vi. 20, vii. 23, and Gal. vi. 17. The confinement of slaves in mines, appears to be referred to in Matt. viii.

12, and xxii. 13, and crucifixion was a punishment almost exclusively reserved for them: whence St. Paul takes occasion to illustrate the love of Christ for fallen man, who, for the joy that was set before him, endured the cross, despising the shame and ignominy of such a death.

CHAPTER VI.

DOMESTIC CUSTOMS AND USAGES OF THE JEWS.

VARIOUS are the modes of address and politeness, which custom has established in different nations. The ordinary formulæ of salutation were—*The Lord be with thee!*—*The Lord bless thee!*—and *Blessed be thou of the Lord!* but the most common salutation was, *Peace* (that is, may all manner of prosperity) *be with thee!* (Ruth ii. 4. Judg. xix. 20. 1 Sam. xxv. 6. 2 Sam. xx. 9. Psal. cxxix 8.) In the later period of the Jewish polity, much time appears to have been spent in the rigid observance of these ceremonious forms: which are alluded to in Matt. x. 12. See also 2 Kings iv. 29.

Respect was shown to persons on meeting, by the salutation of *Peace be with you!* and laying the right hand upon the bosom: but if the person addressed was of the highest rank, they bowed to the earth. Thus, *Jacob bowed to the ground seven times until he came near to his brother Esau.* (Gen. xxxiii. 3.) Sometimes they kissed the hem of the person's garment, and even the dust on which he had to tread. (Zech. viii. 23. Luke viii. 44. Acts x. 26. Psal. lxxii. 9.) Near relations and intimate acquaintances kissed each other's hands, head, neck, beard, (which on such occasions, only, could be touched without affront,) or shoulders. (Gen. xxxiii. 4, xlv. 14. 2 Sam. xx. 9. Luke xv. 20. Acts xx. 17.)

Whenever the common people approached their prince, or any person of superior rank, it was customary for them to prostrate themselves before them. The allusions to this practice, in the Old and New Testaments, are very numerous; as well as to the making of presents to superiors. (See particularly Matt. ii 11.)

When any person visited another, he stood at the gate and knocked, or called aloud, until the person on whom he called admitted him. (2 Kings v. 9—12. Acts x. 17, xii. 13, 16.) Visiters were always received and dismissed with great respect. On their arrival, water was brought to wash their feet and hands, (Gen. xviii. 4, xix. 2,) after which the guests were anointed with oil. David alludes to this in Psal. xxiii. 5, and Solomon, in Prov. xxvii. 9. The same practice obtained in our Saviour's time. (Luke vii. 44, 45.)

The Jews rose early, about the dawn of day, when they breakfasted. They dined about eleven in the forenoon, and supped at five in the afternoon. Their food consisted principally of bread, milk, rice, vegetables, honey, and sometimes of locusts, except at the appointed festivals, or when they offered their feast-offerings: at these times they ate animal food, of which they appear to have been very fond. (Numb. xi. 4.) But they were prohibited from eating the flesh of certain animals, as well as with people of another religion. The pottage which Jacob had prepared, and which was so tempting to Esau as to make him sell his birthright, shows the simplicity of the *ordinary* diet of the patriarchs. Isaac, in his old age, longed for *savoury meat*, which was accordingly prepared for him; (Gen. xxvii. 4. 17;) but this was an unusual thing. The feast with which Abraham entertained the three angels was a calf, new cakes baked on the hearth, together with butter *(ghee)* and milk. (Gen. xviii. 6, 7.) We may form a correct idea of their ordinary food by the articles which were presented to David on various occasions by Abigail, (1 Sam. xxv. 18,) by Ziba, (2 Sam. xvi. 1,) and by Barzillai. (2 Sam. xvii. 28, 29.) Their ordinary beverage was water, which was drawn from the public wells and fountains, (John iv. 6, 7,) and which was to be refused to no one. (John vi. 9. Matt. xxv. 35.) Wine of different sorts, which was preserved in skins, was also drunk by the Jews, after their settlement in the land of Canaan. Red wine seems to have been most esteemed. (Prov. xxiii. 31. Rev. xiv. 20, xix. 3. 18.) The women did not appear at table in entertainments with the men. This would have been then, as it is at this day throughout the East, an indecency. Thus, *Vashti the*

Queen made a feast for the women in the royal house, which belonged to Ahasuerus, (Esther i. 9,) while the Persian monarch was feasting his nobles.

The Hebrews anciently sat at table as we do now; afterwards, they imitated the Persians and Chaldæans, who reclined on table-beds, or couches, while eating; some traces of these couches are, nevertheless, observed in Amos, (vi. 4, 7,) Ezekiel, (xxiii. 47,) and Tobit; (ii. 4;) but this use was not general. We see expressions in the sacred authors of those times, which prove that they also sat at table. At Ahasuerus's banquet, (Esth. i. 6,) the company lay on beds, and also at that which Esther gave the king and Haman. (Esth. vii. 8.) Our Saviour, in like manner, reclined at table, when Mary Magdalen anointed his feet with perfume, (Matt. xxvi. 7,) and when John, at the last supper, rested his head on his bosom. (John xiii. 25.)

When persons journeyed, they provided themselves with every necessary; women and rich men frequently travelled on asses or camels, which carried not only their merchandise, but also their household goods and chattels. The Jews often travelled in *caravans*, or companies, (as the inhabitants of the East do to this day,) especially when they went up to Jerusalem at the three great annual festivals. The *company*, among which Joseph and Mary supposed Jesus to have been, on their return from the passover, when he was twelve years old, (Luke ii. 42—44,) was one of these caravans.

In the East, anciently, as well as in modern times, there were no inns, in which the traveller could meet with refreshment. Hence hospitality was deemed a sacred duty incumbent upon every one. The sacred writings exhibit several instances of hospitality exercised by the patriarchs. (Gen. xviii. 2, 3, &c., xix. 1—3.) St. Paul and St. Peter frequently enforce the sacred duty of hospitality.

CHAPTER VI

ON THE OCCUPATIONS, ARTS, AND SCIENCES OF THE HEBREWS

SECTION I.—Agriculture and Horticulture of the Jews.

AGRICULTURE, including sheep husbandry, was the principal occupation of the patriarchs and their families: and, in succeeding ages, the greatest men, as Moses, David, and others, did not disdain to follow husbandry, however mean that occupation may be accounted in modern times. All the Mosaic statutes, indeed, were admirably calculated to encourage agriculture, as the chief basis of national prosperity, and also to preserve the Israelites detached from the surrounding idolatrous nations.

Although the Scriptures do not furnish us with any *details* respecting the state of agriculture in Judæa, yet we may collect from various passages many interesting hints that will enable us to form a tolerably correct idea of the high state of its cultivation. With the use of manures, the Jews were unquestionably acquainted. Salt, either by itself, or mixed in the dunghill, in order to promote putrefaction, is specially mentioned as one article of manure: (Matt. v. 13. Luke xiv. 34, 35:) and as the river Jordan annually overflowed its banks, the mud deposited when its waters subsided must have served as a valuable irrigation and top-dressing, particularly to the pasture lands. It is probable that, after the waters had thus subsided, seed was sown on the wet soft ground; in allusion to which, Solomon says, *Cast thy bread* (corn or seed) *upon the waters: for thou shalt find it again*, with increase, *after many days.* (Eccles. xi. 1.) And Isaiah, promising a time of peace and plenty, says—*Blessed are ye that sow beside all waters, and send forth thither the feet of the ox and the ass.* (Isa. xxxii. 20.)

The method of managing the ground and preparing it for the seed, was much the same with the practice of the present times; for Jeremiah speaks of ploughing up the fallow ground, (Jer. iv. 3,) and Isaiah of harrowing, or breaking up the clods; (Isa. xxviii. 24;) but Moses, for wise reasons doubtless, gave a positive injunction, that they should not sow their fields with mingled seed.

The kinds of grain sowed by the Jews were fitches, cummin, wheat, barley, and rice: (Isa. xxviii. 25:) there were three months between their sowing and their first reaping, and four months to their full harvest: their barley-harvest was at the passover, and their wheat-harvest at the pentecost. The reapers made use of sickles, and according to the present custom they filled their hands with the corn, and those that bound up the sheaves, their bosom: there was a person *set over the reapers*, (Ruth ii. 5,) to see that they did their work, that they had provision proper for them, and to pay them their wages. Women were employed in reaping as well as the men. The poor were allowed the liberty of gleaning, though the land-owners were not bound to admit them immediately into the field as soon as the reapers had cut down the corn and bound it up in sheaves, but after it was carried off: they might also choose those among the poor, whom they thought most worthy or most necessitous. The conclusion of the harvest, or carrying home the last load, was with the Jews a season of joyous festivity, and was celebrated with a harvest-feast. (Psal. cxxvi. Isa. ix. 3, xvi. 9, 10.(The corn being cut and carried in wagons or carts, (Numb. vii. 3—8. Isa. v. 8, xxviii. 27, 28. Amos ii. 13,) was either laid up in stacks (Exod xxii. 6,) or barns; (Matt. vi. 26, xiii. 30. Luke xiii. 18. 24;) and, when thrashed out, was stored in graneries or garners. (Psal. xliv. 13. Matt. iii. 12.) David had *storehouses in the fields, in the cities, and in the villages, and in the castles.* (1 Chron. xxvii. 25.)

After the grain was carried into the barn, the next process was to thrash, or beat the corn out of the ear; this was performed in various ways. Sometimes it was done by horses (Isa. xxviii. 28,) and by oxen, that trod out the corn, with their hoofs shod with brass. (Mic. iv. 12, 13.) This mode of thrashing is expressly referred to by Hosea, (x. 11,) and in the prohibition of Moses against *muzzling the ox that treadeth out the corn,* (Deut. xxv. 4,) and it obtains in India to this day. Other modes of thrashing are mentioned in Isa. xxviii. 28, Judg. vi. 11, and 1 Chron. xxi. 20. When the corn was thus thrashed, it was dried either in the sun, or by a fire, or in a furnace. This is called *parched corn,* (Levit. xxiii. 14, 1 Sam. xvii. 17 and xxv. 18,) and was sometimes used in this manner for food, without any further preparation; but generally, the parching or drying it was in order to make it more fit for grinding. This process was performed either in mortars or mills, both of which are mentioned in Numb. xi. 8: but mills were chiefly employed for this purpose; and they were deemed of such use and necessity, that the Israelites were strictly forbidden *to take the nether or upper mill-stone in pledge;* the reason of which is added, because this was taking a man's life in pledge; (Deut. xxiv. 6;) intimating that while the mill ceases to grind, people are in danger of being starved.

The grinding at mills was accounted an inferior sort of work, and therefore prisoners and captives were generally put to it. To this work Samson was set, while he was in the prison-house. (Judg. xvi. 21.) There hand-mills were usually kept, by which prisoners earned their living. The expression in Isa. xlvii. 2—*Take the millstones and grind meal*—is part of the description of a slave; but, for the most part, the women-servants were employed in this drudgery, as is evident from Matt. xxiv. 1. This was in use not only among the Jews, but also among the Egyptians and Chaldeans, as appears from Exod. xi. 5, and Lam. v. 13. The various processes of agriculture have furnished the sacred writers with numerous beautiful allusions. Palestine abounded with generous wine; and in some districts the grapes were of superior quality. The canton allotted to Judah was celebrated on this account. In this district were the vales of Sorek and of Eshcol; and the cluster, which the Hebrew spies carried from this last place, was so large as to be carried on a staff between two of them; (Numb. xiii. 23;) Lebanon (Hos. xiv. 7,) and Helbon (Ezek. xxvii. 18,) were likewise celebrated for their exquisite wines. Grapes were also dried into raisins. (1 Sam. xxv. 18. 2 Sam. xvi. 1.)

The ancient Hebrews were very fond of gardens, which are frequently mentioned in the sacred writings; and derive their appellations from the prevalence of certain trees, as the garden of nuts and of pomegranates. (Sol. Song vi. 11, iv. 13.) Besides these and other fruits, which were common in Judæa, (as dates, figs, &c.) they had regular plantations of olives, the oil expressed from which furnished a profitable article of commerce with the Tyrians: (Ezek. xxxii. 17. compared with 1 Kings v. 11:) and among the judgments with which God threatened the Israelites for their sins, it was denounced, that though they had olive trees through all their coasts yet they should not anoint themselves with the oil, for the olive should cast her fruit. (Deut. xxviii. 40.)

Section II. - On the Arts and Sciences of the Jews.

Of the Arts practised by the Hebrews, in the earlier periods of their history, we have but few notices in the sacred writings. From the mention of utensils, ornaments, and other things, which imply some knowledge of the arts, in the book of Genesis, it is evident that considerable progress must have been made in the time of Noah: and it is scarcely credible that the Hebrews could have resided four hundred years in Egypt, without acquiring some knowledge of those arts, which their masters are allowed to have possessed. Soon after the death of Joshua, a place was expressly allotted to artificers: for, in the genealogy of the tribe of Judah, delivered in 1 Chron. iv. 14, we read of a place called the *Valley of Craftsmen*, and (ver. 21. 23,) of a family of workmen of fine linen, and another of potters: and when Jerusalem was taken by Nebuchadnezzar, the enemy *carried away all the craftsmen and smiths.* (2 Kings xxiv. 14.) But, as a proof that their skill in manufactures and trade therein could not be very extensive, we find that the prophet Ezekiel, (chap. xxvii.) in describing the affluence of the goods which came to Tyre, mentions nothing as being brought thither from Judæa, except wheat, oil, grapes, and balm, which were all the natural products of their ground. From Prov. xxxi. 13, it appears that the mistresses of families usually made the clothing for their husbands, their children, and themselves.

Their knowledge in the Liberal Arts does not seem to have greatly exceeded their skill in mechanics. They knew but little of astronomy and the motions of the heavenly bodies. Solomon, indeed, was a noble pattern of knowledge and wisdom. His skill in natural philosophy is sufficiently indicated, when we are told, *that he spake of trees from the cedar tree that is in Lebanon, even to the hyssop that springeth out of the wall; he spake also of beasts, and of fowls, and of creeping things, and of fishes.* (1 Kings iv. 33.) His books of Proverbs and Ecclesiastes abundantly inform us what skill he had in ethics, economics, and politics : but as the wonderful talents, with which he was endued, were the immediate gift of God, and in compliance with his special request for divine wisdom, (2 Chron. i. 7—13,) so singular an instance is no rule, by which we ought to judge of the genius of the whole nation.

Nor did Building or Architecture attain much perfection prior to the reign of the accomplished Solomon. We read, indeed, before the Israelites came into the land of Canaan, that Bezaleel and Aholiab (who were employed in the construction of the tabernacle (excelled *in all manner of workmanship*, (Exod. xxxv. 30—35,) but we are there told, that they had their skill by inspiration from God, and it does not appear that they had any successors : for in the days of Solomon, when the Israelites were at rest from all their enemies, and at full freedom to follow out improvements of every kind, yet they had no professed artists that could undertake the work of the temple ; so that Solomon was obliged to send to Hiram, king of Tyre, for a skilful artist ; (2 Chron. vii. 13, 14 ;) by whose direction the model of the temple, and all the curious furniture of it, was both designed and finished. But, after the Jews were under the influence or power of the Romans, there is no doubt that a better taste prevailed among them. Herod, at least, must have employed some architects of distinguished abilities to repair and beautify the temple, and render it the superb structure, which the description of Josephus shows that it must have been.

We read nothing of the art of Writing, in Scripture, before the copy of the law was given by God to Moses, which was *written* (that is engraven,) *on two tables of stone by the finger of God,* (Exod. xxxi. 18,) and this is called the *writing of God.* (Exod. xxxii. 16.) It is therefore probable that God himself first taught letters to Moses, who communicated the knowledge of them to the Israelites, and they to the other eastern nations. Engraving or sculpture seems, therefore, to be the most ancient way of writing, of which we have another very early instance in Exod. xxxix. 30, where we are told, that " *Holiness to the Lord*" was written on a golden plate, and worn on the high priest's head. And we find that the names of the twelve tribes were commanded to be written on twelve rods. (Numb. xvii. 2.) Afterwards they made use of broad rushes or flags for writing on, which grew in great abundance in Egypt, and are noticed by the prophet Isaiah, when foretelling the confusion of that country. (Isa. xix. 6, 7.)

The other eastern nations made use chiefly of parchment, being the thin skins of animals carefully dressed. The best was made at Pergamos, whence it was called *Charta Pergamena.* It is probable that the Jews learned the use of it from them, and that this is what is meant by a *roll*, (Ezra vi. 2,) and a *roll of a book*, (Jer. xxxvi. 2,) and a *scroll rolled together:* (Isa. xxxiv. 4:) for it could not be thin and weak paper, but parchment, which is of some consistency, that was capable of being thus rolled up. St. Paul is the only person who makes express mention of parchment. (2 Tim. iv. 13.) In Job xix. 24, and in Jer. xvii. 1, there is mention made of pens of iron, with which they probably made the letters, when they engraved on stone or other hard substances: but for softer materials they, in all probability, made use of quills or reeds; for we are told of some in the tribe of Zebulun who *handled the pen of the writer.* (Judg. v. 14.) David alludes to the *pen of a ready writer*, (Psal. xlv. 1,) and Baruch, wrote the words of Jeremiah with ink in a book. (Jer. xxxvi. 18.)

Of the poetry and music of the Hebrews we have more ample information.

The genius of their Poetry having been already discussed in pages 108—111, it is sufficient here to remark, that the effusions of the inspired Hebrew muse infinitely surpass in grandeur, sublimity, beauty, and pathos, all the most celebrated productions of Greece and Rome. Not to repeat unnecessarily the observations already offered on this topic, we may here briefly remark, that the eucharistic song of Moses, composed on the deliverance of the Israelites and their miraculous passage of the Red Sea, (Exod. xv. 1—19,) is an admirable hymn, full of strong and lively images. The song of Deborah and Barak (Judg. v.) and that of Hannah, the mother of Samuel, (1

Sam. ii. 1,) have many excellent flights, and some noble and sublime raptures. David's lamentation on the death of Saul and Jonathan (2 Sam. i. 19—27,) is an incomparable elegy. The gratulatory hymn (Isa. xii.) and Hezekiah's song of praise, (Isa. xxviii.) are worthy of every one's attention. The prayer of Habakkuk (iii.) contains a sublime description of the divine majesty. Besides these single hymns we have the books of Psalms, Proverbs, Ecclesiastes, Canticles, and Lamentations; all of which are composed by different poets, according to the usage of those times. The Psalms are a great storehouse of heavenly devotion, full of affecting and sublime thoughts, and with a variety of expressions admirably calculated to excite a thankful remembrance of God's mercies, and for moving the passions of joy and grief, indignation and hatred. They consist mostly of pious and affectionate prayers, holy meditations, and exalted strains of praise and thanksgiving, intermingled with sublime descriptions, and most beautiful allusions.

Their sacred songs were accompanied with Music, the *nature* of which it is now as difficult to determine, as it is to ascertain with precision the various musical instruments which were in use among them, without entering into details and conjectures which are inconsistent with the plan of this volume. Referring the reader, therefore, to the author's larger work, in which he has attempted to collect the most probable accounts, he will only remark in this place, that, if any conclusions may be drawn concerning the Hebrew music from its effects, the sacred history has recorded several examples of the power and charms of music, to sweeten the temper, to compose and allay the passions of the mind, to revive the drooping spirits, and to dissipate melancholy. It had this effect on Saul, when David played to him on his harp. (1 Sam. xvi. 16. 23.) And when Elisha was desired by Jehoshaphat to tell him what his success against the king of Moab would be, the prophet required a minstrel to be brought unto him: and when he played, it is said, that the *hand of the Lord came upon him;* (2 Kings iii. 15;) not that the gift of prophecy was the natural effect of music, but the meaning is, that music disposed the organs, the humours, and, in short, the whole mind and spirit of the prophet, to receive these supernatural impressions.

But music was not exclusively confined to religious worship. From Gen. xxxi. 27, Isa. v. 2, and xxiv. 8, it appears that music was employed on all solemn occasions of entertaining their friends, and also at other entertainments. That music and dancing were used among the Jews at their feasts, in latter ages, may be inferred from the parable of the prodigal son. (Luke xv. 25.) Further, dancing was also an ordinary concomitant of music among the Jews; sometimes it was used on a religious account. Thus, Miriam with her women glorified God (after the deliverance from the Egyptians) in dances as well as songs, (Exod. xv. 20,) and David danced after the ark. (2 Sam. ii. 16.) It was a thing common at the Jewish feasts, (Judg. xxi. 19, 21,) and in public triumphs, (Judg. xi. 34,) and at all seasons of mirth and rejoicing. (Psal. xxx. 11. Jer. xxxi. 4, 13. Luke xv. 25.) The idolatrous Jews made it a part of the worship which they paid to the golden calf. (Exod. xxxii. 19.) The Amalekites danced after their victory at Ziklag, (1 Sam. xxx. 16,) and Job makes it part of the character of the prosperous wicked, (that is, of those who, placing all their happiness in the enjoyments of sense, forget God and religion,) that their children dance. (Job. xxi. 11.) The dancing of the profligate Herodias's daughter pleased Herod so highly, that he promised to give her whatever she asked, and accordingly, at her desire, and in compliment to her, he commanded John the Baptist to be beheaded in prison. (Matt. xiv. 6, 7, 8.)

The diseases to which the human frame is subject would naturally lead man to try to alleviate or to remove them. Hence sprang the art of Medicine. Anciently, it is said to have been the practice to expose the sick on the sides of frequented ways, in order that those persons who passed along, inquiring into the nature of their complaint, might communicate the knowledge of such remedies as had been beneficial to themselves under similar circumstances. The healing art was unquestionably cultivated; but there is reason to think that the knowledge of the Jews was very limited, and that it extended little beyond the curing of a green wound, or the binding up of fractures. In the case of *internal* disorders, it does not appear to have been customary to call in the aid of a physician. These maladies were regarded as the immediate effect of the divine anger, and inflicted by evil spirits, as the executioners of his vengeance; and this was the reason why religious people generally had recourse to God only, or to his prophets, (see 2 Kings xx. 7,) while the irreligious resorted to false gods, and charms or enchantments. (2 Kings i. 2. Jer. viii. 17.)

Various diseases are mentioned in the sacred writings, as cancers, consumption, dropsy, epilepsy, fevers, gangrenes, hemorrhoids, or piles, leprosy, (concerning which see p. 245, *supra*,) lunacy, palsy, &c. The disease of Saul appears to have been a true melancholy madness; that of Nebuchadnezzar, a hypochondriacal madness; that of Job, an incurable *elephantiasis*, in which the skin becomes uneven and wrinkled with many furrows, like that of an elephant, whence it takes its name.

Lastly, in the New Testament we meet with numerous cases of what are termed *Demoniacal Possession.* Some eminent writers have supposed that the demoniacs, or persons who were possessed by evil spirits, were only lunatics. But it is evident that the persons, who in the New Testament are said to be *possessed with devils*, (more correctly with demons,) cannot mean only persons afflicted with some strange disease: for they are evidently here, as in other places,—particularly in Luke iv. 33—36, 41—distinguished from the diseased. Further Christ's speaking on various occasions to these evil spirits, as distinct from the persons possessed by them,—his commanding them, and asking them questions, and receiving answers from them, or not suffering them to speak,—and several circumstances relating to the terrible preternatural effects which they had upon the possessed, and to the manner of Christ's evoking them,—particularly their requesting and obtaining permission to enter the herd of swine, (Matt. viii. 31, 32,) and precipitating them into the sea;—all these circumstances can *never* be accounted for by any distemper whatever. Nor is it any reasonable objection, that we do not read of such frequent possessions before or since the appearance of our Redeemer upon earth. It seems, indeed, to have been ordered by a special providence, that they should have been permitted to have *then* been more common; in order that He, who came to destroy the works of the Devil, might the more remarkably and visibly triumph over him; and that the machinations and devices of Satan might be more openly defeated, at a time when their power was at its highest, both in the souls and bodies of men; and also, that plain facts might be a sensible confutation of the Sadducean error, which denied the existence of angels or spirits, (Acts xxiii. 8,) and prevailed among the principal men both for rank and learning in those days. The cases of the demoniacs expelled by the apostles were cases of real possessions: and it is a well known fact, that, in the second century of the Christian æra, the apologists for the persecuted believers in the faith of Christ, appealed to their ejection of evil spirits as a proof of the divine origin of their religion. Hence it is evident that the demoniacs were not merely insane or epileptic patients, but persons really and truly vexed and convulsed by unclean demons.

CHAPTER VIII.

ALLUSIONS TO THE THEATRES, TO THEATRICAL PERFORMANCES, AND TO THE GRECIAN GAMES, IN THE NEW TESTAMENT.

I. Theatrical performances were in great request among the Greeks and Romans, and this will account for so many theatres being erected in Judæa, soon after that country became subject to the Roman power. The Epistles of St. Paul, being addressed to Gentiles, abound with elegant allusions drawn from the theatre. Thus, in 1 Cor. vii. 29—31, he refers to the personification of the woes of others, which was common on the stage, while the heart continued unaffected with them, and also to the rapid shifting of the scenes. In 1 Cor. iv. 9, he alludes to the barbarous practice then common in the Roman amphitheatre, where the *bestiarii*, who in the morning combated with wild beasts, had armour with which to defend themselves, and to slay their antagonists: but the *last*, those who were exposed at noon were naked and unarmed, and *set forth* (as our version renders it) to certain and cruel death.

II. But the most splendid and renowned solemnities were the Olympic Games, solemnized every fifth year, in the presence of a cloud of witnesses or spectators, assembled from almost every part of the then known world. The exercises at these games consisted principally in running, wrestling, and the chariot race. The candidates were to be freemen and Greeks, of unimpeachable character; and they were subjected to a long and severe regimen. On the day appointed, the names of the candidates were called over by the heralds: and on a given signal, those who engaged in the foot-race, rushed forward towards the goal, in the presence of the assembled multitude, and especially of the Hellanodics, persons venerable for their years and character, who were appointed judges of the games, and whose province it was to distribute chaplets composed of the fading sprigs of the wild olive, and palm branches, which were conspicuously exposed to the view of the candidates. The knowledge of these circumstances throws much light and beauty on those animating exhortations of St. Paul, in Heb. xii. 1 3. 12, 13. Phil. iii. 12—14. 2 Tim. iv. 7, 8, and 1 Cor. ix. 24, 25. In the two following verses, he alludes to the practice of those who engaged in boxing, as well as to the previous discipline to which all candidates were subjected.

CHAPTER IX.

JEWISH MODE OF TREATING THE DEAD.—FUNERAL RITES.

By the law of Moses a dead body conveyed a legal pollution to every thing that touched it—even to the very house and furniture—which continued seven days. (Numb. xix. 14, 15, 16.) And this was the reason why the priests, on account of their daily ministrations in holy things, were forbidden to assist at any funerals but those of their nearest relatives; nay, the very dead bones, though they had lain ever so long in the grave, if digged up, conveyed a pollution to any who touched them; and this was the reason why Josiah caused the bones of the false priests to be burnt upon the altar at Bethel, (2 Chron. xxxiv. 5,) to the intent that these altars, being thus polluted, might be had in the greater detestation.

When the principle of life was extinguished, the first funeral office among the Jews was to close the eyes of the deceased. This was done by the nearest of kin. Thus, it was promised to Jacob, when he took his journey into Egypt, that Joseph should *put his hands upon his eyes.* (Gen. xlvi. 4.) The next office was the ablution of the corpse. Thus, when Tabitha died, it is said, that they *washed her body, and laid it in an upper chamber.* (Acts ix. 37.) This rite was common both to the Greeks and Romans. In Egypt, it is still the custom to wash the dead body several times. Loud lamentations attended the decease of persons, especially those who were greatly beloved, not only as soon as they had expired, (Gen. l. 1. Matt. ix. 23. Mark v. 38,) but especially at the time of interment. (Gen. l. 10, 11.) In later times, the Jews hired persons, whose profession it was to superintend and conduct these funeral lamentations. (Jer. ix. 17, xvi. 6, 7, xlviii. 36, 37. Ezek. xxiv. 16—18. Amos v. 16:) and in the time of Christ, minstrels and mourners were hired for this purpose. (Matt. ix. 23. Mark v. 38.

After the corpse had been washed it was embalmed in costly spices and aromatic drugs, after which it was closely swathed in linen rollers, probably resembling those of the Egyptian mummies now to be seen in the British Museum. So Nicodemus made preparation for the embalming of Jesus Christ; (John xix. 39, 40;) and Lazarus appears to have been swathed in a similar way, when raised to life again by the omnipotent voice of Jesus Christ. (John xi. 44.) At the funerals of some Jewish monarchs, great piles of aromatics were set on fire, in which were consumed their bowels, armour, and other things. (2 Chron. xvi. 14. Jer. xxxiv. 5.)

The Jews showed great regard for the burial of their dead. To be deprived of interment, was deemed one of the greatest dishonours and calamities that could befall any person. (Psal. lxxix. 2. Jer. xxii. 19, xxxvi. 30.) Their burial-places were in gardens, fields, and the sides of mountains: and over the rich and great were erected splendid monuments. To this practice Jesus Christ alludes in Matt. xxiii. 7. From Isa. lxv. 4, and Mark v. 5, it would seem that some tombs had cupolas over them which afforded shelter, similar to those which modern travellers in the East have seen and described. Family sepulchres were in gardens. (John xix. 41.)

A funeral feast commonly succeeded the Jewish burials. Thus, after Abner's funeral was solemnized, the people came to David to eat meat with him, though they could not persuade him to do so. (2 Sam. iii. 35.) He was the chief mourner, and probably had invited them to this banquet. Of this Jeremiah speaks, (xvi. 7,) where he calls it the *cup of consolation, which they drank for their father or their mother;* and accordingly the place where this funeral entertainment was made is called in the next verse the house of feasting. Hosea calls it the *bread of mourners.* (Hos. ix. 4.)

The usual tokens of mourning, by which the Jews expressed their grief and concern for the death of their friends and relations, were, the rending of their garments, putting on sack-cloth, sprinkling dust upon their heads, wearing mourning apparel, and covering the face and head. (Gen. xxxvii. 34. 2 Sam. xiv. 2, xix. 4.)

Anciently, there was a peculiar space of time allotted for lamenting the deceased, which they called *the days of mourning.* (Gen. xxvii. 41, and l. 4.) Thus, the Egyptians, who had a great regard for the patriarch Jacob, lamented his death *threescore and ten days.* (Gen. l. 3.) The Israelites wept for Moses in the plains of Moab *thirty days.* (Deut. xxxiv. 8.) Afterwards among the Jews the funeral mourning was generally confined to *seven days.* Thus, besides the mourning for Jacob in Egypt, Joseph and his company set apart *seven days* to mourn for his father, when they approached the Jordan with his corpse. (Gen. l. 10.) No particular period has been recorded, during which widows mourned for their husbands. Bathsheba is said, generally, to have *mourned* for Uriah; (2 Sam. xi. 26;) but her mourning could neither be long nor very sincere. The Jews paid a greater or less degree of honour to their kings after their death, according to the merits of their actions when they were alive. On the death of any prince, who had in any way distinguished himself, they used to make lamentations or mournful songs for them. From an expression in 2 Chron. xxxv. 25. *Behold, they are written in the Lamentations*, we may infer that they had certain collections of this kind of composition. The author of the book of Samuel has preserved those which David composed on occasion of the death of Saul and Jonathan, of Abner and Absalom; but we have no remains of the mournful elegy composed by Jeremiah upon the immature death of Josiah, the exemplary king of Judah.

PART IV.

ON THE ANALYSIS OF SCRIPTURE

BOOK I.—ANALYSIS OF THE OLD TESTAMENT

CHAPTER I.

ON THE PENTATEUCH.

THE Pentateuch, by which title the first five books of Moses are distinguished, is a word of Greek original, Πεντατευχος *(Pentateuchos)* from πεντε *(pente)* five, and τευχος *(teuchos)* a book or volume, which literally signifies the five instruments or books; by the Jews it is termed Chometz, a word synonymous with Pentateuch, and also, more generally, the LAW, or the LAW OF MOSES, because it contains the ecclesiastical and political ordinances issued by God to the Israelites. The pentateuch forms, to this day, but one roll or volume in the Jewish manuscripts, being divided only into larger and smaller sections. This collective designation of the books of Genesis, Exodus, Leviticus, Numbers, and Deuteronomy, is of very considerable antiquity, though we have no certain information when it was first introduced. As, however, the names of these books are evidently derived from the Greek, and as the five books of Moses are expressly mentioned by Josephus, who wrote only a few years after our Saviour's ascension, we have every reason to believe that the appellation of Pentateuch was prefixed to the Septuagint version by the Alexandrian translators.

SECTION I.—On the Book of Genesis.

The first book of the Pentateuch, which is called GENESIS, (ΓΕΝΕΣΙΣ,) derives its appellation from the title it bears in the Greek Septuagint Version, ΒΙΒΛΟΣ ΓΕΝΕΣΕΩΣ, (*Biblos Geneseos;*) which signifies the Book of the Generation or Production, because it commences with the history of the generation or production of all things.

Different opinions have been entertained concerning the *time* when Moses wrote it; (for it is indisputably his production;) but the most probable conjecture is that which places it after the departure of the Israelites from Egypt, and the promulgation of the law. It comprises the history of about 2369 years according to the vulgar computation of time, or of 3619 years according to the larger computation of Dr. Hales; and may be divided into four parts, viz.:

PART I. The Origin of the World. (ch. i., ii.)

PART II. The History of the former World. (ch. iii.—vii.)

PART III. The General History of Mankind after the Deluge. (ch. viii.—xi.)

PART IV. The particular History of the Patriarchs. (ch. xii.—l.)

SECTION II.—On the Book of Exodus.

The title of this book is derived from the Septuagint version, and is significant of the principal transaction which it records, namely, the ΕΞΟΔΟΣ (*Exodos,*) EXODUS, or departure of the Israelites from Egypt. It comprises a history of the events that took place during the period of 145 years, from the year of the world 2369 to 2514 inclusive, from the death of Joseph to the erection of the tabernacle. Though the time when it was written by Moses cannot be precisely determined, yet, since it is a history of matters of fact, it must have been written after the giving of the law and the erection of the tabernacle. This book shows the accomplishment of the divine promises made to Abraham, of the increase of his posterity, and their departure from Egypt after suffering great affliction. It contains

I. An Account of the oppression of the Israelites, and the transactions previously to their departure out of Egypt. (ch. i.—xi.)

II. The Narrative of the Exodus, or Departure of the Israelites. (ch. xii., xiii.)

III. Transactions subsequent to their Exodus. (ch. xiv.—xviii.)

IV. The Promulgation of the Law on Mount Sinai. (ch. xix.—xl.)

In ch. xxxii.—xxxiv. are related the idolatry of the Israelites, the breaking of the two tables of the law, the divine chastisement of the Hebrews, and the renewal of the tables of the covenant.

Section III.—On the Book of Leviticus.

Leviticus, by the Septuagint styled ΛΕΥΙΤΙΚΟΝ, *(Levitikon,)* derives its name from the circumstance of its containing the Laws concerning the religion of the Israelites. It is cited as the production of Moses in several books of Scripture; and is of great use in explaining many passages of the New Testament, especially the Epistle to the Hebrews, which would otherwise be inexplicable. The enactments it contains may be referred to the four following heads, viz.:

I. The Laws concerning Sacrifices, in which the different kinds of sacrifices are enumerated, together with their concomitant rites. (ch. i.—vii.)

II. The Institution of the Priesthood, in which the consecration of Aaron and his sons to the sacred office is related, together with the punishment of Nadab and Abihu. (ch. viii.—x.)

III. The Laws concerning Purifications both of the people and the priests. (ch. xi.—xxii.)

IV. The Laws concerning the sacred Festivals, Vows, Things devoted, and Tithes.

Chap. xxvi. contains various prophetic promises and threatenings, which have signally been fulfilled among the Jews. (Compare v. 22, with Numb. xxi. 6. 2 Kings ii. 24, and xvii. 25. with Ezek. v. 17.) The preservation of the Jews to this day as a *distinct* people is a living comment on v. 44.

Section IV.—On the Book of Numbers.

This fourth book of Moses was entitled ΑΡΙΘΜΟΙ, *(Arithmoi,)* and by the Latin translators it was termed

Numeri, *Numbers*, whence our English title is derived; because it contains an account of the numbering of the children of Israel, (related in chapters i.—iii. and xxvi.) It appears from xxxvi. 13, to have been written by Moses, in the plains of Moab. Besides the numeration and marshalling of the Israelites for their journey, several laws in addition to those delivered in Exodus and Leviticus, and likewise several remarkable events, are recorded in this book. It contains a history of the Israelites, from the beginning of the second month of the second year after their departure from Egypt to the beginning of the eleventh month of the fortieth year of their journeyings: that is, a period of thirty-eight years and nine or ten months. (Compare Numb. i. 1, and xxxvi. 13, with Deut. i. 3.) Most of the transactions here recorded took place in the second and thirty-eighth years: "the dates of the facts related in the middle of the book cannot be precisely ascertained." This book may be divided into four parts; viz.:

PART I. The Census of the Israelites, and the marshalling of them into a regular camp, "each tribe by itself under its own captain or chief, distinguished by his own peculiar standard, and occupying an assigned place with reference to the tabernacle." (Numb. i., ii.) The sacred census of the Levites, the designation of them to the sacred office, and the appointment of them to various services in the tabernacle, are related in Numb. iii. and iv.

PART II. The Institution of various Legal Ceremonies. (ch. v.—x.)

PART III. The History of their Journey from Mount Sinai to the Land of Moab, which may be described and distinguished by their eight remarkable murmurings in the way; every one of which was visited with severe chastisement. (ch. xi.—xxi.)

PART IV. A History of the Transactions which took place in the plains of Moab. (ch. xxii.—xxxvi.)

Section V.—On the Book of Deutoronomy.

This fifth book of Moses derives its name from the title ΔΕΥΤΕΡΟΝΟΜΙΟΝ, *(Deuteronomion,)* prefixed to it by the translators of the Septuagint version, which is a compound term, signifying the *second law*, or *the law repeated;* because it contains a repetition of the law of God, given by Moses to the Israelites. From a comparison of Deut. i. 5, with xxiv. 1, it appears to have been written by Moses in the plains of Moab, a short time before his death: and this circumstance will account for that affectionate earnestness with which he addresses the Israelites. The period of time comprised in this book is five *lunar* weeks, or, according to some chronologers, about two months, viz.: from the first day of the eleventh month of the fortieth year, after the exodus of Israel from Egypt, to the eleventh day of the twelfth month of the same year, A. M. 2553, B. C. 1451. This book comprises four parts; viz.:

Part I. A Repetition of the History related in the preceding Books. (ch. i.—iv.)

Part II. A Repetition of the Moral, Ceremonial, and Judicial Law. (ch. v.—xxvi.)

Part III. The Confirmation of the Law. (ch. xxvii.—xxx.)

Part IV. The Personal History of Moses. (ch. xxxi.—xxxiii.)

The thirty-fourth chapter (which relates the death of Moses) has most probably been detached from the Book of Joshua: for Moses could not record his own death.

CHAPTER II.

ON THE HISTORICAL BOOKS.

This division of the sacred writings comprises twelve books, viz.: from Joshua to Esther inclusive: the first seven of these books are, by the Jews, called the *former prophets*, probably because they treat of the more ancient periods of Jewish history, and because they are most justly supposed to be written by prophetical men. The events recorded in these books occupy a period of almost one thousand years, which commences at the death of Moses, and terminates with the great national reform effected by Nehemiah, after the return of the Jews from the Babylonish captivity.

SECTION I.—On the Book of Joshua.

The book of Joshua, which in all the copies of the Old Testament immediately follows the Pentateuch, is thus denominated, because it contains a narration of the achievements of Joshua the son of Nun, who had been the minister of Moses, and succeeded him in the command of the children of Israel. It has always been received by the Jews as a part of their canon of Scripture.

This book of Joshua comprises the history of about seventeen years, or, according to some chronologers, of twenty-seven or thirty years: it relates,

I. The History of the Occupation of Canaan by the Israelites. (ch. i.—xii.)

II. The Division of the Conquered Land. (ch. xiii.—xxii.)

III. The Assembling of the People, the Dying Address and Counsels of Joshua, his Death, and Burial, &c. (ch. xxiii., xxiv.)

SECTION II.—On the Book of Judges.

The book of Judges derives its name from its containing the history of the Israelites, from the death of Joshua to the time of Eli, under the administration of thirteen Judges, and consequently before the establishment of the regal government. It is supposed to have been written by the prophet Samuel: in it are related,

I. The State of the Israelites after the Death of Joshua, until they began to turn aside from serving the Lord. (ch. i.—iii.)

II. The History of the Oppressions of the Israelites, and their Deliverances by the Judges. (ch. iv.—xvi.)

III. An Account of the Introduction of Idolatry among the Israelites, and the consequent corruption of religion and manners among them; for which God gave them up into the hands of their enemies. (ch. xvii.—xxi.)

Section III.—On the Book of Ruth.

The book of Ruth is generally considered as an Appendix to that of Judges, and an introduction to that of Samuel: it is therefore, with great propriety, placed between the books of Judges and Samuel. It relates, with equal beauty and simplicity, the history of a Moabitish damsel, who renounced idolatry, and by marriage was ingrafted among the Israelites. David was descended from her. The adoption of Ruth, a heathen converted to Judaism, into the line of Christ, has generally been considered as a pre-intimation of the admission of the Gentiles into the church. A further design of this book is, to evince the care of Divine Providence over those who sincerely fear God, in raising the pious Ruth from a state of the deepest adversity to that of the highest prosperity.

Section IV.—On the two Books of Samuel.

In the Jewish canon of Scripture these two books form but one, termed in Hebrew the Book of Samuel, probably because the greater part of the first book was written by that prophet, whose history and transactions it relates. According to the Talmudical writers, the first twenty-four chapters of the first book of Samuel were written by the prophet whose name they bear; and the remainder of that book, together with the whole of the second book, was commited to writing by the prophets Gad and Nathan, agreeably to the practice of the prophets, who wrote memoirs of the transactions of their respective times.

The FIRST BOOK of Samuel contains the history of the Jewish church and polity, from the birth of Samuel, during the judicature of Eli, to the death of Saul, the first king of Israel; a period of nearly eighty years, viz.: from the year of the world 2869 to 2949. It comprises,

I. The Transactions under the Judicature of Eli. (ch. i.—iv.)

II. The History of the Israelites during the Judicature of Samuel. (ch. v.—xiii.)

III. The History of Saul and the transactions of his Reign. (ch. xiv.—xxxi.)

The SECOND BOOK of Samuel contains the history of David, the second king of Israel, during a period of nearly forty years, viz.: from the year of the world 2948 to 2988; and, by recording the translation of the kingdom from the tribe of Benjamin to that of Judah, it relates the partial accomplishment of the prediction delivered in Gen. xlix. 10. This book consists of three principal divisions, relating the triumphs and the troubles of David, and his transactions subsequent to his recovery of the throne, whence he was driven for a short time by the rebellion of his son Absalom.

I. The Triumphs of David. (ch. i.—x.)

II. The Troubles of David, and their cause, together with his repentance, and subsequent recovery of the divine favour. (ch. xi.—xxiv.)

III. David's Restoration to his Throne, and subsequent transactions. (ch. xx.—xxiv.)

The two books of Samuel are of very considerable importance for illustrating the book of Psalms, to which they may be considered as a key.

SECTION V.—On the Two Books of Kings.

The two books of Kings are closely connected with those of Samuel. The origin and gradual increase of the united kingdom of Israel, under Saul and his successor David, having been described in the latter, the books now under consideration relate its height of glory under Solomon, its division into two kingdoms, under his son and successor Rehoboam, the causes of that division, and the consequent decline of the two kingdoms of Israel and Judah, until their final subversion; the ten tribes being carried captive into Assyria by Shalmenezer, and Judah and Benjamin to Babylon by Nebuchadnezzar. In the Jewish canon these books constitute but one volume, termed Melakim, or Kings, having been divided at some unknown period into two parts, for the convenience of reading. In the Septuagint and Vulgate copies they are termed the third and fourth book of Kings; they are generally ascribed to Ezra.

The FIRST BOOK OF KINGS embraces a period of one hundred and twenty-six years, from the anointing of Solomon and his admission as a partner in the throne with David, A. M. 2989, to the death of Jehoshaphat, A. M. 3115.

The first book of Kings may be divided into two principal parts, containing, 1. The history of the undivided kingdom under Solomon; and, 2. The history of the divided kingdom under Rehoboam and his successors, and Jeroboam and his successors.

PART I. The History of Solomon's reign (ch. i.—x.) contains a narrative of

1. The latter days of David; the inauguration of Solomon as his associate in the kingdom, and his designation to be his successor. (ch. i. ii. 1—11.)
2. The Reign of Solomon from the death of David to his dedication of the temple. (ii. 12—46, iii.—viii.)
3. The Transactions during the remainder of Solomon's reign. (ix.—xi.)

PART II. The history of the two kingdoms of Judah and Israel. (ch. xi.—xxii.)

1. The accession of Rehoboam, and the division of the two kingdoms. (ch. xi.)
2. The reigns of Rehoboam, king of Judah, and of Jeroboam I. king of Israel. (xii.—xiv.)
3. The reigns of Abijam and Asa, kings of Judah, and the contemporary reigns of Nadab, Baasha, Elah, Zimri, Omri, and the commencement of Ahab's reign. (xv, xvi.)
4. The reign of Jehoshaphat king of Judah, and of his contemporaries Ahab and Ahaziah, (in part,) during which the prophet Elisha flourished. (xvii.—xxii.)

The SECOND BOOK OF KINGS continues the contemporary history of the two kingdoms of Israel and Judah, from the death of Jehoshaphat, A. M. 3115, to the destruction of the city and temple of Jerusalem by Nebuchadnezzar, A. M. 3416, a period of three hundred years. The three last verses of the preceding book have been improperly disjoined from this. The history of the two kingdoms is interwoven in this book, which may be divided into two parts, viz.:

PART I. The contemporary History of the Kingdoms of Israel and Judah, to the end of the former. (ch. i.—xvii.)

Part II. The History of the decline and fall of the kingdom of Judah. (ch. xviii.—xxv.)

Section VI.—On the Two Books of Chronicles.

The Jews comprise the two books of Chronicles in one book, which they call *Dibre Hajamin*, that is, *The Words of Days*, probably from the circumstance of their being compiled out of diaries or annals, in which were recorded the various events related in these books. In the Septuagint version they are termed Παραλειπομενων *(Paraleipomenon,)* or of *Things omitted;* because many things which were omitted in the former part of the sacred history are here not only supplied, but some narrations are also enlarged, while others are added. The appellation of Chronicles was given to these books by Jerome, because they contain an abstract, in order of time, of the whole of the sacred history, to the time when they were written.

These books were evidently compiled from others, which were written at different times, some before and others after the Babylonish captivity: the period of time contained in these books, is about 3468 years. They may be divided into four parts, viz.:

Part I. Genealogical Tables from Adam to the time of Ezra. (1 Chron. i.—ix.)

Part II. The Histories of Saul and David. (1 Chron. ix. 35—44, x.—xxix.)

Part III. The History of the United Kingdom of Israel and Judah under Solomon. (1 Chron. xxix. 23—30. 2 Chron. i.—ix.)

Part IV. The History of the Kingdom of Judah, from the secession of the ten tribes, under Jeroboam, to its termination by Nebuchadnezzar. (2 Chron. x.—xxxvi.)

As the books of Samuel, Kings, and Chronicles, relate the same histories, they should each be constantly read and collated together; not only for the purpose of obtaining a more comprehensive view of Jewish history, but also in order to illustrate from one book what may appear to be obscure in either of the others.

Section VII.—On the Book of Ezra.

The Books of Ezra and Nehemiah were anciently reckoned by the Jews as one volume, and were divided by them into the first and second books of Ezra. The same division is recognised by the Greek and Latin churches; but the third book, assigned to Ezra, and received as canonical by the Greek church, is the same, in substance, as the book which properly bears his name, but interpolated. And the *fourth* book, which has been attributed to him, is a manifest forgery, in which the marks of falsehood are plainly discernible, and which was never unanimously received as canonical either by the Greek or by the Latin church, although some of the fathers have cited it, and the Latin church has borrowed some words out of it. It is not now extant in Greek, and never was extant in Hebrew. Ezra is generally admitted to have been the author of the book which bears his name: every page, indeed, of the book proves that the writer of it was personally present at the transactions which he has recorded.

The book of Ezra harmonizes most strictly with the prophecies of Haggai and Zechariah, which it materially elucidates. (Compare Ezra v. with Hagg. i. 12. and Zech. iii. iv.) It evinces the paternal care of the Almighty over his chosen people, and consists of two parts, viz.:

I. A Narrative of events from the return of the Jews under Zerubbabel to the rebuilding of the temple. (ch. i.—vi.)

II. The arrival of Ezra at Jerusalem, and the Reformation made there by him. (vii.—x.)

The zeal and piety of Ezra appear, in this book, in a most conspicuous point of view: his memory has always been held in the highest reverence by the Jews.

Section VIII.—On the Book of Nehemiah.

Some eminent fathers of the Christian church have ascribed this book to Ezra; but that Nehemiah, whose name it bears, and who was cup-bearer to Artaxerxes Longimanus, was the author of it, there cannot be any reasonable doubt: the whole of it being written in his name, and, what is very unusual when compared with the preceding sacred historians, being written in the first person. His book contains,

I. An Account of Nehemiah's departure from Shushan, with a royal commission to rebuild the walls of Jerusalem, and his first arrival there. (ch. i., ii. 1—11.)

II. An Account of the building of the walls, notwithstanding the obstacles interposed by Sanballat. (ch. ii. 12—20, iii.—vii. 4.

III. The first reformation accomplished by Nehemiah. (ch. vii.—xii.)

IV. The second reformation accomplished by Nehemiah on his second return to Jerusalem, and his correction of the abuses which had crept in during his absence. (xiii.)

The administration of this pious man and excellent governor lasted about thirty-six years, to the year of the world 3574, according to some chronologers, but Dr. Prideaux has, with more probability, fixed it to the year 3595. The Scripture history closes with the book of Nehemiah.

Section IX.—On the Book of Esther.

This book, which derives its name from the Jewish captive whose history it chiefly relates, is by the Jews termed *Megilloth Esther*, or the volume of Esther. The history it contains comes in between the sixth and seventh chapters of Ezra: its authenticity was questioned by some of the fathers, in consequence of the name of God being omitted throughout, but it has always been received as canonical by the Jews. The book consists of two parts, detailing,

I. The promotion of Esther to the throne of Persia; and the essential service rendered to the king by Mordecai, in detecting a plot against his life. (ch. i., ii.)

II. The advancement of Haman, his designs against the Jews, and their frustration; and the advancement of Mordecai. (ch. iii.—x.)

In our copies, the book of Esther terminates with the hird verse of the tenth chapter; but in the Greek and Vulgate Bibles, there are ten more verses annexed to it, together with six additional chapters, which the Greek and Romish churches account to be canonical. As, however, they are not extant in Hebrew, they are expunged from the sacred canon by Protestants, and are supposed to have been compiled by some Hellenistic Jew.

CHAPTER III.

ON THE POETICAL BOOKS.

THOUGH some of the Sacred Writings, which present themselves to our notice in the present chapter, are anterior in point of date to the Historical Books, yet they are usually classed by themselves under the title of the *Poetical Books;* because they are almost wholly composed in Hebrew verse. This appellation is of considerable antiquity. The Poetical Books are five in number, viz.: Job, Psalms, Proverbs, Ecclesiastes, and the Canticles, or Song of Solomon: in the Jewish canon of Scripture they are classed among the Hagiographa, or Holy Writings; and in our Bibles they are placed between the Historical and Prophetical Books.

SECTION I.—On the book of Job.

This book has derived its title from the venerable patriarch Job, whose prosperity, afflictions, and restoration from the deepest adversity, are here recorded, together with his exemplary and unequalled patience under all his calamities. Some critics have doubted, or affected to doubt, the existence of such a character as Job; but that point is satisfactorily determined by the prophet Ezekiel (xiv. 14,) and the apostle James, (v. 11,) both of whom mention him as a real character. The length of his life places him in the patriarchal times: and Dr. Hales, besides other evidences, which cannot here be detailed, has rendered it highly probable that he lived about 184 years before the time of Abraham. He dwelt in Uz or Idumæa.

Among the conflicting opinions which have been advanced respecting the author of this book, the most probable is that of Archbishop Magee, who supposes it to have been originally written by Job, and subsequently transcribed by Moses; who having applied it to the use of the Jews, and given it the sanction of his authority, it thenceforth became enrolled among the sacred writings It has been quoted by almost every Hebrew writer from the age of Moses to that of Malachi. In its form, this poem approximates to the Mekama, or philosophical discourses of the Arabian Poets.

Nothing, perhaps, has contributed more to render the poem of Job obscure, than the common division into chapters and verses; by which not only the unity of the general subject, but frequently that of a single paragraph, or clause, is broken.

The poem may be divided into six parts; viz.: The *first* of these contains the exordium or narrative part, which is written in prose; (ch. i., ii.;) the *second* comprises the *first* debate or dialogue of Job and his friends; (iii.—xiv.;) the *third* includes the *second* series of debate or controversy; (xv.—xxi.;) the *fourth* comprehends the *third* series of controversy; (xxii.—xxxi.;) in *the fifth* part Elihu sums up the argument; (xxxii.—xxxvii.;) and in the *sixth* part Jehovah determines the controversy, Job humbles himself, is accepted, and restored to health and prosperity. (xxxviii.—xlii.)

Independently of the important instruction and benefit which may be derived from a devout perusal of the book of Job, this divine poem is of no small value, as transmitting to us a faithful delineation of the patriarchal doctrines of religion, and particularly the existence of a God, who is the rewarder of them that diligently seek him, and a day of future resurrection, judgment, and final retribution.

Section II.—On the Book of Psalms.

This book is entitled in the Hebrew *Sepher Tehillim*, that is, the *Book of Hymns* or *Praises;* because the praises of God constitute their chief subject matter: and as they were set, not only to be sung with the voice, but also to be accompanied with musical instruments, the Septuagint version designates them Βιβλος Ψαλμων, (*Biblos Psal-*

mon,) the *Book of Psalms*, by which name they are cited in Luke xx. 42; and this appellation is retained in our Bibles. The right of the book of Psalms to a place in the sacred canon has never been disputed: they are frequently alluded to in the Old Testament, and are often cited by our Lord and his apostles as the work of the Holy Spirit. They are generally termed the Psalms of David, that Hebrew monarch being their chief author. Many of them bear his name, and were composed on occasion of remarkable circumstances in his life, his dangers, his afflictions, and his deliverances. Many of them, however, are strictly prophetical of the Messiah, of whom David; was an eminent type: but others were composed during the reign of Solomon, or during and subsequent to the captivity. We have no information when these divine poems were collected into a volume. The Psalms of Degrees, or Odes of Ascension, as Bishop Lowth terms them, are supposed to have derived this name from their being sung, when the people *came up* either to worship in Jerusalem, at the annual festivals, or perhaps from the Babylonish captivity. The word "Selah," which is found in many of the Psalms, appears to have been inserted in order to point out something worthy of most attentive observation.

For a Table of those Psalms which are strictly prophetical of the Messiah, see pp. 102, 103, *supra*.

The book of Psalms, being composed in Hebrew verse, must generally be studied according to the laws of Hebrew Poetry, which have been noticed in pp. 108—111: and this the *English* reader will find little difficulty in accomplishing, in our admirably faithful authorized version. Attention to the following hints will also enable him to enter into their force and meaning.

1. Investigate the Argument of each psalm.

This is sometimes intimated in the prefixed title: but as these inscriptions are not always genuine, it will be preferable, in every case, to deduce the argument from a diligent and attentive reading of the psalm itself, and then to form our opinion concerning the correctness of the title, if there be any.

2. With this view, examine the Historical Origin of the psalm, or the circumstances that led the sacred poet to compose it.

Much advantage and assistance may be derived from studying the psalms *chronologically*, and comparing them with the historical books of the Old

Testament, particularly those which treat of the Israelites and Jews, from the origin of their monarchy to their return from the Babylonish captivity.

3. Attend to the Structure of the psalms.

The psalms, being principally designed for the national worship of the Jews, are adapted to choral singing: attention to this circumstance will enable us better to enter into their spirit and meaning.

For a Table of the Psalms adapted to private reading or devotion, see the APPENDIX, No. IV.

SECTION III.—On the Books of Proverbs.

The book of Proverbs has always been ascribed to Solomon, whose name it bears, though, from the frequent repetition of the same sentences, as well as from some variations in style which have been discovered, doubts have been entertained whether he really was the author of every maxim it comprises. As it is no where said that Solomon himself made a collection of proverbs and sentences, the general opinion is, that several persons made a collection of them: Hezekiah, among others, as mentioned in the twenty-fifth chapter: Agur, Isaiah, and Ezra, might have done the same. This book is frequently cited by the apostles: its scope is to instruct men in the deepest mysteries of true wisdom and understanding, the height and perfection of which is, the true knowledge of the divine will, and the sincere fear of the Lord. (Prov. i. 2—7, ix. 10.) It may be divided into five parts, viz.:

PART I. In the proem or exordium, containing the first *nine* chapters, the teacher gives his pupil a series of admonitions, directions, cautions, and excitements to the study of wisdom.

PART II. extends from chapter x. to xxii. 16, and consists of what may be strictly and properly called *proverbs*, —namely, unconnected sentences, expressed with much neatness and simplicity.

PART III. reaches from chapter xxii. 17, to xxv. inclusive: in this part the tutor drops the sententious style, and addresses his pupil as present, to whom he gives renewed and connected admonitions to the study of wisdom.

The proverbs contained in

PART IV. are supposed to have been selected from

some larger collection of Solomon "by the men of Hezekiah,"—that is, by the prophets whom he employed to restore the service and writings of the Jewish church. (2 Chron. xxxi. 20, 21.) This part, like the second, consists of detached unconnected sentences, and extends from chapter xxv to xxix. Some of the proverbs, which Solomon had introduced into the former part of the book, are here repeated.

Part V. Comprises chapters xxx. and xxxi. In the former are included the wise observations and instructions delivered by Agur, the son Jakeh, to his pupils, Ithiel and Ucal. The thirty-first chapter contains the precepts which were given to Lemuel by his mother, who is supposed by some to have been a Jewish woman married to some neighbouring prince, and who appears to have been most ardently desirous to guard him against vice, to establish him in the principles of justice, and to unite him to a wife of the best qualities. Of Agur we know nothing; nor have any of the commentators offered so much as a plausible conjecture respecting him.

Section IV.—On the Book of Ecclesiastes.

The title of this book, in our Bibles, is derived from the Septuagint version, Εκκλησιαςης, *(Ecclesiastes,)* signifying a a *preacher*, or one who harangues a public congregation. In Hebrew it is termed, from the initial words, *Dibre Coheleth*, "the Words of the Preacher;" by whom may be intended, either the person assembling the people, or he who addresses them when convened. Although this book does not bear the name of Solomon, it is evident from several passages that he was the author of it. Compare ch. i. 12. 16, ii. 4—9, and xii. 9, 10. Its scope is explicitly announced in ch. i. 2, and xii. 13, viz.: to demonstrate the vanity of all earthly objects, and to draw off men from the pursuit of them, as an *apparent* good, to the fear of God, and communion with him, as to the highest and only *permanent* good in this life, and to show that men must seek for happiness beyond the grave. It consists of two parts; viz.:

Part I. The Vanity of all earthly conditions, occupations, and pleasures. (ch. i.—vi. 9.)

PART II. The Nature, Excellence, and Beneficial Effects of true Religion. (ch. vi.—xii. 7.)

The CONCLUSION. (ch. xii. 8—14.)

SECTION V.—On the Song of Solomon.

This book has always been reputed to be the production of the Hebrew monarch. Concerning its structure, there is great difference of opinion among critics, whose various hypotheses are discussed in the author's larger work. The most probable opinion is that which refers it to the idyls of the Arabian Poets. Dr. John Mason Good makes them to be twelve in number; viz.:

IDYL		CHAP.
1	containing	i. 1—8
2		i. 9, ii. 7.
3		ii. 8—17.
4		iii. 1—5.
5		iii. 6, iv. 7.
6		iv. 8, v. 1.
7		v. 2, vi. 10.
8		vi. 11—13.
9		vii. 1—9.
10		vii. 10, vii. 4
11		viii. 5—7.
12		viii. 8—14.

This poem was composed on occasion of Solomon's marriage. That it is a mystical poem, or allegory, all sound interpreters are agreed; though some expositors, who have not entered sufficiently into the spirit and meaning of Oriental poesy, have caused particular passages to be considered as coarse and indelicate, which, in the original, are altogether the reverse; while others have so confounded the literal and allegorical senses as to give neither, distinctly or completely. At the same time, they have applied the figures to such a variety of objects, as to leave the reader still to seek the right; and, by their minute dissection of the allegory, they have not only destroyed its consistency and beauty, but have also exposed the poem to the unmerited ridicule of profane minds. Much, unquestionably, has been done, by later writers, towards elucidating the language and allusions of the Song of Songs by the aid of Oriental literature and manners: but, after all the labours of learned men, there will, perhaps, be found many expressions which are very difficult to us, both as to the literal meaning, and the spiritual instruction intended to be conveyed by them; and some descriptions must not be judged by *modern* notions of delicacy. But the grand outlines, *soberly interpreted*, in the obvious meaning of the allegory, so accord with the affections and experience of the sincere Christian, "that he will hardly ever read and meditate upon them, in a spirit of humble devotion, without feeling a conviction that no other poem, of the same kind, extant in the world, could, without most manifest violence, be so explained as to describe the state of his heart at different times, and to excite admiring, adoring, grateful love to God our Saviour, as this does." (Scott's Pref. to Sol. Song.)

CHAPTER IV.

GENERAL OBSERVATIONS ON THE PROPHETS AND THEIR WRITINGS.

We now enter on the fourth, or prophetical part of the Old Testament, according to the division which is generally adopted, but which (as we have already seen in page 79, *supra*,) forms the second division, according to the Jewish classification of the sacred volume. This portion of the Scriptures is termed *prophetical*, because it chiefly consists of predictions of future events; though many historical and doctrinal passages are interspersed through the writings of the PROPHETS, as there also are many predictions of future events scattered through those books, which are more strictly historical. The authors of these books are, by way of eminence, termed *Prophets*, that is, divinely inspired persons, who were raised up among the Israelites to be the ministers of God's dispensations. The prophets are usually reckoned among sacred persons. See p. 230, 231, *supra;* and some observations on the interpretation of Scripture Prophecy, especially the predictions relative to the Messiah, will be found in pp. 144—148, *supra*.

The prophetical books are sixteen in number, (the Lamentations of Jeremiah being usually considered as an appendix to his predictions,) and, in all modern editions of the Bible, they are usually divided into two classes; viz.: 1. The *Greater Prophets*, comprising the writings of Isaiah, Jeremiah, Ezekiel, and Daniel; who have been thus designated from the size of their books, not because they possessed greater authority than the others. 2. The *Minor Prophets*, comprising the writings of Hosea, Joel, Amos, Jonah, Obadiah, Micah, Nahum, Habakkuk, Zephaniah, Haggai, Zechariah, and Malachi. These books were anciently written in one volume, by the Jews, lest any of them should be lost; some of their writings being very short.

Much of the obscurity which hangs over the prophetic writings may be removed by perusing them in the order of time in which they were probably written; and though the *precise* time in which some of the prophets delivered their predictions, cannot, perhaps, be traced in every instance, yet the following arrangement of the prophets in their supposed order of time, (according to the tables of Blair, Archbishop Newcome, and other eminent critics, with a few variations,) will, we think, be found sufficiently correct for the right understanding of their predictions.

According to the annexed table, the times when the prophets flourished may be referred to three periods; viz.: 1. Before the Babylonian Captivity;—2. Near to and during that event;—and, 3. After the return of the Jews from Babylon. And if, in these three periods, we parallel the prophetical writings with the historical books written during the same times, they will materially illustrate each other.

	Before Christ.		
Jonah	Between 856 and 784.		Jehu and Jehoahaz, according to BishopLloyd; but Joash and Jeroboam the Second, according to Blair.
Amos	Between 810 and 785.	Uzziah, ch. i. 1.	Jeroboam the Second, ch. i. 1.
Hosea	Between 810 and 725.	Uzziah,Jotham,Ahaz,the third year of Hezekiah.	Jeroboam the Second, ch. i. 1.
Isaiah	Between 810 and 749.	Uzziah,Jotham,Ahaz and Hezekiah, chap. i. 1, and perhaps Manasseh.	
Joel	Between 810 and 660, or later,	Uzziah, or possibly Manasseh.	
Micah	Between 758 and 699.	Jotham, Ahaz, and Hezekiah, ch. i. 1.	Pekan ana Hosea.
Nahum	Between 720 and 698	Probablytowards theclose of Hezekiah's reign.	
Zephaniah	Between 640 and 609.	In the reign of Josiah ch. i. 1.	
Jeremiah	Between 628 and 586.	In the thirteenth year of Josiah.	
Habakkuk	Between 612 and 598.	Probably in the reign of Jehoiakim.	
Daniel	Between 606 and 534.	During all the captivity.	
Obadiah	Between 588 and 583.	Between the taking of Jerusalem byNebuchadnezzar, and the destruction of the Edomites by him.	
Ezekiel	Between 595 and 536.	During part of the captivity.	
Haggai	About 520 to 518.	After the return from Babylon.	
Zechariah	From 520 to 518,or longer.		
Malachi	Between 436 and 397.		

CHAPTER V.

ON THE PROPHETS WHO FLOURISHED BEFORE THE BABYLONIAN CAPTIVITY.

SECTION I.—On the Book of the Prophet Jonah.

BEFORE CHRIST, 856—784.

THIS Book is by the Hebrews called *Sepher Jonah*, or the Book of Jonah, from its author Jonah, the son of Amittai, who was a native of Gath-Hepher in Galilee. (Jon. i. 1, with Josh. xix. 13.) He is supposed to have prophesied to the ten tribes, according to Bishop Lloyd, toward the close of Jehu's reign, or in the beginning of Jehoahaz's reign; though other chronologers place him under Joash and Jeroboam II., about forty years later. The scope of this book is to show, by the very striking example of the Ninevites, the divine forbearance and long suffering towards sinners who are spared on their sincere repentance.

The book of Jonah consists of two parts; viz.:

PART I. His first mission to Nineveh, and his attempt to flee to Tarshish, and its frustration, together with his delivery from the stomach of the great fish which had swallowed him. (ch. i., ii.)

PART II. His second mission, and its happy result to the Ninevites, who, in consequence of the prophet's preaching, repented in dust and ashes; (iii. ;) and the discontent of Jonah, who, dreading to be thought a false prophet, repined at the divine mercy in sparing the Ninevites, whose destruction he seems to have expected. (iv.)

The time of Jonah's continuance in the belly of the fish was a type of our Lord's continuance in the grave. (Luke xi. 30.)

SECTION II.—On the Book of the Prophet Amos.

BEFORE CHRIST, 810--785.

AMOS, the third of the minor prophets, is supposed to have been a native of Tekoah, a small town in the kingdom of Judah, situate about four leagues to the south of Jerusalem. He prophesied during the reigns of Uzziah, king of Judah, and of Jeroboam, son of Joash. His prophecy consists of four parts, viz.:

Part I. The Judgments of God denounced against the neighbouring Gentile nations; as

The Syrians, (ch. i. 1—5,) which see fulfilled in 2 Kings xvi. 9; the Philistines, (i. 6—8,) recorded as accomplished in 2 Kings xviii. 8, Jer. xlvii. 1. 5, and 2 Chron. xxvi. 6; the Tyrians, (i. 9, 10,) the Edomites, (i. 11, 12. compared with Jer. xxvi. 9. 21, xxvii. 3. 6, and 1 Macc. v. 3,) the Ammonites, (13—15,) and the Moabites. (ii. 1—3.)

Part II. The Divine Judgments denounced against Judah and Israel. (ch. ii. 4, ix. 1—10.)

Part III. Consolatory Promises to the Church, describing her Restoration by the Messiah. (ch. ix. 11—15.)

Section III.—On the Book of the Prophet Hosea.

BEFORE CHRIST, 810—725.

Hosea, of whose family we have no certain information, prophesied during the reigns of Uzziah, Jotham, and Ahaz, and in the third year of Hezekiah, kings of Judah, and during the reign of Jeroboam II. king of Israel; and it is most probable that he was an Israelite, who lived in the kingdom of Samaria, or of the ten tribes, as his predictions are chiefly directed against their wickedness and idolatry. But, with the severest denunciations of vengeance, he blends promises of mercy. The prophecy of Hosea contains fourteen chapters, which may be divided into five sections, or discourses, exclusive of the title in ch. i. 1, viz.:

Discourse I. Under the figure of the supposed infidelity of the prophet's wife is represented the spiritual infidelity of the Israelites, a remnant of whom, it is promised, shall be saved (ch. i. 2—11,) and they are exhorted to forsake idolatry. (ii. 1—11.) Promises are then introduced, on the general conversion of the *twelve* tribes to Christianity; and the gracious purposes of Jehovah toward the *ten* tribes, or the kingdom of Israel in particular, are represented under the figure of the prophet taking back his wife on her amendment. (ii. 11—23, iii.)

Discourse II. A reproof of the bloodshed and idolatry of the Israelites, against which the inhabitants of Judah are exhorted to take warning: interspersed with promises of pardon. (ch. iv.—vi. 1—3.)

DISCOURSE III. The prophet's exhortations to repentance proving ineffectual, God complains by him of their obstinate iniquity and idolatry, (ch. vi. 4—11, vii. 1—10,) and denounces that Israel will be carried into captivity into Assyria by Sennacherib, notwithstanding their reliance on Egypt for assistance. (vii. 11—16, viii.)

DISCOURSE IV. The captivity and dispersion of Israel is further threatened; (ch. ix., x.) the Israelites are reproved for their idolatry, yet they shall not be utterly destroyed, and their return to their own country is foretold. (xi.) Renewed denunciations are made on account of their idolatry. (xii., xiii. 1—8.)

DISCOURSE V. After a terrible denunciation of divine punishment, intermixed with promises of restoration from captivity, (ch. xiii. 9—16,) the prophet exhorts the Israelites to repentance, and furnishes them with a beautiful form of prayer adapted to their situation; (xiv. 1—3;) and foretells their reformation from idolatry, together with the subsequent restoration of *all* the tribes from their dispersed state, and their conversion to the Gospel. (4—9.)

SECTION IV.—On the Book of the Prophet Isaiah.

BEFORE CHRIST, 810—749.

Though fifth in the order of time, the writings of the prophet Isaiah are placed first in order of the prophetical books, principally on account of the sublimity and importance of his predictions, and partly also because the book, which bears his name, is larger than all the twelve minor prophets put together.

Concerning his family and descent, nothing certain has been recorded, except what he himself tells us, (i. 1,) viz.: that he was the son of Amos, and discharged the prophetic office in the days of Uzziah, Jotham, Ahaz, and Hezekiah, kings of Judah. Concerning the time or manner of his death nothing certain is known. Besides the predictions ascribed to him, it appears from 1 Chron. xxvi. 22, that Isaiah wrote an account of the *Acts of Uzziah*, king of

Judah: this has long since perished. Of all the prophets, none have so clearly predicted the circumstances relative to the advent, sufferings, atoning death, and resurrection of the Messiah, as Isaiah; who has, from this circumstance, been styled the Evangelical Prophet. His predictions (yet unfulfilled) of the ultimate triumph and extension of the Redeemer's kingdom are unrivalled for the splendour of their imagery, and the beauty and sublimity of their language.

PART I. contains a general Description of the State and Condition of the Jews, in the several periods of their history; the Promulgation and success of the Gospel, and the coming of Messiah to judgment. (ch. i.—v.) The predictions in this section were delivered during the reign of Uzziah king of Judah.

PART II. comprises the predictions delivered in the reigns of Jotham and Ahaz. (ch. vi.—xii.)

PART III. contains various predictions against the Babylonians, Assyrians, Philistines, and other nations with whom the Jews had any intercourse. (ch. xiii.—xxiv.)

PART IV. contains a Prophecy of the great calamities that should befall the people of God, His merciful preservation of a remnant of them, and of their restoration to their country, of their conversion to the Gospel, and the destruction of Antichrist. (ch. xxiv.—xxxiii.)

PART V. comprises the historical part of the prophecy of Isaiah. (ch. xxxvi.—xxxix.)

PART VI. comprises a series of prophecies, delivered in all probability, toward the close of Hezekiah's reign. (ch. xl.—lxvi.)

This portion of Isaiah's predictions constitutes the most elegant part of the sacred writings of the Old Testament. The chief subject is the restoration of the church, which is pursued with the greatest regularity. But, as the subject of this very beautiful series of prophecies is chiefly of the consolatory kind, they are introduced with a promise of the restoration of the kingdom, and the return of the Jews from the Babylonian captivity, through the merciful interposition of God. At the same time this redemption from Babylon is employed as an image to shadow out a redemption of an infinitely higher and more important nature. The prophet connects these two events together, scarcely ever treating of the former without throwing in some intimations of the latter; and sometimes he is so fully possessed with the glories of the future more remote kingdom of the Messiah, that he seems to leave the immediate subject of his commission almost out of the question.

SECTION V.—On the Book of the Prophet Joel.

BEFORE CHRIST, 810—660, or later.

Concerning the family, condition, and pursuits of this prophet, nothing certain is known; but from internal evidence, we are authorized to place him in the reign of Uzziah. Consequently he was contemporary with Amos and Hosea, if indeed he did not prophesy before Amos. His book consists of three chapters, which may be divided into three discourses or parts, viz.

PART I. is an exhortation, both to the priests and to the people, to repent, by reason of the famine brought upon them by the palmer-worm, &c. in consequence of their sins; (ch. i. 1—20. ;) and is followed by a denunciation of still greater calamities, if they continued impenitent. (ii. 1—11.)

PART II. An Exhortation to keep a public and solemn fast, (ch. ii. 12—17,) with a promise of removing the calamities of the Jews on their repentance (18—26,) and of the Effusion of the Holy Spirit. (27—32. Compare Acts ii. 17—21.)

PART III. predicts the general Conversion and return of the Jews, and the destruction of their opponents, together with the glorious state of the church that is to follow. (ch. iii.)

SECTION VI.—On the Book of the Prophet Micah.

BEFORE CHRIST, 758—699.

Micah, the third of the minor prophets, was a native of Morasthi, a small town in the southern part of the territory of Judah; and, as we learn from the commencement of his predictions, prophesied in the reigns of Jotham, Ahaz, and Hezekiah, kings of that country; consequently he was contemporary with Isaiah, Joel, Hosea, and Amos. His book contains seven chapters, forming three parts; viz.:

INTRODUCTION, or title. (I. 1.)

PART I. comprises the prophecies delivered in the reign of Jotham king of Judah (with whom Pekah king of Israel was contemporary,) in which the divine judgments are denounced against both Israel and Judah for their sins. (ch. i. 2—16.)

PART II. contains the predictions delivered in the reigns of Ahaz king of Judah (with whom his son Hezekiah was associated in the government during the latter part of his life,) and of Pekah king of Israel, who was also contemporary with him. (ii.—iv. 8.)

PART III. includes the prophecies delivered by Micah during the reign of Hezekiah king of Judah, the first six years of whose government were contemporary with the greater part of the reign of Hoshea, the last king of Israel. (iv. 9—13, v.—vii.)

Chap. v. contains an eminent prediction of the place of the Messiah's Nativity, as well as of his kingdom and conquests.

SECTION VII.—On the Book of the Prophet Nahum.

BEFORE CHRIST, 720—698.

Nahum, a native of Elkosh, or Elkosha, a village in Galilee, is generally supposed to have lived between the Assyrian and Babylonian captivities, about 715 years before the Christian æra. The repentance of the Ninevites, in consequence of Jonah's preaching, being of short duration, Nahum was commissioned to denounce the final and inevitable ruin of Nineveh and the Assyrian empire by the Chaldeans, and to comfort his countrymen in the certainty of their destruction

His prophecy is one entire poem, which, opening with a sublime description of the justice and power of God tempered with long-suffering, (ch. i. 1—8,) foretells the destruction of Sennacherib's forces, and the subversion of the Assyrian empire, (9—12,) together with the deliverance of Hezekiah and the death of Sennacherib. (13—15.) The destruction of Nineveh is then predicted, and described with singular minuteness. (ii., iii.)

Section VIII.—On the Book of the Prophet Zephaniah.

BEFORE CHRIST, 640—609

This prophet, who was "the son of Cushi, the son of Gedaliah, the son of Amariah, the son of Hizkiah," (i. 1,) is supposed to have discharged the prophetic office before the eighteenth year of Josiah; that is, before this prince had reformed the abuses and corruptions of his dominions. His prophecy, which consists of three chapters, may be divided into four sections; viz.:

Sect. I. A denunciation against Judah for their idolatry. (ch. 1.)

Sect. II. Repentance the only means to avert the divine vengeance. (ch. ii. 1—3.)

Sect. III. Prophecies against the Philistines, (ch. ii. 4—7,) Moabites and Ammonites, (8—11,) Ethiopia (12,) and Nineveh. (13—15.) In

Sect. IV. The captivity of the Jews by the Babylonians is foretold, (ch. iii. 1—7.) together with their future restoration and the ultimate prosperous state of the church.

CHAPTER VI.

OF THE PROPHETS WHO FLOURISHED NEAR TO AND DURING THE BABYLONIAN CAPTIVITY.

Section I.—On the Book of the Prophet Jeremiah.

BEFORE CHRIST, 628—586.

The prophet Jeremiah was of the sacerdotal race, being (as he himself records) one of the priests that dwelt at Anathoth, (i. 1,) in the land of Benjamin, a city appropriated out of that tribe to the use of the priests, the sons of Aaron, (Josh. xxi. 18,) and situate, as we learn from Jerome, about three Roman miles north of Jerusalem. He appears to have been very young when called to the prophetic office, in the discharge of which he received much ill treatment from the Jews: he prophesied about forty-two years, and followed the remnant of the Jews on their retiring into Egypt, where he is said to have been put to death by his profligate countrymen. His predictions, which are levelled against the crimes of the Jews, are not arranged in the chronological order in which they were originally delivered. The cause of their transposition it is now impossible to ascertain. The late Rev. Dr. Blayney, to whom we are indebted for a learned version of, and commentary on, the writings of this prophet, has endeavoured, with great judgment, to restore their proper order by transposing the chapters, wherever it appeared to be necessary. According to his arrangement, the predictions of Jeremiah are to be placed in the following order, viz.:

SECTION. I. The prophecies delivered in the reign of Josiah, containing chapters i.—xii. inclusive.

SECTION II. The prophecies delivered in the reign of Jehoiakim, comprising chapters xiii.—xx., xxii., xxiii., xxxv., xxxvi., xlv.—xlviii., and xlix. 1—33.

SECTION III. The prophecies delivered in the reign of Zedekiah, including chapters xxi., xxiv., xxvii.—xxxiv., xxxvii.—xxxix. xlix. 34—39, and l., li.

SECTION IV. The prophecies delivered under the government of Gedaliah, from the taking of Jerusalem to the retreat of the people into Egypt, and the prophecies of Jeremiah delivered to the Jews in that country; comprehending chapters xl.—xliv. inclusive.

In ch. xxiii. 5, 6, is foretold the mediatorial kingdom of the Messiah, who is called the LORD OUR RIGHTEOUSNESS. Again, in Jer. xxxi. 31—36, and xxxiii. 8, the efficacy of Christ's atonement, the spiritual character of the new covenant, and the inward efficacy of the Gospel, are most clearly and emphatically described. Compare Saint Paul's Epistle to the Hebrews, ch. viii. 8—13, and x. 16, *et seq.*

Section II.—On the Lamentations of Jeremiah.

That Jeremiah was the author of the Elegies or Lamentations which bear his name is evident, not only from a very ancient and almost uninterrupted tradition, but also from the argument and style of the book, which corresponds exactly with those of his prophecies. This book consists of five chapters, forming as many pathetic elegies; in the four first of which the prophet bewails the various calamities of his country; the fifth elegy is an epilogue to the four preceding. Dr. Blayney considers it as a memorial representing, in the name of the whole body of Jewish exiles, the numerous calamities under which they groaned; and humbly supplicating God to commiserate their wretchedness, and to restore them to his favour, and to their ancient prosperity.

Section III.—On the Book of the Prophet Habakkuk.

BEFORE CHRIST, 612—598.

Concerning this prophet we have no certain information; he exercised the prophetic office, most probably, in the reign of Jehoiakim, and consequently was contemporary with Jeremiah. His book consists of two parts. In

Part I. which is in the form of a dialogue between God and the prophet, the Babylonish captivity is announced; with a promise, however, of deliverance, and the ultimate destruction of the Babylonian empire.

Part II. contains the prayer or psalm of Habakkuk, in which he implores God to hasten the deliverance of his people. (ii.)

Section IV.—On the Book of the Prophet Daniel.

BEFORE CHRIST, 606—534.

Daniel, the fourth of the greater prophets, if not of royal birth, (as the Jews affirm,) was of noble descent, and was carried captive to Babylon at an early age, in the fourth year of Jehoiachin king of Judah, in the year 606 before the Christian æra, and seven years before the deportation of Ezekiel. Having been instructed in the language and literature of the Chaldæans, he afterwards held a very distinguished office in the Babylonian empire. (Dan. i. 1—4.) He was contemporary with Ezekiel, who mentions his extraordinary piety and wisdom, (Ezek. xiv. 14, 20,) and the latter, even at that time, seems to have become proverbial. (Ezek. xxviii. 3.) Daniel lived in great credit with the Babylonian monarchs; and his uncommon merit procured him the same regard from Darius and Cyrus, the two first sovereigns of Persia. He lived throughout the captivity, but it does not appear that he returned to his own country when Cyrus permitted the Jews to revisit their native land. The time of his death is not certainly known. Although the name of Daniel is not prefixed to his book, the many passages in which he speaks in the first person sufficiently prove that he was the author. His writings may be divided into two parts; viz.:

Part I. comprises the historical portion of this book: it contains a narrative of the circumstances that led to Daniel's elevation. (ch. i.—vi.)

Part. II. comprises various prophecies and visions of things future, until the advent and death of the Messiah, and the ultimate conversion of the Jews and Gentiles to the faith of the Gospel. (ch. vii.—xii.)

This is an amazing series of prophecy, extending through many successive ages from the first establishment of the Persian empire, upwards of 530 years before Christ, to the general resurrection! "What a proof does it afford of a Divine Providence, and of a Divine Revelation! for who could thus declare the things that shall be, with their times and seasons, but He only who hath them in his power: whose dominion is over all, and whose kingdom endureth from generation to generation!"

Section V.—On the Book of the Prophet Obadiah.

BEFORE CHRIST, 588—583.

The time when this prophet flourished is uncertain: rchbishop Newcome places it, with great probability.

between the taking of Jerusalem (which happened in the year 587 before Christ) and the destruction of Idumæa, by Nebuchadnezzar, which took place a very few years after. Consequently he was partly contemporary with Jeremiah, one of whose predictions includes the greater part of Obadiah's book. (Compare Obad. 1—9, with Jer. xlix. 14, 15, 16. 7. 9, 10.) His writings, which consist of only one chapter, unfold a very interesting scene of prophecy, in two parts; viz.:

PART I. is minatory, and denounces the destruction of Edom for their pride and carnal security, (1—9,) and for their cruel insults and enmity to the Jews, after the capture of their city. (10—16.)

PART II. is consolatory, and foretells the restoration of the Jews, (17,) their victory over their enemies, and their flourishing state in consequence. (18—21.)

SECTION VI.—On the Book of the Prophet Ezekiel.

BEFORE CHRIST, 595—536.

Ezekiel, whose name imports the *strength of God*, was the son of Buzi, of the sacerdotal race, and one of the captives carried by Nebuchadnezzar to Babylon with Jehoiachin king of Judah: it does not appear that he had prophesied before he came into Mesopotamia. The principal scene of his predictions was some place on the river Chebar, which flows into the Euphrates about two hundred miles to the north of Babylon, where the prophet resided; though he was, occasionally, conveyed in vision to Jerusalem. He commenced his prophetic ministry in the thirtieth year of his age, according to general accounts; or rather, as Calmet thinks, in the thirtieth year after the covenant was renewed with God, in the reign of Josiah, which answers to the fifth year of Ezekiel's and Jehoiachin's captivity, (Ezek. i. 1, xl. 1,) the æra whence he dates his predictions; and he continued to prophesy about twenty or twenty-one years. The events of his life, after his call to the prophetic office, are interwoven with the detail which he has himself given of his predictions: but the manner of its termination is no where ascertained. His prophecies have always been acknowledged to be canonical, nor was it ever disputed that he was their author: they form, in our Bibles, forty-eight chapters, and, as he is extremely punctual in dating them, we have little or no difficulty in arranging them in chronological order. They may be divided into four parts, viz.:

PART I. Ezekiel's call to the Prophetic office, (ch. i. 1, to the first part of verse 28,) his commission, instructions, and encouragements for executing it (i. 28, latter clause, ii., iii. 1—21.)

PART II. Denunciations against the Jewish People. (ch. iii. 22—27, iv.—xxiv.)

PART III. comprises Ezekiel's Prophecies against various neighbouring nations, enemies to the Jews. (ch. xxv.—xxxii.)

PART IV. contains a series of exhortations and consolatory promises to the Jews, of future deliverance under Cyrus, but principally of their final restoration and conversion under the kingdom of Messiah. (ch. xxxiii.—xlvi.)

CHAPTER VII.

OF THE PROPHETS WHO FLOURISHED AFTER THE RETURN OF THE JEWS FROM BABYLON.

SECTION I.—On the Book of the Prophet Haggai.

BEFORE CHRIST, 520—518.

NOTHING is certainly known concerning the tribe or birth-place of Haggai, the tenth in order of the minor prophets, but the first of the three who were commissioned to make known the divine will to the Jews after their return from captivity. The Jews having for fourteen years discontinued the rebuilding of the temple, this prophet was commissioned to encourage them in their work, in consequence of the edict issued by Cyrus in their favour. Accordingly the work was resumed, and completed in a few years. His prophecy comprises three distinct prophecies or discourses; viz.:

DISCOURSE I. contains a severe reproof of the people, especially of their governor and high-priest, for their delay in rebuilding the temple, which neglect was the cause of the unfruitful seasons, and other marks of the divine displeasure, with which they had been visited. (i. 1—11.) The obedience of the governors and people to the prophet's message is then related. (12—15.)

DISCOURSE II. The prophet comforts the aged men, who, when young, had beheld the splendour of the first temple, and now wept for the diminished magnificence of the second temple, by foretelling that its glory should be greater than that of the first. (ii. 1—2.) This prediction was accomplished by Jesus Christ honouring it with his presence and preaching. Haggai then predicts a fruitful harvest, as a reward for carrying on the building. (10—19.)

DISCOURSE III. The prophet foretells the setting up of Messiah's kingdom under the name of Zerubbabel. (ii 20—23.)

SECTION II.—On the Book of the Prophet Zechariah.

BEFORE CHRIST, 520—518.

Although the names of Zechariah's father and grandfather are specified, (Zech. i. 1,) it is not known from what tribe or family this prophet was descended, nor where he was born; but that he was one of the captives who returned to Jerusalem in consequence of the decree of Cyrus, is unquestionable. As he opened his prophetic commission in the eighth month of the second year of Darius, the son of Hystaspes, that is, about the year 520 before the Christian æra, it is evident that he was contemporary with Haggai, and his authority was equally effectual in promoting the building of the temple.

The prophecy of Zechariah consists of two parts; viz.:

PART I. concerns the events which were then taking place, viz.: the restoration of the temple, interspersing predictions relative to the advent of the Messiah. (ch. i.—vi.) These predictions were delivered in the second year of the reign of Darius, king of Persia.

PART II. comprises prophecies relative to more remote events, particularly the coming of Jesus Christ, and the war of the Romans against the Jews. (vii.—xiv.) These prophecies were announced in the fourth year of Darius's reign.

SECTION III.—On the Book of the Prophet Malachi.

BEFORE CHRIST, 436—397.

Malachi, the last of the minor prophets, delivered his predictions while Nehemiah was governor of Judæa more particularly after his second coming from the Persian court: and he appears to have contributed the weight of his exhortations to the restoration of the Jewish polity, and the final reform established by that pious and excellent governor. The people having relapsed into irreligion, the prophet was commissioned to reprove both priests and people. His writings, which consist of four chapters comprise two prophetic discourses; viz.:

DISCOURSE I. reproves the Jews for their irreverence to God, their benefactor, and denounces divine judgments against them. (ch. i., ii.)

DISCOURSE II. foretells the coming of Christ, and his harbinger, John the Baptist, to purify the sons of Levi, the priests, and to smite the land with a curse, unless they all repented. (iii., iv.)

CHAPTER VIII.

ON THE APOCRYPHA.

BESIDES the Scriptures of the Old Testament, which are universally acknowledged to be genuine and inspired writings, both by the Jewish and Christian churches, there are several other writings, partly historical, partly ethical, and partly poetical, which are usually printed at the end of the Old Testament in the larger editions of the English Bible, under the appellation of the "APOCRYPHA;" that is, books not admitted into the sacred canon, being either spurious, or at least not acknowledged to be divine. These books are deservedly rejected by all Protestants from the canon of Scripture, because they never were recognised as canonical by the Jewish or Christian churches; because they contain many things which are fabulous and contradictory to historical truth, as well as to the canonical Scriptures; and also because they contain passages which are false, absurd, and incredible. These human productions were first enrolled among the divinely inspired writings by the assembly of popish prelates and others, who were convened in what is called the council of Trent.

I. The FIRST BOOK OF ESDRAS is only extant in Greek, and is so called because the events related in it occurred before the Babylonian captivity. It is chiefly historical, and gives an account of the return of the Jews from the Babylonish captivity, the building of the temple, and the re-establishment of divine worship.

II. The SECOND BOOK OF ESDRAS is supposed to have been originally written in Greek, though at present it is only extant in Latin, of which there is an Arabic version, differing very materially from it, and having many interpolations. The author of this book is unknown; but the allusions to Jesus Christ, and to the phraseology of the New Testament, prove it to be the composition of some Jewish Christian. It abounds with absurd rabbinical tales and fables.

III. Concerning the author of the book of TOBIT, or the time when he flourished, we have no authentic information. It professes to relate the history of Tobit and his family, who were carried into captivity to Nineveh by Shalmanezer: but it contains so many rabbinical fables, and allusions to the Babylonian demonology, that many learned men consider it as an ingenious and amusing fiction, calculated to form a pious temper, and to teach the most important duties. The simplicity of its narrative and the pious and moral lessons it inculcates, have imparted to it an interest, which has rendered it one of the most popular of the apocryphal writings.

IV. The BOOK OF JUDITH professes to relate the defeat of the Assyrians by the Jews, through the instrumentality of their countrywoman Judith, whose genealogy is recorded in the eighth chapter; but so many geographical, historical, and chronological difficulties attend this book, that the most eminent critics have considered it rather as a drama, or parable, than a real history. The author is utterly unknown. This book was originally written in Chaldee, and translated into Latin.

V. "THE REST OF THE CHAPTERS OF THE BOOK OF ESTHER, which are found neither in the Hebrew nor in the Chaldee," were originally written in Greek, whence they were translated into Latin, and formed part of the Italic or old Latin version in use before the time of Jerome. Being there annexed to the canonical book, they passed without censure, but were rejected by Jerome in his version, because he confined himself to the Hebrew Scriptures, and these chapters never were extant in the Hebrew language. They are evidently the production of an Hellenistic Jew, but are considered both by Jerome and Grotius as a work of pure fiction, which was annexed to the canonical book of Esther by way of embellishment.

VI. "THE WISDOM OF SOLOMON" is commonly ascribed to that Hebrew monarch, either because the author imitated his sententious manner of writing, or because he sometimes speaks in his name, the better to recommend his moral precepts. It is, however, certain that Solomon was not the author, for it was never extant in Hebrew, nor received into the Hebrew canon, nor is the style like that of Solomon. This book has always been admired for its elegance and for the admirable moral tendency of its precepts. It consists of two parts: the first contains a description or encomium of wisdom. (ch. i.—x.) The second part, comprising the rest of the book, treats on a variety of topics widely differing from the subject of the first; viz.: reflections on the history and conduct of the Israelites during their journeyings in the wilderness, and their subsequent proneness to idolatry.

VII. Although the "WISDOM OF JESUS, THE SON OF SIRACH," or ECCLESIASTICUS, has sometimes been considered as the production of Solomon, yet the style and other internal evidences prove that it could not possibly have been written by the Hebrew monarch. Respecting the author of Ecclesiasticus we have no information beyond what this book itself imparts; viz.: that it was written by a person of the name of Jesus, the son of Sirach, who had travelled in pursuit of knowledge. This man, being deeply conversant with the Old Testament, and having collected many things from the prophets, blended them, as well as the sentences ascribed to Solomon, with the result of his own observation, and thus endeavoured to produce a work of instruction that might be useful to his countrymen. This book was written in Hebrew, or rather the Syro-Chaldaic dialect, then in use in Judæa, and was translated by his grandson into Greek, for the use of the Alexandrian Jews, who were ignorant of the language of Judæa. The translator himself is supposed to have been a son of Sirach, as well as his grandfather, the author. The book was probably written about the year 232 B. C., when the author might be seventy years of age; and it was translated about sixty years after.

This book has met with general and deserved esteem in the Western church, and was introduced into the public service by the venerable reformers and compilers of our national liturgy

It commences with an exhortation to the pursuit of wisdom: this is followed by numerous moral sentences or maxims, arranged in a less desultory manner than the proverbs of Solomon, as far as the forty-fourth chapter, at which the author begins his eulogy of the patriarchs, prophets, and celebrated men among the Jews, to the end of the fiftieth chapter. And the book concludes with a prayer.

VIII. It is alike uncertain by whom, or in what language, the BOOK OF BARUCH was written; and whether it contains any matters historically true, or whether the whole is a fiction. The principal subject of the book is an epistle, pretended to be sent by Jehoiakim and the captive Jews in Babylon, to their brethren in Judah and Jerusalem. The last chapter contains an epistle which falsely bears the name of Jeremiah.

IX. "THE SONG OF THE THREE CHILDREN" is placed in the Greek version of Daniel, and also in the Vulgate Latin version, between the twenty-third and twenty-fourth verses of the third chapter. It does not appear to have ever been extant in Hebrew, and although it has always been admired for the piety of its sentiments, it was never admitted to be canonical, until it was recognised by the council of Trent.

X. THE HISTORY OF SUSANNA is evidently the work of some Hellenistic Jew: and in the Vulgate version it forms the thirteenth chapter of the book of Daniel. Some modern critics consider it to be both spurious and fabulous.

XI. "The History of the Destruction of BEL AND THE DRAGON" was always rejected by the Jewish church; it is not extant either in the Hebrew or the Chaldee language. Jerome gives it no better title than that of *the Fable of Bel and the Dragon;* nor has it obtained more credit with posterity, except with the Romish clergy present at the council of Trent, who determined it to be a part of the canonical Scriptures. The design of this fiction is to render idolatry ridiculous, and to exalt the true God; but the author has destroyed the illusion of his fiction by transporting to Babylon the worship of animals, which was never practised in that country.

XII. "The Prayer of Manasses, king of Judah, when he was holden captive in Babylon," though not unworthy of the occasion on which it is pretended to have been composed, was never recognised as canonical. It is rejected as spurious even by the church of Rome.

XIII. The two books of Maccabees are thus denominated, because they relate to the patriotic and gallant exploits of Judas Maccabeus and his brethren: they are both admitted into the canon of Scripture by the church of Rome.

1. The first book contains the history of the Jews, from the beginning of the reign of Antiochus Epiphanes to the death of Simon, a period of about thirty-four years. It was originally written in the Syro-Chaldaic language, and was most probably composed in the time of John Hyrcanus, when the wars of the Maccabees were terminated, either by Hyrcanus himself, or by some persons employed by him. From the Syro-Chaldaic it was translated into Greek, and thence into Latin. Our English version is made from the Greek. The first book of Maccabees is a most valuable historical monument.

2. The second book of Maccabees is very inferior to the preceding, and consists of several pieces compiled by an unknown author; it must therefore be read with great caution. It contains the history of about fifteen years, from the execution of the commission of Heliodorus, who was sent by Seleucus to bring away the treasures of the Temple, to the victory obtained by Judas Maccabeus over Nicanor, that is, from the year of the world 3828 to 3843. Two ancient translations of this book are extant, one in Syriac, the other in Latin: the version in ou Bibles was executed from the Greek.

CHAPTER II.

ON THE HISTORICAL BOOKS OF THE NEW TESTAMENT.

SECTION I.—On the Name and Number of the Canonical Gospel

THE word ΕΥΑΝΓΕΛΙΟΝ, *(Euangelion,)* which we translate Gospel, among Greek profane writers signifies any good tidings,* and corresponds exactly with our English word Gospel, which is derived from the Saxon words ᵹoꝺ, *God* or *good*, and ꞅpel, *word* or *tiding*, and denotes God's word or *good tidings.* In the New Testament this term is confined to the glad tidings of the actual coming of the Messiah, and is even opposed to the prophecies concerning Christ. (Matt. xi. 5, Rom. i. 1, 2.) Hence Ecclesiastical writers gave the appellation of Gospels to the lives of Christ—that is, to those sacred histories in which are recorded the "good tidings of great joy to all people," of the advent of the Messiah, together with all its joyful circumstances: and hence the authors of those histories have acquired the title of EVANGELISTS. Besides this general title, the sacred writers use the term Gospel, with a variety of epithets, derived from the nature of its contents. See instances in Eph. i. 13, vi. 15, Rom. i. 1. 3, and 2 Cor. v. 19.

The Gospels which have been transmitted to us are four in number: and we learn from ecclesiastical history, that four, and four only, were ever received by the Christian church as the genuine and inspired writings of the evangelists. And it is a considerable advantage, that a history, of such importance as that of Jesus Christ, has been recorded by the pens of separate and independent writers; for, by the contradictions, whether real or apparent, which are visible in these accounts, (but which admit of easy

* From ευ (*eu*) good, and αγγελια (*angelia*) a message or tidings.

solution by any attentive reader,) they have incontestably proved that they did not unite with a view of imposing a fabulous narrative on mankind. And in all matters of consequence, whether doctrinal or historical, there is such a manifest agreement between them as is to be found in no other writings whatever.

Section II.—On the Gospel by Saint Matthew.

Matthew, surnamed Levi, was the son of Alpheus, but not of that Alpheus, or Cleopas, who was the father of James, mentioned in Matt. x. 3. He was a native of Galilee, but of what city in that country, or of what tribe of the people of Israel, we are not informed. Before his conversion to Christianity, he was a publican or tax-gatherer, under the Romans, and collected the customs of all goods exported or imported at Capernaum, a maritime town on the sea of Galilee, and also received the tribute paid by all passengers who went by water. While employed "at the receipt of custom," Jesus called him to be a witness of his words and works, thus conferring upon him the honourable office of an apostle. From that time he continued with Jesus Christ, a familiar attendant on his person, a spectator of his public and private conduct, a hearer of his discourses, a witness of his miracles, and an evidence of his resurrection. After our Saviour's ascension, Matthew continued at Jerusalem with the other apostles, and with them, on the day of Pentecost, was endued with the gift of the Holy Spirit. Of how long he remained in Judæa after that event, or of where he died, we have no authentic accounts. He is generally allowed to have written first of all the evangelists, though a considerable difference of opinion exists as to the language in which and the time when his Gospel was composed. Some critics think that its original language was Hebrew; others, Greek; while a third class decide in favour of a Hebrew and Greek original. The reasons on which these several opinions are founded are detailed in the author's larger Introduction, which do not admit of abridgment. the most probable is that, which determines that Matthew wrote a Hebrew Gospel for the Hebrew Christians, about the year 37, and afterwards a Greek Gospel, about the year 61. The present Greek Gospel has every internal mark of being an original writing: and the disappearance of the Hebrew Gospel is sufficiently accounted for, not only by the prevalence of the Greek language, but also by the fact that it was so corrupted by the Ebionites (a sect contemporary with St. John,) as to lose all its authority in the church. The authenticity of his Gospel was never doubted.

The voice of antiquity accords in testifying that St. Matthew wrote his Gospel in Judæa for the Jewish nation while the church consisted wholly of the circumcision, that is, of Jewish and Samaritan believers, but principally Jewish: and that he wrote it primarily for their use, with a view to confirm those who believed, and to convert those who believed not, we have, besides historical facts, very strong presumptions from the book itself. Every circumstance is carefully pointed out, which might conciliate the faith of that nation; and every unnecessary expression is avoided, that might in any way tend to obstruct it. The Gospel of St. Matthew consists of four parts; viz.:

PART I. treats on the Infancy of Jesus Christ. (ch. i., ii.)

PART II. records the Discourses and Actions of John the Baptist and of Jesus Christ, preparatory to our Saviour's commencing his public ministry. (ch. iii. iv. 1—11.)

PART III. relates the Discourses and Actions of Christ in Galilee, by which he demonstrated that he was the Messiah. (ch. iv. 12.—xx. 16.)

PART IV. contains the Transactions relative to the passion and resurrection of Christ. (ch. xx. 17,—xxviii.)

SECTION III.—On the Gospel by Saint Mark.

This evangelist, whose Hebrew name was John, was nephew to Barnabas, (Col. iv. 10,) and the son of Mary, a pious woman in Jerusalem, at whose house the apostles and first Christians often assembled. (Acts xii. 12.) He is supposed to have adopted the surname of Mark, when he left Judæa to preach the Gospel in foreign countries

The consent of antiquity attests that he wrote his Gospel in Greek, under the inspection of the apostle Peter, at Rome, and between the years 60 and 63. It may be divided into three parts; viz.:

PART I. The Transactions from the Baptism of Christ to his entering on the more public part of his Ministry. (ch. I. 1—10.)

PART II. The Discourses and Actions of Jesus Christ to his going up to Jerusalem to the fourth and last Passover. (ch. i. 14,—x.)

PART III. The Passion, Death, and Resurrection of Christ. (ch. xi.—xiv.)

SECTION IV.—On the Gospel by Saint Luke.

St. Luke was descended from Gentile parents, and in his youth had embraced Judaism, from which he was converted to Christianity. He was for the most part the companion of the apostle Paul: and as no ancient writer has mentioned his suffering martyrdom, it is probable that he died a natural death. The genuineness and authenticity of his Gospel and of the Acts of the Apostles were never doubted. The Gospel appears to have been written about the year 63 or 64: it was written for Gentile Christians, and the events which he has recorded are *classed*, after the manner of some ancient profane writers, instead of being disposed in chronological order, as St. Matthew has related them. The Gospel of St. Luke may be divided into five classes or sections; viz.:

CLASS I. contains the narrative of the birth of Christ, together with all the circumstances that preceded, attended, and followed it. (ch. i. ii. 1—40.)

CLASS II. comprises the particulars relative to our Saviour's infancy and youth. (ch. ii. 41—52.)

CLASS III. includes the preaching of John. and the baptism of Jesus Christ, whose genealogy is annexed. (ch. iii.)

CLASS IV. comprehends the discourses, miracles, and actions of Jesus Christ during the whole of his ministry. (ch. iv.—ix. 50.) This appears evident; for, after Saint Luke had related his temptation in the wilderness, (ch. iv.

1—13,) he immediately adds, that Christ returned to Galilee, (14,) and mentions Nazareth, (16,) Capernaum, (31,) and the lake of Gennesareth; (v. 1;) and then he proceeds as far as ix. 50, to relate our Saviour's transactions in Galilee.

Class V. begins with chap. ix. 51, and contains an account of our Saviour's last journey to Jerusalem. Consequently, this class comprises every thing relative to his passion, death, resurrection, and ascension. (ix. 51—62, x.—xxiv.)

Section V.—On the Gospel by Saint John

Saint John, the evangelist and apostle, was the son of Zebedee, a fisherman of the town of Bethsaida, on the sea of Galilee, and the younger brother of James the elder. His mother's name was Salome. He was eminently the object of our Lord's regard and confidence; and was, on various occasions, admitted to free and intimate intercourse with him, so that he was characterized as "the disciple whom Jesus loved." (John xiii. 23.) Hence we find him present at several scenes, to which most of the other disciples were not admitted. He died a natural death about the year 100. He wrote his Gospel in Greek, most probably about the year 97: it has been universally received as genuine: indeed, besides the uninterrupted testimony of Christian antiquity, the circumstantiality of its details prove that his book was written by an eyewitness of the transactions it records.

The general design of Saint John, in common with the rest of the evangelists, is, as he himself assures us, to prove that Jesus is the Messiah, the Son of God, and that believing, we may have life through his name. (xx. 31.) But, besides this, we are informed by ancient writers, that there were two especial motives that induced Saint John to compose his Gospel. One was, to supply those important events in our Saviour's life which had been omitted by the other evangelists; the other motive was, that he might refute the heresies of Cerinthus and the Nicolaitans, who had attempted to corrupt the Christian doctrine. Of the Nicolaitans nothing certain is known: but, concerning the tenets of the Cerinthians, the following particulars (taken from the author's larger Introduction) are necessary to be known in order to understand the design of the evangelist in composing his Gospel.

Cerinthus was by birth a Jew, who lived at the close of the first century: having studied literature and philosophy at Alexandria, he attempted, at length, to form a new and singular system of doctrine and discipline, by a monstrous combination of the doctrines of Jesus Christ, with the opinions and errors of the Jews and Gnostics. From the latter he borrowed their *Pleroma*, or fulness, their *Æons*, or spirits, their *Demiurgus*, or creator of the visible world, &c. and so modified and tempered these fictions as to give them an air of Judaism, which must have considerably favoured the progress of his heresy. He taught, that the most high God was utterly unknown before the appearance of Christ, and dwelt in a remote heaven called ΠΛΗΡΩΜΑ (*Plerōma*) with the chief spirits, or æons. That this supreme God first generated an *only begotten* SON, ΜΟΝΟΓΕΝΗΣ (*Monogenes*, who again begat the WORD, ΛΟΓΟΣ (*Logos*,) which was inferior to the first-born. That CHRIST was a still lower æon, though far superior to some others. That there were two higher æons, distinct from Christ; one called ΖΩΗ (*Zōe*,) or LIFE, and the other ΦΩΣ (*Phōs*,) or the LIGHT. That from the æons again proceeded inferior orders of spirits, and particularly one *Demiurgus*, who created this visible world out of eternal matter. That this Demiurgus was ignorant of the supreme God, and much lower than the æons, which were wholly invisible. That he was, however, the peculiar God and protector of the Israelites, and sent Moses to them, whose laws were to be of perpetual obligation. That Jesus was a mere man, of the most illustrious sanctity and justice, the real son of Joseph and Mary. That the æon Christ descended upon him in the form of a dove, when he was baptized, revealed to him the unknown Father, and empowered him to work miracles. That the æon LIGHT entered John the Baptist in the same manner, and, therefore, that John was in some respects preferable to Christ. That Jesus, after his union with Christ, opposed himself with vigour to the God of the Jews, at whose instigation he was seized and crucified by the Hebrew chiefs, and that when Jesus was taken captive, and came to suffer, Christ ascended up on high, so that the man Jesus alone was subjected to the pains of an ignominious death. That Christ will one day return upon earth, and renewing his former union with the man Jesus, will reign in Palestine a thousand years, during which his disciples will enjoy the most exquisite sensual delights

Bearing these dogmas in mind, we shall find that Saint John's Gospel is divided into three parts, viz.

PART I. contains doctrines laid down in opposition to those of Cerinthus. (John i. 1—18.)

PART II. delivers the proofs of those doctrines in a historical manner. (i. 19,—xx. 29.

PART III. is a conclusion, or appendix, giving an account of the person of the writer, and of his design in writing his Gospel. (xx. 30, 31, xxi.)

SECTION VI.—On the Acts of the Apostles.

The Book of the ACTS of the APOSTLES forms the fifth and last of the historical books of the New Testament, and connects the Gospels with the Epistles; being a useful postscript to the former, and a proper introduction to the latter. That Saint Luke was the author of the Acts of the Apostles, is evident, both from the introduction, and from the unanimous testimonies of the early Christians. The Gospel and the Book of the Acts of the Apostles are both inscribed to Theophilus: and in the very first verse of the Acts there is a reference made to his Gospel, which he calls "*the former Treatise.*" On this account Dr. Benson and some other critics have conjectured that Saint Luke wrote the Gospel and Acts in one book, and divided it into two parts. From the frequent use of the first person plural, it is clear that he was present at most of the transactions he relates. To the genuineness and authenticity of this book, which was written about the year 63, all the Christian Fathers bear unanimous testimony.

The acts of the apostles may be divided into three principal parts; viz.:

PART I. contains the Rise and Progress of the mother church at Jerusalem, from the time of our Saviour's ascension to the first Jewish persecution. (ch. i.—viii.)

PART II. comprises the Dispersion of the Disciples—the propagation of Christianity among the Samaritans—the conversion of Saint Paul, and the foundation of a Christian church at Antioch. (ch. viii. 5, xii.)

PART III. describes the conversion of the more remote Gentiles, by Barnabas and Paul, and, after their separation, by Paul and his associates, among whom was Luke himself during the latter part of Paul's labours. (ch. xiii.—xxviii.)

The Acts of the Apostles afford abundant evidence of the truth and divine original of the Christian religion; for we learn from this book, that the Gospel was not indebted for its success to deceit or fraud; but it was wholly the result of the mighty power of God, and of the excellence and efficacy of the saving truths which it contains. The general and particular doctrines comprised in the Acts of the Apostles, are perfectly in unison with the glorious truths revealed in the Gospels, and illustrated in the apostolic Epistles; and are admirably suited to the state of the persons, whether Jews or Gentiles, to whom they were addressed. And the evidences which the apostles gave of their doctrine, in their appeals to prophecies and miracles, and the various gifts of the Spirit, were so numerous and so strong, and at the same time so widely adapted to every class of persons, that the truth of the religion which they attest cannot be reasonably disputed.

In perusing this very interesting portion of sacred history, it will be desirable constantly to refer to the accompanying map of the Travels of the Apostles, particularly those of Saint Paul.

CHAPTER II.

ON THE EPISTOLARY OR DOCTRINAL WRITINGS OF THE NEW TESTAMENT, PARTICULARLY THOSE OF SAINT PAUL.

SECTION I.—A Brief Account of the Apostle Paul.—Nature of the Epistolarly Writings of the New Testament.

I. A BRIEF Account of Saint Paul.

SAUL, also called PAUL, (by which name this illustrious apostle was generally known after his preaching among the Gentiles, especially among the Greeks and Romans,) was a Hebrew of the Hebrews, a descendant of the patriarch Abraham, of the tribe of Benjamin, and a native of Tarsus, then the chief city of Cilicia. By birth he was a citizen of Rome, a distinguished honour and privilege, which had been conferred on some of his ancestors for services rendered to the commonwealth during the wars. His father was a Pharisee, and he himself was educated in the most rigid principles of that sect; but he was also early initiated into Greek literature at Tarsus: and his parents completed his education by having him taught the art of tent-making, in conformity with the custom of the Jews at that time. It appears from Acts xxiii. 16—22, and Rom. xvi. 7. 11. 21, that his sister's son and some others of his relations were Christians, and had embraced the Gospel before his conversion; but Saul himself was an inveterate enemy of the Christian name and faith, until his conversion in A.D. 35, on the road to Damascus whither he was going with letters of commission from the high priest and elders, or sanhedrin, to the synagogue of the Jews at Damascus, empowering him to bring to Jerusalem any Christians, whether men or women, whom he might find there.

Shortly after his baptism, and the descent of the Holy Spirit upon him, Saul went into Arabia; (Gal. i. 17;) and during his residence in that country he was fully instructed, as we may reasonably think, by divine revelation, and by diligent study of the Old Testament, in the doctrines and duties of the Gospel. Three years after his conversion, he returned to Damascus, A.D. 38, (Gal. i. 18,) and boldly preached the Gospel to the Jews, who, rejecting his testimony, as an apostate, conspired to kill him; but, the plot being communicated to Saul, he escaped from Damascus privately by night, and went up to Jerusalem, for the first time since his conversion. After some hesitation on the part of the Christians in that city, he was acknowledged to be a disciple. He remained at Jerusalem only fifteen days, during which his boldness in preaching the Gospel so irritated the Hellenistic Jews, that they conspired against him; "*which when the brethren knew, they brought him down to Cæsarea Philippi, and sent him forth to Tarsus.*" (Acts ix. 28—30.)

From that time (A.D. 39) to the year 58, the apostle preached the Gospel in various parts of Asia Minor and in Greece with great energy and success; but, being rescued from a tumultuous assembly of Jews, who would have put him to death, at Jerusalem, (Acts xxi, xxii.) he was sent Cæsarea by the tribune Lysias, who directed the Jewish council to accuse him before Felix, the Roman procurator. By this officer he was detained in prison two years; and, his cause being heard before Festus the successor of Felix, the apostle appealed to the imperial tribunal, and was sent to Rome, (Acts xxiv.—xxvii.) A.D. 60. Here he was confined two years, from A.D. 61 to 63. As Saint Luke has not continued Saint Paul's history beyond his first imprisonment at Rome, we have no authentic record of his subsequent travels and labours from the spring of A.D. 63, when he was released, to the time of his martyrdom. This is said to have taken place by decapitation, June 29, A.D. 66, at Aquæ Salviæ, three miles from Rome. Fourteen epistles are extant bearing the name of this distinguished "apostle of Jesus Christ," whose life and labours have justly been considered as an irrefragable proof of the truth of the Christian revelation.

II. Nature and Design of the Epistolary Writings of the New Testament

The Epistles, or letters addressed to various Christian communities, and also to individuals, by the apostles Paul, James, Peter, and John, form the second principal division of the New Testament. These writings abundantly confirm all the material facts related in the Gospels and Acts of the Apostles. The particulars of our Savour's life and death are often referred to in them, as grounded upon the undoubted testimony of eye-witnesses, and as being the foundation of the Christian religion. The speedy propagation of the Christian faith, recorded in the Acts, is confirmed beyond all contradiction, by innumerable passages in the Epistles, written to the churches already planted; and the miraculous gifts, with which the apostles were endued, are often appealed to in the same writings, as an undeniable evidence of the divine mission of the apostles.

Though all the essential doctrines and precepts of the Christian religion were unquestionably taught by our Saviour himself, and are contained in the Gospels, yet it is evident to any person who attentively studies the Epistles, that they are to be considered as commentaries on the doctrines of the Gospel, addressed to particular Christian societies or persons, in order to explain and apply those doctrines more fully, to confute some growing errors, to compose differences and schisms, to reform abuses and corruptions, to excite the Christians to holiness, and to encourage them against persecutions. And since these Epistles were written (as we have already shown) under divine inspiration, and have uniformly been received by the Christian church as the productions of inspired writers, it consequently follows, (notwithstanding some writers have insinuated that they are not of equal authority with the Gospels, while others would reject them altogether,) that what the apostles have delivered in these Epistles, as necessary to be believed or done by Christians, must be as necessary to be believed and practised in order to salvation, as the doctrines and precepts delivered by Jesus Christ himself, and recorded in the Gospels; because in writing these Epistles, the sacred penmen were the servants, apostles, ambassadors, and ministers of Christ, and stewards of the mysteries of God, and their doctrine; and precepts are the will, the mind, the truth, and the commandments of God himself. On account of the fuller displays of evangelical truth contained in this portion of the sacred volume, the Epistles have by some divines been termed the DOCTRINAL BOOKS of the New Testament.

The Epistles contained in the New Testament are twenty-one in number, and are generally divided into two classes; viz.: the fourteen Epistles of Saint Paul, and the seven Catholic or general Epistles, written by the apostles James, Peter, John, and Jude : the reason of this appellation will be found in Chapter III. Sect. I. page 338. *infra.*

The general plan on which the Epistles are written, is, *first*, to discuss and decide the controversy, or to refute the erroneous notions, which had arisen in the church, or among the persons to whom they are addressed, and which was the occasion of their being written; and, *secondly*, to recommend the observance of those duties, which would be necessary, and of absolute importance to the Christian church in every age, consideration being chiefly given to those particular graces or virtues of the Christian character, which the disputes that occasioned the Epistles might tempt them to neglect.

The observations on the Doctrinal interpretation of Scripture, in pp. 149—151, will be found useful in studying the Epistles. A Table of the times, when they were most probably composed, will be found in the Appendix, No. II.

Section. II.—On the Epistle to the Romans.

The Epistle to the Romans, though seventh in order time, is placed first of all the apostolical letters, either from the pre-eminence of Rome, as being the mistress of the world, or because it is the longest and most comprehensive of all Saint Paul's Epistles. Various years have been assigned for its date : but the most probable date is that, which refers this Epistle to the end of 57, or the beginning of 58 ; at which time Saint Paul was at Corinth.

Christianity is generally supposed to have been first planted at Rome by some of those "strangers of Rome, Jews, and proselytes," (Acts ii. 10,) who heard Peter preach, and were converted at Jerusalem on the day of Pentecost.

The occasion of writing this Epistle may be easily collected from the Epistle itself. It appears that Saint Paul, who had been made acquainted with all the circumstances of the Christians at Rome by Aquila and Priscilla, (Rom. xvi. 3,) and by other Jews who had been expelled from Rome by the decree of Claudius, (Acts xviii. 2,) was very desirous of seeing them, that he might impart some spiritual gift; but, being prevented from visiting them, as he had purposed, in his journey into Spain, he availed himself of the opportunity that presented itself to him by the departure of Phœbe to Rome, to send them an Epistle. Finding, however, that the church was composed partly of Heathens who had embraced the Gospel, and partly of Jews, who, with many remaining prejudices, believed in Jesus as the Messiah; and finding, also, that many contentions arose from the Gentile converts claiming equal privileges with the Hebrew Christians, (which claims the latter absolutely refused to admit, unless the Gentile converts were circumcised,) he wrote this Epistle to compose these differences, and to strengthen the faith of the Roman Christians against the insinuations of false teachers; being apprehensive lest his involuntary absence from Rome should be turned by the latter to the prejudice of the Gospel.

This Epistle consists of four parts; viz.:

PART I. The introduction. (ch. i. 1—13.)

PART II. contains the Doctrinal Part of the Epistle concerning justification. (i. 16—32, ii.—xi.)

PART III. comprises the Hortatory or Practical Part of the Epistle, (ch. xii.—xv. 1—14,) in which the apostle exhorts Christian believers to dedicate themselves to God, and how they should demean themselves to one another.

PART IV. The Conclusion, in which Saint Paul excuses himself, partly for his boldness in thus writing to the Romans, (xv. 14—21,) and partly for not having hitherto come to them, (22,) but promises to visit them, recommending himself to their prayers; (23—33;) and sends various salutations to the brethren at Rome. (xvi.)

In perusing this Epistle, it will be desirable to read at least the eleven first chapters *at once*, uninterruptedly; as every sentence, especially in the argumentative part, bears an intimate relation to, and is dependent upon the whole discourse, and cannot be understood unless we comprehend the scope of the whole. Further, in order to enter fully into its spirit, we must enter into the spirit of a Jew in those times, and endeavour to realize in our own minds his utter aversion from the Gentiles, his valuing and exalting himself upon his relation to God and to Abraham, and also upon his law, pompous worship, circumcision, &c, as if the Jews were the only people in the world who had any right to the favour of God.

Section III.—On the First Epistle to the Corinthians.

This Epistle was written from Ephesus, about the year 57: its genuineness was never disputed.

Christianity was first planted at Corinth, by St. Paul himself, who resided here a year and six months, between the years 51 and 53. The church consisted partly of Jews, and partly of Gentiles, but chiefly of the latter; whence the apostle had to combat, sometimes with Jewish superstition, and sometimes with Heathen licentiousness. On Saint Paul's departure from Corinth, he was succeeded by Apollos, "an eloquent man, and mighty in the Scriptures," who preached the Gospel with great success. (Acts xviii. 24—28.) Acquila and Sosthenes were also eminent teachers in this church. (xviii. 3. 1 Cor. i. 1.) But shortly after Saint Paul quitted this church, its peace was disturbed by the intrusion of false teachers, who made great pretensions to eloquence, wisdom, and knowledge of their Christian liberty, and thus undermined his influence and the credit of his ministry. Hence two parties were formed, one of which contended strenuously for the observance of Jewish ceremonies, while the other, misinterpreting the true nature of Christian liberty, indulged in excesses which were contrary to the design and spirit of the Gospel. One party boasted that they were the followers of Paul; and another, that they were the followers of Apollos. To correct these and other abuses, and also to answer some queries which the Christians at Corinth had proposed to the apostle, was the design of this Epistle, which divides itself into three parts; viz.:

Part I. The Introduction, (ch. i. 1—9,) in which Saint Paul expresses his satisfaction at all the good he knew of them, particularly at their having received the gifts of the Holy Spirit for the confirmation of the Gospel.

PART II. contains the Treatise, or Discussion of various particulars, adapted to the state of the Corinthian church; which may be commodiously arranged into two sections.

SECT. 1. contains a reproof of the corruptions and abuses which disgraced the church. (i. 10.—vi. 1—20.

SECT. 2. contains an answer to the questions which the Corinthian church had proposed to the apostle. (vii.—xv.)

PART III. contains the conclusion, comprising directions relative to the contributions for the saints at Jerusalem, promises that the apostle would shortly visit them, and salutations to various members of the church at Corinth. (xvi.)

SECTION IV.—On the Second Epistle to the Corinthians.

This Epistle was written from Macedonia, most probably from Philippi, and within a year after the preceding Epistle, that is, early in the year 58: its genuineness was never doubted. Compelled to vindicate his apostolic character, Saint Paul here furnishes us with many interesting details respecting his personal history and sufferings for the name and faith of Christ. He commends the faithful members of the church at Corinth, for their obedience to his injunctions contained in his former Epistle, and particularly for excommunicating an incestuous person; and excites them to finish their contributions for their poor bre thren in Judæa.

This epistle consists of three parts, viz.:

PART I. The Introduction. (ch. i. 1, 2.)

PART II. The Apologetic Discourse of Saint Paul; in which

1. He justifies himself from the imputations of the false teacher and his adherents, by showing his sincerity and integrity in the discharge of his ministry; and that he acted not from worldly interest, but from true love for them, and a tender concern for their spiritual welfare. (i. 3—24, ii.—vii.)

2. He exhorts them to a liberal contribution for their poor brethren in Judæa. (viii., ix.)

3. He resumes his apology; justifying himself from the charges and insinuations of the false teacher, and his followers; in order to detach the Corinthians from them, and to re-establish himself and his authority. (x.—xiii. 10.)

PART III. The Conclusion. (xiii. 11—14.)

Section V.—On the Epistle to the Galatians.

The Epistle to the Galatians, among whom Christianity had been planted by Saint Paul himself, was most probably written from Corinth, about the latter end of the year 52, or early in 53. The apostle's design in writing it was, first, to assert his apostolical character and authority, and the doctrine which he taught, in opposition to the erroneous tenets of a Judaising teacher; and, secondly, to confirm the Galatian churches in the faith of Christ, especially with respect to the important point of justification by faith alone; to expose the errors which had been disseminated among them, by demonstrating to them the true nature and use of the moral and ceremonial law; and to revive those principles of Christianity which he had taught when he first preached the Gospel to them.

This Epistle is written with great energy and force of language, and affords a fine specimen of Saint Paul's skill in conducting an argument. It consists of three parts, viz.:

Part I. The Introduction. (ch. i. 1—5.)

Part II. The Treatise, or Discussion of the subjects which had occasioned this Epistle: in which the apostle first vindicates his doctrine and authority; (ch. i. 6—24, ii.;) and then disputes against the advocates for circumcision, (iii.—v. 9,) and gives the Galatian Christians various instructions for their conduct. (v. 10—26, vi. 1—10.)

Part III. The Conclusion, which is a summary of the topics discussed in this Epistle, terminates with an apostolic benediction. (vi. 11—18.)

Section VI.—On the Epistle to the Ephesians.

Ephesus was the metropolis of the proconsular Asia, distinguished for the magnificent temple of Diana, there erected, as well as for the accomplishments, luxury, and lasciviousness of its inhabitants. Christianity was first planted here, about A. D. 54, by Saint Paul; who wrote this E istle, (the genuineness of which is undisputed,) about the year 61, during the early part of his imprisonment at Rome. In this animated epistle he shows the grand design of the Gospel, and exhorts his converts against those evil practices and customs to which they had been addicted when Heathens, (ch. i.—iii.,) and which, as believers in Christ, they had renounced. He then urges them to walk in a manner becoming their profession, in the faithful discharge both of the general and common duties of religion, and of the special duties of particular relations, (iv., v. 1—9,) and encourages them to war the spiritual warfare, and concludes with his apostolic benediction. (vi. 10—24.)

Section VII.—On the Epistle to the Philippians.

This Epistle was written to the Philippians towards the close of Saint Paul's first imprisonment at Rome, about the end of the year 62, or early in 63: its genuineness was never questioned. Its scope is to confirm them in the faith of the Gospel, (ch. i. 1—20,) and to encourage them to walk in a manner becoming their holy profession. (i. 21—30, ii.) He then cautions them against those Judaising teachers who preached Christ through envy and strife, (iii., iv. 1,) and concludes with various exhortations, at the same time testifying his gratitude to them for their Christian bounty to him during his imprisonment. (iv. 2—23.)

Section VIII.—On the Epistle to the Colossians.

This Epistle bears so close a resemblance to that addressed to the Ephesians, that they ought to be read together, in order to be fully understood. It is not known by whom Christianity was first planted at Colossæ: from internal evidence we are enabled to refer its date to the year 62. No doubt was ever entertained respecting its genuineness.

The scope of the Epistle to the Colossians is, *first*, to show, in opposition to the errors of some Judaising teachers, that all hope of man's redemption is founded on Christ our Redeemer, in whom alone all complete fulness, perfections, and sufficiency, are centred; (ch. i., ii. 1—7;)

secondly, to caution the Colossians against the insinuations of Judaising teachers, and also against philosophical speculations and deceits, and human traditions, as inconsistent with Christ, and his fulness for our salvation ; (ii. 8—23;) and to excite the Colossians, by the most persuasive arguments, to a temper and conduct worthy of their sacred character. (iii., iv. 1—6.) The Epistle concludes with matters chiefly of a private nature, except the directions for reading it in the church of Laodicea, as well as that of Colossæ. (iv. 7—18.)

The Epistle *from* Laodicea, mentioned in ch. iv. 16, which some have supposed to have been an epistle *to* the church at Laodicea, was most probably the Epistle to the Ephesians; Laodicea being within the circuit of the Ephesian church.

Section IX.—On the First Epistle to the Thessalonians

Thessalonica was a large and populous city and seaport of Macedonia, the capital of one of the four districts into which the Romans divided that country after its conquest by Paulus Æmylius. Besides being the seat of the proconsul of Macedonia, Thessalonica was commodiously situated for commerce, which was carried on by its inhabitants to a considerable extent: the Jews were very numerous here. Christianity was first planted here by St. Paul, A. D. 50. The first Epistle to the Thessalonians was the earliest of all that apostle's writings: its date is referred to the year 52, and its genuineness has never been questioned.

St. Paul having heard a favourable report of the steadfastness of the Thessalonians in the faith of Christ, wrote this Epistle to confirm them in that faith, and to animate them to a holy conversation, becoming the dignity of their high and holy calling. With this view, after a short introduction, (ch. i. 1—4,) he proceeds to show the divine origin of the Christian revelation, by the four following arguments; viz.:

I. The miracles wrought by the first preachers of the Gospel, in attestation of their divine commission. (i. 5

II. That their character, behaviour, and views, evidenced its truth. (ii., iii.)

III. That the first preachers of the Gospel delivered to their disciples, from the very beginning, precepts of the greatest strictness and holiness ; so that, by the sanctity of its precepts, the Gospel is shown to be a scheme of religion, every way worthy of the true God, and highly beneficial to mankind. (iv. 1—12.) The practical directions introduced in this part of the Epistle were admirably suited to the state of the Thessalonian church.

IV. That Jesus Christ, the Author of our religion, was declared to be the Son of God and the Judge of the world by his resurrection from the dead ; and that, by the same miracle, his own promise, and the predictions of his apostles, concerning his return from Heaven to reward the righteous and punish the wicked—especially those who obey not the Gospel—are rendered absolutely certain. (iv. 13—18, v. 1—11.)

The Epistle concludes with various practical advices and instructions. (v. 12—28.)

Section X.—On the Second Epistle to the Thessalonians.

This Epistle was evidently written soon after the first : (A. D. 52 :) its scope principally is, to rectify a mistake of the Thessalonians, who, from misunderstanding a passage in his former letter, imagined that the day of judgment was at hand. This Epistle consists of five parts ; viz. :

Part I. The Inscription. (i. 1, 2.)

Part II. Saint Paul's Thanksgiving and Prayer for them. (i. 3—12.)

Part III. The Rectification of their Mistake, and the Doctrine concerning the man of sin. (ii.)

Part IV. Various Advices relative to Christian virtues, particularly,

i. To Prayer, with a prayer for the Thessalonians. (iv. 1—5.)
ii. To correct the disorderly. (iv. 6—16.)

Part V. The Conclusion. (ii. 17, 18.)

Section XI.—On the First Epistle to Timothy.

Timothy, to whom this Epistle was addressed, was a native of Lystra, a city of Lycaonia, in Asia Minor. His father was a Greek, but his mother was a Jewess, (Acts xvi. 1,) and, as well as his grandmother *Lois*, a person of excellent character. (2 Tim. i. 5.) The pious care they took of his education soon appeared to have the desired success; for we are assured by Saint Paul, that, from his childhood, Timothy was well acquainted with the Holy Scriptures. (2 Tim. iii. 15.) It is generally supposed that he was converted to the Christian faith during the first visit made by Paul and Barnabas to Lystra. (Acts xiv.) From the time of his conversion, Timothy made such proficiency in the knowledge of the Gospel, and was so remarkable for the sanctity of his manners, as well as for his zeal in the cause of Christ, that he attracted the esteem of all the brethren in those parts. Accordingly, when the apostle came from Antioch, in Syria, to Lystra, the second time, they commended Timothy so highly to him, that Saint Paul selected him to be the companion of his travels, having previously circumcised him, (Acts xvi. 1—3,) and ordained him in a solemn manner by imposition of hands, (1 Tim. iv. 14. 2 Tim. i. 6,) though at that time he probably was not more than twenty years of age. (1 Tim. iv. 12.) From this period frequent mention is made of Timothy, as the attendant of Saint Paul in his various journeys, assisting him in preaching the Gospel, and in conveying his instructions to the churches.

The date of this Epistle has been much disputed, some writers placing it so early as the year 56, and others so late as the year 64. The latter is considered the most probable. This Epistle has always been acknowledged to be the undisputed production of Saint Paul

Timothy having been left at Ephesus, to regulate the affairs of the church in that city, Saint Paul wrote this Epistle chiefly to instruct him in the choice of proper officers in the church, as well as in the exercise of a regular ministry. Another, and very important part of the apostle's design, was to caution this young evangelist against the influence of those false teachers, who, by their subtle distinctions, and endless controversies, had corruptted the purity and simplicity of the Gospel; to press upon him, in all his preaching, a constant regard to the interests of practical religion; and to animate him to the greatest diligence, fidelity, and zeal, in the discharge of his office. The Epistle, therefore, consists of three parts; viz.:

PART I. The introduction. (ch. i. 1, 2.)

PART II. Instructions to Timothy how to behave in the administration of the church at Ephesus. (ii.—vi. 19.)

PART III. The Conclusion. (vi. 20, 21.)

SECTION XII.—On the Second Epistle to Timothy.

This Epistle was written during Saint Paul's second imprisonment, and not long before his martyrdom, most probably in the month of July or August, A. D. 65.

The immediate design of Saint Paul, in writing this Epistle to Timothy, was to apprise him of the circumstances that had befallen him during his second imprisonment at Rome, and to request him to come to him before the ensuing winter. But, being uncertain whether he should live so long, he gave him in this letter a variety of advices, charges and encouragements for the faithful discharge of his ministerial functions, with the solemnity and affection of a dying parent; in order that, if he should be put to death before Timothy's arrival, the loss might, in some measure, be compensated to him by the instructions contained in this admirable Epistle. With this view he exhorts him to stir up the gift which had been conferred upon him; (2 Tim. i. 2—5;) not to be ashamed of the testimony of the Lord, nor of Paul's sufferings; (6—16;) to hold fast the form of sound words, and to guard inviolable that good deposit of Gospel doctrine, (i. 13, 14,) which he was to commit to faithful men who should be able to teach others; (ii. 1, 2;) to endure, with fortitude, persecutions for the sake of the Gospel; (ii. 3—13;) to suppress and avoid logomachies; (14. 23;) to approve himself a faithful minister of the word; (15—22;) and to forewarn him of the perils of the last days, in consequence of wicked hypocritical seducers and enemies of the truth, who, even then, were beginning to rise in the church.

These Saint Paul admonishes Timothy to flee, giving him various cautions against them. (iii.)

This Epistle affords a beautiful instance of the consolations which the Gospel imparts to all that truly believe it. "Imagine," says a learned commentator of the 18th century, (Dr. Benson ;)—"Imagine a pious father, under sentence of death for his piety and benevolence to mankind, writing to a dutiful and affectionate son, that he might see and embrace him again before he left the world; particularly that he might leave with him his dying commands, and charge him to live and suffer as he had done: and you will have the frame of the apostle's mind, during the writing of this whole Epistle." (Pref. to 2 Tim. p. 517.)

Section XIII.—On the Epistle to Titus.

Titus was a Greek, and one of St. Paul's early converts, who attended him and Barnabas to the first council at Jerusalem, A. D. 49, and afterwards on his ensuing circuit. (Tit. i. 4. Gal. ii. 1—3. Acts xv. 2.) Subsequently, he was confidentially employed by the apostle on various occasions; and, as appears from this Epistle, was specially appointed by him to regulate the Christian churches in that island. Whether Titus ever quitted Crete, we know not; neither have we any certain information concerning the time, place, or manner of his death; but, according to ancient ecclesiastical tradition, he lived to the age of ninety-four years, and died and was buried in that island.

This Epistle, the genuineness of which was never questioned, is supposed to have been written after St. Paul's liberation from his first imprisonment, A. D. 64. Titus having been left in Crete to settle the churches in the several cities of that island, according to the apostolical plan, Saint Paul wrote this Epistle to him, that he might discharge his ministry among the Cretans with the greater success, and to give him particular instructions concerning his behaviour towards the Judaising teachers, who endeavoured to pervert the faith, and disturb the peace of the Christian church. The Epistle, therefore, consists of three parts.

Part I. The inscription. (ch. i. 1—4.)

PART II. Instructions to Titus. 1. Concerning the ordination of elders, that is, of bishops and deacons. (i. 5—16.)—2. To accommodate his exhortations to the respective ages, sexes, and circumstances of those whom he was commissioned to instruct; and, to give the greater weight to his instructions, he admonishes him to be an example of what he taught. (ii.)—3. To inculcate obedience to the civil magistrate, in opposition to the Jews and Judaising teachers, who, being averse from all civil governors, except such as were of their own nation, were apt to imbue Gentile Christians with a like seditious spirit, as if it were an indignity for the people of God to obey an idolatrous magistrate; and also to enforce gentleness to all men. (iii. 1—7.)—4. To enforce good works, avoid foolish questions, and to shun heretics. (iii. 8—11.)

PART III. An invitation to Titus, to come to the apostle at Nicopolis, together with various directions. (iii. 12—15.)

SECTION XIV.—On the Epistle to Philemon.

Philemon was an inhabitant of Colossæ, most probably a converted Gentile, and it should seem, an opulent and benevolent Christian. As it is evident, from the Epistle itself, that St. Paul was under confinement when he wrote it, and as he expresses (verse 22) his expectation of being shortly released, it is probable that it was written during his first imprisonment at Rome, toward the end of A. D. 62, or early in 63; and was sent, together with the Epistles to the Ephesians and Colossians, by Tychicus and Onesimus. Though some, formerly, questioned the genuineness of this Epistle, the attestations it has received, from the earliest antiquity, are deemed sufficient to establish that point. The design of this short but beautiful and persuasive letter is, to recommend Onesimus, formerly the runaway slave of Philemon, (but now a Christian convert,) to his master, and induce him to receive him again into his house. Whether Philemon pardoned or punished Onesimus, we have no information.

Section XV.—On the Epistle to the Hebrews.

The Hebrews, to whom this Epistle is addressed, were Jewish Christians, resident in Palestine: and, though considerable difference of opinion exists concerning its author, yet the similarity of its style and expressions to that of St. Paul's other Epistles, proves that it was written by him in Greek, and not in Hebrew, as some eminent critics have supposed. The absence of his name is accounted for by the consideration that he withheld it, lest he should give umbrage to the Jews. This Epistle was written from Rome, not long before he left Italy; viz.: at the end of A. D. 62, or early in 63.

The occasion of writing this Epistle will be sufficiently apparent from an attentive review of its contents. The Jews did every thing in their power to withdraw their brethren, who had been converted, from the Christian faith: to specious arguments, drawn from the excellency of the Jewish religion, they added others more cogent, namely, persecution and menaces. The object of the apostle, therefore, in writing this letter, is to show the deity of Jesus Christ, and the excellency of his Gospel, when compared with the institutions of Moses; to prevent the Hebrews, or Jewish converts, from relapsing into those rites and ceremonies which were now abolished; and to point out their total insufficiency, as means of reconciliation and atonement. The reasonings are interspersed with numerous solemn and affectionate warnings and exhortations, addressed to different descriptions of persons. At length St. Paul shows the nature, efficacy, and triumph of faith, by which all the saints in former ages had been accepted by God, and enabled to obey, suffer, and perform exploits in defence of their holy religion; from which he takes occasion to exhort the Hebrew Christians to steadfastness and perseverance in the true faith.

The Epistle to the Hebrews consists of three parts, viz.:

Part I. demonstrates the Deity of Christ, by the explicit declarations of Scripture concerning his superiority to angels, to Moses, to Aaron, and the whole Jewish priesthood, and the typical nature of the Mosaic ritual. (ch. i.—x. 18.

PART II. comprehends the Application of the preceding arguments and proofs, (x. 19—39, to xiii. 1—19,) in which the Hebrews are exhorted to steadfastness in the faith of Christ, and are encouraged by the examples of believers in former ages. (ch. x. 19—39, to xiii. 1—19.)

PART III. The conclusion, containing a prayer for the Hebrews, and apostolical salutations. (ch. xiii. 20—25.)

CHAPTER III.

ON THE CATHOLIC EPISTLES.

SECTION I.—On the Genuineness and authenticity of the Catholic Epistles.

THE Epistles of Saint Paul are followed in the canon of the New Testament by seven Epistles, bearing the names of the apostles James, Peter, Jude, and John. For many centuries, these Epistles have been generally termed *Catholic*, or General Epistles, because they are not addressed to the believers of some particular city or country, or to individuals, as Saint Paul's Epistles were, but to Christians in general, or to Christians of several countries.

Although the authenticity of the Epistle of James, the second of Peter, the Epistle of Jude, and the second and third Epistles of John, was questioned by some ancient fathers, as well as by some modern writers, yet we have every reason to believe that they are the genuine and authentic productions of the inspired writers whose names they bear. The claims to authenticity of these disputed Epistles are briefly noticed in the following sections. Indeed, the ancient Christians had such good opportunities for examining this subject, they exercised so much caution in guarding against imposition, and so well founded was their judgment concerning the books of the New Testament, that no writing which they pronounced genuine has yet been proved spurious; nor have we, at this day, the least reason to believe any book to be genuine which they rejected.

Section II.—On the General Epistle of James.

James, the author of this Epistle, was the son of Alpheus, or Cleophas, and is by St. Paul termed the 'Brother," or near relation of our Lord, (Gal. i. 18,19,) and is also generally termed "the Less," partly to distinguish him from the other James, and probably, also, because he was lower in stature. That he was an apostle evident from various passages in the New Testament, though it does not appear when his designation to this office took place. He was honoured by Jesus Christ with a separate interview soon after his resurrection. (1 Cor. xv. 7.) He was distinguished as one of the apostles of the circumcision; (Acts i. 13;) and soon after the death of Stephen, A. D. 34, he seems to have been appointed president, or bishop of the Christian church at Jerusalem, to have dwelt in that city, and to have presided at the council of the apostles, which was convened there A. D. 49. On account of his distinguished piety and sanctity, he was surnamed "the Just." He is said to have been stoned to death by the Jews, A. D. 62; and most learned men agree in placing his Epistle in the year 61. Though its authenticity has been doubted by some critics, we have every reason to believe it genuine, because it is cited by two of the apostolic fathers (those who immediately succeeded the apostles of Jesus Christ,) and by several succeeding writers. But the most decisive proof of its canonical authority is, that the Epistle of Saint James is inserted in the Syriac version of the New Testament, executed at the close of the first, or early in the second century, in which the second Epistle of Peter, the second and third of John, the Epistle of Jude, and the Book of Revelation are omitted.

The persons to whom this Epistle is addressed were Hebrew Christians, who were in danger of falling into the sins which abounded among the Jews of that time. The apostle, therefore, cautions them against those sins, and comforts them under the persecutions to which they were exposed; and in the course of his epistle he takes occasion, in chap. ii. 14—26, to rectify the notions of the Hebrew Christians concerning the doctrine of *justification by faith.* For as they were not to be justified by the *law*, but by the method proposed in the Gospel, and that method was said to be *by faith, without the works of the law;* they, some of them weakly, and others, perhaps, wilfully, perverted that discovery; and were for understanding, by faith, a bare assent to the truth of the Gospel, without that living, fruitful, and evangelical faith, which "worketh by love," and is required of all that would be saved.

The Epistle of Saint James divides itself into three parts, exclusive of the Introduction; (ch. i. 1;) viz.:

PART I. contains Exhortations to patience, humility, and suitable dispositions for receiving the word of God aright. (ch. i. 2—27.)

PART II. censures and condemns various sinful practices and erroneous notions; and here their mistaken notions of justification by faith without works, are corrected and illustrated by the examples of Abraham and Rahab. (ii.—v. 1—6.)

PART III. comprises various Exhortations and Cautions. (v. 7—20.)

SECTION III.—On the First General Epistle of Peter.

Simon, surnamed Cephas or Peter, which appellation signifies a stone or rock, was the son of Jonas or Jonah, and was born at Bethsaida, on the coast of the sea of Galilee. He had a brother, called Andrew, and they jointly pursued the occupation of fishermen on that lake. These two brothers were hearers of John the Baptist; from whose express testimony, and their own personal conversation with Jesus Christ, they were fully convinced that he was the Messiah; (John i. 35—42;) and, from this time, it is probable that they had frequent intercourse with our Saviour, and were witnesses of some of the miracles wrought by him, particularly that performed at Cana in Galilee. (John ii. 1, 2.) Both Peter and Andrew seem to have followed their trade, until Jesus Christ called them to "follow him," and promised to make them "both fishers of men." (Matt. iv. 18, 19, Mark i. 17. Luke v. 10.) From this time they became his companions.

and when he completed the number of his apostles they were included among them. Peter, in particular, was honoured with his master's intimacy, together with James and John: he is frequently mentioned in the Gospels, and in the former part of the Acts of the Apostles. We know nothing of his personal history after the apostolic council, related in Acts xv., (which is the last place where he is mentioned by Luke,) until many years afterwards, ecclesiastical history informs us, that he received the crown of martyrdom at Rome, A.D. 63, during the Neronian persecution; being crucified with his head downwards. The genuineness and authenticity of his first Epistle were never disputed: it was addressed to the same persecuted Hebrew Christians to whom Saint James and Saint Paul respectively wrote their letters. Its design is partly to support them under their afflictions and trials, and also to instruct them how to behave under persecution: and, as their character and conduct were liable to be aspersed and misrepresented by their enemies, they are exhorted to lead a holy life, that they might stop the mouths of their enemies, put their calumniators to shame, and win others over to their religion, by their holy and Christian conversation.

The Epistle may be conveniently divided into four sections, exclusive of the introduction and conclusion.

The Introduction. (ch. i. 1, 2.)

Section I. contains an exhortation to the Jewish Christians to persevere steadfastly in the faith, and to maintain a holy conversation, amid all their sufferings and persecutions. (i. 3—25, ii. 1—10.)

Section II. comprises exhortations, 1. To a holy conversation in general. (ii. 11, 12.) 2. To a particular discharge of their several duties, as dutiful *subjects* to their sovereign, (13—15,) who at this time was the ferocious Nero; as *servants* to their masters; (16—25;) and as *husbands* to their wives. (iii. 1—13.)

Section III. contains an exhortation to patience, submission, and to holiness of life, enforced by considering the example of Christ, (iii. 14—18,) and various other examples and affecting considerations. (iii. 19—22, iv. 1—19.)

Section IV. Directions to the ministers of the churches,

and to the people, how to behave towards each other. (v. 1—11.)

The Conclusion. (v. 12. 14.)

SECTION. IV.—On the Second General Epistle of Peter.

Though some doubts have been entertained respecting the authenticity of this Epistle, which has been received as the genuine production of St. Peter ever since the fourth century, except by the Syrian church, in which it is read as an excellent book, though not of canonical authority; yet we have the most satisfactory evidence of its genuineness and authenticity. It is cited or alluded to by three apostolic fathers, and by another writer of the second century: and though no writer in the third century appears to have cited it, yet ever since the fourth century it has been recognised as a genuine and canonical epistle. It was also addressed to Hebrew Christians under persecution, and a short time before the apostle's martyrdom, most probably early in the year 65. This Epistle consists of three parts; viz.:

PART I. The Introduction. (ch. i. 1, 2.)

PART II. Having stated the blessings to which God had called them, the apostle exhorts the Christians, who had received these precious gifts, to endeavour to improve in the most substantial graces and virtues. (i. 3—21, ii.) He then guards them against scoffers and impostors, who, he foretells, would ridicule their expectation of Christ's coming. (iii. 1—14.)

PART III. The Conclusion, in which the apostle declares the agreement of his doctrine with that of St. Paul (iii. 15, 16,) and repeats the sum of the Epistle. (iii 17, 18.)

SECTION V.—On the First General Epistle of Saint John.

The canonical authority of this Epistle, which appears to have been written A.D. 68 or 69, was never questioned: independently of historical or external testimony, we have the strongest internal evidence that this Epistle was written by the apostle John, in the very close analogy of its sentiments and expressions to those of his Gospel. Artless simplicity and benevolence, blended with singular modesty and candour, together with a wonderful sublimity of sentiment, are the characteristics of this Epistle, which is justly considered a catholic epistle; it being written for the use of Christians of every denomination and of every country, and designed to guard them against erroneous and licentious tenets, and to animate them to communion with God and a holy life. This Epistle consists of six sections, besides the conclusion, which is a recapitulation of the whole.

Sect. 1. asserts the true divinity and humanity of Christ, in opposition to the false teachers, and urges the union of faith and holiness of life as absolutely necessary to enable Christians to enjoy communion with God. (ch. i. 1—7.)

Sect. 2. shows that all have sinned, and explains the doctrine of Christ's propitiation. (i. 8—10, ii. 1, 2.) Whence the apostle takes occasion to illustrate the marks of true faith, viz.: Obeying his commandments, and sincere love of the brethren: and shows that the love of the world is inconsistent with the love of God. (ii. 3—17.)

Sect. 3. asserts Jesus to be the same person with Christ, in opposition to the false teachers who denied it. (ii. 18—29.)

Sect. 4. On the privileges of true believers, and their consequent happiness and duties, and the marks by which they are known to be "the sons of God." (iii.)

Sect. 5. contains criteria by which to distinguish Antichrist and false Christians, with an exhortation to brotherly love. (iv.)

Sect. 6. shows the connexion between faith in Christ, the being born of God, love to God and his children, obedience to his commandments, and victory over the world; and that Jesus Christ is truly the Son of God, able to save us, and to hear the prayers we make for ourselves and others. (v. 1—16.)

The conclusion, which is a summary of the preceding treatise, shows that a sinful life is inconsistent with true Christianity; asserts the divinity of Christ; and cautions believers against idolatry. (v. 17—21.

The preceding is an outline of this admirable Epistle; which, being designed to promote right principles of doctrine and practical piety in conduct, abounds, more than any book of the New Testament, with criteria by which Christians may soberly *examine themselves whether they be in the faith*. (2. Cor. xiii. 5.)

Considerable discussion has taken place respecting the genuineness of the clause in 1 John v. 7, 8. which runs thus: "in heaven the Father, the Word and the Holy Ghost, and these three are one. And there are three that bear witness in earth." Of the evidence for and against this passage the author has given a copious ab stract in the fourth volume of his larger Introduction which does not admit of abridgment. The humble reader of the Bible, however, need not entertain any apprehension lest any of the truths of the true and proper deity of our Lord and Saviour Jesus Christ should be weakened. Much as has been written on this topic, the question cannot yet be considered as decided, while it is known that many hundred manuscripts of the New Testament still remain uncollated. Even, should it *ultimately* appear that the disputed clause is spurious, its absence will not diminish the weight of irresistible evidence which other undisputed passages of holy writ afford to the doctrine of the Trinity. "The proofs of our Lord's true and proper Godhead remain *unshaken*—deduced from the prophetic descriptions of the Messiah's person in the Old Testament—from the ascription to him of the attributes, the works, and the homage, which are peculiar to the Deity—and from those numerous and important relations, which he is affirmed in Scripture to sustain towards his holy and universal church, and towards each of its true members."*

SECTION VI.—On the Second and Third Epistles of Saint John.

Although some doubts were, in the *fourth* century, entertained respecting the canonical authority of these Epistles, yet that point has long been considered as determined by the fact that these Epistles have been cited by Christian writers of the *third* century, as well as by many in the ages immediately following. The similarity of style also attests that they are the productions of the same author as the first epistle of St. John, who probably wrote them about A.D. 68 or 69.

The SECOND EPISTLE is addressed to an eminent Christian matron, the *Lady* Electa, whom the apostle commends for her virtuous and religious education of her children; and who is exhorted to abide in the doctrine of Christ, to persevere in the truth, and carefully to avoid the delusions of false teachers. But chiefly the apostle beseeches this

* Eclectic Review, vol. v. part i. p. 249.

Christian matron to practise the great and indispensable commandment of Christian love and charity.

The THIRD EPISTLE of St. John is addressed to a converted Gentile, a respectable member of some Christian church, called Gaius or Caius: most probably Gaius of Corinth, (1 Cor. i. 14,) whom St. Paul calls his "host, and the host of the whole church." (Rom. xvi. 23.) The scope of this Epistle is to commend his steadfastness in the faith, and his general hospitality, especially to the ministers of Christ; to caution him against the ambitious and turbulent practices of Diotrephes, and to recommend Demetrius to his friendship; referring what he further had to say to a personal interview.

SECTION VII.—On the General Epistle of Jude.

Jude, or Judas, who was surnamed Thaddeus and Lebbeus, and was also called the brother of our Lord, (Matt. xiii. 55,) was the son of Alpheus, brother of James the Less, and one of the twelve apostles. We are not informed when, or how he was called to the apostleship; and there is scarcely any mention of him in the New Testament, except in the different catalogues of the twelve apostles. Although the epistle which bears his name, was rejected in the early ages of Christianity, by some persons, we have satisfactory evidences of its authenticity; for it is found in all the ancient catalogues of the sacred writings of the New Testament; it is asserted to be genuine by Christian fathers of the third and following centuries; and independently of this external evidence, the genuineness of the Epistle of St. Jude is confirmed by the subjects discussed in it, which are in every respect worthy of an apostle of Jesus Christ. There is great similarity between this Epistle and the second chapter of St. Peter's second Epistle. Jude addressed his letter to all who had embraced the Gospel; its design is to guard them against the false teachers who had begun to insinuate themselves into the Christian church; and to contend with the utmost earnestness and zeal for the true faith, against the dangerous tenets which they disseminated, resolving the whole of Christianity into a speculative belief and outward profession of the Gospel. And having thus cancelled the obligations of morality and personal holiness, they taught their disciples to live in all manner of licentiousness, and at the same time flattered them with the hope of divine favour, and of obtaining eternal life. The vile characters of these seducers are further shown, and their sentence is denounced; and the Epistle concludes with warnings, admonitions, and counsels to be lievers how to persevere in faith and godliness themselves, and to rescue others from the snares of the false teachers.

CHAPTER IV.

ON THE REVELATION OF ST. JOHN THE DIVINE.

It is a remarkable circumstance that the authenticity of this book was very generally, if not universally, acknowledged during the first two centuries, and yet in the third century it began to be questioned. This seems to have been occasioned by *some* absurd notions concerning the Millenium, which a few well-meaning but fanciful expositors grounded on this book; which notions their opponents injudiciously and presumptuously endeavoured to discredit, by denying the authority of the book itself. So little, however, has this portion of holy writ suffered from the ordeal of criticism, to which it has in consequence been subjected, that, (as Sir Isaac Newton has long since remarked) there is no other book of the New Testament so strongly attested, or commented upon so early, as the Apocalypse, or Revelation of Saint John; for, besides the strong internal evidence afforded by the similarity of its style to that of the apostle's other writings, we have an unbroken series of external, or historical testimony, from the apostolic age downwards. The revelations contained in this book were made to Saint John during his exile in the isle of Patmos, toward the end of Domitian's reign, though the book containing them could not have been published until after his release, on the emperor's death, in the year 96, and after his return to Ephesus. The year 96 or 97, may therefore be considered as its true date. The scope of this book is twofold: *first*, generally to make known to the apostle "the things which are," (i. 19,) that is, the then present state of the Christian churches in Asia; and, *secondly* and principally, to reveal to him "the things which shall be hereafter," or the constitution and fates of the Christian church, through its several periods of propagation, corruption and amendment, from its beginning to its consummation in glory. The Apocalypse, therefore, consists of two principal divisions, or parts; viz.:

After the title of the book. (ch. i. 1—3.)

Part I. contains the "*things which are*—" that is, the then present state of the church: it includes the Epistles to the seven Asiatic Churches of Ephesus, Smyrna, Pergamos, Thyatira, Sardis, Philadelphia, and Laodicea. (i. 9—20, ii., iii.) These churches, in the Lydian, or Proconsular Asia, are supposed to have been planted by the apostle Paul, and his assistants during their ministry. They lie nearly in an amphitheatre, and are addressed according to their geographical positions, as may be seen on reference to our Map of the Travels of the Apostles. These seven Epistles contain excellent precepts and exhortations, commendations and reproofs, promises and threatenings, which are calculated to afford instruction to the Universal Church of Christ at all times.

Part II. contains a Prophecy of "*the things which shall be hereafter*," or the future state of the church through succeeding ages, from the time when the apostle beheld the apocalyptic visions, to the grand consummation of all things. (ch. iv.—xxii.)

Although many parts of the Apocalypse are necessarily obscure to us, because they contain predictions of events still future, yet enough is sufficiently clear to convey to us the most important religious instruction. The Revelation of St. John is to us precisely what the prophecies of the Old Testament were to the Jews, nor is it in any degree more inexplicable. "No prophecies in the Revelation can be more clouded with obscurity, than that a child should be born of a pure virgin—that a mortal should not see corruption—that a person despised and numbered among malefactors should be established for ever on the throne of David. Yet still the *pious Jew* preserved his faith entire amidst all these wonderful, and, in appearance, contradictory intimations. He looked into the holy books in which they were contained, with reverence, and with an eye of patient expectation 'waited for the consolation of Israel.' We, in the same manner, look up to those prophecies of the Apocalypse, for the full consummation of the great scheme of the Gospel; when Christianity shall finally prevail over all the corruptions of the world, and be universally established in its utmost purity."*

* Gilpin's Exposition of the New Testament, vol. ii. p. 428.

APPENDIX.

No. I.

TABLES OF WEIGHTS, MEASURES, AND MONEY, MENTIONED IN THE BIBLE.

Chiefly extracted from Dr. Arbuthnot's Tables of Ancient Coins, Weights, and Measures.

1. *Jewish Weights reduced to English Troy weight.*

	lbs.	oz.	pen.	gr.
The geran, one twentieth of a shekel	0	0	0	12
Bekah, half a shekel	0	0	5	0
The shekel	0	0	10	0
The maneh, 60 shekels	2	6	0	0
The talent, 50 maneh or 3000 shekels	125	0	0	0

2. *Scripture Measures of Length reduced to English measure.*

								Eng. feet.	inch.
A digit								0	0.912
4	A palm							0	3.648
12	3	A span						0	10.944
24	6	3	A cubit					1	9.888
96	24	6	2	A fathom					3.552
144	36	12	6	1.5	Ezekiel's reed			10	11.328
192	48	16	8	2	1.3	An Arabian pole		14	7.10
1920	480	160	80	20	13.3	10	A schœnus or measuring line	145	11.04

3. *The long Scripture measures.*

						Eng. miles.	paces.	feet
A cubit						0	0	1.824
400	A stadium or furlong					0	145	4.6
2000	5	A sabbath day's journey				0	729	3.0
4000	10	2	An eastern mile			1	403	1.0
12000	30	6	3	A parasang		4	153	3.0
96000	240	48	24	8	A day's journey	33	172	4.0

4. *Scripture Measures of capacity for liquids, reduced to English wine measure.*

							Gal.	pints.
A Caph							0	0.625
1.3	A log						0	0.833
5.3	4	A cab					0	3.333
16	12	0	A hin				1	2
32	24	6	2	A seah			2	4
96	72	18	6	3	A bath or ephah		7	4
960	720	180	60	20	10	A kor or koros, chomer or homer	75	5

5. *Scripture Measures of capacity for things dry, reduced to English corn measure.*

							Pecks.	gal.	pints.
A gachal							0	0	0.1416
20	A cab						0	0	2.8333
36	1.8	An omer or gomer					0	0	5.1
120	6	3.3	A seah				1	0	1
360	18	10	3	An ephah			3	0	3
1800	90	50	15	5	A letech		16	0	0
3600	180	100	30	10	2	A chomer, homer, kor, or coros	32	0	1

6 *Jewish Money reduced to the English standard.*

					l.	*s.*	*d.*
A gerah					0	0	1.2687
10	A bekah				0	1	1.6875
20	2	A shekel			0	2	3.375
1200	120	50	A maneh, or mina Hebraica		5	14	0.75
60000	6000	3000	60	A talent	342	3	9
A solidus aureus, or sextula, was worth					0	12	0
A siclus aureus, or gold shekel, was worth					1	16	6
A talent of gold was worth					5475	0	0

In the preceding table, silver is valued at 5*s.* and gold at 4*l.* per oz.

7. *Roman Money, mentioned in the New Testament, reduced to the English standard.*

	l.	*s.*	*d.*	far.
A mite, (Λεπτον or Ασσαριον)	0	0	0	0¾
A farthing (Κοδραντης) about	0	0	0	1½
A penny or denarius (Δηναριον)	0	0	7	2
A pound or mina	3	2	6	0

No. II.

A TABLE

OF THE ORDER AND DATES OF THE BOOKS OF THE NEW TESTAMENT, AND OF THE PLACES WHERE THEY ARE SUPPOSED TO HAVE BEEN WRITTEN.

I. THE HISTORICAL BOOKS.

GOSPELS.	PLACES.	A. D.
Matthew (Hebrew) ——— (Greek)	Judæa	37 or 38 61
Mark	Rome	between 60 and 63
Luke (Gospel) —— (Acts of the Apostles)	Greece	63 or 64
John	Ephesus	97 or 98

II. THE EPISTLES OF PAUL

EPISTLES.	PLACES.	A. D.
1 Thessalonians	Corinth	52
2 Thessalonians	Corinth	52
Galatians	Corinth	At the close of 52 or early in 53
1 Corinthians	Ephesus	56
Romans	Corinth	About the end of 57 or the beginning of 58
2 Corinthians	Macedonia (perhaps from Philippi)	58
Ephesians	Rome	61
Philippians	Rome	Before the end of 62 or the beginning of 63
Colossians	Rome	62
Philemon	Rome	About the end of 62 or early in 63
Hebrews	Italy (perhaps from Rome)	About the end of 62 or early in 63
1 Timothy	Macedonia	64
Titus	Macedonia	64
2 Timothy	Rome	65

III. THE CATHOLIC, OR GENERAL EPISTLES.

EPISTLES.	PLACES.	A. D.
James	Judæa	61
1 Peter	Rome	64
2 Peter	Rome	about the beginning of 65
1 John	Unknown (perhaps Ephesus)	68 or early in 69
2 and 3 John	Ephesus	68 or early in 69
Jude	Unknown	64 or 65
The Revelation of St. John	Ephesus	96 or 97

No. III.

A TABLE

OF THE PSALMS, CLASSED ACCORDING TO THEIR SEVERAL SUBJECTS, AND ADAPTED TO THE PURPOSES OF PRIVATE DEVOTION.

I. *Prayers.*

1. Prayers for pardon of sin, Psal. vi. xxv. xxxviii. li. cxxx. Psalms styled penitential, vi. xxxii. xxxviii. li. cii. cxxx. cxliii.
2. Prayers, composed when the Psalmist was deprived of an opportu nity of the public exercise of religion, Psal. xlii. xliii. lxiii. lxxxiv.
3. Prayers, in which the Psalmist seems extremely dejected, though not totally deprived of consolation, under his afflictions, Psal. xiii. xxii. lxix. lxxvii. lxxxviii. cxliii.
4. Prayers, in which the Psalmist asks help of God, in consideration of his own integrity, and the uprightness of his cause, Psal. vii. xvii. xxvi. xxxv.
5. Prayers, expressing the firmest trust and confidence in God under afflictions, Psal. iii. xvi. xxvii. xxxi. liv. lvi. lvii. lxi. lxii. lxxi. lxxxvi.
6. Prayers, composed when the people of God were under affliction or persecution, Psal. xliv. lx. lxxiv. lxxix. lxxx. lxxxiii. lxxxix. xciv. cii. cxxiii. cxxxvii.
7. The following are likewise prayers in time of trouble and affliction, Psal. iv. v. xi. xxviii. xli. lv. lix. lxiv. lxx. cix. cxx. cxl. cxli. cxlii.
8. Prayers of intercession, Psal. xx. lxvii. cxxii. cxxxii. cxliv.

II. *Psalms of Thanksgiving.*

1. Thanksgivings for Mercies vouchsafed to particular persons, Psal. ix. xviii. xxi. xxx. xxxiv. xl. lxxv. ciii. cviii. cxvi. cxviii. cxxxviii. cxliv.
2. Thanksgivings for mercies vouchsafed to the Israelites in general, Psal. xlvi. xlviii. lxv. lxvi. lxviii. lxxvi. lxxxi. lxxxv. xcviii. cv. cxxiv cxxvi. cxxix. cxxxv. cxxxvi. cxlix.

III. *Psalms of Praise and Adoration, displaying the Attributes of God.*

1. General acknowledgments of God's goodness and mercy, and particu larly his care and protection of good men, Psal. xxiii. xxxiv. xxxvi. xci. c. ciii. cvii. cxvii. cxxi. cxlv. cxlvi.
2. Psalms displaying the power, majesty, glory, and other attributes of the Divine Being, Psal. viii. xix. xxiv. xxix. xxxiii. xlvii. l. lxv. lxvi. lxxvi. lxxvii. xciii. xcv. xcvi. xcvii. xcix. civ. cxi. cxiii. cxiv. cxv. cxxxiv. cxxxix. cxlvii. cxlviii. cl.

IV. *Instructive Psalms.*

1. The different characters of good and bad men: the happiness of the one, and the misery of the other: are represented in the following psalms i. v. vii. ix. x. xi. xii. xiv. xv. xvii. xxiv. xxv. xxxii. xxxiv. xxxvi. xxxvii l. lii. liii. lviii. lxxiii. lxxv. lxxxiv. xci. xcii. xciv. cxii. cxix. cxxi. cxxv cxxvii. cxxviii. cxxxiii.
2. The excellence of God's laws, Psal. xix. cxix.
3. The vanity of human life, Psal. xxxix. xlix. xc.
4. Advice to magistrates, Psal. lxxxii. ci.
5. The virtue of humility, Psal. cxxxi.

V. *Psalms more eminently and directly Prophetical.*

Psal. ii. xvi. xxii. xl. xlv. lxviii. lxxii. lxxxvii. cx. cxviii.

VI. *Historical Psalms.*

Psal. lxxviii. cv. cvi.

No. IV.

A TABLE,

OR LIST, OF SELECT CHAPTERS OF THE HOLY SCRIPTURES,

Forming an Epitome of the Bible, and adapted to Family, or Private Reading.

☞ *The following arrangement of Chapters from the Sacred Scriptures is not offered with a view to supersede a regular and orderly perusal of the word of God. Having devoted a considerable portion of his life to the preparation of his larger "Introduction to the Study and Knowledge of the" entire "Holy Scriptures," the author trusts that he shall be acquitted of such an intention. The present selection of chapters is offered, in consequence of a wish which he has often heard expressed, that some list were extant, which should, in a short compass, present the most important portions of the sacred volume to the attention of individuals possessing but little leisure to make a selection for themselves, and who were desirous of becoming acquainted with the leading facts, doctrines, and precepts of the Bible. The author will rejoice if his attempt shall lead any one to a more frequent and attentive study of that holy volume. To any of his readers, who may be desirous of perusing the* entire *Scriptures in chronological order, (and who may be able to purchase them,) he can with confidence recommend the Rev. George Townsend's four volumes on the Harmony of the Old and New Testaments.*

Part I.—A Selection of Chapters, forming a Series of the Sacred History of the Old Testament.

GENESIS.

Section
1. An Account of the Origin of the World and of the six days' Creation, chap i., ii. 1—6.
2. A more particular Account of the Creation of Man. The Garden of Eden described. The Formation of Woman and Institution of Marriage, chap. ii. 7—24.
3. The Fall of Man. The first Promise of the Redeemer. Expulsion of Adam and Eve from Paradise, chap. ii. 25, iii.
4. The Birth of Cain and Abel. Murder of Abel. History of other descendants of Adam to Lamech, chap. iv.
5. Genealogy of the Patriarchs from Adam to Noah, chap. v.
6. The Increase of Wickedness in the World. The Deluge threatened. Noah commanded to prepare the Ark, chap. vi.
7. Noah and his Family enter the Ark. Account of the Destruction of the former World by the Deluge, chap. vii.
8. The Waters subside. Noah and his Family quit the Ark. History of the Renovation of the World, chap. viii.
9. The Covenant of God with Noah. His intoxication, chap. ix.
10. The erection of the Tower of Babel attempted. The confusion of Tongues, and the dispersion of Mankind, chap. xi.
11. The call of Abraham. He goes into Egypt, chap. xii.
12. Abraham and Lot return from Egypt and separate, chap. xiii.

Section

13. Abraham blessed by Melchizedek, King of Salem, chap. xiv.
14. God renews his promises to Abraham, chap. xvii.
15. Three Angels visit Abraham. His Intercession for Sodom and Gomorrah, chap. xviii.
16. The Destruction of Sodom and Gomorrah, chap. xix. 1—26.
17. Abraham commanded to sacrifice his only Son, Isaac. He prepares to obey, and receives the divine benediction, chap. xxii. 1—19.
10 Isaac marries Rebekah, chap. xxiv.
19. The Birth of Esau and Jacob. Esau despises his birthright, chap. xxv. 20—34.
20. The Promise of God to Isaac, chap. xxvi. 1—6.
21. Jacob surreptitiously obtains Isaac's blessing, chap. xxvii. 1—40.
22. Esau menaces Jacob. The marriage of Esau. Jacob's vision at Beth-el, and his vow, chap. xxvii. 41—46, xxviii.
23. Jacob entertained by Laban. His Marriage, chap. xxix.
24. Joseph sold into Egypt, chap. xxxvii.
25. The Imprisonment of Joseph by Potiphar, chap. xxxix.
26. Joseph, in prison, interprets the dreams of Pharaoh's chief Baker and chief Butler, chap. xl.
27. The deliverance of Joseph. His advancement in the court of Pharaoh, chap. xli.
28. The first journey of Joseph's Brethren into Egypt, to buy corn, chap. xlii.
29. Jacob persuaded to send Benjamin into Egypt. Joseph entertains his Brethren, chap. xliii.
30. Joseph makes himself known to his Brethren, chap. xliv., xlv.
31. Jacob settles in Egypt with his family, chap. xlvi.
32. Joseph presents certain of his Brethren unto Pharaoh.—His administration in Egypt, chap. xlvii. 1—26.
33. Jacob's last days.—He is visited by Joseph, whose children he blesses, chap. xlvii. 27—31, xlviii.
34. Jacob's Prophetic Benediction of his Children, chap. xlix.
35. The Burial of Jacob. Death and Burial of Joseph, chap. l.

EXODUS.

36. The Oppression of the Children of Israel by Rameses Miamoun, the King who knew neither Joseph nor his services, chap. i.
37. The Birth and Preservation of Moses. His flight into Midian, chap. ii.
38. God appears unto Moses, and calls him to be the deliverer of the Israelites, chap. iii., iv.
39. Moses and Aaron apply to Pharaoh, in the name of God, and on behalf of the Israelites, chap. v.
40. God renews his promise of deliverance to the Israelites, chap. vi. 1—12.
41. The interview of Moses with Pharaoh. The first plague, chap. vii.
42. Pharaoh hardens his heart. The second, third, and fourth plagues, chap. viii.
43. The fifth, sixth, and seventh plagues, chap. ix.
44. The eighth and ninth plagues, chap. x.
45. The Death of the First Born threatened, chap. xi.
46. The Institution of the Passover. The Departure of Israel from Egypt, chap. xii.
47. The Israelites' miraculous passage of the Red Sea. Pharaoh and his army drowned, chap. xiv.
48. The Song of Moses, for the deliverance of the Israelites. The bitter waters of Marah sweetened, chap. xv.
49. The Israelites miraculously fed in the Desert, chap. xvi.
50. Their murmurs at Rephidim. Water miraculously given them from the rock at Horeb, chap. xvii.

Section

51. The Arrival of Moses' wife and children with Jethro. The counsel given by the latter to Moses, chap. xviii.
52. The preparation of the Israelites for renewing their covenant with God, chap. xix.
53. The Promulgation of the Moral Law, chap. xx.
54. Moses called to ascend Mount Sinai. The Covenant ratified, chap. xxiv.
55. The people request Aaron to make the Golden Calf. The Punishment of the Idolaters, chap. xxxii.
56. Moses removes his tent from the camp. The people mourn, chap. xxxiii.
57. The Tables of the Law renewed. Various instructions given to Moses, chap. xxxiv.

NUMBERS.

58. Moses despatches Spies into the land of Canaan, chap. xiii.
59. The murmurs of the people. Joshua's attempt to pacify them, chap. xiv.
60. The Rebellion and Punishment of Korah, Dathan, and Abiram, and their associates, chap. xvi.

DEUTERONOMY.

61. Discourse of Moses to the Israelites, relating the events that took place in the wilderness from their leaving Mount Horeb, until their arrival at Kadesh, chap. i.
62. Renewal of the Covenant with the People of Israel, chap. xxix.
63. Promises of Pardon to the Penitent. Good and evil set before them, chap. xxx.
64. Joshua appointed to be the successor of Moses. A solemn charge given to him, chap. xxxi. 1—27.
65. The people convened to hear the prophetical and historical Ode of Moses, chap. xxxi. 28—30. xxxii.
66. Moses' Prophetic Blessing of the twelve Tribes. Their peculiar felicity and privilege in having THE LORD for their God and Protector, chap. xxxiii.
67. The Death and Burial of Moses, chap. xxxiv.

JOSHUA.

68. The Call and Appointment of Joshua to be Captain-General of the people of God, chap. i.
69. The Miraculous Passage of the Israelites over Jordan, and the setting up of twelve memorial stones, chap. iii., iv.
70. Joshua, stricken in years, gives his first charge to the people of Israel, chap. xxiii.
71. Joshua's second charge to the Israelites, chap. xxiv.

JUDGES.

72. The people chastised for their sins. Judges raised up. Their administration, chap. ii

I SAMUEL.

73. The Birth of Samuel, chap. i.
74. The Hymn of Hannah. Depraved conduct of Eli's Sons, chap. ii.
75. The call of Samuel, and his establishment in the Prophetic Office, chap. iii.
76. The Israelites demand a king, chap. viii.
77. Saul anointed king, chap. ix., x.
78. Saul rejected by God, chap. xiii.

Section

79. The anointing of David to be king over Israel, chap. xvi.
80. David's Combat and Victory over Goliath, chap. xvii. 1—54.
81. Saul's Life in David's power, in the cave at Engedi, who magnanimously spares it, chap. xxiv.
82. David spares the Life of Saul a second time, chap. xxvi.
83. The suicide of Saul, after his total discomfiture by the Philistines, chap. xxxi.

2 SAMUEL.

84. David anointed king over Israel. His victories, chap. v.
85. The Bringing up of the Ark to Jerusalem, and the Divine Promises made to him, chap. vi., vii.
86. The Sin and Repentance of David, chap. xi., xii.
87. David's Psalm of Praise, on a general review of the mercies of his life, and of the many deliverances he had experienced, chap. xxii.

1 KINGS.

88. The death of David, and Accession of Solomon, chap. ii.
89. The commencement of Solomon's Reign, chap. iii.
90. The Dedication of the Temple, and the Sublime Prayer of Solomon on that occasion, chap. viii.
91. Divine Vision to Solomon. His Opulence and Commerce, chap, ix.
92. The death of Solomon, and accession of Rehoboam, chap. xi.
93. The Revolt of the Ten Tribes under Jeroboam, who forms the Kingdom of Israel. chap. xii.
94. The Reigns of Rehoboam king of Judah, and of Jeroboam king of Israel, chap. xiv.
95. The Reign of Ahab, against whom Elijah prophesieth. Miracles wrought by the Prophet, chap. xvii.
96. The Prophets of Baal slain, chap. xviii.
97. Elijah's Flight to Horeb. Transactions there, chap. xix.

2 KINGS.

98. The translation of Elijah, chap. ii.
99. Miracles wrought by his successor, Elisha, chap. iv.
100. The Healing of Naaman, and punishment of Gehazi, chap. v.
101. Miracle wrought by Elisha. The Syrian army smitten with blindness. chap. vi.
102. Hoshea, the last king of Israel, dethroned by Shalmaneser, and the Israelites carried captive into Assyria, chap. xvi.
103. The reign of Hezekiah. His danger from Sennacherib's besieging Jerusalem, chap. xvii.
104. The deliverance of Hezekiah, chap xix.
105. The pious reign of Josiah, chap. xxii., xxiii. 1—30.
106. The reigns of Jehoahaz, Jehoiakim, Jehoiachin, and Zedekiah, the last kings of Judah, chap. xxiii. 31—37. xxiv.
107. Rebellion of Zedekiah against Nebuchadnezzar. Jerusalem taken; the temple burnt; and the Jews carried into captivity to Babylon chap. xxv.

EZRA.

108. Edict of Cyrus, permitting the Jews to return into Judæa and rebuild the temple, chap. i.
109. The building of the second temple commenced, but hindered by the Samaritans, chap. iii. iv.
110. Edict of Darius in favour of the Jews. The temple finished and dedicated. chap. v., vi.

ESTHER.

Section

111. Haman, prime minister of Ahasuerus, from motives of hatred towards Mordecai, forms a plan to massacre the Jews throughout Persia, chap. iii.
112. Esther, the niece of Mordecai, apprises the king of Haman's sanguinary design, chap. vii.
113. The Advancement of Mordecai. The deliverance of the Jews, chap. viii., ix., x.

EZRA.

114. Ezra the priest returns to Jerusalem with a commission from Artaxerxes Longimanus, king of Persia, in favour of the Jews, chap. vii.

NEHEMIAH.

115. Departure of Nehemiah for Jerusalem, with a royal commission, in favour of the Jews, chap ii.
116. Jerusalem and the Temple being rebuilt, Ezra and Nehemiah convene the people, to hear the law read, chap. viii.

PART II.—A Selection of Chapters, forming a series of the Gospel History

Section

1. The Birth of John the Baptist and of Jesus Christ announced, Luke i. 1—56.
2. John the Baptist born. The prophetic hymn of Zacharias, Luke i 57—80.
3. The Nativity and Infancy of Jesus Christ, Luke ii.
4. The Arrival of the Wise Men from the East to adore Jesus Christ, Matt. ii.
5. The Ministry of John the Baptist. The Baptism of Christ, Luke iii.
6. The Temptation of Jesus Christ. He beginneth to preach, Matt. iv. 1—17.
6. Christ preacheth at Nazareth. Various Miracles wrought by Christ, Luke iv. 14—44.
7. Testimony of John the Baptist to Jesus Christ, John i.
8. Christ's Miracle at Cana in Galilee, John ii.
9. His Conversation with Nicodemus, John iii.
10. His Discourse with the Woman of Samaria, John iv.
11. Peter, James, John, and Matthew become Christ's stated disciples, Luke v.
12. Jesus Christ heals a Paralytic at the Pool of Bethesda, John v.
13. The twelve Apostles appointed, Luke vi.
14. Christ's Sermon on the Mount, Matt. v.—vii.
    - § 1. Who only are truly happy. The duty of Christians to be exemplary, Matt. v. 1—16.
    - § 2. The design of Christ's coming; viz.: to ratify the divine law, v. 17—20, which had been much impaired by the traditions of the Pharisees. 1. IN RESPECT OF ITS EXTENT: this is exemplified in what concerns *Murder*, 21—26; *Adultery*, 27—30; *Divorce*, 31, 32; *Oaths*, 33—37; *Retaliation*, 38—42; the Love of our Neighbour, 43—48. 2. IN RESPECT OF MOTIVE: where the end is applause, the virtue is destroyed. This is exemplified in *Almsgiving*, vi. 1—4; *Prayer*, 5—15; and *Fasting*, 16—18.
    - § 3. Heavenly Mindedness enforced by various considerations vi. 19—34.

Section

§ 4. Cautions against *rash judgments of others*, vii. 1—5; various *admonitions*, 6—14; warnings against *false teachers*, who are commonly known by their actions, 15—20; the wisdom of adding practice to knowledge, and the insignificancy of the latter without the former, 21—29.

15. Jesus Christ heals the Centurion's Servant, and restores to life the Widow's Son at Nain, Luke vii. 1—17.
16. Christ's reply to the inquiry of John the Baptist's Disciples, and his discourse to the people concerning John, Luke vii. 18—35.
17. Christ pardons a woman who had been a sinner, Luke vii. 36—50.
18. The parable of the Sower. Who are Christ's Disciples, Luke viii. 1—21.
19. Christ stills a tempest by his command, and heals a demoniac at Gadara, Luke viii. 22—39.
20. Christ cures an issue of blood, and raises the daughter of Jairus to life, Luke viii. 40—56.
21. Christ heals a paralytic and two blind men, Matt. ix.
22. The Mission of the Apostles. Five thousand men miraculously fed, Luke ix. 1—27.
23. Christ feedeth five thousand men. Peter's confession, John vi.
24. Christ performs various miracles, Matt. xv.
25. Christ foretells his death and resurrection, Matt. xvi.
26. The transfiguration of Jesus Christ, and the miracle which followed it, Matt. xvii.
27. The Mission of the Seventy Disciples, Luke x. 1—24.
28. The Parable of the benevolent Samaritan. Christ visits Martha and Mary, Luke x. 25—42.
29. Jesus goes to Jerusalem to the Feast of Tabernacles, John vii.
30. Jesus Christ teaches in the Temple, John viii.
31. Christ heals a man who had been born blind, John ix.
32. Instructions concerning Prayer. The Scribes and Pharisees reproved. Luke xi.
33. Cautions against hypocrisy. The Care of Divine Providence, Luke xii. 1—34.
34. Admonition to be prepared for Death, Luke xii. 35—48.
35. Christ reproacheth the people for not knowing the time of Messiah's coming. Common reason sufficient to teach men repentance, Luke xii. 49—59.
6. Design of God's Judgments. An infirm woman healed. Parable of the Mustard-seed, which prophetically represents the spread of the Gospel, Luke xiii. 1—20.
37. Christ's journey to Jerusalem to keep the Feast of Dedication. His lamentation over the judicial blindness of Jerusalem, Luke xiii. 22—35.
38. A dropsical man healed on the Sabbath-day. The parable of the great Supper, Luke xiv. 1—24.
39. Courage and perseverance shown to be requisite in a true Christian. The unprofitableness of an unsound Christian, Luke xiv. 25—35.
40. Christ illustrates the joy of the angels in heaven over repenting Sinners, by the Parables, 1. Of the *lost sheep*, Luke xv. 1—7; 2. Of the *lost piece of money*, 8—10; and, 3. Of the *Prodigal Son*, 11—32.
41. Parable of the Unjust Steward. The Pharisees reproved for their hypocrisy and covetousness, Luke xvi. 1—18.
42. The Parable of the rich man and Lazarus, Luke xvi. 19—31.
43. The duty of not giving offence. Ten lepers healed, Luke xvii. 1—19.
44. Christ discourses concerning his second coming, Luke xvii. 20—37.
45. Encouragement to perseverance in prayer, illustrated by the parable of the Importunate Widow. Parable of the Pharisee and Publican, or Tax-gatherer, Luke xviii. 1—14.
46 Christ encourages young children to be brought to him; again foretells his death; and cures a blind man near Jericho, Luke xviii. 15—42

Section

47. Parable of the Labourers in the vineyard. Humility inculcated. Two blind men receive their sight, Matt. xx.
48. The Resurrection of Lazarus, John xi. 41—44.
49. Account of the different effects produced by this miracle on the Jews, John xi. 45—57, xii. 1—11.
50. The Conversion of Zaccheus, Luke xix. 1—10.
51. Parable of the nobleman going into a distant country to receive a kingdom, Luke xix. 11—28.
52. Christ's lowly, yet triumphal entry into Jerusalem. He weeps over her impending calamities, and expels the traders out of the temple, where he teaches the people, Luke xix. 29—48.
53. Christ confutes the chief-priests, scribes, and elders, 1. By a question concerning the baptism of John, Luke xx. 1—8; 2. By the Parable of the Labourers in the vineyard, 9—19; and, 3. By showing the lawfulness of paying tribute unto Cæsar, 20—26.
54. The Sadducees and Scribes severally confuted. The Charity of a poor widow commended, Luke xx. 27—47, xxi. 1—4.
55. Christ discourses on the destruction of the temple; and enforces the duty of watchfulness, Luke xxi. 5—38.
56. Christ's Prophetic Discourse concerning the destruction of Jerusalem, and the end of the World, Matt. xxiv.
57. Parables of the Ten Virgins, and of the Talents. The last Judgment described, Matt. xxv.
58. Christ washes his apostle's feet; predicts the treachery of Judas, and Peter's denial, John xiii.
59. Christ celebrates the passover; institutes the Lord's Supper; and again warns Peter that he would deny him, Luke xxii. 1—38.
60. Christ's last discourse with his disciples, John xiv.—xvi.
61. Christ's last prayer for his disciples, and for all who in future ages should believe in him, John xvii.
62. Judas betrays Jesus; who retires to the garden of Gethsemane. Peter's denial of Christ, who is arraigned before Pilate, John xviii.
63. Christ condemned and crucified, Luke xxiii.
64. The Resurrection of Jesus Christ, Matt. xxviii. 1—15.
65. Christ appears to two disciples on their way to Emmaus, Luke xxiv. 13—35; and also to the assembled disciples, 36—48. The Ascension of Christ, 49—53.

THE ACTS OF THE APOSTLES.

66. The transactions before and after Christ's ascension into heaven. Matthias elected an apostle, chap. i.
67. The Descent of the Holy Spirit upon the Apostles on the day of Pentecost, and Peter's discourse to the people in consequence of it, chap. ii.
68. Peter and John heal a lame man. Peter's discourse to the people, chap. iii.
69. A great multitude converted by the preaching of Peter. The apostles are put in prison, and released, chap. iv. 1—32.
70. Unanimity of the first Christians; their charity. Hypocrisy and punishment of Ananias and Sapphira, chap. iv. 33—37, v. 1—11.
71. The apostles being imprisoned, are released by an angel. Gamaliel's counsel concerning them, chap. v. 12—42.
72. Seven persons chosen to superintend the distribution of alms, chap. vi. 1—8.
73. Stephen falsely accused. His discourse. He is condemned and stoned, chap. vi. 9—15, to viii. 1, first clause of the verse.
74. Persecution of the Christians at Jerusalem. A church planted at Samaria, chap. viii. 1, and at that time, &c. 2—25.
75. Conversion of the Ethiopian Eunuch, chap. viii. 26—40
76. Conversion, baptism, and first preaching of Saint Paul, chap. ix. 1—31.

Section
77. Peter heals Æneas, and raises Dorcas to life, chap. ix. 32. 43.
78. Peter instructed by a vision concerning the calling of the Gentiles. The conversation of Cornelius and his family, chap. x., xi. 1—18.
79. The first Gentile Church founded at Antioch, chap. xi. 19—30.
80. The apostle James put to death by Herod Agrippa. His miserable death, chap. xii.
81. The planting of several churches in the isle of Cyprus, at Perga, in Pamphilia, and Antioch, in Pisidia, chap. xiii.
82. The gospel preached at Iconium, Lystra, and Derbe. Paul returns to Antioch, chap. xiv.
83. Discussion of the question by the apostles at Jerusalem, concerning the necessity of circumcision, and observing the law. Their letter to the churches on this subject, chap. xv. 1—35.
84. Paul's second departure from Antioch. He preaches the gospel in various countries, particularly at Philippi, in Macedonia. The conversion of the Philippian gaoler, chap. xv. 36—41, xvi.
85. The journeys and apostolical labours of Paul, and his associates, at Thessalonica, Berea, and Athens. His masterly apology before the court of the Areopagites, chap. xvii.
86. Paul's journey to Corinth, and thence to Antioch, chap. xviii. 1—22.
87. Paul's third departure from Antioch. Consequences of his preaching at Ephesus, chap. xviii. 23—28, xix.
88. The labours of Paul in Greece and Asia Minor. His journey toward Jerusalem, chap. xx.
89. On his arrival at Jerusalem Paul relates the fruits of his ministry chap. xxi.
90. The Jews demanded the death of Paul, who pleads his privilege as a Roman citizen, chap. xxii.
91. Paul pleads his cause before the council. A conspiracy is formed against his life. He is sent to Cæsarea, chap. xxiii.
92. Paul accused before Felix, pleads his own cause. Effects of his preaching upon the conscience of Felix, chap. xxiv.
93. Paul pleads his cause before Festus, the successor of Felix. His innocence admitted by the Roman Governor, chap. xxv.
94. Paul's defence before king Agrippa, chap. xxvi.
95. Narrative of Paul's Voyage from Cæsarea. He is shipwrecked on the isle of Malta, chap. xxvii.
96. His voyage from Malta to Rome, where he preaches the Gospel to the Jews, and resides for two years, chap. xxviii.

Part III.—Select Chapters taken from the Apostolic Epistles.

Section
1. The blessed consequences of our Justification by Jesus Christ, Rom. v.
2. Eulogium and Description of Charity, 1 Cor. xiii.
3. The Resurrection of Jesus Christ.—Victory over death and sin 1 Cor. xv.
4. A Future Life.—The love of Christ, 2 Cor. v.
5. Spiritual blessings in Christ Jesus, Eph. i.
6. Various Duties of the Christian Life, Eph. iv.—vi.
7. Exhortations to Christian Holiness, Phil. iv.
8. The excellence of Godliness, 1 Tim. vi.
9. The supreme Deity and Dignity of Jesus Christ, his superiority to angels, and our duty in consequence, Heb. i., ii. 1—4.
10. Exhortations to perseverance, Heb. xii.
11. Exhortations and Cautions, James v

Section

12. Exhortation to steadfastness in the faith of Christ, from a consideration of the peculiar blessings and privileges conferred by Christ, 1 Pet. i., ii. 1—10.
13. Exhortation to various civil and relative duties, 1 Pet. ii. 11—25, iii. 1—13.
14. The hope and conduct of a Christian, 2 Pet. i.
15. The second advent of Christ, 2 Pet. iii.
16. The Love of God opposed to that of the world, 1 John iii.
17. Exhortation to Brotherly Love, 1 John iv.

No. V.

LIST, comprising the most NECESSARY WORKS upon the Holy Scriptures, which the author trusts will be found sufficient for all ordinary purposes of study.

D'Allemand's Edition of the Hebrew Bible.

Rev. E. Valpy's Edition of the Greek Testament, with Notes. In 3 vols. 8vo.

Vetus Testamentum Græcum (Valpy's Edition,) 8vo.

Holy Bible, with marginal renderings and references, 8vo.

Rev. Geo. Townsend's Harmony of the Old Testament, 2 vols. 8vo.

——————Harmony of the New Testament, 2 vols. 8vo.

Introduction to the Critical Study and Knowledge of the Holy Scriptures. By the author of this volume, 4 vols. 8vo.

Professor Lee's Lectures on the Hebrew Language, 8vo.; or,

Mr. Yeates's Hebrew Grammar, 8vo.

Gibb's Hebrew and English Lexicon, 8vo; or,

Parkhurst's Hebrew and English Lexicon, 8vo.

——————Greek Lexicon to the New Testament, edited by the Rev. H. J. Rose.

Winer's Greek Grammar of the New Testament, 8vo.

Robinson's Greek and English Lexicon to the New Testament, 8vo.; or,

Wahl's Clavis Philologica Novi Testamenti

Rev. Dr. D'Oyly's and Bp. Mant's Commentary on the Bible, 3 vols, 4to.

Rev. Matthew Henry's, or Rev. Tho. Scott's Commentary on the Bible, each 6 vols. 4to., and Rev. W. Burkitt's Expository Notes, &c. on the New Testament, will be found particularly useful for practical and expository study.

Bp. Horne's Commentary on the Psalms, 2 vols. 8vo.

Rev. Messrs. Elsley's and Slade's Annotations on the New Testament, 5 vols. 8vo.

Rev. S. T. Bloomfield's Recensio Synoptica Annotationis Sacræ, &c. 7 vols. 8vo.

Rev. Dr. Doddridge's Family Expositor, 6 vols. 8vo.

Rev. Dr. Robinson's Biblical and Ecclesiastical Dictionary, 8vo.

Dr. Harris's Natural History of the Bible, 8vo.

Rev. Geo. Holden's Testimonies to the Deity of Christ, 8vo.

Rev. Dr. J. P. Smith's Scripture Testimony to the Messiah, 3 vols 8vo.
Rev. J. Butterworth's Concordance, 8vo.
Bp. Gastrell's Christian Institutes, 12mo.; or,
Mr. Warden's System of Revealed Religion, 2 vols. 8vo.
Bp. Newton's Dissertations on the Prophecies, 2 vols. 8vo.

Should more extended commentaries be required than those here specified, the reader is referred to the works of Dr. A. CLARKE, and others, which are enumerated in the Appendix to Vol II of the author's larger Introduction.

No. VI.

A CONCISE CHRONOLOGICAL TABLE OF THE PRINCIPAL EPOCHS MENTIONED IN THE OLD AND NEW TESTAMENTS.

I. OLD TESTAMENT HISTORY.

	B C.
The Creation of the World	4004
Noah born	2948
Peleg, (son of Heber.)—Division of the earth into families and languages	2247
Abraham born	1996
Call of Abraham	1921
Ishmael, son of Abraham and Hagar, born	1910
Destruction of Sodom, Gomorrah, and the cities of the plain	1898
Covenant with Abraham renewed	1898
Birth of Isaac	1871
Isaac marries Rebekah	1856
Jacob marries Leah and Rachel	1759
Joseph sold into Egypt	1728
Jacob and his family go into Egypt	1706
Death of Jacob	1689
Death of Joseph	1635
A Revolution in Egypt.—The Israelites persecuted	1577
Birth of Moses	1571
The Exodus from Egypt	1491
The Delivery of the Law	1490
The death of Moses; the entrance of the Israelites into the promised land, under Joshua	1451
The Administration of the Elders and Judges, after the death of Joshua	1443, &c.
Saul appointed and consecrated king	1095
The accession of David to the throne	1055
The reign of Solomon alone	1014
The dedication of the temple	1004
Accession of Rehoboam, and the secession of the ten tribes under Jeroboam	975

Kings of Israel for 264 Years.	B. C.	*Kings of Judah for 388 Years.*	B. C.
Jeroboam I.	975	Rehoboam	975
		Jerusalem taken by Shishak king of Egypt. The Temple plundered	975
Nadab	954	Abijah	958
Baasha	953	Asa	955
Elah	930		
Zimri conspires against Elah, and reigns seven days at Tirza			
Omri	929		
Ahab	918	Jehoshaphat	914
Ahaziah	897		
Jehoram, or Joram	896	Joram	889
Jehu	884	Ahaziah	885
		Athaliah	884
Jehoahaz	856	Amaziah	838
Joash	839		
Jeroboam II.	823	Uzziah, or Azariah	809
An interregnum of eleven years begins	784		
Zachariah son of Jeroboam	773		
Shallum reigned one month	772		
And slain by Menahem	770		
Pekahiah	760	Uzziah	
Pekah	758	Jotham	757
Anarchy for nine years	738	Ahaz	741
Hoshea	729	Hezekiah	726
End of the kingdom of Israel, after it had subsisted two hundred and fifty-four years.			

Kings of Judah alone.

	B. C.
Manasseh	697
Amon	642
Josiah	640
Jehoaz, son of Josiah	609
Jehoiakim	608
Jeconiah, Coniah, or Jehoiakim, son of Jehoiakim	599
Zedekiah, uncle of Jeconiah, originally named Mattaniah	597
Zedekiah revolts against the Chaldæans	590
The siege of Jerusalem by Nebuchadnezzar.—Zedekiah's Flight. He is deprived of sight.—Jerusalem taken, and the temple burnt	588

Beginning of the seventy years' captivity.—The destruction of the kingdom of Judah, after it had subsisted four hundred and sixty-eight years from the commencement of David's reign;

	B.C
and three hundred and eighty-eight years from the separation between Judah and the ten tribes	
Daniel's three companions cast into the fiery furnace	560
Nebuchadnezzar's death	
Evil-Merodach succeeds him; reigns but one year	
Belshazzar his son succeeds him	559
Cyrus liberates the Persians, and takes the title of king	558
Belshazzar's impious feast; his death	556
Darius the Mede succeeds Belshazzar	
Daniel's prophecy of the seventy weeks. (Dan. ix., x.)	555
Daniel cast into the lion's den	552
Cyrus sets the Jews at liberty, and permits their return into Judæa	547
The Jews, returning from captivity, renew the sacrifices in the temple	546
Darius, otherwise Ahasuerus, acknowledged king of the Persians	521
Haggai the prophet	520
Zechariah begins to prophesy	519
Darius allows the Jews to rebuild their temple	518
Here, properly, end the seventy years of captivity foretold by Jeremiah, which began A. M. 3416	
The dedication of the temple of Jerusalem, rebuilt by Zerubbabel	515
Haman vows the destruction of the Jews, and procures from Ahasuerus an order for their extermination	508
Esther obtains a revocation of this decree	
Haman hung on the gallows he had prepared for Mordecai	
The Jews punish their enemies at Shushan, and throughout the Persian empire	508
Xerxes succeed Darius	485
Xerxes dies; Artaxerxes succeeds him	473
He sends Ezra to Jerusalem. (Ezra vii. 1. 7, 8.)	467
Ezra reforms abuses among the Jews	466
Dedication of the walls of Jerusalem by Nehemiah	454
Nehemiah renews the covenant of Israel with the Lord	453
Nehemiah returns to king Artaxerxes	441
Nehemiah comes a second time into Judæa, and reforms abuses	439
Zechariah prophesies under his government; also Malachi, whom several have confounded with Ezra.	

II. New Testament History.

From the Birth of Jesus Christ, to the Completion of the Canon of the New Testament.

	Y. of J. C.
The birth of our Lord and Saviour Jesus Christ, the 4th year before A. D.	1
The circumcision of Jesus Christ	1
Wise men come to worship Jesus Christ	

Event	Y. of J.C.
Purification of the holy virgin.—Jesus presented in the temple	
Flight into Egypt	
Massacre of the innocents at Bethlehem	
Herod dies	
Archelaus appointed king of Judæa by his will	
Return of Jesus Christ out of Egypt; he goes to dwell at Nazareth	
Archelaus banished to Vienna in Gaul	9
Jesus Christ, at twelve years of age, goes into the temple of Jerusalem	12
John the Baptist begins to preach	32
Jesus Christ baptized by John the Baptist	33
Jesus goes into the desert	
The second passover of our Saviour's public ministry	34
Our Saviour's sermon on the mount	
Mission of the apostles into several parts of Judæa	35
John the Baptist slain by order of Herod, at the instigation of Herodias	
Lazarus falls sick and dies	36
Jesus comes to Jerusalem to be present at his THIRD and LAST passover;—	
Institutes the Lord's supper; is betrayed and crucified.—His resurrection and appearance to many.—Ascension into Heaven, and the miraculous effusion of the Holy Spirit	
Seven deacons chosen	37
Stephen martyred	37
Saul persecutes the church	37
Conversion of Saul	38
Paul a prisoner at Rome	64
Paul set at liberty	66
Paul's second imprisonment at Rome	68
Paul and Peter put to death there	69
The Emperor Vespasian enters Judæa	70
Jerusalem taken by Titus, and the Temple burnt	73
John banished to Patmos	95
John liberated	99
John writes his Gospel and Revelation	100

No. VII.

A TABLE OF THE PRINCIPAL PROPHECIES RELATIVE TO THE

MESSIAH,

WITH THEIR ACCOMPLISHMENT, AS RELATED IN THE NEW TESTAMENT.

1. *That* A MESSIAH *should come.*

Prophecy. Gen. iii. 15. *He* (the seed of the woman) shall *bruise* thy head, and thou shalt *bruise* his heel. Compare Gen. xxii. 18, xii. 3, xxvi. 4, xxviii. 4, and Psal. lxxii. 17. Isa. xl. 5. The glory of the Lord shall be revealed, and all flesh shall see it together. Hagg. ii. 7. The desire of *all* nations shall come.

Fulfilment. Gal. iv. 4. When the fulness of time was come, God sent forth his son, made of a *woman*, (four thousand years after the first prophecy was delivered.) Rom. xvi. 20. The God of peace shall *bruise* Satan under your feet shortly. 1 John iii. 8. The Son of God was manifested that he might destroy the works of the *Devil*, (that old *serpent*, Rev. xii. 9.) See also Heb. ii. 14. Luke ii. 10. I bring you good tidings of great joy, which shall be to *all* people.

2. *The* TIME *when he should come.*

Prophecy. Gen. xlix. 10. The sceptre *shall not* depart from Judah, nor a lawgiver from between his feet, *until* Shiloh come. The Messiah was to come at a time of universal peace, and when there was a general expectation of him; and while the second temple was standing seventy weeks (of years, i. e. 490 years) after the rebuilding of Jerusalem. See Hagg. ii. 6—9; Dan ix. 23—25; Mal. iii. 1.

Fulfilment. When the Messiah came, the sceptre *had departed* from Judah; for the Jews, though governed by their own rulers and magistrates, yet were subject to the paramount authority of the Roman emperors; as was evinced by their being subject to the enrolment of Augustus, paying tribute to Cæsar, and not having the power of life and death. Compare Luke ii. 1. 3—5; Matt. xxii. 20, 21; and the parallel passages; and John xx. 10. 15. When Jesus Christ came into the world, the Roman wars were terminated, the temple of Janus was shut, and universal peace reigned throughout the Roman empire; and all nations, both Jews and Gentiles, were expecting the coming of some extraordinary person. See Matt. ii. 1—10; Mark xv. 43; Luke ii. 25. 38; and John i. 19—45. for the expectation of the Jews. The two Roman historians, Suetonius and Tacitus, confirm the fulfilment of the prediction, as to the expectation of the Gentiles.

3. *The* DIGNITY OF HIS CHARACTER,—*that the Messiah should be God and Man together.*

Prophecy. Psal. ii. 7. Thou art my *Son*, this day have I begotten thee. Psal. cx. 1. The Lord said unto my Lord. Isa. ix. 6. The mighty *God*, the everlasting Father. Mic. 5. 2. Whose goings forth have been from of old, from everlasting.

Fulfilment. Heb. i. 8. Unto the *Son*, he saith, "Thy throne, O God, is for ever and ever." Compare Matt. xxii. 42—55; Acts ii. 34, 35; Cor. xv. 24; Heb. i. 13. Matt. i. 23. They shall call his name Emmanuel, that is, *God* with us. John i. 1. 14. The *Word* was with God, and the *Word* was *God*. The *Word* was made flesh and dwelt among us Rom. ix. 5.

Of whom (the fathers) as concerning the flesh Christ came, who is *God* over all, blessed for ever. See also Col. ii. 9; 1 John v. 20.

4. *From* WHOM *he was to be descended.*

Prophecy. From the first woman. Gen. iii. 15. From *Abraham* and his descendants, Gen. xii. 3, xviii. 18; viz.: *Isaac*, Gen. xxvi. 4; *Jacob*, Gen. xxviii. 14; *Judah*, Gen. xlix. 10; *Jesse*, Isa. xi. 1; *David*, Psal. cxxxii. 11, lxxxix. 4, 27; Isa. vi. 13, 14, ix. 7; Jer. xxiii. 5, and xxxiii. 20, 21.

Fulfilment. Gal. iv. 4. When the fulness of time was come, God sent forth his son, made of a woman.

Acts iii. 25. The covenant which God made with our fathers, saying unto *Abraham*, "And in thy seed shall all the nations of the earth be blessed." See Matt. i. 1. Heb. vii. 14. It is evident that our Lord sprang out of *Judah*. Rom. xv. 12, Isaiah saith there shall be a root of *Jesse*. John vii. 42, Hath not the Scripture said, that Christ cometh of the seed of *David*. See also Acts ii. 30, xiii. 23; Luke i. 32.

5. *That the Messiah should be born of a* VIRGIN.

Prophecy. Isa. vii. 14. Behold a *Virgin* shall conceive and bring forth a *Son*.

Jer. xxxi. 22. The Lord hath created a new thing on the earth; a woman shall compass a man. (N. B. *The ancient Jews applied this prophecy* to the Messiah, whence it follows, *that the later interpretations* to the contrary *are only to avoid the truth which we profess*; viz.: *That Jesus was born of a virgin, and therefore is* THE CHRIST, or Messiah. Bp. Pearson on the Creed, Art. III. p. 171. edit. 1715. folio.)

Fulfilment. Matt. i. 24, 25. Joseph took his wife and knew her not, till she had brought forth her first born son. Compare Luke i. 26—35. Matt. i. 22, 23. All this was done, that it might be fulfilled, which was spoken of the Lord by the prophet, saying, 'Behold a *virgin* shall be with child, and shall bring forth a son.'

6. *The* PLACE *where the Messiah was to be born.*

Prophecy. Mic. v. 2. Thou *Bethlehem* Ephratah, though thou be little among the thousands of Judah; yet out of thee shall he come forth unto me that is to be ruler in Israel.

Fulfilment. Luke ii. 4—6. All went to be taxed (or enrolled,) every one into his own city. And Joseph also went up from Galilee, with Mary his espoused wife, unto *Bethlehem*; and, while they were there *she brought forth her first born son.* Compare also Luke ii. 10, 11. 16, and Matt. ii. 1. 4—6. 8.11; John vii. 42.

7. *That a* PROPHET, *in the spirit and power of Elias, or Elijah, should be the Messiah's forerunner and prepare his way.*

Prophecy. Malachi iii. 1, and iv. 5; Isa. xl. 3; Luke i. 17. Behold I will send my messenger, and he shall prepare my way before me.

Fulfilment. Matt. iii. 1. In those days came *John the Baptist* preaching in the wilderness of Judæa, saying, Repent ye, the kingdom of heaven is at hand. Matt. xi. 14; Luke vii. 27, 28. This is Elias which was for to come.

8. *That he should begin to publish the Gospel in* GALILEE.

Prophecy. Isa. ix. 1, 2. In *Galilee* of the nations, the people that walked in darkness have seen a great light.

Fulfilment. Matt. iv. 12. 17. Now when Jesus heard that John was cast into prison, he departed into *Galilee.* From that time Jesus began to preach and to say, Repent, for the kingdom of heaven is at hand.

9. *That the Messiah was to be a* PROPHET *and* LEGISLATOR *like unto Moses, but superior to him, who should change the law of Moses into a new and more perfect law, common both to Jews and Gentiles, and which should last for ever.*

The law of Moses was promulgated to the Jewish people exclusively, and was full of burdensome ceremonies; the sacrifices enjoined by it were to be performed only at Jerusalem, and it was delivered by a man to man. But,

Prophecy. 1. The Messiah is foretold to be a *prophet like unto Moses.* Deut. 15. 18. "The Lord thy God will raise up unto thee a prophet from the midst of thee, of thy brethren, like unto me. Unto him shall ye hearken." For Moses differs from all the other Old Testament prophets in this, that he was truly a legislator, the friend of God, Exod. xxxiii. 11, and was distinguished by the multitude of his miracles, Deut. xxxiv. 11.

2. The Messiah was to *enact a new law*, Isa. iv. 3. Out of Zion shall go forth the law, and the word of the law from Jerusalem.

3. This law was to be *common to all nations ;* see Isa. ii. 2, 3, and li. 4, 5.

4. The new law, or covenant of the Messiah, was to endure for ever; see Isa. lix. 21; Jer. xxxi. 34; Ezek. xxxvi. 27, xxxvii. 26; Isa. lv. 3, lxi. 8; Jer. xxxii. 40; Ezek. xxxiv. 25; Dan. vii. 13, 14; Isa. xliii. 6, lxii. 2.

Fulfilment. Christ is a prophet infinitely superior to Moses:

1. *As to his person.* Heb. iii. 5, 6. Moses, verily, was faithful in all his house, as a *servant*, for a testimony of those things which were to be spoken after; but Christ as a *Son* over his own house, whose house are we.

2. *As to his law.* Heb. vii. 18, 19. There is a disannulling of the commandment going before, for the weakness and unprofitableness thereof; for the law made nothing perfect, but the bringing in of a *better hope* (i.e. of a new law,) did, by the which we draw nigh to God.

The law of Moses belonged to one nation only, but the Gospel, which is the law of Christ, is designed *for all nations.* Compare Nos. 3 and 4 of the preceding predictions, with Matt. xxviii. 19, 20; Mark xvi. 20; and Col. i. 23.

3. *As to the benefits he has conferred.* Moses delivered the Israelites from their cruel bondage in Egypt; he was the mediator of the covenant between God and his people; he conducted them through the desert into Canaan, and interceded with God for them; but all these were only temporal benefits. On the other hand, Christ *saves* ALL that truly believe in him, and unfeignedly repent, *from* the guilt, the power, and the punishment of *their sins*, Matt. i. 23. He hath obtained a more excellent ministry, by how much also he is the mediator of a better covenant, which was established upon better promises, Heb. viii. 6. See also Heb. vii. 22, ix. 15, xii. 24; 2 Cor. iii. 6. Christ has reconciled the world unto God, 2 Cor. v. 19; 1 John ii. 2; and has given us an example that we should follow his steps, 1 Pet. ii. 21—23. As our forerunner, he hath entered into heaven, that where he is, there his followers may be also, Heb. vi. 20, ix. 24; John xiv. 2, 3; and as an *advocate* he ever liveth to make intercession for all that come unto God by him, 1 John ii. 1; Heb. vii. 25.

4. *As to the circumstances of his death.* Moses died, in one sense, for the iniquities of his people. Their rebellion, which was the occasion of it, drew down the divine displeasure upon them, and upon him. See Deut. i. 37. Moses, therefore, went up, in the sight of the people, to the top of Mount Nebo, and there he died, when he was in perfect rigour. Christ suffered for the sins of mankind, and was led up in the presence of the people to Calvary, where he died in the flower of his age.

"Let us search all the records of universal history, and see if we can find a man who was so like to Moses as Christ was. If we cannot find such a one, then we have found HIM, of whom Moses in the law and the prophets did write, to be Jesus of Nazareth, THE SON OF GOD."

10. *That the Messiah should confirm his doctrine by great* MIRACLES.

Prophecy. Isa. xxxv. 5, 6. Then the *eyes* of the *blind* shall be *opened*, and the *ears* of the *deaf* shall be *unstopped;* then shall the *lame* man *leap* as a hart, and the *tongue* of the *dumb* sing.

Fulfilment. Matt. xi. 4, 5. Jesus . . . said, "Go and show John those things which ye do hear and see: the *blind* receive their *sight*, and the *lame walk;* the lepers are cleansed, and the *deaf hear*."

11. *In what manner the Messiah was to make his public entry into* JERUSALEM.

Prophecy. Zech. ix. 9. Rejoice greatly, O daughter of Jerusalem, behold thy King cometh unto thee; he is just, and having salvation, lowly, and riding upon an ass, even upon a colt, the foal of an ass.

Fulfilment. Matt. xxi. 7—10. The disciples, brought the ass and the colt, and put on them their clothes, and set him (Jesus) thereon, (that is, *upon the clothes.*) And great multitudes spread their garments, &c. &c. Matt. xxi. 4, 5. *All this was done*, that it might be fulfilled which was spoken by the prophet, saying, Tell ye the daughter of Zion, "Behold thy King cometh," &c. &c.

12. *The* CIRCUMSTANCES *of his* SUFFERINGS *and* DEATH.

1. *That the Messiah should be poor and despised, and be betrayed by one of his own disciples, for thirty pieces of silver;* (at that time the ordinary price of the vilest slave;) *with which the potter's field should be purchased.*

Prophecy. Isa. liii. 3. There is no beauty that we should desire him. He is despised and rejected of men, a man of sorrows, and acquainted with grief; and we hid as it were our faces from him; he was despised, and we esteemed him not. Ps. xli. 9, and Ps. lv. 12—14. Yea, mine own familiar friend in whom I trusted, who did eat of my bread, hath lift up his heel against me. Zech. xi. 12. So they weighed for my price *thirty pieces of silver*. Zech. xi. 13. And the Lord said unto me, Cast it unto the potter: a goodly price that I was prized at of them! And I took the thirty pieces of silver, and cast them to the potter in the house of the Lord.

Fulfilment. Luke ix. 58. The Son of Man hath not where to lay his head. 2 Cor. viii. 9. For your sakes he became poor. John xi. 35. JESUS WEPT. Luke xxii. 3, 4. Then Satan entered into Judas, being one of the twelve, and he went his way, and communed with the chief priests how he might betray him unto them. Matt. xxvi. 14. And Judas went unto the chief priests, and said unto them, What will ye give me, and I will deliver him unto you? and they covenanted with him for *thirty pieces of silver*. Matt. xxvii. 3—8. Then Judas, who had betrayed him, brought again the thirty pieces of silver, saying, I have sinned in that I have betrayed innocent blood; and he cast down the pieces of silver in the temple, and departed, and went and hanged himself. And the chief priests took the silver, and they said, it is not lawful to put it into the treasury, because it is the price of blood. And they took counsel, and bought with them the *potter's field*, to bury strangers in.

2. *That the Messiah should* SUFFER *pain and death for the sins of the World.*

Prophecy. Psal. xxii. 16, 17. For dogs, (that is, the *Heathens*, whom the Jews called dogs,) have compassed me; the assembly of the wicked have inclosed me; they have pierced my hands and my feet. I may tell all my bones; they look and stare upon me. Isa. l. 6. I gave my *back* to the *smiters*, and my cheeks to them that plucked off the hair. I hid not my face from *shame* and spitting. Isa. liii. 5. 8. He was wounded for our transgressions: he was bruised for our iniquities: by his stripes we are healed. He was cut off out of the land of the living: for the transgression of my people was he striken. Isa. liii. 12. And he *bare* the sin of *many*, and made *intercession* for the transgressors.

Fulfilment. John xix. 1, 2. Then Pilate took Jesus, and *scourged* him. And the soldiers platted a crown of thorns, and they *smote* him with the palms of their hands. Matt. xxvii. 30; Mark xv. 19. And they did *spit* upon him, and *smote* him on the head, Mark xv. 25. And they crucified him. 1 Pet. ii. 23, 24. Who, when he was reviled, reviled not again; when he suffered, he threatened not. Who bare *our* sins in his own body on the *tree*, (the cross.) Luke xxiii. 34. *Then*, said Jesus, "*Father, forgive them, for they know not what they do.*"

3. *That the Messiah should be cruelly* MOCKED *and* DERIDED.

Prophecy. Psal. xxii. 12, 13. 7, 8. Many bulls have compassed me; strong bulls of Bashan, (that is, the wicked and furious Jews, who, like the beasts fattened on the fertile plains of Bashan, "waxed fat and kicked," became proud and rebellious,) have beset me round. They gaped upon me with their mouth; as a ravening and roaring lion. All they that see me, laugh me to scorn; they shoot out the lip, saying, *he trusted in God that he would deliver him: let him deliver him*, seeing he delighted in him.

Fulfilment. Matt. xxvii. 39. 41, 42; Mark xv. 31, 32; Luke xxiii. 35, 36. And they that passed by, reviled him, wagging their heads. Likewise also the chief priests, and the rulers also with them, derided, *and* mocking, said among themselves, with the scribes and elders, "He saved others; himself he cannot save; if he be the Christ, the chosen of God, let him now come down from the cross, and save himself, that we may see, and we will believe him. *He trusted in God, let him deliver him* now, if he will have him." And the soldiers also mocked him, saying, "If thou be the King of the Jews, save thyself."

4. *That vinegar and gall should be offered to the Messiah upon the cross, and that his garments should be divided, and lots cast for his vesture.*

Prophecy. Psal. lxix. 21. They gave me also gall for my meat, and in my thirst they gave me vinegar to drink. Psal. xxii. 18. They part my garments among them, and cast lots upon my vesture.

Fulfilment. John xix. 29. Matt. xxvii. 48; Mark xv. 36. And they filled a sponge with vinegar, and put it upon hyssop, and put it to his mouth, John xix. 23, 24. And the soldiers, when they had crucified Jesus, took his garments, and made four parts, to every soldier a part: and also his coat: now the coat was without seam. They said, therefore, let us not rend it, but cast lots, whose it shall be.

5. *That not a* BONE *of the Messiah should be* BROKEN.

Prophecy. Psal. xxxiv. 20. He keepeth all his bones: not one of them is broken. Zech. xii. 10. And they shall look upon me whom they have *pierced.*

Fulfilment. John xix. 32—34. Then came the soldiers, and brake the legs of the first, and of the other which was crucified with him; but when they came to Jesus, and saw that he was dead already, they brake not his legs. But one of the soldiers, with a spear, pierced his side, and forthwith there came out blood and water.

6. *That the Messiah should* DIE *with malefactors, but be buried honourably.*

Prophecy. Isa. liii. 9. And he made his grave with the wicked, and with the rich in his death.

Fulfilment. Matt. xxvii. 38. 57—60. Then were there two thieves crucified with him. There came a rich man of Arimathea, named Joseph, and begged the body of Jesus; and he wrapped it in a clean linen cloth, and laid it in his own new tomb.

13. *That the Messiah should* RISE FROM THE DEAD *and* ASCEND INTO HEAVEN.

Prophecy. Psal. xvi. 9, 10. My flesh also shall rest in hope. For thou wilt not leave my soul in *hell*, (the separate state of departed spirits,) neither wilt thou suffer thy holy one to see corruption. Isa. liii. 10. When thou shalt make his soul an offering for sin, he shall prolong his days. Jesus Christ also foretold his own resurrection; see Mark viii. 31, x. 34; Luke ix. 22: John ii. 19. 21, x. 17. Psal. lxviii. 18. Thou hast *as-*

cended up on high; thou hast led captivity captive; thou hast received gifts for men, that the Lord God might dwell among them.

Fulfilment. Acts ii. 31. David spake before of the resurrection of Christ, that his soul was not left in *hell;* (Hades, or the separate state;) neither did his flesh see corruption. See also Acts xiii. 35. Matt. xxviii. 5, 6. The angels said unto the Woman, "He is not here, for he is *risen*, as he said." See Luke xxiv. 5, 6. 1 Cor. xv. 4. He rose again the third day, according to Scriptures: Acts i. 3. He showed himself alive after his passion, by many infallible proofs. Mark xvi. 19; Luke xxiv. 51; Acts i. 9. So then, after the Lord had spoken to them, while he was blessing them, and while they beheld him, he was parted from them, and *carried up* into heaven, and sat at the right hand of God. Compare also 1 Pet. iii. 22; 1 Tim. iii. 16; Heb. vi. 20.

14. *That the Messiah should send the* Holy Spirit, *the Comforter.*

Prophecy. Joel ii. 28. I will pour out my Spirit upon all flesh; and your sons and your daughters shall prophesy. Jesus Christ promised, and foretold the gift of the Holy Spirit, in John vii. 38, 39, xiv. 16, 17. 26, xv. 26, xvi. 7. 13; Acts i. 4, 5. 8.

Fulfilment. See all these promises and predictions fulfilled in Acts ii. 1—4, iv. 31, viii. 17, x. 44, xi. 15.

15. *The* Abolition of the Jewish covenant *by the introduction of the Gospel.*

Prophecy. Behold the days come, saith the Lord, that I will make a new covenant with the house of Israel, and with the house of Judah: not according to the covenant that I made with their fathers, in the *day* that I took them by the hand to bring them out of Egypt; which my covenant they brake, though I was a husband to them, saith the Lord. But this shall be the covenant, that I will make with the house of Israel: After those days, saith the Lord, I will put my law in their inward parts, and write it in their hearts, and will be their God, and they shall be my people. And they shall teach no more every man his neighbour, and every man his brother, saying, "Know the Lord:" for they shall all know me, from the least of them unto the greatest of them, saith the Lord: for I will forgive their iniquity, and I will remember their sin no more. The *Fulfilment* of this prediction is shown at length by St. Paul, in the eighth chapter of the Epistle to the Hebrews, verses 7—13.

The old covenant is abolished, and its observance rendered impossible by the expulsion of the Jews from Judæa and Jerusalem, and by the utter destruction of that temple and altar, on which the whole of the Jewish Worship depended. It is, therefore, as impossible to doubt that the Mediator of the new covenant *is* come, as to question those external facts which prove that the ancient covenant subsists no longer.

16. *That there is salvation* only *through Christ.*

Prophecy. Zech. xiii. 1. In that day there shall be a fountain opened to the house of David, and to the inhabitants of Jerusalem, for sin, and for uncleanness. Mal. iv. 2. Unto you that fear my name, shall the Sun of Righteousness arise, with healing in his wings, Isa. liii. 11. By his knowledge shall my righteous Servant justify many. Isa. lix. 20. The Redeemer shall come to Sion, and unto them that turn from transgression in Jacob. See Rom. ix. 26. Ps. cxviii. 22. The stone which the builders refused, the same is become the head-stone of the corner, Isa. xxviii. 16; Mark xii. 10.

Fulfilment. John iii. 16. God so loved the world, that he gave his only begotten Son, that whosoever believeth in him, should not perish but have everlasting life. Compare also 1 Thes. v. 9; John xvii. 3. Luke xxiv. 47. That repentance and remission of sins should be preached in his name. See also Acts x. 43, Acts xiii. 38, 39. Through this man is preached unto you the forgiveness of sins; and by him all that believe are justified. Acts iv. 11, 12. This is the stone which was set at naught of you builders, which is become the head of the corner. Neither is there salvation in any other: for there is none other name under Heaven given among men, whereby we must be saved.

17. *Of the necessity of believing in Christ, and the danger of rejecting him.*

Deut. xviii. 15.19. The Lord will raise up unto thee a prophet, unto him shall ye hearken. whosoever will not hearken unto my words, which he shall speak in my name, I will require it of him. [In Acts iii. 20, this prediction is cited and applied to Jesus Christ.] Numb. xv. 30, 31. The soul that doth aught presumptuously, reproacheth the Lord; and that soul shall be cut off from among his people, because he hath despised the word of the Lord. Ps. ii. 12. Kiss the son, lest he be angry, and ye perish from the right way.

John iii. 18. He that believeth on him is not condemned; but he that believeth not is condemned already, because he hath not believed in the name of the only Son of God. Heb. ii. 3. How shall we escape if we neglect so great salvation. Heb. x. 26. 29. If we sin wilfully, after that we have received the knowledge of the truth, there remaineth no more sacrifice for sins, but a certain fearful looking for of judgment and fiery indignation, which shall devour the adversaries. He that despised Moses' law died without mercy, under two or three witnesses; of how much sorer punishment shall he be thought worthy, who hath trodden under foot the Son of God, and hath counted the blood of the covenant, wherewith he was sanctified, an unholy thing, and hath done despite unto the Spirit of grace. *The Lord shall be revealed from Heaven, with his mighty angels, in flaming fire, taking vengeance on them that know not God, and that obey not the gospel of our Lord Christ,* 2 Thess. i. 7, 8.

"The testimony of Jesus is the spirit of prophecy," Rev. xix. 10: and of that testimony, it were easy to have offered hundreds of instances, equally striking with those above given. Copious as the preceding table of prophecies is, the selection has necessarily been restricted to *the principal,* in order that this article might not be extended to an undue length. A more copious table is given in the appendix to the first volume of the author's Introduction to the Critical Study and Knowledge of the Holy Scriptures. To conclude, it is worthy of remark, that most of the prophecies concerning the Messiah were revealed nearly, and some of them more than three thousand years ago, and yet scarcely one of them can be applied to any man that ever lived upon earth, except to him, who is Immanuel, God with us, the Lord Jesus Christ, to whom "give all the prophets witness," Acts x. 43. The more we contemplate these astonishing FACTS, the more deeply we investigate the wonderful display of Divine power, wisdom, and goodness, the more we shall be disposed to exclaim, with the amazed centurion, "*Truly this was* THE SON OF GOD."

A CONCISE

GEOGRAPHICAL INDEX

OF THE

PRINCIPAL PLACES MENTIONED IN THE SCRIPTURES, ESPECIALLY IN THE NEW TESTAMENT

ABANA and PHARPAR, two rivers of Damascus, mentioned in 2 Kings v. 12. The valley of Damascus, which lay between Libanus and Anti-Libanus, was watered by five rivers, of which these were the two principal. Both descended from Mount Hermon: the latter flowed by the walls of Damascus; the former flowed through the city and divided it into two parts. These rivers are not now to be distinguished.

ABARIM, mountains of. See pp. 177, 178.

ABEL, *Abel-beth-Maacha*, or *Abel-main*, a city in the northern part of the canton allotted to the tribe of Naphtali. (2 Sam. xx. 14—22. 1 Kings xv. 20. 2 Kings xv. 29.)

ABEL-MEHOLAH was the native country of Elisha. (1 Kings xix. 16.) Not far from hence, Gideon obtained a victory over the Midianites. (Judg. vii. 22.)

ABEL-SHITTIM was a town in the plains of Moab, beyond Jordan, opposite Jericho. Here the Israelites fell into idolatry, and worshipped Baal-Peor, seduced by Balak; and here God severely punished them by the hands of the Levites. (Numb. xxv. 1, &c.)

ABILENE. See p. 164, *supra*.

ACCHO. See PTOLEMAIS.

ACELDAMA, (or the Field of Blood,) the name given to a field purchased with the money for which Judas had betrayed Jesus. It was appropriated as a place of burial for strangers (Acts i. 19. Matt. xxvii. 7, 8.)

ACHAIA, in a *wider* sense, comprised Peloponnesus and the whole of Greece, properly so called. (2 Cor. xi. 10.) In a *stricter* sense, Achaia is the northern region of Peloponnesus, of which Corinth was the capital.

ACHMETHA. See ECBATANA.

ACHOR, a valley in the territory of Jericho, and in the canton of the tribe of Benjamin, where Achan was stoned. (Josh. vii. 24.)

ACKSHAPH, a city belonging to the tribe of Asher. The king of Ackshaph was conquered by Joshua, (xii. 20.)

ADMAH, or ADAMA, one of the five cities destroyed by fire from heaven, and afterwards overwhelmed by the waters of the Dead Sea. (Gen. xix. 21.)

ADRAMYTTIUM, a maritime town of Mysia, in Asia Minor, for which Paul embarked in his first voyage to Italy. (Acts xxvii. 12.)

ADRIA, mentioned in Acts xxvii. 27, is the Adriatic Sea, now called the Gulf of Venice.

ÆNON, or ENON, signifies the place of springs, where John baptized. (John iii. 23.) It is uncertain where it was situated, whether in Galilee or Judæa.

AHAVA, a river of Babylonia, or of Assyria, where Ezra assembled those captives whom he afterwards brought into Judæa. (Ezra viii. 15.)

AJALON, a city in the canton of the tribe of Dan, assigned to the Levites of Kohath's family. It was situated between Timnath and Beth-Shemesh, and is probably the city alluded to in Josh. x. 12.

ALEXANDRIA, a city of Egypt, built by Alexander the Great, celebrated for the magnificence of its edifices, and for the extensive commerce carried on by its inhabitants, especially in corn. Alexandria was the native place of Apollos. (Acts xviii. 24.)

Amphipolis, a city between Macedon and Thrace, but dependant on Macedon, mentioned in Acts xvii. 1.

Anathoth, a city in the tribe of Benjamin, memorable as being the birthplace of the prophet Jeremiah. (Josh. xxi. 18. Jer. 1. 1.)

Antioch, the metropolis of Syria, was erected, according to some writers, by Antiochus Epiphanes, according to others, by Seleucus Nicanor, the first king of Syria after Alexander the Great, in memory of his father Antiochus, and was the royal seat of the kings of Syria. For power and dignity it was little inferior to Seleucia or Alexandria. The distinctive name of Christians was here first applied to the followers of Jesus Christ. (Acts xi. 19. 26.)

Antioch of Pisidia, a city of Phrygia, but thus denominated because it was attached to the province of Pisidia. (Acts xiii. 14.)

Antipatris, a small town which was situated in the road from Jerusalem to Cæsarea. It was formerly called Capharsalma; but, being rebuilt and beautified by Herod the Great, it was by him named Antipatris in honour of his father Antipater. Hither St. Paul was brought after his apprehension at Jerusalem. (Acts xxiii. 31.)

Apollonia, a city of Macedonia Prima, through which Paul passed, in his way to Thessalonica. (Acts xvii. 1.)

Arabia, the name of a large region, including the peninsula which lies between Syria, Palestine, the Arabian and Persian Gulfs, and the Indian Ocean or Sea of Arabia. Its inhabitants are supposed to be principally descended from Ishmael. It is distinguished into three parts, Arabia *Felix*, *Petræa*, and *Deserta*; but these divisions were not anciently known to the inhabitants of the East, nor are they observed in the Bible.

1. Arabia Felix lies between the ocean on the south-east, and the Arabian and Persian Gulfs. It is a fertile region, especially in the interior, producing various species of odoriferous shrubs and fragrant gums; as, frankincense, myrrh, cassia, &c. The Queen of Sheba (1 Kings x. 1,) is supposed to have reigned over part of this region.

2. Arabia Petræa received its name from the city Petra, and lies on the south and south-east of Palestine; extending to Egypt, and including the peninsula of mount Sinai. It is remarkable for its mountains and sandy plains.

3. Arabia Deserta lies between the other two, and extends northward along the confines of Palestine, Syria, Babylonia, and Mesopotamia; including the vast deserts which lie within these limits, and which are inhabited only by wandering tribes of savage Arabs.

Aram, fifth son of Shem, was father of the people of Syria, who, from him, are called Aramæans. The region which in the Old Testament is denominated Aram, is a vast tract, extending from Mount Taurus south as far as Damascus, and from the Mediterranean Sea in an eastern direction beyond the Tigris into Assyria. Different parts of this region are called by different names; as, *Aram Naharaim*, or Syria of the Two Rivers, that is *Mesopotamia; Aram of Damascus; Aram of Soba; Aram Bethrehob;* and *Aram of Maacha;* because the cities of Damascus, Soba, Bethrehob, and Maacha, were in Syria; or at least, because Syria contained the provinces of Soba, Maacha, Rehob, &c.

Ararat, a celebrated mountain in the Greater Armenia; on which Noah's ark rested after the deluge. (Gen. viii. 4.)

Arimathea, a small town to which Joseph belonged, who begged the body of Jesus from Pilate: (Matt. xxvii. 57:) it was about thirty-six or thirty-seven miles distant from Jerusalem.

Arnon (River.) See p. 173, *supra*.

Ashdod. See Azotus, p. 377, *infra*.

Asia, one of the largest divisions of the old world, is not mentioned in the Old Testament. In the New Testament it is always taken for Asia Minor, as it includes the proconsular Asia, which comprised the four regions of Phrygia, Mysia, Caria, and Lydia. In this proconsular Asia were the seven churches of Ephesus, Laodicæa, Pergamos, Philadelphia, Sardis, Smyrna, and Thyatira.

Assos, a maritime city of Mysia, according to some geographers, but of Troas, according to others. It is mentioned in Acts xx. 13, 14.

Assyria, a country of Asia, the boundaries of which it is difficult to assign. Three of its monarchs are particularly mentioned in the Old Testament, viz. Tiglath-pileser, Shalmaneser, and Sennacherib. The former, having defeated Rezin, king of Damascus, and taken that city, put an end to the kingdom there erected by the Syrians. He also entered the kingdom of Israel, conquered Pekah, and carried away part of the ten tribes beyond the river Euphrates. Shalmaneser, the successor of Tiglath-pileser, came into Syria, A. M. 3280, B. C. 724, and desolated the country of the Moabites, agreeably to the prophecy of Isaiah, (xvi. 1,) delivered three years before. He then attacked Samaria, and completed the misfortunes of the Israelites who remained, by carrying them into captivity beyond the Euphrates. Thus terminated the kingdom of Israel, A. M. 3283, B. C. 721. (2 Kings xvii. 3, xviii. 9—11.) Hezekiah, by the special protection of God, escaped the fury of Shalmaneser, to whom, however, he became tributary, and the Assyrian returned in triumph to Nineveh. He was succeeded on the throne by his son Sennacherib, A. M. 3287, B. C. 717. He invaded the kingdom of Judah, during the reign of Hezekiah, who had refused to pay the tribute stipulated by Shalmaneser; but an angel of Jehovah slew one hundred and eighty-five thousand of his troops. (2 Kings xix. 35.) Sennacherib returned to Nineveh, where two of his sons, weary of his tyranny and savage temper, slew him while he was worshipping in the temple of Nisroch his god, and immediately fled into the mountains of Armenia. (2 Kings xix. 37. Tobit i. 21.) He was succeeded by his son Esarhaddon.

Athens, the capital of Attica, and the chief city of ancient Greece. It was distinguished by the military talents, but still more by the learning, eloquence, and politeness of its inhabitants. Saint Paul coming hither, A. D. 3?, found them plunged in idolatry, occupied in inquiring and reporting news, curious to know every thing, and divided in opinion concerning religion and happiness. (Acts xvii.) The great apostle of the Gentiles, taking opportunities here to preach Jesus Christ, was carried before the judges of the tribunal, called the Areopagus; where he gave an illustrious testimony to truth, and a remarkable instance of powerful reasoning. (See an account of the Areopagus in p. 194, *supra.*)

Attalia, a maritime city of Pamphylia, and the chief residence of the prefect. It derived its name from king Attalus, its founder. Hither St. Paul went from Perga in Pamphylia. (Acts xiv. 25.)

Azotus, or Ashdod, a city of Judæa, is situated between Gaza and Jamnia, or Jafnia, in a pleasant plain. Here the ark of Jehovah triumphed over the Philistine idol Dagon, (1 Sam. v. 2,) and Philip the Evangelist was found, after he had baptized the Ethiopian eunuch. (Acts viii. 40.) It is at present an inconsiderable place.

Babylon, the metropolis of the Chaldæan, or Babylonish Empire, was situated on the river Euphrates, and was celebrated for its extent and for the magnificence of its edifices. The most terrible denunciations were uttered against it by the Hebrew Prophets, especially Isaiah; the literal fulfilment of whose predictions has been shown by various modern travellers.

Bashan, or Batanæa. See p. 164, *supra.*

Berea, a city of Macedonia, where Paul preached the Gospel with great success. Acts xvii. 10.

Besor, Brook. See p. 173, *supra.*

Bethany, a town of Judæa, where Lazarus dwelt, and where he was raised from the dead, was fifteen furlongs east from Jerusalem, on the way to Jericho. (John xi. 8.) But the tract of ground which bore that name reached within eight furlongs of Jerusalem, it being only a sabbath-day's journey from it; (Luke xxiv. 50 Acts i. 12;) and then began the tract called

Bethphage, from the *φαγη*, that is, the green figs, that grew upon it which ran along so near to Jerusalem, that the utmost street within the walls was called by that name.

Bethlehem was a celebrated city about six miles south-west from Jerusalem. In Matt. ii. 1. 5. it is called Bethlehem of Judæa, to distinguish it from another town of the same name situated in Lower Galilee, and mentioned in Josh. xix. 15. In Luke ii. 4, it is called the *city of David*, because David was born and educated there. (Compare John vii. 42, and 1 Sam. xvi. 1. 18.) This city, though not considerable for its extent or riches, is of great dignity as the appointed birth-place of the Messiah. (Matt. ii. 6. Luke ii. 6—15.)

Bethsaida was the name of two towns or villages.

1. Bethsaida of Galilee was situated in Galilee, on the western shore of the lake of Gennesareth, a little south of Capernaum. It was the birth-place of the Apostles Philip, Andrew, and Peter.

2. The other Bethsaida lay in Gaulonitis, on the eastern side of the lake, and near the place where the Jordan enters it. This town was enlarged by Philip, tetrarch of that region, who called it Julias, in honour of Julia, the daughter of Augustus.

Bithynia, a region of Asia Minor, bounded on the north by the Euxine Sea, on the south by Phrygia, on the west by the Propontis, and on the east by Galatia. Saint Peter addressed his first epistle (among others) to the Hebrew Christians who were scattered throughout Bithynia. (1 Pet. i. 1.)

———

Cæsarea of Palestine, so called as being the metropolis of Palestine and the residence of the Roman proconsul, was formerly named the tower of Strato; but its harbour being extremely incommodious, Herod the Great erected a spacious mole, and greatly enlarged and beautified the city, which he denominated Cæsarea, in honour of the emperor Augustus. It is very frequently mentioned in the New Testament; and was about thirty-five miles from Jerusalem.

Cæsarea Philippi (formerly called Paneas) was situated at the foot of mount Paneas, near the springs of the Jordan. It was at first called Lais or Lechem, (Judg. xviii. 7,) and after it was subdued by the Danites (v. 29,) it received the appellation of Dan. Cæsarea was a day's journey from Sidon; a day and a half from Damascus. Philip the tetrarch built it, or, at least, embellished and enlarged it. and named it Cæsarea, in honour of Tiberius, afterwards, in compliment to Nero, it was called Neronias. The woman who was troubled with an issue of blood, and healed by our Saviour, (Matt. ix. 20. Luke viii. 43.) is said to have been of Cæsarea Philippi.

Cana, a small town of Galilee, situated on a gentle eminence to the west of Capernaum. Here Jesus Christ performed the miracle of turning water into wine. (John ii. 7—10.)

Canaan, Land of. See p. 159, *supra*.

Capernaum, a town of Galilee. situated on the coast of the Lake of Gennesareth, on the borders of the tract occupied by the tribes of Zebulun and Nephthalim. This place is celebrated for the *many mighty works* and discourses performed by our Saviour, which brought a heavy wo upon the inhabitants for their infidelity. (Matt. xi. 23.)

Cappadocia, a fertile region of Asia Minor, mentioned in Acts ii. 9, and also by the apostle Peter, who addresses his first Epistle to the Hebrew Christians who were dispersed through Pontus, Galatia, *Cappadocia*, Bithynia, and Asia Minor.

Carmel, Mount. See p. 176, *supra*.

Cedron or Kedron, Brook. See p. 173, *supra*.

Cenchrea, a haven on the east of the isthmus of Corinth, to which city it was considered as a kind of subsidiary port. It is mentioned in Acts xviii. 18.

Chaldæa, a country of Asia, lying near the junction of the Tigris and Euphrates, the capital of which was Babylon, whence it was also denominated Babylonia. In ancient times it was known by the names Shinar, Shinaar, &c.

Chios (Acts xx. 15,) is an island of the Ægean Sea, between Lesbos and Samos, celebrated in ancient and in modern times, for its wine, figs, marble, and white earth.

CHITTIM. *The land of Chittim,* and *the isles of Chittim,* denote in general, the maritime countries and islands of the Mediterranean, Greece, Italy, Crete, Cyprus, Corsica, &c.

CHORAZIN, a small town situated on the western coast of the Sea of Galilee, at no great distance from Capernaum. It was one of those places where very many of our Saviour's miracles were performed, whose inhabitants he upbraided for their infidelity. (Matt. xi. 21. Luke x. 13.)

CILICIA, a country of Asia Minor, between Pamphylia on the west, and Pieria on the east, the Mount Taurus on the north, and the Cilician Sea on the south, celebrated on the account of Cicero, proconsul there, but more on the account of St. Paul's birth at Tarsus, a city of Cilicia. (Acts xxii. 3.)

CLAUDA, an island near Crete, situated near the southern and western sea. It is mentioned in Acts xxvii. 16; as also is

CNIDUS, (xxvii. 7,) which was a city and promontory of Paria, memorable for the worship of Venus.

COLOSSÆ, or COLASSÆ, was a city of Phrygia Pacatiana in Asia Minor, situated near the conflux of the Lycus and the Meander, not far from the cities of Hierapolis and Laodicea, with which it was destroyed by an earthquake, not long after St. Paul wrote his epistle to the Colossians.

Coos, an island in the Ægean Sea, lying off the coast of Caria in Asia Minor, near the cities of Myndos and Cnidus. It is mentioned in Acts xxi. 1.

CORINTH, the metropolis of Achaia Proper, was situated on the isthmus which connects the Peloponnesus with the main land. It was distinguished as the seat of commerce, arts, and wealth. St. Paul resided here for some time, about A. D. 52. and collected a Christian Church, the numerous members of which were not afterwards exempt from the common vices of the place.

CYPRUS, an island in the Mediterranean Sea, situated between Cilicia and Syria, and anciently celebrated for the profligacy of its inhabitants, whose principal deity was the impure goddess Venus. Here Paul and Barnabas landed, A. D. 44, and successfully preached the Gospel. (Acts xiii. 4. *et seq.* xxi. 3.)

CYRENE, the principal city of the province of Lybia in Africa, which was thence sometimes demonstrated Cyrenaica, and which, by the evangelist Luke, is paraphrastically called *Lybia about Cyrene.* (Acts ii. 10)

DALMANUTHA. See MAGDALA.

DAMASCUS, a city of Syria, situated in the valley between Libanus and Antilibanus, watered by the rivers Abana and Pharphar. (2 Kings v. 12.) It is celebrated for its antiquity, and for being still one of the richest and most magnificent cities of the Levant, but most of all for being the place of the miraculous conversion of St. Paul.

DEAD SEA. See p. 174. *supra.*

DECAPOLIS. See p. 165. *supra.*

DERBE, a city of Lycaonia, near Isauria, not far from the Cilician range of Mount Taurus. It was the country of Timothy, and is mentioned in Acts xiv. 6.

EBAL (Mount.) See p. 177. *supra.*

EGYPT, a country of Africa, bounded on the east by Arabia Petræa and the Red Sea, or Arabian gulf; on the west, by Lybia, and Marmarica; on the south by Ethiopia, and on the north by the Mediterranean Sea. In the earliest times, this country was divided into Upper Egypt, or Thebais, (the Pathros of Scripture,) and Lower Egypt. The whole region was known to the ancient Hebrews by the name of Mizraim; and the princes who governed it, were, in virtue of their office, styled Pharaohs, or kings, until the time of Solomon, after which they are designated in the Scriptures by their proper names. After the captivity, Egypt became a place of great resort to the Jews.

ELAH, Valley of. See p. 178. *supra.*

EMMAUS, a small village of Judæa, distant sixty furlongs from Jerusalem. It is memorable for the very interesting conversation between Jesus Christ and two of his disciples in the evening of the day of his resurrection. (Luke xxiv.)

EPHESUS, a city on the western coast of Asia Minor, and the metropolis of the proconsular Asia, was celebrated for the magnificent temple erected there in honour of Diana. In the time of Saint Paul, this city abounded with orators and philosophers; and its inhabitants, in their Gentile state, were celebrated for their idolatry and skill in magic, as well as for their luxury and lasciviousness. Ephesus is now under the dominion of the Turks, and is in a state of almost total ruin.

EPHRAIM, a considerable city of Judœa, eight miles north of Jerusalem, and near a desert of the same name; to which Jesus Christ retired after he had raised Lazarus from the dead. (John xi. 54.)

GADARA, the metropolis of Perœa, or the region beyond Jordan, was situated on the eastern shore of the lake of Gennesareth, opposite to Tiberias, from which it was about 7 or 8 miles distant. Few of its inhabitants were Jews.

GALATIA, a province of Asia Minor, bounded on the west by Phrygia, on the east by the river Halys, on the north by Paphlagonia, and on the south by Lycaonia. The Galatians were the descendents of those Gauls who, finding their own country too small to support its redundant population, emigrated from it after the death of Alexander the Great, B. C. 278. During the reign of Augustus (A. U. C. 529, B. C. 26.) Galatia was reduced into a Roman province, and was thenceforh governed by the Roman laws, under the administration of a proprœtor. This country was the seat of colonies from various nations, among whom were many Jews; and from all these St. Paul appears to have made numerous converts to Christianity. (Gal. i. 2. 1 Cor. xvi. i. 1 Tim. iv. 10. 1 Pet. i. 1.)

GALILEE, Upper and Lower. See p. 163. *supra.*

GALILEE, Sea of. See p. 174. *supra.*

GAULONITIS. See p. 164. *supra.*

GAZA, a very celebrated city of the Jews, distant about 60 miles south-west from Jerusalem: it was one of the five cities of the Philestines, which fell by lot to the tribe of Judah. (Josh. xv. 47. The city of Gaza, mentioned in Acts viii. 26, was erected near the site of old Gaza, which, after being taken by Alexander the Great, was subsequently destroyed (B. C. 96,) by Alexander Jannæus, a prince of the Jews.

GENNESARETH, the name of a region and lake, in the vicinity of which were several towns, where Jesus Christ dwelt, taught, and performed miracles. See a notice of the lake of Gennesareth in p. 174. *supra.*

GERGESA, a city annexed to Peræa, and supposed to have been situated in the country adjacent to Gadara. (Matt. viii. 28. Luke viii. 26.)

GEPIZIM, Mount. See p. 177. *supra.*

GETHSEMANE, a garden beyond Kedron, at the foot of Mount Olivet, so called from the wine-presses in it: it is memorable in the evangelical history, as being the scene of our Saviour's agony.

GILEAD, Mountains of. See p. 236. *supra.*

GOLGOTHA. See p. 222. *supra.*

GOMORRAH, one of the cities which formerly occupied the region now covered by the Dead Sea, for the history of its destruction see Gen. xix.

GREECE, in the Scriptures, often comprehends all the countries inhabited by the descendants of Javan, as well in Greece as in Ionia, and Asia Minor. Since the time of Alexander the Great, the name of Greeks is taken in a more uncertain and enlarged sense, because the Greeks being masters of Egypt and Syria, of the countries beyond the Euphrates, &c. the Jews called all those Gentiles Greeks.

HEBRON, a city of Judæa, was situated on an eminence, twenty miles southward of Jerusalem, and twenty miles north from Beersheba. It was a place of considerable note in the early history of the Hebrews. Here Zechariah and Elizabeth resided, and John the Baptist was born.

HIERAPOLIS, a city of Phrygia, in the vicinity of Colosse and Loadicea. (Col. iv. 13.)

HINNOM, Valley of See p. 238 *supra.*

HOLY LAND. See p. 213. *supra.*

HOREB, a mountain in Arabia Petræa, so near mount Sinai that Horeb and Sinai seem to be two hills of the same mountain. (Exod. iii. 1—3. xvii. 6. 1 Kings xix. 8.)

ICONIUM, a large city of Asia Minor: here St. Paul preached in the Jewish Synagogue, and made many proselytes. (Acts xiv. 1—3.)

ILLYRICUM, a province lying to the north and north-west of Macedonia, along the eastern coast of the Adriatic Gulf, or Gulf of Venice. Hither, St. Paul informs Timothy, Titus went (2 Tim. iv. 10; and in Rom. xv. 19, he says that he preached the Gospel *from Jerusalem round about unto Illyricum.*

ISRAEL, Land of. See p. 159, *supra.*

——, Kingdom of. See pp. 162, 163. *supra.*

——, Mountains of. See p. 176, *supra.*

ITURÆA. See p. 164. *supra.*

JABBOK, Brook. See p. 173, *supra.*

JACOB'S WELL. See p. 233, *supra.*

JERICHO, a celebrated city in the tribe of Benjamin, of which frequent mention is made in the New Testament: it was about 19 miles distant from Jerusalem. The country around Jericho was the most fertile part of Palestine. In the time of our Saviour, Jericho was one of the cities appropriated for the residence of the priests and Levites, 12,000 of whom dwelt there; and as the way thither from Jerusalem was rocky and desert, it was greatly infested with thieves; this circumstance marks the admirable propriety with which our Lord made it the scene of his beautiful parable of the *good Samaritan.* (Luke x. 30—37.) It is now a miserable village.

JERUSALEM, City of. See pp. 165, 168. *supra.*

JEZREEL, Plain of. See p. 179, *supra.*

JOPPA, now called Jaffa, was anciently the chief part of Judæa: it lies on the Mediterranean, about west north-west of Jerusalem. This place is supposed to be of great antiquity. The Gospel was early planted here. (Acts ix., x., xi.)

JORDAN, River. See p. 172. *supra*

JUDAH, Desert of. See p. 180, *supra.*

—— Kingdom of. See p. 162, *supra.*

—— Mountains of, 175, 176.

—— Wilderness of, 180.

JUDÆA, Country of. See p. 163, *supra.*

KANA, Brook of. See p. 173, *supra.*

KEDRON, Cedron, or Kidron, Brook of. See p. 173, *supra.*

KISHON, Brook of. See p. 173, *supra.*

LAND of Canaan, 159.

—— Holy, 159, 160.

—— of Israel, 159.

—— of Promise, 159.

LAODICEA, a city of Asia Minor, in the vicinity of Colossæ and Hierapolis; together with which cities it was destroyed by an earthquake, about A. D. 65 or 66. Not a vestige of its former magnificence remains. (Col. ii. 1. iv. 13. 15, 16. Rev. i. 11.)

LASÆA, a maritime city of Crete, visited by St. Paul. (Acts xxvii. 8.)

LEBANON, Mount. See pp. 175, 176, *supra.*

LIBYA, a region of Africa, lying west of Egypt, on the southern coast of the Mediterranean Sea. (Acts ii. 10.)

LYBONIA, a region of Asia Minor, bounded on the north by Galatia; on the east by Cappadocia; on the south, by Isauria and Cilicia, and on the west by Phrygia. Of its various cities, Iconium, Derbe, and Lystra, are mentioned in Acts xiv. 6.

LYDDA, a large village of Palestine, not far from Joppa. (Acts ix. 32. 34. 38.)

LYSTRA, a city of Asia Minor, now called Latik. (Acts xiv. 6. 8. 10, 11, 21. xvi. 1.)

MACEDONIA, a region lying north of Greece Proper: it was bounded on the north by the mountains of Hæmus, on the south by Epirus and Achaia, on the east by the Ægean, on the west by the Ionian and Adriatic seas. To this country, whose metropolis was then Thessalonica, St. Paul was called by a vision; (Acts

xvi. 9:) and the churches planted by him in it, are celebrated for their great charity, and ready contribution to the distressed Jews in Judæa. (2 Cor. viii. ix.)

MAGDALA, a city and territory beyond Jordan, on the western side of the lake Gennesareth. It reached to the bridge above Jordan, which joined it to the other side of Galilee, and contained within its precincts DALMANUTHA; hence, while Matthew says, (xv. 19,) *Christ came into the coasts of Magdala*, St. Mark says, more particularly, (viii. 10,) that *he came into the parts of Dalmanutha.*

MEDIA, a vast region of Asia, having on the north the Caspian Sea, on the West Armenia and Assyria, on the south Persia, on the east Hyrcania and Parthia. In the Babylonian captivity, the Jews were carried captive into Assyria, and placed in the cities of the Medes. (2 Kings xvii. 6, and xviii. 11.) Hence, we find many of them and their proselytes at Jerusalem, when the Holy Ghost fell on the apostles. (Acts ii. 9.)

MELITE, or Malta, an island in the Mediterranean Sea, on which St. Paul was wrecked. (Acts xxviii. 1.)

MESOPOTAMIA, a famous province, situated between the rivers Tigris and Euphrates. The Hebrews call it *Aram Naharaim*, or Aram of the rivers; because it was first peopled by Aram, father of the Syrians, and is situated between two rivers.

MIDIAN, in Arabia Petræa, the land into which Moses fled from the Egyptians. (Acts vii. 29.) Here Jethro lived. (Exod. xii. 11.)

MIGDOL, a frontier town of Lower Egypt, toward the Red Sea, between which and that sea the Israelites encamped. (Exod. xiv. 1.)

MILETUS, a seaport of Asia Minor, and a city of Ionia, where Saint Paul delivered to the elders of the church of Ephesus, that affecting discourse which is recorded in Acts xx. 17—35. There was another Miletus in Crete, where St. Paul left Trophimus sick. (2 Tim. iv. 20.)

MITYLENE, a celebrated city, the capital of the island of Lesbos. It was visited by St. Paul, as related in Acts xx. 14.

MYRA, a city on the coast of Lycia, one of the south-western provinces of Asia Minor. (Acts xxvii. 5.)

MYSIA, the north-western province of Asia Minor. It was bounded on the north by Bithynia, on the east by Phrygia Minor, on the west by Troas, on the south by the river Hermus.

NAIN, a small city or town of Galilee, not far from Capernaum, at the gates of which Jesus Christ raised to life a widow's only son. (Luke vii 11—15.)

NAZARETH, a small city of Lower Galilee, celebrated as having been the place where our Saviour was educated, where he preached and whence he was called a Nazarene.

NEBO. See p. 178, *supra*.

NINEVEH, the metropolis of the Assyrian empire. It was celebrated for its extent, magnificence, and the vast number of its inhabitants. Its site can no longer be ascertained.

OLIVES, Mount of, a ridge lying east of Jerusalem (of which it had a commanding view,) and separated from it by the valley of the Cedron.

OPHIR, a country on the eastern coast of Africa, (by the Arabians termed Zanguebar;) most probably the small country of Sofala, whither Solomon sent a fleet aided by the subjects of Hiram king of Tyre, and from which they brought back gold. (1 Kings ix. 27, 28. 2 Chron. viii. 17, 18.) and also *almug trees and precious stones*. (1 Kings x. 11.)

PALESTINE. See page 160, *supra*.

PAMPHYLIA, a province of Asia Minor, having to the south the Pamphylian sea, mentioned Acts xxvii. 5. Cilicia to the east, Pisidia to the north (whence we find Saint Paul passing through Pisidia to Pamphylia, Acts xiv. 24, and from Pamphylia to Pisidia, Acts xiii. 14.) and Lycia to the west. The cities mentioned in the Scripture as belonging to it, are Perga and Attalia. (Acts xiii. 13.)

PAPHOS, the metropolis of the island of Cyprus (Acts xiii. 4. 6,) and the residence of the preconsul Numerous Jews dwelt here.

Parthians, mentioned in Acts ii. 9, were Jews, who were born or resided in Parthia, a region of Asia situated between Media and Mesopotamia.

Patara, a maritime city of Lycia, mentioned in Acts xxi. 1.

Patmos, an island in the Ægean Sea, whither the apostle and evangelist John was banished, A.D. 94, and where he had the revelations which he has recorded in the Apocalypse.

Peræa. See p. 164 *supra*.

Pergamus, a city of Mysia, and the capital of the powerful kingdom of Pergamus: it was celebrated for the noble library collected by the kings of the race of Attalus. (Rev. i. 11, ii. 12.)

Pharpar. See Abana, p. 375.

Philadelphia, a city of Asia Minor, derived its name from its founder, Attalus Philadelphus, and is situated about twenty-seven miles to the south-east of Sardis. Not long before the date of the Apocalyptic Epistle, this city had suffered so much from earthquakes, that it had been in a great measure deserted by its inhabitants; which may in some degree account for the poverty of this church as described in this Epistle.

Philippi was a city of Macedonia *Prima*, or the first of the four parts into which that province was divided. It was of moderate extent, and situated on the confines of Thrace. Christianity was first planted at Philippi, by Saint Paul, A.D. 50, the particulars of which are related in Acts xvi. 9—40.

Philistines. See p. 215, *supra*.

Phœnice, or Phœnix a city and harbour on the south-eastern coast of Crete. (Acts xxvii. 12.)

Phœnicia, or Phœnice, a narrow region of country on the eastern coast of the Mediterranean, between Judæa and Syria. Its principal cities were Ptolemais, Sidon, and Tyre.

Phrygia, an inland province of Asia Minor, bounded on the north by Bithynia; on the east by Galatia; on the south by Pamphylia, and Lycia; and on the west by Lydia and Mysia. Its chief cities, mentioned in the New Testament, are Laodicea and Hierapolis. (Col. ii. 1.)

Pisgah, Mount. See p. 178, *supra*.

Pisidia, a region of Asia Minor, having Pamphylia on the south, Galatia on the north, Isauria on the east, and Phrygia on the west. Its chief city was Antioch in Pisidia, (Acts xiii. 14,) so called to distinguish it from Antioch in Syria. —

Pontus, a province of Asia Minor, having the Euxine sea on the north, Cappadocia on the south, Paphlagonia and Galatia on the east, and the Lesser Armenia on the west. (Acts ii. 9. 1 Pet. i. 1.)

Promise, Land of. See p. 159 *supra*.

Ptolemais, anciently called Accho (Judg. i. 31,) and now known by the name of Acre, is situated on the shore of the Mediterranean Sea, on the confines of Lower and Upper Galilee. Here St. Paul rested for one day on his journey from Ephesus to Jerusalem. (Acts xxi. 7.)

Puteoli (at present called Pozzuolo) a city and haven in the kingdom of Naples, eight miles from that city. (Acts xxviii. 13.)

Rama, Ramah, or Ramathaim, a small town in the tribe of Benjamin, a few miles north of Jerusalem, between Gibeah and Bethel. It is frequently mentioned in the Old Testament.

Ramoth, a famous city in the mountains of Gilead, often called Ramoth-gilead, and sometimes Ramoth, and sometimes Ramoth-mizpeh, or the Watch-Tower, (Josh. xiii. 26.) This city belonged to the tribe of Gad. It was assigned to the Levites, and was one of the cities of refuge beyond Jordan. (Deut. iv 43. Josh. xx. 8, and xxi. 38.)

Red Sea, called also the Arabian Gulf, separates Egypt on the west from Arabia on the east. The name in Hebrew signifies the "weedy sea," or the sea of weeds; (which appellation it still retains in the Coptic language.) It is thus denominated either from the variety of sea-weeds said to be visible on its shores at low water, or from the quantity of white coral, spread everywhere over its bottom. We derive the name "Red Sea" from the Greeks. Most probably this sea was anciently called the sea of Edom, from its neighbouring coast: and as Edom signifies *Red* in Hebrew, the Greeks, not understanding the meaning of the appellation, translated it, as we have done after them, the Red Sea

RHEGIUM, a seaport town in Italy, opposite to Sicily. (Acts xxviii. 13.)

RHODES, the capital of an island of the same name, lying off the coast of Caria. (Acts. xxi. 1.)

ROME, the celebrated metropolis of the Roman Empire.

SALT SEA. See p. 174, *supra.*

SAMARIA, Region of. See p. 163 *supra.*

SAMARIA, City of the ancient capital of the kingdom of Israel, was situated on a hill which derived its name from Semer or Shemer, of whom it was purchased by Omri, king of Israel, B. C. 921, who made it the seat of his government, and called it Samaria, (Heb. *Shomeron,*) from its former owner. By his successors it was greatly improved and fortified. After having been destroyed by Shalmaneser, king of Assyria, and rebuilt during the reign of Alexander, B. C. 449, it was again destroyed by John Hyrcanus. It was afterwards wholly rebuilt, and considerably enlarged by Herod, surnamed the Great, who gave it the name of Sebaste, and erected a temple there in honour of the Emperor Augustus.

SAMOS, an island of the Archipelago, on the coast of Asia Minor. (Acts. xx. 15.)

SAMOTHRACIA, an island of the Ægean Sea, Saint Paul, departing from Troas for Macedonia, arrived first at Samothracia, and then landed in Macedonia. (Acts xvi. 11.)

SARDIS, the capital of Lydia, was situated at the foot of Mount Tmolus, on the banks of the river Pactolus: it was celebrated for the wealth, and for the voluptuous and debauched manners of its inhabitants. (Rev. i. 11, iii. 1. 4.) Sardis is at present reduced to a miserable village, called Sart.

SAREPTA, or Zarephath, (Luke iv. 26,) was a city in the territory of Sidon, between that city and Tyre, (1 Kings. xvii. 9. Luke iv. 26.)

SARON, a spacious and fertile vale, between Lydda and the sea, which contained several villages. (Acts ix. 35.)

SHUSHAN, the capital of Susiana, a province of Elam or Persia, which Daniel terms the palace, (viii. 2,) because the Chaldæan monarchs had a royal palace here. This once splendid metropolis is now a mere wilderness.

SICHEM, *Sychar,* or *Shechem,* a city of Samaria, about forty miles distant from Jerusalem, which became the metropolis of the Samaritans after the destruction of Samaria by Hyrcanus. In the vicinity of this place is Jacob's well, (John iv. 6,) memorable for our Saviour's conversation with the Samaritan woman.

SIDDIM, vale of. See p. 178, *supra.*

SIDON, or ZIDON, a very ancient and celebrated port and city, originally the metropolis of Phœnicia, is situated on the Mediterranean Sea. Sidon has always been famous for its great trade and navigation; at present it is called Said.

SIHOR RIVER. See p. 173, *supra.*

SILOAM, Fountain. See p. 175, *supra.*

SINAI, a mountain in Arabia Petræ, where the law was given. It had two tops: the one lower, called Horeb, or the Mount of God, (Exod. iii. 1,) where he appeared to Moses in a flame of fire in a bush; this Horeb is therefore called Sinai by Saint Stephen. (Acts vii. 30.) See HOREB, p. 380, *supra.*

SMYRNA, a city of Asia Minor, was situated between forty and forty-five miles to the north of Ephesus, of which city it was originally a colony. It was one of the most opulent and powerful cities of that region; but is now celebrated chiefly for the number, wealth and commerce of the inhabitants.

SODOM, the chief of the Pentapolitan cities, or five cities of the plain, gave the name to the whole land. It was burnt with three other cities, by fire from heaven, for the unnatural lusts of their inhabitants.

SODOM, Sea of. See p. 174, *supra.*

SYRIA, the name of a large district of Asia, lying in the widest acceptation of the name between Palestine, Mount Taurus, and the Tigris, and thus including Mesopotamia, or Syria of the two rivers, (in Hebrew, Aram Naharaim.) In the New Testament, Syria may be considered as bounded on the west and north-west by the Mediterranean Sea, and by Mount Taurus; on the east by the Euphrates: and on the south by Arabia Deserta and Palestine, or rather Judæa, for the name Syria includes the northern part of Palestine. The valley between the ridges of Libanus and Anti-Libanus, was called Cœlo-Syria, or Cœle-Syria; which appellation was also sometimes extended to the neighbouring country. At the time of the Jewish exile, Syria and Phœnicia were subject to the king of Babylon, and they afterward were tributary to the Persian monarchs. After the country fell into the hands of the Romans, Syria was made the province of a proconsul. (Robinson's Gr. and English Lexicon to the New Testament, p. 731.)

SYRO-PHŒNICIA is Phœnicia properly so called, of which Sidon was the capital; which having by right of conquest been united to the kingdom of Syria, added its old name Phœnicia to that of Syria. The Canaanitish woman is called a Syro-Phœnician, (Mark vii. 26,) because she was of Phœnicia, which was then considered as making part of Syria. St. Matthew calls her a Canaanitish woman, (Matt. xv. 22. 24,) because this country was really peopled by the Canaanites, Sidon being the eldest son of Canaan. (Gen. x. 15.)

TABOR, or THABOR, Mount. See p. 177, *supra*.

TARSUS, a rich and populous city, the capital of Cilicia. It was celebrated in the Scriptures as being the place whither Jonah designed to flee, and where St. Paul was born.

THESSALONICA, a large and populous city and seaport of Macedonia, the capital of one of the four districts into which the Romans divided that country after its conquest by Paulus Æmilius. It was situated on the Thermian Bay, and was anciently called Thermæ; but, being rebuilt by Philip, the father of Alexander, after his victory over the Thessalians, it then received the name of Thessalonica. It was inhabited by Greeks, Romans, and Jews; from among whom St. Paul collected a numerous church. (Acts xvii. 1. 11. 13.)

THYATIRA, a city of Asia Minor, was a considerable city on the road from Pergamos to Sardis, and about 48 miles eastward of the former. It is called by the Turks Ak-hisar.

TIBERIUS, (John vi. 1—23. xxi. 1,) still called by the natives Tabaria, or Tabbareean, was anciently one of the principal cities of Galilee: it was built by Herod the Great, and so called in honour of the emperor Tiberius. The privileges conferred upon its inhabitants by Herod, caused it in a short time to become a place of considerable note: it was situated in a plain near the lake of Gennesareth, which is thence termed the *Lake* or *Sea of Tiberias;* for a notice of which see p. 174, *supra*.

TRACHONITIS. See p. 164, *supra*.

TROAS, a port and town of Mysia, visited by St. Paul in his apostolic journeys: it was situated on the western coast, at some distance to the southward of the supposed site of ancient Troy.

TROGYLLIUM (Acts xx. 15,) a promontory at the foot of Mount Mycale, opposite to, and about five miles fr[illegible]. Samos.

TYRE, a celebrated city and seaport of Phœnicia, that boasted of a very early antiquity. Even in the time of Joshua it was strongly fortified; for it is called the *strong city Tyre*. (Josh. xix. 29.) After the time of David, Tyre is frequently mentioned in the Old Testament, where its inhabitants are represented as filled with pride and luxury, and all the vices attendant on prosperity and immense wealth. Judgments are denounced against them by the prophets, in consequence of their idolatry and wickedness; and the destruction of their city is foretold. After this destruction the great body of the inhabitants fixed themselves on an island opposite the former city, about 30 stadia from the main land, where they erected another city. This also soon became opulent and powerful: it was taken by Alexander the Great, after an obstinate siege of seven months, in the year 332, B. C. After many subsequent reverses of fortune, and various changes of masters, Tyre at length fell under the dominion of the Romans, and continued to enjoy its commercial prosperity. (Robinson's Lexicon, p. 772.) Tyre is now a miserable place, called Sur, whose inhabitants support themselves by fishing.

ZAREPHATH. See SAREPTA. p. 384, *supra*.

ZIDON. See SIDON, p. 384, *supra*.

II

INDEX OF MATTERS

NEW BOOKS.

Arthur in America.

Addresses delivered in New-York by Rev. Wm. Arthur, A. M. With a Biographical Sketch of the Author. Also, the Address of Rev. Dr. Adams at the Broadway Tabernacle. "To get, to keep, to give." With a portrait. Edited by W. P. STRICKLAND, D. D. Carlton & Porter. Price 55 cents.

A most interesting and instructive volume. The claims of *systematic* benevolence are forcibly urged. The wants of Ireland are set forth with great eloquence. The speech of Dr. Adams is refreshing, emanating as it does from an eminent divine in *one* Church advocating a great evangelical enterprise in *another* communion.—*Southern Christian Advocate.*

Revised History of the Bible Society.

History of the American Bible Society. Revised and brought down to the present time. 8vo., 500 pages. By WILLIAM P. STRICKLAND, D. D. Harper & Brothers.

Strickland's Biblical Literature.

A Manual of Biblical Literature. By WILLIAM P. STRICKLAND, D. D. 404 pages. Carlton & Porter. Muslin, 80 cents.

The work is divided into nine parts, treating severally of Biblical Philology, Biblical Criticism, Biblical Exegesis, Biblical Analysis, Biblical Archæology, Biblical Ethnography, Biblical History, Biblical Chronology, and Biblical Geography. This enumeration will suffice to show the extent of the range of topics embraced in this volume. Of course they are treated summarily; but the very design of the author was to prepare a compendious *manual*, and he has succeeded excellently.—*Methodist Quarterly Review.*

Christianity Demonstrated

By Facts drawn from History, Prophecy, and Miracles. Price $1.

Sketches of Western Methodism.

By Rev. JAMES B. FINLEY. With a likeness of the "Old Chief." 560 pages. Price $1.

This highly popular work, embracing a history of Methodism in the Great West from its introduction toward the close of the eighteenth century, with a description of the toils and sacrifices of the early pioneers, by one who was himself an actor in the scenes, and containing graphic sketches of many of the lives of the most prominent in the field of itinerant labor, with many incidents of thrilling interest in relation to backwoods life, has already, within a space of less than two years, reached a sale of *seventeen thousand.* Whoever wants a reliable history of life and manners in the West will be interested in reading this book.

Light of the Temple.

By WILLIAM P. STRICKLAND. Price 75 cents.

Astrologers of Chaldea;

Or, the Life of Faith. By WILLIAM P. STRICKLAND. Price 75 cents.

NEW BOOKS,

PUBLISHED BY CARLTON AND PORTER,

200 Mulberry-street, New-York.

FOR SALE ALSO BY J. P. MAGEE, 5 CORNHILL, BOSTON, AND H. H. OTIS, SENECA-STREET, BUFFALO.

Heroes of Methodism.

The Heroes of Methodism. Containing Sketches of Eminent Methodist Ministers, and Characteristic Anecdotes of their Personal History. By Rev. J. B. WAKELEY, of the New-York Conference. With Portraits of Bishops Asbury, Coke, and M'Kendree. Large 12mo., pp. 470. Price $1 00, with the usual discount to wholesale purchasers.

Dr. M'Clintock, who examined the work in manuscript, and is familiar with it, says, in the April number of the Quarterly Review: "It is a work of great interest to the Methodist public, and will doubtless have a great run."

With laudable industry, Mr. Wakeley has gleaned, from a great variety of sources, anecdotes and illustrations of the life and character of men to whom not only the Church of which they were ministers, but the world at large, and more especially these United States, are largely indebted. They were the pioneers of Christianity, men of burning zeal and undaunted perseverance; spending their lives for the welfare of their fellow-men—in journeyings often, in perils of waters, in perils of robbers, in perils by their own countrymen, in perils in the city, and most especially in perils in the wilderness. With equal truth may it be said also of these heralds of salvation, that they were "In weariness and painfulness, in watchings often, in hunger and thirst, in fastings often, in cold and nakedness." The perusal of this volume cannot fail to kindle anew the flagging zeal of the successors of these truly great men. We have entered into their labors, and it is owing to the blessing of the great Head of the Church upon *their* toil that *we* have such a goodly heritage. Mr. Wakeley has executed his task with ability, and his beautifully printed volume, illustrated with portraits of Asbury, Coke, and M'Kendree, will doubtless have, as it deserves, a wide circulation.—*National Magazine.*

Pioneers of the West.

The Pioneers of the West; or, Life in the Woods. By W. P. STRICKLAND. Price $1.

The table of contents is quite attractive: The West; Pioneer Explorers of the West; Hunters of the West; Pioneer Settlers; Pioneer Preachers; Pioneer Institutions and Professional Men; Pioneer Boatmen; The Prophet Francis; Logan, the Mingo Chief; The Mountain Hunter; Indian Captivity; The "Old Chief," or, the Indian Missionary; The Hermit; Panther Hunting; The Squatter Family; The Lost Hunter; Wisconsin Schoolma'am. These vivid pictures are sketches from life. The author takes his readers with him as he traces the path of the pioneer explorer, settler, hunter, or preacher, and we follow the blazed path in the wilderness, and witness the thrilling scenes which start up on every hill, and in every valley, and glen, and river, until the blood chills at some deed of savage warfare, or warms at the recital of some of the thrilling scenes and heroic incidents with which the work abounds. The interest is kept up through the whole volume, and the reader closes with the conviction that truth is as strange and as entertaining as fiction, and certainly more instructive. The book is embellished with some fine wood-cuts.—*Christian Advocate and Journal*

BOOKS AND PERIODICALS.

CARLTON & PORTER,

Agents of the Methodist Book Concern, 200 Mulberry-street, New-York, would call attention to a few of their numerous publications.

THE SUNDAY SCHOOL ADVOCATE

Is a beautifully illustrated child's paper, edited by the distinguished friend of children, the veritable FRANCIS FORRESTER, and is issued semi-monthly. The nineteenth volume will commence in October, 1859. The circulation is over 200,000 copies. Price 25 cents single, and 20 cents per copy when ten or more copies are ordered to one address.

SABBATH-SCHOOL BOOKS.

Of these we have about 1,100 bound volumes, besides multitudes of Question Books, Hymn Books, Picture Books, Catechisms, Cards, and Tracts, adapted to children of all ranks and ages, and we are adding to the number monthly. They are being ordered and prized by schools of all denominations.

Then we have a large list of other works, beautifully illustrated for gift-books for children and youth, which are equal to any in the land, such as,

Harry Budd	**Price $0 50**	**Poor Nelly**	**Price $0 32**
Illustrated Olio	**0 70**	**Pictorial Gatherings**	**0 65**
Six Steps to Honor	**0 65**	**Here and There**	**0 15**
Uncle Toby's Library, 12 vols.	**2 00**	**Historical Series, 10 vols**	**2 50**
Pictorial Catechism	**0 70**	**Henry's Birthday**	**0 35**
Child's Sabbath-Day Book	**0 25**	**Bird-Book**	**0 70**

To these we may add the popular volumes, entitled,

Pilgrim's Progress	**Price $1 50**	**Young Man's Counselor**	**Price $0 55**
Path of Life	**0 50**	**Young Lady's Counselor**	**0 55**
Manly Character	**0 40**	**Young Man Advised**	**0 75**
Bridal Greetings	**0 30**	**Frank Harley**	**0 20**
Chart of Life	**0 60**	**Ministering Children**	**0 90**
The Successful Merchant	**0 40**	**Object of Life**	**0 75**

HIBBARD ON THE PSALMS,

Giving the time when, and the circumstances under which each Psalm was written, is a new and splendid work for preachers, teachers, and for reading in family worship. Price, $2 00.

We have BIBLES also, Royal Octavo and Imperial Quarto, in different styles of binding, ranging in prices from $8 to $50 per copy. Besides, we have a large list of Miscellaneous Works of various sizes and costs, on moral and religious subjects, which only need to be known to be appreciated.

Catalogues will be sent, gratuitously, to all who order, and on receiving the retail price of any of our books, we will forward said books free of charge. Orders sent to us as above, or to J. P. MAGEE, No. 5 Cornhill, Boston; or J. L. READ, Pittsburgh, Pa.; or to H. H. OTIS, Buffalo, N. Y.; or SWORMSTEDT & POE, Cincinnati, or any other Methodist Booksellers, will receive prompt attention.

BOOKS PUBLISHED BY CARLTON & PORTER,
200 Mulberry-Street, New York.

Harmony of Divine Dispensations.

Harmony of the Divine Dispensations. Being a Series of Discourses on Select Portions of Holy Scripture, designed to show the Spirituality, Efficacy, and Harmony of the Divine Revelations made to Mankind from the Beginning. With Notes, Critical, Historical, and Explanatory. By GEORGE SMITH, F. A. S., Member of the Royal Asiatic Society, of the Royal Society of Literature, Fellow of the Genealogical and Historical Society, etc., etc.

8vo., pp. 319. Sheep $1 50
———— Half calf 2 00

This is a new work, being reprinted from the London edition to correspond with the "Patriarchal Age," "Hebrew People," and "Gentile Nations," by the same distinguished author. It will be sold in connection with the others, or separately. It is a profound work, and will have a large sale.

Lady Huntingdon Portrayed.

Including Brief Sketches of some of her Friends and Co-laborers. By the Author of "The Missionary Teacher," "Sketches of Mission Life," etc.

Large 16mo., pp. 319. Muslin $0 75
———— Morocco 1 75

Hibbard on the Psalms.

The Psalms Chronologically Arranged, with Historical Introductions, and a General Introduction to the whole Book. By F. G. HIBBARD.

8vo., pp. 589. Muslin $2 00
———— Half Morocco 2 50
———— Morocco 5 00

This book occupies an important place in Biblical interpretation, and is a valuable contribution to Biblical literature.

The Object of Life:

A Narrative Illustrating the Insufficiency of the World, and the Sufficiency of Christ. With four Illustrations.

Large 16mo., pp. 357. Price $0 75
———— Morocco 1 75

The Living Way;

Or, Suggestions and Counsels concerning some of the Privileges and Duties of the Christian Life. By Rev. JOHN ATKINSON.

16mo., pp. 139. Price $0 40

www.ingramcontent.com/pod-product-compliance
Lightning Source LLC
LaVergne TN
LVHW011150110826
845150LV00006B/1208
* 9 7 8 1 4 2 5 5 4 5 8 9 5 *